SOCIAL CAPITAL, SOCIAL SUPPORT AND STRATIFICATION

Social Capital, Social Support and Stratification

An Analysis of the Sociology of Nan Lin

Edited by

Ronald S. Burt
Booth School of Business, University of Chicago, USA

Yanjie Bian
Department of Sociology, University of Minnesota, USA

Lijun Song
Department of Sociology, Vanderbilt University, USA

Nan Lin
Department of Sociology, Duke University, USA

EE Edward **Elgar**
PUBLISHING

Cheltenham, UK • Northampton, MA, USA

Published by
Edward Elgar Publishing Limited
The Lypiatts
15 Lansdown Road
Cheltenham
Glos GL50 2JA
UK

Edward Elgar Publishing, Inc.
William Pratt House
9 Dewey Court
Northampton
Massachusetts 01060
USA

A catalogue record for this book
is available from the British Library

Library of Congress Control Number: 2019951650

This book is available electronically in the **Elgar**online
Social and Political Science subject collection
DOI 10.4337/9781789907285

MIX
Paper from
responsible sources
FSC FSC® C013604
www.fsc.org

ISBN 978 1 78990 727 8 (cased)
ISBN 978 1 78990 728 5 (eBook)

Printed and bound by CPI Group (UK) Ltd, Croydon CR0 4YY

Contents

Acknowledgements

The editors and publishers wish to thank the authors and the following publishers who have kindly given permission for the use of copyright material.

American Sociological Association for articles: Nan Lin, Ronald S. Simeone, Walter M. Ensel and Wen Kuo (1979), 'Social Support, Stressful Life Events, and Illness: A Model and an Empirical Test', *Journal of Health and Social Behavior*, **20** (2), June, 108–19; Nan Lin, Walter M. Ensel and John C. Vaughn (1981), 'Social Resources and Strength of Ties: Structural Factors in Occupational Status Attainment', *American Sociological Review*, **46** (4), August, 393–405; Nan Lin, Xiaolan Ye and Walter M. Ensel (1999), 'Social Support and Depressed Mood: A Structural Analysis', *Journal of Health and Social Behavior*, **40** (4), December, 334–59.

Taylor and Francis Group LLC (Books) for excerpt: Nan Lin (2001), 'Building a Network Theory of Social Capital', in Nan Lin, Karen Cook and Ronald S. Burt (eds), *Social Capital: Theory and Research*, Chapter 1, Aldine Transaction: New Jersey, USA, 3–29.

University of Chicago Press for articles: Nan Lin and Yanjie Bian (1991), 'Getting Ahead in Urban China', *American Journal of Sociology*, **97** (3), November, 657–88; Nan Lin and Wen Xie (1988), 'Occupational Prestige in Urban China', *American Journal of Sociology*, **93** (4), January, 793–832.

Every effort has been made to trace all the copyright holders but if any have been inadvertently overlooked the publishers will be pleased to make the necessary arrangement at the first opportunity.

ntroduction

here are moments in the order of things during which scholarly thinking takes a turn. What /as a productive way of looking at things is put aside in transition to something new. The ransition is occasionally based on solid evidence, sometimes an escape from boredom, erhaps too often it is a group of scholars hoping to find identity by institutionalizing new /ords. Whatever the reason for it, the transition puts a spotlight on individual character. The onservative hangs onto the old, peeled away eventually at death's door. The faddish jumps on ne new, nervously eyeing the horizon for the next something new. Thankfully there are also eople – in some circles known as entrepreneurs, or creatives, or network brokers – for whom ransition is an opportunity to mix bits of the old and new to better understand the world.

This book is about transitions associated with the spread of social network imagery in ociology. The thread that holds together our selected transitions is a network broker who was rotagonist in all three: Nan Lin. Chapter 2 is about the entry of social network imagery into neories of stratification and achievement, with advantage termed social capital, a complement the earlier focus on human capital. Drawing on his background in social networks and tratification, Nan was early to bring network data into the Blau and Duncan occupational chievement models dominant during the 1970s. The heart of Lin's synthesis is that people are efined by their position in macro-structure (rather than the micro-structure around them), and elationships are presumed to be portals through which one person has rights to the resources f the other. To provide a sense of the transition as Nan dealt with it, we include as Chapters and 4 two of Nan's most cited papers on networks and social capital in their original. Chapter is about the entry of social network imagery into theories of social support, expanding linical psychology into social psychology. Drawing on his background in social networks, nd sharing interests with his wife Alice, a senior administrator in the New York State social ervices organization, Nan was early to bring network data into research on social support. rom his social capital image of a person's network providing access to needed resources, lan crafted a unique perspective for conceptualizing, measuring, and modeling social support. Iere again, to provide a sense of the transition Nan experienced, we include as Chapters 6 and two of Nan's most cited papers on social support in their original form. Chapter 8 is about ne renovation of Chinese sociology from disdained ideology to admired social science. A ond visitor to his homeland China, Nan was articulate, charming, and generous, in the right lace at the right time to bring state-of-the-art sociology to China when China was ready to sten. With Nan's background in social networks informing his view of sociology, it is no urprise that social network imagery is prominent in contemporary Chinese sociology. Ieginning with Blau and Duncan's model as a comparative baseline for rigorous empirical esearch, Nan expanded into indigenous images such as "local state socialism," "centrally nanaged capitalism," and "sentiment-based *guanxi*." Again to illustrate Nan's synthesis, we nclude as Chapters 9 and 10 two of Nan's most cited China papers.

The book speaks to the general audience of people interested in social capital, social support, or stratification – and people interested in academic entrepreneurs like Nan. The book is also aimed at the many students and colleagues who have experienced Nan's patient generosity. This is not the place for a greeting-card display of sentimentality. We leave that to you, if you are interested. Ask any student or colleague of Nan's what it was like to work with him. Each has his or her story sure to induce a smile on any but the most truculent. Mr. Burt's stories come from his experience as a college and graduate student with Nan in the 1970s. Mr. Bian's come from his experience as a graduate student with Nan in the 1980s and early 1990s. Ms. Song's come from her experience as a graduate student with Nan in the 2000s. One and all experienced Nan as a turning point in their lives. We close in Chapter 11 with Nan's reflections on what he learned making the contributions detailed in the preceding chapters.

PART I

SOCIAL CAPITAL

[2]

Nan Lin and social capital

Ronald S. Burt

Nan Lin's work on social capital is a significant, unique contribution. My purpose here is to explain that statement by looking at the work in historical context. Figure 2.1 is an index for much of the story to be told. The horizontal axis is time, beginning in 1975 when Nan Lin was at the State University of New York at Albany (now the University of Albany), through his 1990 move to Duke University, and on to 2010.

Bars above the horizontal axis show citations to Nan Lin's 15 most prominent works. White bars refer to works on social support (included in Figure 2.1 because they are among Lin's most-cited works, see Chapter 5). Dark bars refer to works on social capital. For example, Lin's (2001a) *Social Capital* book is a "hit" cited in 9,945 subsequent works. My selection of Lin's 15 most prominent works is arbitrary. I chose 15 because the last five of the 15 are works on social support, which provide a substantive boundary for the most prominent works on social capital. Work after 2001 has not found the broad audience of the earlier work. An edited book on international studies of social capital, Lin and Erickson (2008a), is the most cited of the later works. I include the book in Figure 2.1 to provide a sense of scale for earlier works. Later works have not had as many years to accumulate citations as have earlier works, but there has been a decade since the 2008 book, and almost two decades since the burst of prominent work at the turn of the century, so constituencies have had time to develop.[1]

I am mindful that citation prominence indicates use, not quality. There are some works by some people that are widely discussed and cited because they make few intellectual demands of readers, and strategies for gaming citation counts are often noted by pundits, perhaps because citations are so often mentioned during promotion and recruitment decisions, and during introductions to prominent speakers.[2] Nevertheless, citations are signal in their own right: They are a familiar index of academic significance, easily replicated by other scholars, and strongly correlated with work quality.[3] For the task at hand, citations are a helpful focus on prominent works.

Works below the horizontal are reference points in the intellectual context for Lin's work on social capital. Works are listed by author, date and number of citations. For example, Freeman's (1977) article introducing betweenness, and his companion article generalizing to network centrality (Freeman 1978), together have received 20,393 citations. There is an element of personal choice here, and some of the listed works do not mention the term "social capital" (e.g., Freeman 1977; Granovetter 1985; Watts and Strogatz 1998), but they are all frequently cited in social capital theory and research, and the listed items include the most highly-cited work by each author.

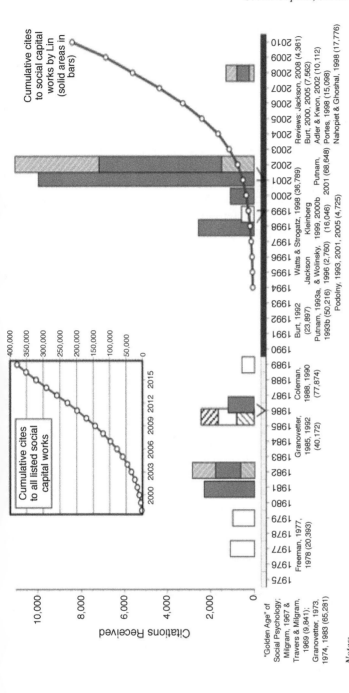

Notes:
Bars above the horizontal axis indicate Google Scholar citations to Lin's most cited works by others as of July 2018. Citations to work by others are given in parentheses below the horizontal. Years to the left are at the University of Albany. Years to the right are at Duke University. White bars are social support research. Dark bars are social capital research. Solid areas show citations to work Lin wrote or co-authored. Upward stripe areas show citations to books Lin edited. Downward stripe areas show citations to chapters not by Lin in books Lin edited. From left to right, the publications are (see references): Dean and Lin 1977; Lin et al. 1979 (Chapter 6 in this book); Lin et al. 1981a (Chapter 3 in this book, includes citations to companion work, Lin et al. 1981b); Marsden and Lin 1982 (solid area refers to Lin's 1982 chapter in the book; cites to the reprinted Granovetter 1983 chapter are excluded); Lin et al. 1986 (solid area refers to chapters authored or co-authored by Lin); Lin and Dumin 1986; Lin and Ensel 1989; Lin et al. 1999 (Chapter 7 in this book); Lin 2000; Lin 2001a; Lin et al. 2001 (solid area refers to Lin 2001b, which is Chapter 4 in this book); Lin and Erickson 2008a (solid area refers to chapters Lin wrote or co-authored).

Figure 2.1   Nan Lin and social capital

Social capital provides collaborative coordination (closure)

Social capital is a metaphor for advantage provided by the social network around a person, group, organization, geographic region, or other unit of analysis. The term became popular in sociology, then political science and economics, following Coleman's prominent article and subsequent book (78,000 cites in Figure 2.1; Coleman 1988, p. S98, 1990, esp. Chapter 12):

> Social capital is defined by its function. It is not a single entity but a variety of different entities, with two elements in common: they all consist of some aspect of social structures, and they facilitate certain actions of actors – whether persons or corporate actors – within the structure.

As Becker (1975) used the term "human capital" to refer to sources of differences in economic achievement that remain after familiar economic variables had been held constant,[4] Coleman (1988, 1990) used the term "social capital" to refer to sources of differences in educational achievement that remain after familiar sociological variables had been held constant. Specifically (Coleman 1991, p. 22):

> We searched for an explanation of why the performance of children in religiously-grounded private schools was greater than that of comparable children in public or independent private schools. ... the social milieu that was relevant for explaining the effectiveness of religiously-grounded schools was ... the community of adults outside the school. We found that when that community was strong, as it more often was in religiously-grounded schools, it provided a resource (which we then termed "social capital") that was important for students' achievement and for their staying in school until graduation.

Such intuitions about social context providing advantage can be expressed with a variety of metaphors, and defined in a variety of ways, an opportunity to which many have risen (see the diffuse discussion of social capital in Wikipedia). I provide exegesis of neither social capital metaphors, nor Nan Lin's perspective on social capital.[5] I focus on Lin's significant contributions in the broader context of work on social capital.

The complexity of social capital discussion is greatly simplified if one focuses on the network models used to conceptualize and study social capital. In large part, the models build on two facts established to the far left in Figure 2.1, during the 1950s "golden age" of social psychology (especially Festinger et al. 1950; Asch 1951; Leavitt 1951; Katz and Lazarsfeld 1955): (1) people cluster into groups as a result of interaction opportunities defined by the places where people meet; and (2) communication is more frequent and influential within than between groups such that people in the same group come to resemble one another's opinion and behavior.

Social capital work initially focused on closure, the extent to which the people in a network are strongly connected with one another. The gist of the idea is that closure facilitates trust and reputation: the more connected the people in a network, the more likely that opinion and behavior "deviant" from the usual will be detected and chastised, distinguishing reputable individuals and creating a reputation cost for such behavior, making such behavior less likely, which lowers the risk of trust within the network, thereby increasing the probability of trust. Closure creates a reputation cost for deviant behavior such that people in the network can more easily coordinate with one another on shared opinions and behavior.

Closure is the condition Coleman invokes as social capital – leveraging his research on peer pressure in social groups (Coleman et al. 1957; Coleman 1961). He goes so far as to speculate that "reputation cannot arise in an open structure" (Coleman 1988, p. S107, which turns out to be an empirical regularity if not a necessity, Burt 2005, pp. 208–11; 2010, pp. 163–71). Further to the right of Coleman in Figure 2.1, you see Putnam's (1993a, esp. Chapter 6) widely-cited book adapting Coleman's image of closure as social capital to describe the success of civic government as a function of social capital indicated by local participation measures such as newspaper readership, memberships in voluntary associations and trade unions (previously termed "civic culture," Putnam et al. 1983), which Putnam provocatively extends in an accompanying piece (Putnam 1993b) and later book (Putnam 2001) to describe the social well-being of communities (cf. Wellman 1979; Fischer 1982 on personal networks of social support, Hampton and Wellman 2018 for a nuanced view from inside the internet, and Chapter 5 regarding Nan Lin's work on social support). Just before Coleman in Figure 2.1, you see Granovetter (1985, 1992) on the implications of closure for behavior in economic transactions "embedded" in networks, which was the inspiration for Uzzi's (1996, 1997, 1999) well-known empirical work on trust and performance associated with closure (see also Acheson 1988; Greif 1989; Barker 1993; Bernstein 1992 on social enforcement provided by closure; and for review, Burt 2005, Chapters 3–4). Further outside sociology, closure is the portal through which Jackson and Wolinsky (1996) bring economics into Figure 2.1 by proposing economic models of more and less stable networks (see Hummon 2000; Doreian 2006 for network analyst work with the Jackson and Wolinsky models, and Jackson 2008 in Figure 2.1 for a broad review in economics of network stability and interpersonal influence, for which Krackhardt 2009 provides an enthusiastic network analyst review). Closure continues to be studied in computational social science more generally (Easley and Kleinberg 2010 for review), but rarely in terms of social capital so much as in terms of strong connections producing interpersonal influence (Salganik et al. 2006; Aral et al. 2009) or efficient coordination (Kearns et al. 2006; Shirado and Christakis 2017).[6]

Social capital provides creative achievement (brokerage)
From continuous conversation within a group, people create systems of behaviors, opinions, phrasings and symbols defining what it means to be a member. Beneath familiar arguments and experiences are new, emerging arguments and experiences awaiting a label, the emerging items more understood than said within the group. What was once explicit knowledge interpretable by anyone becomes tacit knowledge more meaningful to insiders than to outsiders. With time, information in the group can become "sticky" – nuanced, interconnected meanings difficult to understand by people in other groups (Von Hippel 1994). Much of what we know is not easily understood beyond our colleagues. For reasons of a division of labor, in which groups become increasingly specialized, or for reasons of simple random variation in the independent evolution of separate groups (Salganik et al. 2006) – holes tear open in the flow of information between groups. These holes in the social structure of communication, or more simply "structural holes" (Burt 1992), are missing relations indicating where information is likely to differ on opposite sides of the hole and not flow easily across the hole. In short, the network structure of variably connected groups indicates where information is relatively homogeneous (within group) and likely to be heterogeneous (between groups).

Providing illustration for the subsequent discussion, Figure 2.2 is a sociogram of the social network among senior managers in a large European organization. Each symbol represents a person. Lines indicate frequent and substantive discussion between connected people. People are close together in the sociogram to the extent that they have a strong connection with each other and with the same colleagues (spring embedding algorithm, Borgatti 2002). Note the groups distinguished by relations dense within group relative to sparse relations across the structural holes between groups. To the east in the sociogram, company leaders in the United States are strongly connected with one another with little connection overseas. To the northeast, company leaders in Asia are strongly connected to one another with little connection outside Asia. To the southeast, an important group in the company's research and development (R&D) operations is little connected to the rest of company leadership. Business practice varies between the clusters. People in the R&D cluster are guided by state-of-the-art scientific practice. People in the American cluster are adapted to American legal code, business practice, and local institutions. Similarly, people in the Asia, European, front office and back-office clusters work in their local language, within the social and professional institutions associated with each cluster.

Where closure is about the substance and correlates of dense connections within a group, a logical next step is to study the substance and correlates of connections between groups. As closure within groups is grounded in the golden age of social psychology, so too are images of people moving information between groups. The connections between groups are "bridge" relations, the people involved at each side of the bridge will come to be termed "brokers," and their network behavior "brokerage," corresponding to Merton's (1949 [1968]; Gouldner 1957) "cosmopolitans" and Katz and Lazarfeld's (1955) "opinion leaders" (see Burt 1999, 2005, pp. 84–6, for discussion of the analogy between network brokers and opinion leaders). In graph theory, a "bridge" connects two people who cannot otherwise be connected indirectly, but it is customary to discuss as bridges any connection between groups unlikely to otherwise connect. In Figure 2.2 for example, the person labeled "Bill" is a network broker on bridge connections between the organization's operations in Europe and Asia. The person labeled "Bob" is a network broker on bridge connections between operations in Europe and the United States. Nan Lin's work on social capital is primarily in this second line of work as an explanation for why certain people have an advantage in securing attractive jobs. Therefore, I focus on brokerage as social capital.

Initial foundation in Boston

The initial foundation for network models of brokerage was laid in the late 1960s with empirical work by young people affiliated with Harrison White in Harvard's Social Relations Department.[7] It would be difficult to overstate the importance of this initial work for the network models developed in subsequent years. The work appears to the far left in Figure 2.1: Milgram's small-world projects, and Granovetter's dissertation on what became known as "weak ties." The work begins with a paper circulated in the late 1950s by Pool and Kochen, respectively political scientist at MIT and mathematician at the IBM research institute (eventually published as Pool and Kochen 1978). Pool and Kochen asked how closely connected two randomly drawn people would be in a population of multiple groups. Even with bold assumptions, Pool and Kochen conclude they cannot answer the question without further research, but believe the probability of connection is low, decreasing with the number of separate groups in a population

In the mid-1960s, Stanley Milgram, an assistant professor in the Social Relations Department at Harvard, thought he might be able to skip the math to answer the Pool and Kochen question

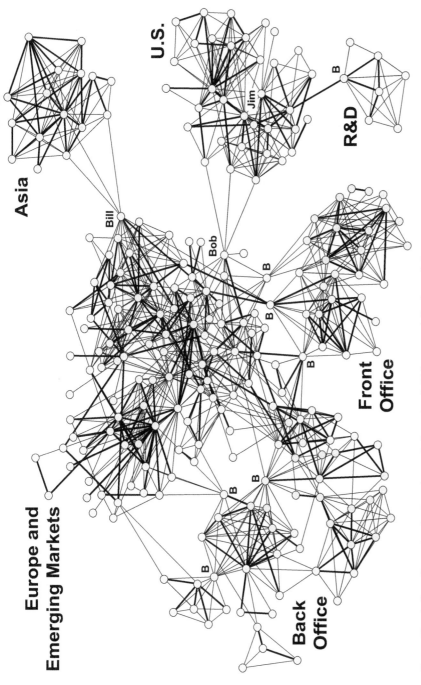

Note: Lines indicate frequent and substantive work discussion; bold lines especially close relations.

Source: Adapted from Burt (2019).

Figure 2.2 Multi-group social network at the top of a large organization

empirically. Armed with an initial $680 research budget (Milgram 1967, p. 63), he asked people of diverse occupations in Kansas and Nebraska to send a message to a target person in the Boston area by relaying the message through friends of friends. Each person had to know on a first-name basis the person to whom they forwarded the message. Consistent with Pool and Kochen's analysis, most messages never reached the target person (71 percent, Travers and Milgram 1969, p. 431), but those that did required a median of five intermediaries, mode of six (Milgram 1967, p. 65; Travers and Milgram 1969, p. 437), from which "six" became the popular answer to Pool and Kochen's question, and a "six degrees of separation" metaphor was born. Milgram (1967) named his data collection strategy the "small world" method, the phenomenon the "small world" problem, and began studying message chains for the social stratification they implied (Travers and Milgram 1969; Korte and Milgram 1970).

A couple of years later, a graduate student in the department, Mark Granovetter, ran a small study to determine how social contacts helped in job search (Granovetter reports a research budget under $900; another project with high intellectual impact per research dollar). Survey respondents were led in 1968 through a set of questions similar to what are today discussed as name generators and interpreters (Marsden 2011), to sketch a picture of the respondent's current network (literally a picture drawn during the interview on a piece of paper, with the respondent at the center of the page surrounded by cited contacts and reported connections among the contacts). Granovetter then asked whether any of the people in the pictured network helped the respondent get his current job. Disappointed from repeated responses of "no, no one here helped," Granovetter asked whether any person had helped the respondent get his current job. "Oh yes, there was John." When asked why John was not in the pictured network, respondents explained that John was an old friend from school, or a friend in the old neighborhood – someone with whom the respondent currently had little contact. Thus, relations not currently close or frequent came into Granovetter's analysis as "weak ties," and the weak-tie hypothesis was born, to be compellingly elaborated in Granovetter (1973).[8]

The argument begins with an intuitive definition of tie strength as a function of time together, emotional closeness, confiding and reciprocal services,[9] grounded in the central prediction from closure – relations are stronger in more closed networks[10] – then takes the prediction to the extreme of saying weak ties do not exist between two people strongly tied to mutual friends,[11] whereupon weak ties refer to bridge relations between separate groups. By this reasoning, weak ties are significant for search and diffusion (illustrated in Granovetter's job-search dissertation and Milgram's small-world studies) and significant for social integration within a broader community (illustrated by Granovetter 1973 using Gans' 1962 analysis of Boston's Italian West End).

Breakthrough: social resources
Nan Lin was well familiar with the early work on small worlds and weak ties. He and Granovetter were together for a couple of years as assistant professors in the Sociology Department at Johns Hopkins University, where Granovetter made a 1971 presentation on the "strength of weak ties." Lin – who was taught in graduate school by Everett Rogers about earlier research on networks and social psychology in the diffusion of information and behavior – must have been quick to recognize the research implications of the empirical results on small worlds and weak ties.

One of Lin's first projects after moving to Albany in 1971 was to run with student colleagues a modified version of Korte and Milgram's (1970) stratification study (see Chapter 11 in this book on that early, fruitful period). Lin et al. (1977, 1978) describe their project in which 298 volunteers initiated 375 messages of which 30 percent reached the destination person. By recording the occupation of the intermediary friends through whom messages were sent, Lin and his colleagues could show that successful chains tended to involve messages sent to friends in higher prestige occupations before "dipping" down to the prestige of the destination person's occupation. Unsuccessful chains, that is, chains which never reached their destination person, tended to involve messages sent between friends in occupations of similar prestige. Lin et al. (1978, p. 160) interpret this finding in terms of people in higher prestige occupations having a broader view of society: "If a given social structure is viewed as pyramidal, then the higher the prestige of an actor's position in the pyramid, the more panoramic view he has of the structure, especially the levels below him." More, the successful chains tended to involve "weak" ties of less-frequent contact rather than "strong" ties of family and neighbors (Lin et al. 1978, p. 163, brackets inserted): "the participants in the successful chains tended to utilize fewer strong ties in their forwarding effort. The successful terminals [intermediaries who reached the destination person] dramatically showed that they had weak ties with the targets."

Armed with results from his small-world study, Lin ran in 1975 a survey of the surrounding tri-city area of Albany, Schnectedy, and Troy (I will reference the study by date) to make statistical inferences about weak ties as a factor in job search and occupational achievement. His baseline was the well-known work by Blau and Duncan (1967) showing that the correlation in the United States between occupational status for father and son depends on the son's education. Better educated sons end up in occupations of higher status, regardless of their father's occupational status, where occupational status is measured by Duncan's socioeconomic index (SEI) defined by the education, income and social standing of an occupation (Duncan 1961). In addition to questions needed to replicate Blau and Duncan's work, Lin asked respondents to describe how they secured their first full-time job, and current job. Lin was especially interested in relationships with personal contacts who provided "the information that led" the respondent to his job (Lin et al. 1981b, p. 1179 for question wording, Chapter 3 in this book).[12]

Two results from the 1975 survey shape Lin's future thinking about social capital. First, the distinction between strong and weak ties matters less than the occupational status reached through either kind of tie. Table 2.1 displays the evidence for this first result in a form more familiar to contemporary readers than the path diagrams used in the original article (Lin et al. 1981a, p. 398, Chapter 3 in this book). The occupation status of a respondent's job is predicted in Table 2.1 by the occupational status of the contact whose information led to the job, and the strength of the relationship between respondent and contact (a binary distinction between friends, neighbors, and relatives as strong ties versus acquaintances or indirect connections such as friends of friends as weak ties). Table 2.1 shows that contact status matters for the status of a respondent's first and current job (t-tests over 11.0), while strength of connection with the contact matters not at all (t-tests under 1.0).

For respondents led to their job through a personal contact, the second key result from Lin's 1975 survey is that respondents who begin in lower-status occupations reach high-status occupations through weak ties to their contacts (Lin et al. 1981a, p. 399). The result is consistent with Granovetter's (1973) argument: Connections between a low-status person and

Table 2.1   Tie strength, contact status, and achieved status

	Status of First Job	**Status of Current Job**
Status of Contact Who Connected Respondent to Job	.659 (11.25)	.645 (11.09)
Strength of Respondent Tie to the Contact	.036 (0.61)	−.117 (−0.04)
R^2	.42	.47
N	204	171

Note: Standardized regression coefficients are presented with t-test statistics in parentheses. Coefficients and test statistics are computed from correlations and standard deviations in Table 1 of Lin et al. (1981a; included in this book as Chapter 3; number of observations here is the smaller of the two in their table). Job status is the socioeconomic status of a person's occupation (SEI, based on Duncan 1961), contact is the person cited by the respondent as providing "the information that led" the respondent to his first and current job (contacts for each job could be different, see Lin et al. 1981b, p. 1179 for question wording), and tie strength is a dummy variable equal to one if respondent and contact were strongly connected (friends, neighbors, or relatives) versus acquaintance or indirect connection such as a friend of a friend.

a high-status person are likely to be bridge relations between groups far apart in social structure, and such relations are expected to be weak rather than strong.

Lin emerges from his small-world study and 1975 Albany survey knowing that contact occupational status distinguishes successful small-world chains, and dominates weak ties in job search. Lin proposes a "social resources" perspective on network advantage: the resources reached through a network matter more for achievement than the structure of the network, particularly resources indicated by occupational status in a hierarchical pyramid of statuses. Networks matter for advantage, but as a function of the resources held by people in the network rather than the network's structure. The cornerstone publication – the first solid bar in Figure 2.1 – is Lin's 1981 article in the *American Sociological Review* (ASR) with two of his students, Ensel and Vaughn. An individual's social resources are defined as (Lin et al. 1981a, p. 395, Chapter 3 in this book): "the wealth, status, power as well as social ties of those persons who are directly or indirectly linked to the individual." And those social resources are distributed in a hierarchical pyramid, as Lin and his colleagues continue on the same page:

> This proposal conceives of the social structure as comprising a network of persons whose positions are ranked according to certain normative honors and rewards, such as wealth, status and power. It further assumes that the structure has a pyramidal shape in terms of the accessibility and control of such honors and rewards. A position nearer to the top of the structure has greater access to and control of honors and rewards not only because more honors and rewards are attached to the position intrinsically, but also because the higher position has greater access to positions elsewhere (primarily lower) in the rankings.

In a companion article, Lin et al. (1981b) use the 1975 survey data to report a strong role for contact status in the baseline Blau and Duncan model. Also in 1981, Lin convened a conference of network analysts at Albany where he presented social resources as (Lin 1982, p. 131) "a theory explaining why certain goal-oriented actions are more successful than others." Lin's (1982) succinct chapter in the book resulting from the conference (Marsden and Lin 1982) repeats key findings from Lin's projects described above along with more elaborate discussion of the pyramid image of resource distribution than was possible within the space limits of the 1981 ASR article (e.g., Lin 1982, p. 136).

In addition to providing data on the use of social resources in job search, Lin's 1975 survey provided data on the extent to which respondents had access to social resources more generally. Respondents were asked whether they had personal contacts (friends, family, or acquaintances) in each of 20 target occupations that varied from low to high status (Lin and Dumin 1986, p. 372 for wording). Adumbrating future research practice by Lin and colleagues, Lin and Dumin (1986) – the third prominent social-capital work in Figure 2.1 – gave each respondent two scores to measure his access to social resources: the highest occupational status in which he has a personal contact (to be termed "upper reachability" in Lin's 2001 book), and the range of statuses in which he has personal contacts (status of highest-status occupation in which respondent has a contact minus status of lowest-status occupation in which he has a contact, to be termed "heterogeneity" in Lin's 2001 book). The two scores are closely correlated (.77, Lin and Dumin 1986, p. 381). Consistent with the proposed hierarchical distribution of social resources, respondents with fathers in occupations of higher status have personal contacts in occupations of high and varied status (Lin and Dumin 1986, p. 376): "the strength of a higher position is due to its access to higher occupations while maintaining its access to lower occupations." Also consistent with the hierarchical distribution (as well as earlier work on social distance, Laumann 1966), relations are fewer and weaker between people in occupations more different in status (Lin and Dumin 1986, p. 378).

In all, the 1970s were an exciting, breakthrough period in Nan Lin's work on social capital, visible in subsequent prominent publications in the 1980s indicated by the three dark bars in Figure 2.1. Lin continues through the 1980s to use his resources perspective to understand advantage from an individual's place in macro social structure.

From weak ties to structural holes[13]

Bridge-and-cluster structures such as those illustrated in Figure 2.2 give people two broadly distinct ways to create value: specialize within a cluster (closure), or integrate across clusters (brokerage). Closure is about strengthening connections within a cluster to gain advantage by improving coordination so we become more reliable and efficient in doing what we currently do (e.g., Jim in the Figure 2.2 U.S. cluster). Brokerage is about connecting across clusters to synthesize productive new practice from diverse bits of information otherwise segregated in separate clusters, with the goal of devising more productive, perhaps different, ways of doing what we currently do. The individuals labeled "Bill" and "Bob" in Figure 2.2 are example network brokers, as are several other people identified with the letter "B" in the figure. Network brokers contrast local operations with operations elsewhere. Might operations over here be a benchmark for us? Might there be a synthesis of operations in those two groups that would give us a competitive advantage?

Broker advantage

Network brokers like Bill and Bob have three information advantages: breadth, timing and arbitrage. With respect to breadth, Bill and Bob's bridge relations across groups give them access to more diverse information. Bob looking at European operations can see where certain practices in America could be an improvement. Bill looking at European operations can see where certain practices in Asia could be an improvement. With respect to timing, Bill and Bob are positioned at crossroads in the flow of information between groups, so they are early to learn about activities in other groups and are often the person introducing to one group information from another. There is no one other than Bob and Bill positioned to look at European operations through an American or Asian lens. Bill and Bob are more likely to know when it would be rewarding to bring together separate groups, which gives them a disproportionate say in whose interests are served when the contacts come together, which brings in arbitrage: Network brokers have an advantage in translating opinion and behavior familiar from one group into the dialect of a target group. Bob and Bill can express their proposals from overseas in terms familiar to their European colleagues. Bob and Bill's relations overseas are weaker than their relations within Europe, but it is not the weakness of their overseas relations that provides value – it is the lack of alternative routes for information flow. Bob's relations with American colleagues, and Bill's relations with Asian colleagues, are bridge relations.

Advantage is less about getting novel information than it is about applying novel interpretations to existing information, and combining previously disparate bits of information into novel interpretations (Burt 2007, 2010). Network structure indicates how a person interprets information. It is one thing to be exposed to diverse knowledge and practice that defines an opportunity. It is quite another to recognize and develop the opportunity. Diverse information is today readily available from professionals, social media, or word of mouth. It is easy to look up a concept in Wikipedia and cite a reputable article on the concept. It is quite another to know the concept well enough to transform it into ideas more appealing to a target audience. Relative to a person who has spent their time in a single line of work, a person connected to multiple lines of work is more likely to see a novel solution that integrates or synthesizes knowledge or practice across previously separate lines. The same holds for recombinant information across multiple countries, industries, disciplines, or projects.

Beyond network brokers having information advantages that manifest in them reaching higher socioeconomic status than peers, a by-product of them exercising their advantages is that they look creative. To their European colleagues, for example, Bill and Bob will appear to be creative. The European colleagues are not familiar with American or Asian operations, so good ideas articulately proposed by Bill or Bob from their contacts overseas look like creative innovations to the Europeans. Suppose that Bob and Jim in Figure 2.2 have the same idea for an entrepreneurial spin-off from the organization. Jim knows how to express the idea in terms of American operations. The more nuanced the idea, the more embedded in American operations, and the more different the American versus European operations (as indicated by the structural hole between the two in Figure 2.2), then the less successful Jim will be in explaining the value of the idea to potential investors at the European headquarters. Jim can only explain in terms of American operations. Bob is embedded in European operations and familiar with American operations, so he is better positioned to explain the value of the idea to potential investors in familiar terms.

In sum, network structure is a proxy for the distribution of information, a structural hole is a context for potentially valuable action moving information across the hole, brokerage is the act of coordinating across the hole, and network brokers are the coordinators. Network brokers are entrepreneurs operating somewhere between the force of corporate authority and the dexterity of markets, building bridges between disconnected parts of markets and organizations where it is valuable to do so. They translate what is known here into what can be understood and seen to be valuable over there. Network brokers are the social mechanism that clears a sticky-information market.

Distinguishing network brokers
In his initial small-world report, Milgram discusses a phenomenon he terms "funneling" in which certain individuals appeared in multiple completed chains (e.g., contacts Jacobs and Jones in Milgram 1967, p. 67). Individuals in multiple completed chains have more bridge connections across groups, so the individuals are portals for search efforts from outside the local network. The individuals through whom funneling is more likely are the opinion leaders that Katz and Lazarsfeld (1955) initially described in mass media advertising, and the people who later become known as network brokers. Being able to distinguish the network brokers in a population is essential to empirical research on the correlates of network advantage. In their early effort, Katz and Lazarsfeld (1955, Appendix D) distinguished opinion leaders by asking a survey respondent about specific instances when she influenced others ("Have you recently been asked for your advice about..."), and whether the respondent saw herself as relatively influential ("Compared with other women in your circle of acquaintances, are you more or less likely than any of them to be asked your advice on...").

Network measures of brokerage in the 1970s built on the earlier foundation in two broadly distinct directions: counts of the structural holes to which a person – or any network element more generally – has access, and measures of the lack of access. None of the measurement proposals in the 1970s and 1980s mentions the phrase "structural hole," which is introduced later to capture the earlier intuitions. I use the term here because intuitions for the early network broker focus on the gaps in social structure now known as structural holes. Betweenness and constraint are illustrative, often-used measures.

Freeman (1977, 1978) proposes a "network betweenness" index, which is a count of the number of structural holes to which a network element has monopoly access (for related count measures, see Cook et al. 1983; Gould and Fernandez 1989, and Freeman et al. 1991 extending Freeman's index to continuous measures of connections; Everett and Borgatti 2005 with special reference to ego networks and the tendency for ego-network brokers to be central in the broader network beyond their own). A quick intuition for Freeman's betweenness index is communicated in Figure 2.3. Ego has five contacts, three from within his own group, and one each from two other groups. Betweenness is the sum of disconnects between contacts for which ego is the only connection. The first row of the table in Figure 2.3 shows that the relationship between contacts one and five is a structural hole for which ego is the only connection. Ego has monopoly access to the hole. Ego's betweenness increases by one. The same for the structural hole between contacts two and five. There is less exclusive access to the hole between contacts two and three. Ego shares access with contact one, so ego's betweenness only increases by a half. Across all pairs of contacts, ego has a score of 5.5, indicating that he has monopoly access to five and a half structural holes.

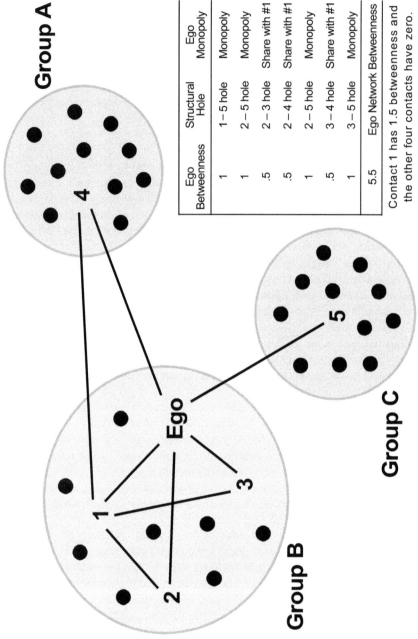

Ego Betweenness	Structural Hole	Ego Monopoly
1	1 – 5 hole	Monopoly
1	2 – 5 hole	Monopoly
.5	2 – 3 hole	Share with #1
.5	2 – 4 hole	Share with #1
1	2 – 5 hole	Monopoly
.5	3 – 4 hole	Share with #1
1	3 – 5 hole	Monopoly
5.5	Ego Network Betweenness	

Contact 1 has 1.5 betweenness and the other four contacts have zero.

Note: Network betweenness is 5.5, network constraint is .48, and relations outside ego's network are not indicated.

Figure 2.3   Sociogram of ego's network

Burt (1980, 1982, 1992, pp. 54 ff.; Burt et al. 1980) proposes a "network constraint" index, applied first to intergroup relations, then to interpersonal relations. Detailed discussion of the index with comparison to betweenness is available in recent reviews (Burt 2010, pp. 293ff., 2019; Burt et al. 2013). The intuition for the index is that little is known about how information advantage increases with more access to more structural holes, but we can clearly define what it means to have no access. The intuition is nicely illustrated by the way Granovetter (1983, p. 202) says that his weak-tie argument predicts success:

> It follows then, that individuals with few weak ties will be deprived of information from distant parts of the social system and will be confined to the provincial news and views of their close friends. This deprivation will not only insulate them from the latest ideas and fashions but may put them in a disadvantaged position in the labor market, where advancement can depend, as I have documented elsewhere (1974), on knowing about appropriate job openings at just the right time.

Granovetter does not say that having many weak ties is an advantage (which would expose him to the Table 2.2 prediction problem discussed below). He says the lack of weak ties – in other words, no bridges to other groups – is a disadvantage. Network constraint measures the extent to which ego's network provides no access to structural holes. Each of ego's contacts has a constraint score of zero to one measuring the extent to which ego cannot avoid the contact. The constraint a contact poses for ego decreases with network size (because it is more difficult for ego to avoid someone in a smaller network), increases with network density (because it is more difficult for ego to avoid someone when everyone is strongly interconnected), and increases with network hierarchy, or centralization (because it is more difficult for ego to avoid someone when everyone is tied to a central leader, illustrated by contact 1 in Figure 2.3). The sum of ego's contact scores is ego's network constraint score.

The ego network in Figure 2.3 is listed with a betweenness score of 5.5 and a constraint score of .48. Without a frame of reference, it is difficult to know whether those scores indicate little or a lot of access to structural holes. Betweenness and constraint scores are plotted in Figure 2.4 for an area probability survey of 700 Chinese entrepreneurs in the Jiangsu, Shanghai and Zhejiang provinces. The networks are discussed elsewhere with success correlates (Burt and Burzynska 2017; Burt and Opper 2017; Burt 2019). For the purposes here, two points are illustrated in Figure 2.4. First, the network in Figure 2.3 provides slightly more access to structural holes than is average for the Chinese entrepreneurs: ego's 5.5 betweenness is higher than the 3.6 median in Figure 2.4, and ego's .48 constraint is lower than the .57 median constraint score. Second, betweenness measures access to structural holes while constraint measures the lack of access, so it is not surprising to see in Figure 2.4 the strong −.92 correlation between the measures.[14]

Over the last thirty years, betweenness, constraint and related network metrics have appeared in a burgeoning literature on the emotional, perceptual and success correlates of structural holes. Reviews are typically incomplete because the literature is expanding so quickly (tens of thousands of Google cites to network betweenness and constraint). The reviews to the right in Figure 2.1 are portals into the literature, but the key point is that people with less access to structural holes are less successful than peers in terms of more positive work evaluations, higher compensation and faster promotion to senior rank. More recently, evidence has also accumulated on the expected creativity association with structural holes. Network brokers are high on creativity when creativity is measured by supervisor's summary

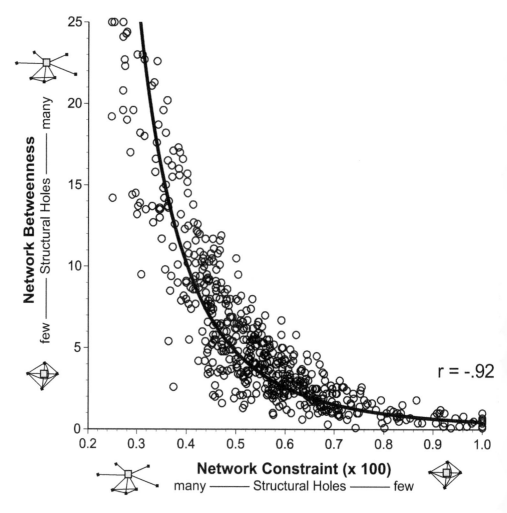

Figure 2.4   Network betweenness versus network constraint for an area probability sample of 700 Chinese entrepreneurs

opinion of a subordinate's work (Perry-Smith 2006; Jang 2018; Carnabuci and Quintane 2018), by senior executive opinion of a manager's best idea for improving the organization (Burt 2004, 2005, Chapter 2), or by external critical opinion of final product (Fleming and Marx 2006; Fleming et al. 2007; deVaan et al. 2015; Soda et al. 2018).

Weak prediction from weak ties[15]
With all the evidence of advantage associated with bridge ties, why do the results in Table 2.1 show a negligible success association with weak ties? Granovetter (1983, p. 208) comments on the Table 2.1 results by emphasizing that weak ties per se are not valuable (brackets added, italics in original): "The argument of SWT [strength of weak ties] implies that only *bridging* weak ties are of special value to individuals; the significance of weak ties is that they are far

more likely to be bridges than are strong ties." Thus, it makes sense that Lin finds weak ties consequential for respondents of low status contacting high status people because those ties are bridge relations between occupations distant from one another. Still, if weak ties are bridges, and bridges are valuable, then the success association with weak ties in Table 2.1 should be stronger, as argued by Lin et al. (1981a, Chapter 3 in this book).

Weak ties tend not to be bridges
The problem is that weak ties tend not to be bridges. Bridge relations tend to be weak ties, but weak ties tend not to be bridges. "The strength of weak ties" is a catchy title, but the title accurate to the argument would be "The strength of bridges," which would not have been as engaging for a 1970s audience of sociologists.

Table 2.2 illustrates the prediction problem using the association between weak ties and bridges. Rows sort your relations into two categories of strength: Strong ties are your frequent, close contacts. Weak ties are less close friends and acquaintances. People typically have more weak than strong ties. Columns in Table 2.2 distinguish relations between people in your social group, however groups are defined, versus bridge relations to people in other groups. The relations in Figure 2.2 between Bill and his Asian contacts are bridge ties. Bill's bridge ties to Asia are the only connection between two otherwise separate clusters of strongly interconnected people (cf. Granovetter 1973, p. 1365). From what we know about how relations develop, bridges form less often than relations between socially similar people (McPherson et al. 2001). Relations within group include strong ties to close friends and colleagues seen often, but also include many weak ties to friends of those close contacts, and friends of friends – people in your line of work or your social group who you meet occasionally, or rarely, if at all.

Cells in Table 2.2 show the relative frequencies expected under independence. Strong ties occur much less often than weak, and ties between groups occur much less often than ties within groups, so strong ties between groups are expected to be rare. Weak ties occur much more often than strong, and ties within groups occur much more often than ties between groups, so weak ties within groups are expected to be the most numerous of all combinations in Table 2.2.

Table 2.2   Strong and weak ties within and across groups

	Location in Social Structure		
Tie Strength	**Within Group**	**Between Groups**	**Total**
Weak Tie	many	some	More
Strong Tie	some	rare	Less
Total	More	Less	

Note: Reproduced from Burt (1992, p. 43) with permission from Harvard University Press.

For illustration, consider the person labeled Bill in Figure 2.2. Bill has two strong ties with colleagues in Europe. He has 12 weak ties, 9 with European colleagues and 3 with his Asian contacts. Bill's 14 ties are relatively close relations elicited by the survey used to gather the data for Figure 2.2 ("Who are the people with whom you have had the most frequent and substantive work discussion in the last six months?"). Through his 14 cited contacts, Bill has weaker, uncited ties to friends and friends of friends who might have been cited under a more thorough inventory of relationships. Bill's office is in Europe so he is especially likely to have spoken to, bumped into, or worked with, friends of his 11 cited European colleagues. Consistent with the distribution of his cited colleagues in versus beyond Europe, the bulk of Bill's weak ties are expected with other people in his own social cluster, people who share his European perspective and behavior.

Prediction

The weak-tie argument is about weak ties that are bridges, an argument about both the strength of relations and their location – because a bridge is at once two things: a chasm spanned, and the span itself. By title and subsequent application, the weak tie argument is about the strength of relations that span chasms, that is, structural holes, between social clusters – but it is the chasm spanned that generates information benefits. Whether a relation is strong or weak, it generates information benefits when it is a bridge over a structural hole. In other words, information benefits vary not across the rows of Table 2.2, but across the columns, higher from bridge relations.

This is accurately represented in the weak tie argument because the argument focuses on the two cells in the second column of Table 2.2. The argument predicts that relations between social clusters, the bridges that provide information benefits, are more likely weak than strong. In the second column of Table 2.2, weak tie bridges are more likely than strong tie bridges. To simplify his argument, Granovetter makes this tendency absolute by ruling out strong tie bridges (the "rare" cell in Table 2.2 corresponds to Granovetter's 1973, p. 1363 "forbidden triad"). He (1973, p. 1364) says:

> A strong tie can be a bridge, therefore, only if neither party to it has any other strong ties, unlikely in a social network of any size (though possible in a small group). Weak ties suffer no such restriction, though they are certainly not automatically bridges. What is important, rather, is that all bridges are weak ties.

Ruling out strong-tie bridges simplifies the theoretical argument, but is inconsistent with the empirical evidence that later emerged. Bridges do tend to be weak, but not always, and strong bridges can be more valuable than weak for moving information from one social cluster to another for coordination (Uzzi 1996; Tortoriello and Krackhardt 2010; Aral and Van Alstyne 2011), diffusion in general (Burt 1999, 2010, pp. 353–61; Reagans and McEvily 2003; Centola and Macy 2007; Tortoriello et al. 2012; Masuda et al. 2018), or job search in particular (Bian 1997). In fact, strong-tie bridges are essential to the power of *guanxi* in China (Bian 2019; Burt and Burzynska 2017; Burt et al. 2018; Burt and Batjargal 2019).

Therefore, using weak ties to measure information advantage (row contrast in Table 2.2) obscures the connection between information advantage and bridge relations (column contrast in Table 2.2). Most weak ties are in-group connections that provide little or no information advantage (upper-left cell in Table 2.2). Research using the rows in Table 2.2 to measure network advantage can be expected to yield weak results on average, and at best inconsistent results, depending on how relations are sampled for study. It is not surprising that weak ties have a negligible association with success in Table 2.1.

Consolidation: social resources as social capital
Fortified by the results from his 1975 Albany survey, and successful publication during the 1980s, Nan Lin enters the 1990s with a move to Duke University and a focus on contact resources as the key to network advantage. The lack in Figure 2.1 of prominent works by Lin during the 1990s implies a period of quiet. In fact, these were years of consolidation: intense reading, writing and re-writing from which Lin emerges at the end of the decade with his most prominent work, indicated in Figure 2.1 by the four bars over 1999, 2000 and 2001.

Initial Social Capital *book*
I have a sense of activity during this period because in 1993 I was asked to review a proposal to Cambridge University Press for what would become Lin's *Social Capital* book. In 1993, the book had a different title, and indeed was a different book. The proposed book was entitled *Social Resources and Social Action*, a book intended to bring together research during the 1980s in Lin's social resources perspective. To give you a sense of the book, this was my summary evaluation:[16]

> This is likely to be a significant work. The book addresses a substantively important question, for which there are large book-buying audiences, and Nan Lin is the optimum person to write it. The book will be a summary statement of evidence and argument on the question of how networks provide access to action-relevant resources (e.g., knowing the right people gives you access to better jobs). There are three sections of material; two chapters lay out the argument, six chapters review evidence, and the concluding four chapters are two that refine the argument (Chap. 10 on variation in weak tie effectiveness, Chap. 12 on social resources versus social capital) and two that link the argument to related substantive topics (Chap. 9 on social support and distress, Chap. 11 on rational choice arguments about group formation).
>
> Such a book has at least five constituencies (more on this below): (a) libraries, (b) people interested in network analysis on any substantive topic (small audience across disciplines), (c) people interested in social support (large audience in sociology and social welfare), (d) people interested in group formation and mobilization (large audience in sociology and political science; check the numbers on Dave Knoke's book in your series), and (e) people interested in job search and stratification (large audience in sociology and economics; check the numbers on Ron Breiger's book in your series).
>
> Nan Lin has three qualities that make him the ideal author of this book: (a) He has done more research on the topic than anyone else. (b) Nan's writing clearly communicates empirical research results. (c) Nan's research is based on probability surveys of heterogeneous populations (versus the non-probability surveys typical in network analysis) and such evidence is needed to make people in the book's target audience take the book seriously.
>
> In sum, get this book. It contains authoritative evidence, on an important question, that has large constituencies ready for the book. I believe that the book will sell and will do honor to the series.

continued with comments around three points: focusing on essential elements in the social resources argument, bridging the argument to the substantive interests of target audiences, and framing the argument more clearly with respect to alternatives. The third point in particular is relevant to this chapter. Quoting again from my comments to Cambridge, I was concerned about:

> ...the inattention in the prospectus to positioning "social resources" research relative to "social capital" research. The issue is mentioned in the prospectus and is one of the final chapters in the book. Not enough. Positioning social resources relative to social capital is one of the two or three most critical issues for the success of this book. It isn't just that social resource and social capital research seem to overlap (as stated on page 3 of the prospectus); they can be viewed as synonyms. Two points: (a) "Social resources" and "social capital" explanations are functionally identical; both are advanced as the social alternative to explaining achievement in terms of personal attributes. Achievement is a function of who you are, but it is also a function of who you know and have known. In the social capital argument, "social capital" is contrasted with "human capital" (which is the aggregate of resources you control personally; e.g., looks, charm, education, personal finances, etc.). Social capital is the aggregate of resources you control jointly via your social relations with other people and their relations with one another. The same null hypothesis is the foundation for the "social resources" argument. The research shows how "who you know" is an advantage above and beyond your personal skills and background. (b) More of the target audience studying political mobilization and job search behavior is, I believe, predisposed to the term social capital because social capital is the term used by prominent theorists (such as Bourdieu and Coleman). Even people doing important social resources research (such as Flap and Marsden) have discussed their work in terms of social capital. The point here is that social resources versus social capital is a critical issue to resolve in the first section of the book. An important part of stating the theoretical argument is to distinguish it from its alternatives. Social capital is a critical alternative. In fact, I would include a sentence or two distinguishing social resources from social capital in the dust jacket text just to get prospective buyers into the book.

Social capital frame on a social resources mechanism
The fact that the book title changed from social resources in the proposal to social capital at publication could be taken to imply my comments had their desired effect. That would be an erroneous inference. It turns out that I had learned from Nan Lin to such an extent that I thought similarly to him about marketing an idea. While working on this chapter in 2018, I went back through my folder of materials on Nan Lin and discovered my 1993 comments. The date surprised me. Why was the 1993 book delayed until 2001? Puzzled, and feeling I knew him well enough to ask, I wrote to Nan, attached my 1993 comments as a reminder, and asked about the delay. Given Nan's work ethic, I had written in my 1993 comments that I suspected the book was already drafted by the time I sent in my comments. Nan responded that he did not receive my, or any other, reviewer comments on the proposal. The publication delay was solely due to his independent extensive writing and re-writing (italics added):[17]

> It took me almost ten years to produce the book and it was all my doing. I must have done close to ten drafts. I remember somewhere along the line I decided to discard the entire manuscript and start all over. The main struggle was the framing. Issue one, whether social resources or social capital. I eventually decided to use social capital because its definition (at least Bourdieu's) was almost the same and I wanted to absorb that literature and felt I could offer a better theory with an extensive research program. Issue two: once I decided to do that, I wanted to start with "capital" which was left undefined by others working on social capital. That meant reading Marx's *The Capital* (the English version) thoroughly so that I could employ his definition but not his entire theory, with confidence. Then, I had to rewrite most of the remaining chapters in this framework.

Thus is a classic produced. Re-framing social resources as social capital facilitated interest spilling over from social capital into social resources. The line graph in Figure 2.1 of Google citations to Lin's listed social capital works follows a power function that closely resembles the increase in citations to all social capital works (displayed in the inset graph).[18]

The *Social Capital* book is the anchor for Lin's four prominent social capital works at the turn of the century. Figure 2.5 here is an executive overview providing thumbnail chapter descriptions. Chapters 5 and 6 are the core of the book. Lin states his theory in Chapter 5 (summary on pages 75–6). The chapters preceding are reviews of social thought about capital, resources and choice. Lin (2001b, Chapter 4 in this book) is an exegesis of Part I of the book (including thoughts from Chapter 13 on expressive motivation to form ties, drawing on Lin's social support work, see Chapter 5 in this book). Chapter 6 of Lin's book is largely a reprint of Lin's (1999a) review of research replicating key results in Lin et al. (1981a, Chapter 3 in this book), results reviewed above in the discussion around Table 2.1. Chapter 7 is a concrete example study in China. The fourth of Lin's four Figure 2.1 prominent social capital works at the turn of the century, Lin (2000), is a review of research on people disadvantaged in their access to social capital ("capital deficit") or returns to social capital ("returns deficit"). The review is a nice complement to the book in connecting the example analysis of gender inequality in Chapter 7 to the broader literature on inequality. Subsequent chapters in the book provide bridges to other research areas. The bridges are imaginatively sketched and a wise provision to facilitate interested outsiders making use of Lin's social resource perspective.

Social resources continue at the core of the theory. Lin (1999a, p. 471) initially explains, and repeats in his book (2001a, p. 82), that he is not replacing social resources with social capital so much as he is using social capital as a theoretical concept measured in terms of social resources:

> The convergence of the social resources and social capital theories complements and strengthens the development of a social theory focusing on the instrumental utility of accessed and mobilized resources embedded in social networks. It places the significance of social resources in the broader theoretical discussion of social capital and sharpens the definition and operationalization of social capital as a research concept. ... The following discussion reflects the merged notions of social capital and social resources. At the empirical and research levels, social resources are used, whereas at the general theoretical level, social capital is employed.

Harking back to his 1980s definition of advantage in terms of access to social resources in a hierarchical pyramid, Lin proposes that social capital (2001a, p. 29, italics in original): "should be defined as *resources embedded in a social structure that are accessed and/or mobilized in purposive actions*."

Social resources and network status

An individual's social resources were initially defined as (Lin et al. 1981a, p. 395, Chapter 3 in this book): "the wealth, status, power as well as social ties of those persons who are directly or indirectly linked to the individual." Free of journal space constraint, the definition expands with illustrations in the book (Lin 2001a, p. 43):

> We define *social resources*, or *social capital*, as those resources accessible through social connections. Social capital contains resources (e.g., wealth, power, and reputation, as well as social networks) of other individual actors to whom an individual actor can gain access through direct or indirect social

Part I. Theory and Research (exegesis in Lin 2001b)

1   Theories of Capital: The Historical Foundation – review of capital metaphors (Marx, Schultz, Becker)

2   Social Capital: Capital Captured through Social Relations – review of social capital metaphors (Bourdieu, Coleman)

3-4   Resources, Hierarchy, Networks, and Homophily: The Structural Foundation and Resources, Motivations, and Interactions: The Action Foundation – resources are action-enabling qualities such as wealth, status, power associated with a high position in a hierarchical, pyramidal social structure; social resources are resources obtained through connections with others (cf., network status)

5   The Theory and Theoretical Propositions – core theory anchored on three indicators of access to social resources: upper reachability, heterogeneity, and extensity of embedded resources

6   Social Capital and Status Attainment: A Research Tradition – core evidence; review of work connecting ego occupational prestige with contact occupational prestige in job search after the analysis in 1981 ASR paper (from Lin 1999)

7   Inequality in Social Capital: A Research Agenda – example social capital study of gender inequality in China (augmented in Lin 2000)

Part II. Conceptual Extensions

8   Social Capital and the Emergence of Social Structure: A Theory of Rational Choice – bridge to rational choice models of endogenous social structure (from Lin 1994)

9   Reputation and Social Capital: The Rational Basis for Social Exchange – bridge to research on social exchange theory, especially Blau and Homans more than Cook and Emerson

10   Social Capital in Hierarchical Structures – bridge to intra-organizational research on mobility in the style of Blau's structural sociology of opportunity constraints (from Lin 1990)

11   Institutions, Networks, and Capital Building: Societal Transformations – bridge to institutional research, DiMaggio and Powell more than Selznick, with examples from women's studies and the communist revolution in China

12   Cybernetworks and the Global Village: The Rise of Social Capital – bridge to debate over the decline in social capital

Part III. Epilogue

13   The Future of the Theory

Figure 2.5   The 2001 book

ties. They are resources embedded in the ties of one's networks. Like personal resources, social resources may include material goods such as land, houses, car, and money and symbolic goods such as education, memberships in clubs, honorific degrees, nobility or organizational titles, family name, reputation, or fame.

In both definitions, resources are loosely defined as a broad variety of qualities that could help a person pursue his or her interests. As such, Lin's social resources are analogous to a network concept of action-enabling unobserved qualities that has a long history in sociology. I mention the analogy because it is a bridge between network models of social capital and Lin's unique perspective on social capital. The analogous concept was popularized in sociology as network status by Podolny (1993, 2001, 2005), but goes back to Moreno's (1934, p. 102) measure of choice status (number of sociometric citations a person receives, now discussed as indegree), to weighted variations on choice status, factor analysis of network data, and later variations on power or network centrality used today (Bonacich 1972, 1987; Mizruchi et al. 1986; Newman 2006), including Google's page rank algorithm (see Wikipedia; Kleinberg 1999). In fact, Coleman (1990, p. 302) cites Lin's social resources perspective in his own discussion of social capital as social resources (cf. Bourdieu and Wacquant 1992, p. 116), and sometimes explicitly uses the network model of status as a measure of the resources a person has to pursue his or her interests (Coleman 1973).

The intuition for network status is that a person's level of action-enabling qualities, or resources, can be inferred from the way people around the person defer to him or her. Ego has resources to the extent that ego is sought out by people who themselves have resources. Ego's status, S_e, is a function of the status of the people who seek ego's attention:

$$S_e = \Sigma_j \, z_{je} \, S_j = z_{1e} \, S_1 + z_{2e} \, S_2 + z_{3e} \, S_3 + \ldots$$

where z_{je} is the extent to which ego is sought out by contact j, and S_j is contact j's status. Ego has high status to the extent that he or she is the object of interest from many high-status people (z_{je} high when S_j is high). Ego's status is low to the extent that no one is interested in ego (z_{je} equal zero), or the only people interested are themselves low-status (S_j low when z_{je} is high). The model is used to infer relative status from a network of connections. It works well for a center–periphery structure of people or organizations in which everyone is at least indirectly connected, and the structure varies from a core of well-connected central elements to weakly-connected elements at the periphery.[19]

Lin's key insight was that – in a probability sample of a large heterogeneous general population – occupations form a hierarchical, center–periphery macro structure, and Duncan's (1961) socioeconomic index (SEI) indicates a person's status in the structure by the income and education characteristic of the person's occupation. Therefore, we do not need to know the network structure of relations among occupations, or around a person, to know the person's status with respect to social resources. For many research purposes, network structure around ego can be replaced with macro structure around ego's occupation, so ego's status is defined by the SEI scores of ego's network contacts. In job search, for example, ego has advantage to the extent that he or she is referred to a job interview by a contact with high status rather than a low-status contact – the former carries more weight with his or her recommendation, and has better access to information on opportunities (either directly or indirectly through others).

This is not a simple descriptive matter of network composition, illustrated by the proportion of ego's contacts who are family, or contact distribution across ages, or political beliefs. Laumann (1966) had already done that when he mapped social relations within and across occupational categories (an acknowledged precedent Lin et al. 1981a, Chapter 3 in this book; Lin and Dumin 1986). But Laumann focused on ego's social psychology, asking whether people prefer connections within their own occupational status versus occupations of higher status. In contrast, Lin proposed to study ego's contacts as portals into the social resources distributed in the occupational structure.

The central prediction from Lin's insight replacing local network structure with macro structure is a "social resources" or "social-capital" proposition (respectively, Lin 1999a, p. 470 and 2001a, p. 75) that people connected with individuals in higher SEI occupations have more access to social resources, so they should be more successful than otherwise similar people without such contacts. This prediction was well supported initially (reported in Table 2.1) and subsequently (Lin 1999a, p. 474, 2001a, p. 84), and corresponds to research reporting higher success for individuals and organizations with high network status (Podolny 2005; Sauder et al. 2012).

The related, second prediction from Lin's insight is the same prediction lagged in time: Ego's current situation benefits from a good beginning. The "strength-of-position" proposition (Lin 1999a, p. 470 and 2001a, p. 76) is "the better the position of origin, the more likely the actor will access and use better social capital." The iconic example in Lin's work is a son's kinship relation to his father, through which the son has access to the social resources of the father's occupation. The "strength-of-position" prediction is addressed in fewer studies than the central "social-capital" prediction (Lin 1999a, p. 474, 2001a, p. 84), but was already widely familiar in sociology from Blau and Duncan's (1967) study of the extent to which sons in high status occupations came from fathers in high status occupations.[20]

Social resources and network brokerage
Beyond providing a measure of social resources used in a specific action, such as job search, Lin goes on to measure a person's access to social resources more generally. Network data are required to compute the network betweenness or network constraint scores measuring a person's access to the advantages of structural holes (Figure 2.3), but with local network structure replaced by macro structure, and sorted on a vertical axis of differentiation by socioeconomic status (SEI), we don't need to gather network data. We can make inferences about the diversity of opinion and practice to which a person is exposed from the SEI diversity of occupations with which a person has contact, that is to say, from the separate social structure positions with which a person has contact. This methodology in the 1975 Albany survey, analyzed in Lin and Dumin (1986), is retrospectively termed "position generator" methodology (Lin 1999a).

Survey network data are usually generated by a mix of "name generator" and "name interpreter" questions (e.g., Marsden 2011). Name generators ask for the names of people with whom the respondent has a certain kind of relationship. For example, the General Social Survey asks for the names of people with whom the respondent discusses important matters. Name interpreters ask for characteristics of the people named; for example, how long the respondent has known each one, frequency of contact, the nature of the respondent's relationship with each one, and so on. The combination provides data on the structure of the social environment around a respondent.

Lin's 1975 Albany survey used a "position generator" (a bit of a misnomer since positions are target occupations selected prior to field work by the person who designs the questionnaire). Instead of asking for the names of people with whom the respondent has a specified kind of relationship, the respondent is asked about personal contacts in target occupations (compare Killworth and Bernard's 1978 reverse small world for related methodology and Van der Gaag and Snijders 2005 on getting past occupation to social resources directly). For example, Table 2.3 lists the 20 target occupations that Lin selected for the 1975 Albany survey (selected to represent more familiar occupation titles and occupations that span SEI scores for occupations, see Lin 1999a, pp. 478–80, 2001b, pp. 87–92, Chapter 4 in this book, for advice on selecting target occupations). Respondents are given a card listing the occupations (out of order, without SEI scores) and asked a generator such as (this one from Lin 2001a, p. 88): "Would you please tell me if you happen to know someone (on a first-name basis) who has each job?" The respondent is not asked to name the contact, just think of the contact. If the respondent knows more than one person in an occupation, the respondent is asked to think about the person they have known the longest. The respondent is then asked a series of interpreter questions about the respondent's relationship with the contact (how long known, nature of relationship, and so on; for examples, see Lin 1999a, p. 477, 2001a, pp. 88 and 124, 2001b, p. 18, Chapter 4 in this book). After completing interpreter questions about the respondent's contact in one occupation, the respondent is asked about a contact in the next occupation.

Lin (2001a, p. 76) focuses on three social capital measures. "Upper reachability" is the highest status score a respondent can reach. If ego in Figure 2.3 were interviewed via a position generator, we would know that he has at least one personal contact in all three groups in the figure. If the groups were ordered by status A, B, then C, ego's upper reachability would be the status score for Group A. Contact 2's upper reachability would be the status score for Group B. With respect to the target occupations in Table 2.3, upper reachability would be 92.3 for a person who knows a lawyer by his first name.

Lin's second measure, "heterogeneity," is the spread of status scores across a respondent's contacts, defined by the maximum minus the minimum score. For ego in Figure 2.3, heterogeneity would be the difference between Group A status and Group C status. For a respondent who responds to Table 2.3 knowing a lawyer, a department head, a teacher, and a janitor on a first name basis, heterogeneity is 79.6 (92.3 minus 12.7). Lin's third measure, "extensity," is the number of target groups in which a respondent has personal contacts. For ego in Figure 2.3, extensity would be three. The above example response to Table 2.3 elicits personal contacts in four occupations, so extensity would be four.

The validity of Lin's insight about replacing local network structure with macro structure is supported by strong correlations between his social resource measures and network brokerage measures of access to structural holes. This was first pointed out by Campbell et al. (1986) and reinforced with national data by Marsden (1987). Using data available at the time from probability sample network surveys, Campbell et al. show that people with higher socioeconomic status have larger, less dense, more heterogeneous networks – in other words, people high in socioeconomic status have access to more diverse contacts, and so to more opportunities to broker information between contacts.

The association can be displayed more precisely with richer data on network status, betweenness and constraint. Kleinberg (2000b) argues the conclusion that people who provide local bridges are likely to provide bridges to outside groups, and Everett and Borgatti (2005)

Table 2.3   Target occupations in the original position generator

Upper White Collar Occupations

92.3	Lawyer
86.9	Engineer
75.1	Manager
70.6	Department Head
62.0	Small business owner
59.8	Union official
44.2	Teacher

Upper Blue Collar Occupations

49.7	Foreman
44.0	Skilled Worker
27.0	Mechanic/Repairman
21.0	Machinist

Lower White Collar Occupations

66.0	Insurance Agent
61.9	Secretary
49.4	Salesman
45.0	Office Machine Operator
44.0	Office Clerk

Lower Blue Collar Occupations

18.2	Guard/Watchman
17.0	Waiter/Bartender
12.7	Janitor/Porter
7.9	Laborer

Note: From Lin and Dumin (1986, p. 374), these are the 20 target occupations used in the 1975 Albany survey, each preceded by its Duncan socioeconomic index (SEI) score.

report a high correlation between ego-network betweenness and centrality in the broader network. Table 2.4 shows correlations among network measures of brokerage and network status measures of social resources computed for the management network in Figure 2.2. Social resources are measured by network status – ego's own status in the management network, in addition to the upper reachability and heterogeneity of ego's personal contacts. Upper reachability is the status of the highest-status person connected to ego. Heterogeneity is the difference between the highest and the lowest-status person connected to ego.

I take away three points from Table 2.4. First, the two measures of access to structural holes are strongly correlated (–.87), as illustrated for the Chinese entrepreneurs in Figure 2.4. Managers constrained by a closed network by definition have little betweenness access to structural holes. Second, the three network measures of social resources are closely correlated with one another, as has been reported with status measured by occupation SEI scores in large probability surveys with the position generator (e.g., Lin 2001a, p. 109). Third, the two network measures of access to structural holes are strongly correlated with all three network measures of social resources. Figure 2.6 shows the data behind the correlations in Table 2.4 for network constraint. Upper reachability and heterogeneity decrease systematically with increasing network constraint. In other words, the more closed the network around a manager, the less likely he or she has contact with high-status executives, and the more limited the status levels to which he or she does have access.

Empirical overlap notwithstanding, brokerage and social resource explanations for network advantage are conceptually distinct. As discussed with respect to Figure 2.2, the network brokerage measures are expected to predict success because ego develops skills in recombining and communicating diverse opinion and practice in his or her network. It is not access to the

Table 2.4   Social resources and network brokerage correlations for the Figure 2.2 management network

	Network Brokerage		Social Resources		
	EgoNetwork Betweenness	Network Constraint	Network Status	Upper Reachability	Heterogeneity
Betweenness	1.00				
Constraint	−.87	1.00			
Status	.65	−.85	1.00		
Upper Reach	.58	−.72	.89	1.00	
Heterogeneity	.70	−.71	.73	.85	1.00
Mean	112.44	.15	1.00	2.18	1.42
Standard Deviation	299.59	.07	.98	1.42	.95

Note: These are social capital measures for the people in the Figure 2.2 management network. Relations are scaled on a continuum from one to zero of especially close, close, less than close, distant. Two-step indirect connections are included in the computations here so that status varies more smoothly over the structural holes between groups (A and B disconnected in Figure 2.2 are here connected by their maximum indirect connection $z_{ak} \times z_{kb}$ through a third person k). Betweenness and network constraint (Figure 2.4) are expressed as log scores for the correlations (nonlinear association with social resources in Figure 2.6), but raw scores for the mean and standard deviation. Network status is the left-hand eigenvector of the network (endnote 19), normalized by its mean, so status scores are a person's status as a multiple of mean status. Upper reachability is the highest status of a person's contacts. Heterogeneity is the spread of status in a person's network, computed as upper reachability minus the lowest status of a person's contacts. Figure 2.6 displays the data for the correlations between constraint and social resources. Here and in Figure 2.6, the 4% of extreme outliers created by people most isolated in the network are deleted (to simplify the display, but as in Figure 2.4, the correlations are not greatly affected: e.g., −.72 correlation above and in Figure 2.6 is −.73 using all the data and −.74 with 5% Winsorized data).

resources held by others that is valuable so much as ego's developed skill in recombinant information. The social resource measures are expected to predict success because contacts share their valuable resources with ego, but heterogeneity and extensity are also measures of diverse opinion and practice among a person's contacts. In other words, Lin's measures of heterogeneity and extensity are also measures of access to structural holes, as illustrated in Table 2.4 and Figure 2.6.

More, and there are reasonable arguments for and against this presumption: the social resources argument assumes an idealized *guanxi* quality to relationships (Lin 2001c; Bian 2018, 2019; and Chapter 8 in this book regarding Lin's view of *guanxi*). The argument assumes that I have access to the resources of the people I know on a first-name basis; as if they would feel guilty for not sharing with me. Podolny (2001) provocatively characterizes such explanations as "pipe" images of networks in that the connection between two people is like a pipe in a plumbing system whereby what is in one of the people automatically flows to the

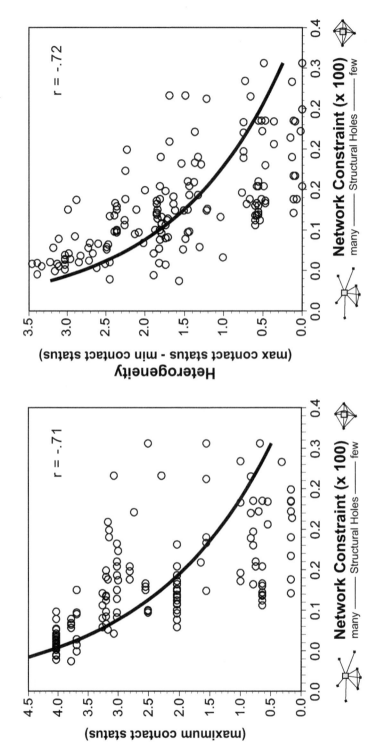

Figure 2.6   Social resources and network constraint in the Figure 2.2 management network

other. The structural hole argument of ego becoming skilled in detecting and communicating good ideas from exposure to diverse opinion and behavior makes a less demanding assumption. Ego is not presumed to have access to alter resources. Rather, value is created by ego from exposure to diversity in ego's surrounding social environment.

For example, the top of the graph to the left in Figure 2.6 shows many network brokers (low constraint) with access to contacts at the highest level of network status. These contacts are C-suite executives at the top of business functions (CEO, CFO, COO, etc.), and senior people next in line to occupy a position in the C-suite. Many people are on a first name basis with these top executives. That does not mean they all have access to C-suite resources. The CEO cannot endorse everyone seeking his or her endorsement. However, a large audience of people can benefit in their work by having a sense of C-suite opinion and practice.

To what extent, when and how often are the alternative explanations correct? The associations in Table 2.4 and Figure 2.6 strongly reject a null hypothesis of brokerage independent of social resources (-15.48 and -15.02 routine t-tests for the two graphs in Figure 2.6), but wide variation around the regression lines in Figure 2.6 shows that access to structural holes is not the same thing as access to social resources (see Van der Gaag et al. 2008 for more extreme differences). Perhaps access to the social resources of high-status contacts are how network advantage works for people low in the social order (as first reported in Lin et al. 1981a, Chapter 3 in this book), but the recombinant information and communication advantages of access to structural holes is how network advantage works for people high in the social order – a provocative empirical question for future research. The provocation is enhanced by research showing that returns to brokerage increase with social standing in the form of authority, network status and reputation (Burt 1997; Rider 2009; Burt and Merluzzi 2014). To my knowledge, Lin's social resource measures have not been used in the way illustrated in Figure 2.6, perhaps because network status is typically analyzed as a characteristic of ego rather than a characteristic distributed across ego's contacts. The simultaneous use of Lin's positional measures with more traditional network measures seems to me a promising way to explore the interface between brokerage and social resources jointly predicting who has social advantage in an organization, or beyond, in the general population.

Generalization
The four turn-of-the-century works just discussed provide a broad foundation for the third phase of Lin's work on social capital. The subsequent years have been spent showing how the social resources perspective articulated in *Social Capital* can be useful in understanding a broader range of phenomena related to social capital, in a diversity of social contexts. Three books have been produced. So, Lin and Poston (2001) contains chapters on networks and social resource use in China, Hong Kong and Taiwan. Lin and Erickson (2008a) – the most cited of Lin's social capital works after 2001, included as the bar to the far right in Figure 2.1 – contains chapters on China, Europe and the United States, with attention to the Putnam hypothesis of declining social capital (also see W. Chen 2014), a methodological discussion of position generators versus other social capital measures (Van der Gaag et al. 2008), and an updated review of the social resources perspective, with attention to replication in different countries, causality, and an overview of the book's chapters (Lin and Erickson 2008b). Lin et al. (2014a) contains chapters on China, Taiwan and the United States reporting variations in networks and social resources across the countries, over the life cycle, across gender, across

instrumental versus emotional tasks (for more detail, see the section in Chapter 8 in this book on "Lin's tri-society project on social capital"). Most chapters in the above books reach relatively specialized audiences, so they have not generated the broad attention generated by the earlier work. Rather, the books deepened and widened the evidential base for a social resource perspective.

Ongoing developments

I had two goals in writing this chapter. First, I wanted to honor Nan Lin for the many things he taught me, and to celebrate what I see as his unique and prominent contributions to the study of social capital. Second, I wanted to sketch a bridge to facilitate intellectual traffic between Lin's social resource perspective and network models of brokerage and closure providing advantage.

In pursuit of the goals, I provided an overview of social capital, discussed key works in the development of social capital as a network concept, and discussed Lin's significant contributions to that development through three phases in his work (breakthrough, consolidation and generalization). The breakthrough insight was to analyze instrumental action with macro occupational structure replacing local network structure. Instead of analyzing success contingent on the structure of the social environment around ego, ego was analyzed for his or her location in the broader social structure of occupations. Ego's contacts became portals into social resources distributed in the occupational structure. Lin consolidated his breakthrough during the 1990s into a unique perspective on social capital, operationalized through position generators, then showed with colleagues in the years after his *Social Capital* book that the theory generalized across countries. In a sentence, the heart of Lin's perspective on social capital is that people are defined by their position in macro-structure (rather than the micro-structure around them), and relationships are presumed to be portals through which one person has rights to the resources of the other. Nevertheless, the measures used to operationalize Lin's macro-structural perspective are closely correlated with, if conceptually distinct from, the network betweenness and network constraint measures used to operationalize micro-structural concepts of advantage.

Research developments by Lin and his many colleagues have enlightened the network brokerage tradition on social capital. In addition to the work already discussed generalizing *Social Capital* to other countries, ongoing work in brokerage includes research showing that information is the active ingredient for broker advantage, with network structure simply a proxy for information (e.g., Aral and Van Alstyne 2011 on diverse information sometimes occurring in closed network; Goldberg et al. 2016 on brokers doing better when they communicate in language familiar to colleagues), research on the personality of brokers (Mehra et al. 2001; Burt 2012), research showing the importance of selection into networks by exogenous processes (Kleinbaum and Stuart 2014) or emotions (Smith et al. 2012), and the feedback of networks affecting perception (Freeman 1992; Janicik and Larrick 2005; Burt 2010, Chapter 8, 2017).

The most obvious development in ongoing work has been the exhilarating entry of analysts from the natural sciences, in particular, from computer science, engineering and physics (see Freeman 2011 for a hopeful description). An especially consequential contribution from the new entrants is Watts and Strogatz's (1998) network model of Milgram's small world. The model was quickly accepted as a standard (36,789 Google citations in Figure 2.1), especially with recognition of the internet as a small world so software browsers needed to be optimized for brokerage search process (Kleinberg 1999, 2000a, 2000b). In Watts and Strogatz's model, people are characterized by two network measures: the density of surrounding relations (clustering) and the average length of connections to other people (path distance). A small world is a network containing groups within which clustering is higher than expected by random chance, and bridge connections make the average path distance between individuals about the same or less than expected by random chance.

The management network in Figure 2.2 is such a small world. On average, managers live in a dense social circle of interconnected colleagues, but there are sufficient brokers in the organization so that path distances between managers are not much higher than would be expected by random chance. The managers are at once safe in their local group at the same time that they are connected across groups.[21]

We knew from experience – and the repeated experience of analysts back to the 1950s – that networks tend to be bridge and cluster structures as illustrated in Figure 2.2, but with the Watts and Strogatz methodology we have a platform for showing that bridge and cluster structures occur across a great variety of networks (e.g., film actor network, a power grid network, and a worm network in Watts and Strogatz, plus many others subsequently), and endure despite varied and substantial exogenous shock (e.g., Kogut and Walker 2001 for a sociological view of the stable small world of German corporations, cf. Kogut 2012).

Within a stable small world, the bridge relations that distinguish network brokers tend to be less stable than relations embedded in the groups (Burt 2005, pp. 197–208), but here too there is stability in the roles individuals play. Several theoretical models describe how advantage will be distributed in stable "equilibrium" networks (Goyal and Vega-Redondo 2007; Ryall and Sorenson 2007; Buskens and van de Rijt 2008; Kleinberg et al. 2008; Reagans and Zuckerman 2008). The models are pessimistic about individuals maintaining access to structural holes, though people seem able to muddle through (Burger and Buskens 2009): the people who have advantaged access to holes today are often the people who had network advantage yesterday. Archives of digital data allow network dynamics to be studied in ways not possible previously. For example, Kleinbaum (2012) uses 250 million email messages among 30,000 employees to construct employee networks over a six-year interval, showing that employees with atypical careers develop increasing access to structural holes. He is further able to show selection and retention effects in which employees with broader networks are more likely to rotate into corporate staff roles, which increases the breadth of their networks, which is retained network when the employee returns to a line job (Kleinbaum and Stuart 2014). Foster et al. (2015) infer from extensive publication records stable scientist dispositions toward seeking rare large reward from innovative brokerage or small likely reward from small variation on established knowledge. Quintane and Carnabuci (2016) use email data over the course of a year to describe a process of hole decay in which broker employees connect across certain holes, those holes close, then the brokers move to new places in the network. These studies corroborate earlier evidence with more limited data of continuing access to brokerage opportunities (Zaheer and Soda 2009; Sasovova et al. 2010; Burt and Merluzzi 2016).[22]

Acknowledgement

I am grateful to the University of Chicago Booth School of Business for financial support during the work reported here, and appreciate comments on draft manuscripts from Yanjie Bian, Nan Lin, and Sonja Opper.

Notes
1. Citations for Figure 2.1 were tabulated during the last week of July, 2018. I looked at three sources for this exercise: Web of Science, Microsoft Academic and Google Scholar. The Web of Science reliably counts citations from journal articles. Google Scholar and Microsoft Academic expand coverage to include conference papers, theses and dissertations and other material posted on scholarly websites. When I obtained the Figure 2.1 citation counts, Lin's (2001a) book, *Social Capital*, had been cited by 248 journal articles according to the Web of Science, 9,946 works according to Microsoft Academic and 9,945 works according to Google Scholar. I put aside the Web of Science because I wanted to include the broader range of scholarly works covered by Microsoft Academic and Google Scholar. I use Google Scholar because I found it easier to get annual counts, and target specific works, especially book chapters in scholar profiles (Cothran 2011).
2. For example, Delgado López-Cózar et al. (2014) ran an experiment in which they posted to a university website six fake documents containing massive citations to themselves, which resulted in a substantial increase in their Google Scholar citations. The results are a useful reminder for some purposes, but irrelevant to my purpose here because I do not expect such behavior from the scholars in Figure 2.1.
3. The correlation is about .7 in physics (Cole and Cole 1967, p. 380n), and likely higher in sociology, given quality a more subjective judgment in sociology (Cole and Cole 1971).
4. From the preface to the first edition (Becker 1975, p. xvii): "The origins of this study can be traced both to the finding that a substantial growth in income in the United States remains after the growth in physical capital and labor has been accounted for and to the emphasis of some economists on the importance of education in promoting economic development."
5. Nan Lin provides his own exegesis (see Lin 2001b [Chapter 4 in this book] on Part I of *Social Capital*; Lin 1999a and Lin and Erickson 2008b, on empirical support; with Fu and Lin 2015 an inventory in preparation). On the broad topic of social capital, see Nahopiet and Ghoshal (1998) and Adler and Kwon (2002), with Kwon and Adler (2014) providing succinct update (also the diffuse discussion of social capital on Wikipedia). On connections between social capital and network structure see Burt (2000, 2005; Burt et al. 2013) and Moody and Paxton (2009).
6. It might seem odd to focus on network models used to conceptualize and study social capital – perhaps less odd when discussing Lin, but odd in the broader arena of social capital. Moody and Paxton (2009, p. 1491) report: "4.5% of abstracts for articles on social networks mention social capital, and just about 2% of those on social capital explicitly mention social networks." The word "explicit" is to be emphasized in Moody and Paxton's report. There is a great deal of work on social capital that refers to networks without explicitly mentioning network structure, treating networks as an unobserved transcendental force somehow responsible for social norms of trust, cooperation and resulting prosperity. Fukuyama (1995) is one of Moody and Paxton's cited examples. It does "not rest on explicit network connections" (Moody and Paxton 2009, p. 1494), but it is an argument about trust and cooperation within closed networks. Of 180 instances of "network" in Fukuyama's book, 10 are about trust and cooperation between group members, 16 are about electronic networks, versus 154 about trust and cooperation between interconnected employees within and across organizations, sometimes business groups such as Keiretsu, sometimes family, but consistently trust and cooperation between interconnected people – a standard closure story. Putnam (1993a) adapted Coleman's (1988) closure argument to describe trust and cooperation within Italian communities, and Fukuyama (1995) adapted both their arguments to describe trust and cooperation within and between networked organizations. What is missing in Fukuyama's story, and this is what I take to be Moody and Paxton's point, is attention to how networks are responsible for trust and cooperation. Moody and Paxton argue the virtues of increasing the overlap between work on social capital and social networks. Their reasons of rigor, clarity, and extension are well advised (in addition to replication more likely with increased rigor and clarity). I take the path here of putting aside social capital work in which social networks are left a metaphorical transcendental force.
7. White (1970, p. 259) thanks Milgram for suggesting White's small-world analysis, and Milgram (1967, p. 65; Travers and Milgram 1969, p. 436) cites White's analysis. With respect to the subsequent work on weak ties between groups, White was Granovetter's dissertation chairman (Granovetter 1974, p. ix), and see Lee's (1969, pp. xiv–xv) appreciation to White for his advice on her dissertation project in which she describes how women searched through networks for a then-illegal abortionist, similar in many ways to Granovetter's later dissertation on job search. It would be interesting to know what other Department dissertations in the late 1960s leveraged the small world metaphor.
8. I paraphrased this treasured discovery story from my memory of conversation in 1980 over dinner with Mark in Albany, New York. I have repeated the story often to students, but this chapter is the first time I put it in print, so I sent my text by email to Mark to check for accuracy. Mark confirmed the story, but also graciously gave

credit to having heard a lecture by Harrison White about the Rapoport and Horvath (1961) article which demonstrated to Mark the connective power of weak ties, which perhaps predisposed graduate student Granovetter to think of asking about contacts not listed on the respondent's pictured network. A draft of the 1973 weak-ties paper went out for journal review in 1969.

9. Granovetter (1973, p. 1361): "the strength of a tie is a (probably linear) combination of the amount of time, the emotional intensity, the intimacy (mutual confiding), and the reciprocal services which characterize the tie." Subsequent empirical research shows that tie strength varies on at least two independent dimensions, frequency versus emotional closeness (Marsden and Campbell 1984; Burt 2005, p. 52, 2010, pp. 286–8), and with respect to information transfer in particular, Brashears and Quintane (2018) make a good case for distinguishing frequency from capacity and redundancy, but the intuitive sense of strength as a joint function of frequency and closeness is sufficient for this discussion.

10. Granovetter (1973, p. 1362): "The hypothesis which enables us to relate dyadic ties to larger structures is: the stronger the tie between A and B, the larger the proportion of individuals in S to whom they will both be tied, that is, connected by a weak or strong tie. This overlap in their friendship circles is predicted to be least when their tie is absent, most when it is strong, and intermediate when it is weak."

11. Referring to a triad of two disconnected people with a close mutual friend as "forbidden," Granovetter (1973, pp. 1363–4, italics in original) concludes: "Now, if the stipulated triad is absent, it follows that, except under unlikely conditions, *no strong tie is a bridge*."

12. Lin's 1975 survey is also noteworthy as an early example of network items in a survey of a probability sample of people in a heterogeneous population, which allowed Lin to draw statistical inferences about the general population. Most prior network research used cluster samples of people in a group, organization, or neighborhood. The 1965–66 Detroit Area Survey (Laumann 1973), based on a modified probability sample of the Detroit area, was the primary precursor to Lin's 1975 survey, and the 1977–78 Northern California Community Study (Fischer 1982) based on a stratified probability sample of the San Francisco Bay Area was the next step forward, both of which facilitated inclusion of network items in the 1985 General Social Survey with a national probability sample (Burt 1984; Marsden 1987). The subsequent step is to gather comparable network data from probability samples in multiple countries, as was done with Lin's position generator in the 2017 International Social Survey Programme, which includes probability samples of respondents in 50 countries (Bian and Ikeda 2014). Representative sample surveys are one of Lin's three primary contributions to Chinese sociology (see Chapter 8).

13. Portions of this section are adapted from introductions to the network theory for other audiences, most recently entrepreneurship (Burt 2019).

14. The data in Figure 2.4 are simplified in two ways for their use here. First, I reduced the observed six levels of connection strength to three to have an abundance of structural holes. Any relationship less than close is treated as a hole. The three strength scores are 1 for especially close, .57 for close, and 0 for anything less than close (scaling in Burt and Burzynska 2017, pp. 255–7). Constraint scores are computed in the usual way, but the betweenness scores illustrated in Figure 2.3 with binary data now have three levels: ego's access to a structural hole between contacts A and B can be 1 for ego especially close to both A and B, or .57 for ego especially to A while just close to B, or .32 for ego close to both A and B but not especially to either. Second, I removed the distraction of outlier scores. The correlation in Figure 2.4 is unaffected (−.92 for all data, −.93 for 1 percent Winsorized data, −.92 in Figure 2.4 for extreme 1 percent deleted from the data).

15. Portions of this section are adapted from Burt (1992, pp. 27–30).

16. The text is from my 18 August 1993 email comments to Mark Granovetter recommending Nan Lin's book for Mark's "Structural Analysis in the Social Sciences" book series with Cambridge University Press.

17. This quoted text is taken, with permission, from Nan Lin's 22 September 2018 email response to my inquiry.

18. I am comfortable using the Google citations to compare relative growth in attention to topics, but cautious about absolute levels. The volume of intellectual content available for digital search has expanded exponentially since Google's 1998 incorporation. Google citations to most topics can be expected to begin low in the 1990s and grow rapidly thereafter. For Figure 2.1, I arbitrarily began the count of citations to Lin's prominent social capital publications in 1994.

19. Scores for network status are computed as the left-hand eigenvector corresponding to the largest eigenvalue of a network matrix. If the rows are normalized to sum to one (so relations indicate each person's allocation of network time and energy to contacts) or each column sums to one (relations indicate the share of attention to each person that comes from specific contacts), the largest eigenvalue equals one and the equation in the text is the left-hand eigenvector. Under different names, the network status model has general use in the social sciences. For example, if the network relations used to compute status describe flows between kinds of goods as in an input–output table, network status corresponds to price under perfect competition (e.g., Hicks 1939, appendices). Network status has no absolute value; people have more or less status than other people, as a product has price higher or lower than the price of another product. I express status here relative to the network average, so a status score of 1.0 indicates a person whose status is average, and a score of 3.0 indicates a person whose status

is three times that of the average person. Eigenvector scores are routinely available in network analysis software.

20. Lin (1999a) focuses on three predictions: the two I discuss in the text – the "social resources" and "strength of position" predictions, plus a third from Lin et al. (1981) concerning weak ties. The "strength of weak tie" prediction is that "the weaker the tie, the more likely ego will have access to better social capital for instrumental action" (Lin 2001a, p. 76). This prediction is not supported in the 1975 Albany study (discussed here in Table 2.1) except for the case when a weak tie is a bridge from low to high occupational SEI, which is consistent with my Table 2.2 explanation that weak ties are social capital only when they are bridges across structural holes. Lin's intuition for the third prediction might be better stated as a "strength of bridges" prediction, which takes us to the next section, on social resources and network brokerage.

21. There are 236 managers in the Figure 2.2 network and 979 symmetric connections. To get benchmark clustering and path distance scores for a corresponding random network, I averaged each of the two measures across 20 networks of 236 people in which 979 symmetric connections are distributed at random (Erdös-Rényi random graphs). The observed structure is dramatically more clustered than would be expected if connections were random: .70 clustering coefficient for the observed structure versus .04 if relations were random between the managers. Yet people are connected almost as well as would be expected in a random network: The average manager's path distance to another person is 4.2 steps, which is about one and a half intermediaries longer than expected in a network of random connections among the 236 managers (4.2 – 2.8 = 1.4 steps).

22. The stability research in this paragraph is less interesting in Lin's social resource perspective because social resource measures are anchored in a continuing structure of occupations. One example of stability work on social resources is W. Chen's (2014) chapter in the most recent of Lin's edited social capital books. Using position generator data for a national probability sample of Americans in 2004/05 and again in 2007, Chen reports a more than random association over time in the number of occupations in which a person has contacts (extensity variable in Lin's triad of upper reach, heterogeneity and extensity).

[3]

SOCIAL RESOURCES AND STRENGTH OF TIES: STRUCTURAL FACTORS IN OCCUPATIONAL STATUS ATTAINMENT*

NAN LIN
State University of New York at Albany

WALTER M. ENSEL
Albany Medical College

JOHN C. VAUGHN
National League for Nursing

For a class of social actions such as seeking a job, the socioeconomic standings of the contact (social resources) an individual uses will probably be very important in achieving a desired result. Drawing upon data from a sample of working males aged 21–64 in the metropolitan area of Albany-Troy-Schenectady, New York, we found that the job seeker's personal resources (initially his family background, but more importantly later his educational and occupational achievements) as well as his use of weak ties affect his ability to reach a contact of high status. The contact's status, in turn, has a strong and direct effect on the prestige of the attained job. As job experience increases, a person relies more on constructed rather than ascribed relations and the strong tie between his contact and the hiring firm becomes increasingly important.

The prevailing model of the status attainment process (Blau and Duncan, 1967; Duncan, Featherman, and Duncan, 1972; Sewell and Hauser, 1975; Jencks et al., 1972; Jencks and Rainwater, 1977; Featherman and Hauser, 1978) analyzes the demographic and distributive process of achievement and locates the occupational status which a person with certain personal resources can reasonably expect to attain. Criticism that the model lacks structural and relational concerns challenges the assumption that the labor market is essentially an open and competitive arena where specifications for a job and the necessary skills and competence are easily matched and where information about job and applicant availability is widely diffused (Rees and Schultz, 1970; U.S. Department of Labor, 1975). Researchers have been generally uncon-

* Direct all correspondence to Nan Lin, Department of Sociology, State University of New York at Albany, 1400 Washington Avenue, Albany, New York 12222.

An earlier version was read at the Annual Meetings of the American Sociological Association, New York, August, 1980. The study reported herein was partially supported by a research and development grant (No. 91-36-75-14) from the Manpower Administration, U.S. Department of Labor. We are grateful to Bonnie Erickson, Mark Granovetter, and Glenna Spitze for their comments on earlier drafts.

vinced that luck or chance largely accounts for the variation of occupational achievement which this prevailing model does not explain (Jencks, et al., 1972).

These criticisms do not reflect a lack of research into mobility patterns at the structural or institutional levels. Several studies, for example those by White (1970), Spilerman (1977), and Sorensen (1977), have investigated macro-level issues such as the movements of vacancies and occupants in a structure. The analysis of dual markets and, more recently, of segmentation of occupational and industrial groupings has attempted to show mobility restrictions and patterns embedded in the structure of the labor market (Gordon, 1972; Edwards, Reich, and Gordon, 1975). Stolzenberg (1978) has discussed how organizations affect status attainment. There have not, however, been sufficient studies of the process by which an individual gets a prestigious job or of the structural factors which help determine an individual's occupational status attainment.[1]

Our paper is not an attempt to construct a universal structural theory of status attainment; we focus on that portion of the process in which the job seeker evokes social relations. We do not even identify all the structurally relevant elements in this process. Rather, our effort is to demonstrate the fruitfulness of analyzing the status attainment process in terms of two particular structural factors, social resources and the strength of social ties.

NOTIONS OF STRENGTH OF TIES AND
SOCIAL RESOURCES

Granovetter (1973:1361) has defined the strength of a tie as a "combination of the

[1] Recognition of structural factors is evident in the status attainment literature. For example, Duncan, et al. (1968) demonstrated the reciprocal effect of friends' aspirations on ego's own occupational and educational aspirations, but their model did not include any status attainment measures. Sewell and Hauser (1975) examined interpersonal influence as social psychological factors in their study of status attainment among male Wisconsin high-school graduates. They found that certain factors (parents' encouragement, teachers' encouragement, and friends' plans to attend college) helped explain educational attainment, but not occupational attainment (pp. 94–6, 186).

amount of time, the emotional intensity, the intimacy (mutual confiding), and the reciprocal services which characterize the tie." He sees weak ties as allowing a person to reach beyond his or her small, well-defined social circle in order to make connections with parts of the social structure not directly accessible to him or her. Weak ties serve as channels through which "ideas, influences and information socially distant from ego may reach him" (p. 1371). Granovetter speculated that the use of weak ties plays an important role in diffusing information and influence, providing opportunities for mobility, and helping the community to function. Boorman (1975) has demonstrated mathematically that under certain assumptions economic actors will maximize their benefits by maintaining weak ties and not strong ties.

Granovetter studied a random sample of professional, technical, and managerial personnel who had recently found new jobs through social contacts to determine how frequently the job seeker and the contact saw each other. He found that 16.7% of the job seekers saw their contact often at the time of the job search, 55.6% occasionally, and 27.8% rarely. Assuming frequency to indicate strength of tie, Granovetter concluded that job seekers used weak ties rather than strong ones. Further, he found those who had used weak ties were more satisfied with their new jobs than those who had used strong ties.

It is temping to go one step further and speculate that weak ties rather than strong ones are advantageous to individuals seeking higher status jobs. This is reasonable if we make certain assumptions, including the usual assumption that the overwhelming majority of job seekers prefer a more prestigious job to one with less prestige. We ignore the situation in which a job seeker must choose between two or more identically prestigious jobs. We may assume, in addition, that labor market information is not distributed uniformly in the social structure. The wider people cast their social nets, the more likely they are to gather information about a specific job. We also assume that the credibility of the referring person or agent

SOCIAL RESOURCES AND STRENGTH OF TIES   395

influences an employer's decision to hire a particular person. It follows that a person is more likely to find the "right" or "influential" contact if he/she looks beyond his/her immediate social circle. These assumptions need not hold simultaneously, because some contacts will provide only information (knowledge about the precise job requirements and procedures for applying it) and others will exercise influence (ability to link the person to a particular segment of the labor market and enhance his/her chances of finding a job there). Nonetheless, these assumptions lead us to hypothesize that the strength of the tie used in job-seeking is negatively related to the occupational status one attains. In general, we should find that weak rather than strong ties help the job seeker find the desired job.

More recently, we (Lin, Vaughn, and Ensel, 1981) have focused on the social resources embedded in an individual's social network. Social resources are defined as "the wealth, status, power as well as social ties of those persons who are directly or indirectly linked to the individual." Lin (Lin, Dayton, and Greenwald, 1978) proposed that an individual's access to the social resources is instrumentally important. This proposal conceives of the social structure as comprising a network of persons whose positions are ranked according to certain normative honors and rewards, such as wealth, status, and power.[2] It further assumes that the structure has a pyramidal shape in terms of the accessibility and control of such honors and rewards.[3] A position nearer to the top of the structure has greater access

to and control of honors and rewards not only because more honors and rewards are attached to the position intrinsically, but also because the higher position has greater access to positions elsewhere (primarily lower) in the rankings. In other words, a higher position commands a greater number of social resources.

The concept of social resources encompasses two components: social relations and the resources embedded in positions reached through such relations. The concept contrasts and complements the concept of personal resources as described in the social mobility and status attainment literature (Sorenson, 1977). While personal resources involve the individual's wealth, status, and power, social resources are embedded in the positions of contacts an individual reaches through his social network. These characteristics include but are broader than the reputational or prestigious characteristics as emphasized in the works of Laumann (1966) and Goode (1978). Our definition of resources is also consistent with Goode's four types of resources in the social-control processes: force, wealth, prestige, and friendship-love-affection (pp. 2–6). The last type delineates certain forms of social relations.

It would follow, then, that when seeking a job an individual will gain more by contracting someone upward in the hierarchical structure, who has, in other words, greater social resources. We hypothesize that reaching greater social resources is positively related to occupational status attainment.

Drawing upon data collected from a representative sample of males in the 21–64 age range among the noninstitutional civilian labor force, we (Lin, Vaughn and Ensel, 1981) identified those who had used social contacts in seeking first and current jobs. We then incorporated the contact's occupational status (Duncan's SEI score) into the basic Blau-Duncan status achievement model. The contact-status variable increased significantly the portion of the explained variance both for the first and current job statuses (about 10% in each case). Further, when we decomposed the effects, we found that the direct effects of

[2] The view that social structure consists of interlocking positions has gained support recently (White et al., 1976; Boorman and White, 1976; Burt, 1977). The social resources approach suggests that there should be some hierarchical order among clusters of positions, and its empirical demonstration awaits research efforts (see Burt, 1979, and Breiger, 1980, for approaches to flushing out such relationships).

[3] Violation of the pyramidal shape of a structure does not affect the general formulation. However, it is convenient to construct such an image to describe the panoramic view from the top toward the bottom of the structure and to indicate the relative number of occupants at each level of the structure. Sorensen's modelling of job earnings distribution (1977, Equations 1 and 2) assumes a similarly pyramidal inequality in society.

family background and education were much reduced and that much of the family-background effect was transmitted indirectly through the contact-status variable. We concluded, therefore, that "when one's social network is utilized for job seeking, his attained occupational status depends chiefly on his education and the social resources embedded in the network, which in turn depend largely on his ascribed status (family background)."

Strength of tie and social resources are, of course, related. They are concepts articulating an individual's interactions with structures of statuses and roles (Granovetter, 1979), and thus seem to be useful concepts in our attempt to bring social structure into an analysis of the status attainment process.

Conceptual Integration

The strength-of-ties literature has produced a hypothesis consistent with the well-known homophily (or like-me) principle (Homans, 1950; Laumann, 1966; Laumann and Senter, 1976; Verbrugge, 1979). This principle states that social interactions tend to take place among individuals with similar attributes. If frequent interaction indicates strong ties, then we may derive from the homophily principle the proposition that strong ties link persons of similar attributes. An extension of this would suggest that the heterophily principle (the linking of people with dissimilar attributes) should be more prominent among weak ties. Presumably, then, when seeking a job weak ties rather than strong ties will provide the seeker with a more extensive reach and hence with a greater likelihood of contacting people who possess job-related information and influence.

However, if the distribution of job information and influence is not random, but is part of the hierarchical structure of social resources, then the probability of an individual's gaining access to job information and influence increases when he or she makes contact with positions higher up in the structure. In other words, the heterophily principle may be ineffective if the positions reached are horizontal or lower in the structure relative to the per-

son's initial status. We may call the tendency to contact positions at higher status levels in the structure the *prestige principle* (Laumann, 1966). It is the prestige principle, then, rather than the heterophily principle, that ought to operate if job seekers wish to maximize their chances of finding contacts who are sources of job information and influence. It is here that the linkage between the strength of ties and social resources occurs. If we assume that social resources, and hence job information and influence, increase at higher levels of the hierarchical structure, then an individual can most easily reach upward in a structure if he or she uses weak ties.

What we envision is a process whereby a job seeker reaches up to a contact as a source of the information or influence the job seeker needs to find a prestigious job. The job obtained is usually at a lower level than the ultimate source of information or influence. This process is illustrated in Figure 1. The first hypothesis states that for a given status level of the ego (E), the status of the contact reached (C or C') is a function of the strength of the tie between the ego and the contact: weaker ties tend to reach contacts at higher levels (C rather than C'). A second hypothesis states that the status of the destination (D or D')—the job obtained—is a direct function of the status level of the contact (C or C') and an

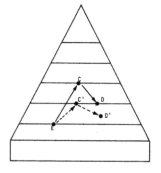

E = Ego's original status.

C, C' = Status of the contact.

D, D' = Status of the destination.

Figure 1. The Use of Social Resources in a Hierarchical Social Structure

indirect function of the strength of the tie between the ego and the contact.

THE DATA AND ANALYSES

The data were from a modified random sample of males, 20–64 years of age, who resided in the tri-city area of Albany-Schenectady-Troy, New York, in the spring of 1975, and who were then or had been members of the United States civilian labor force. The total sample consisted of 399 respondents.

We asked each respondent whether any personal or impersonal channels were effective in helping him to get his first and current jobs. Three types of channels were used to find first and current jobs. For the first job, 57% of the respondents used personal contacts, 22% went directly to an employer, and 21% used formal channels. For the current job, 59% used personal contacts, 17% applied directly to an employer, and 24% used formal channels. To ascertain the effects of type of channel used on status of first and current jobs, we entered three dummy variables based on the above categories into a regression along with the basic status attainment variables. Only the use of formal channels showed a small positive effect on current job. While there was no evidence that the use of personal contacts had any significant effect on the attainment process, our conceptual model had led us to believe that the characteristics of the contacts used might have an effect on the occupational status attained.

We shall discuss further only those respondents who utilized social ties as channels in seeking their first or current jobs.

When a respondent mentioned a personal contact, we identified the contact's attributes. We measured social resources by the contact's occupational status (Duncan's SEI). Thus, there are two social resources measures: the occupational status of the contact used for the first job (O_{TW}) and the occupational status of the contact used for the current job (O_{TY}). We also obtained data on each contact's educational achievement, an alternative measure of social resources which we will discuss later.

We indexed the strength of the tie between the respondent and the contact as being either (1) weak, that is, acquaintances and indirect ties (e.g., friend's relatives, relative's friends), or (2) strong, that is, relatives, friends, and neighbors.[4] This variable was identified as S_{TW} for the relationship between the respondent and the contact relative to seeking the first job and as S_{TY} for that in seeking the current job. (In addition, we examined whether it was the respondent or the contact who initiated the interaction or whether the contact came about by chance. As it turned out, this variable did not have any significant effects, either direct or indirect, on the job the respondent attained.)

Effects of Strength of Tie and Social Resources on Attained Status

In the first phase of the data analysis we examined the interrelationships among the strength of tie between each respondent and the personal contact he utilized, the occupational status of the contact, and the attained occupational status of the respondent. We conducted separate analyses relative to the first and current jobs (see Table 1).

Comparing the contact's status with the occupational status attained by the respondent makes it evident that the former is significantly higher than the latter ($\overline{X}_{OTW} > \overline{X}_W$ and $\overline{X}_{OTY} > \overline{X}_Y$). This observation contradicts what the like-me principle would predict. If a person were best served in the social structure by ties with persons of similar status, as dictated by the like-me principle, we should have observed the respondent and his contact to have similar status. Instead, our results are consistent with the prestige principle: job seekers seem to reach upward when using contacts to get a job.

As expected, the zero-order correlations show significant relationships among

---

[4] We have here classified neighbors as strong ties, although we recognize that some researchers have called them weak ties (e.g., Wellman, 1979). However, given the fact that less than 3% of all individuals in our sample used neighbors to attain either first or current jobs (see Table 2), this classificatory difference does not appear very significant. For other possible criteria for measuring the strength of ties, see Granovetter, 1973.

Table 1. Means, Standard Deviations, and Zero-Order Correlations for the Strength of Tie, Contact Status, and Attained Status

	Seeking First Job				
	S_{TW}	O_{TW}	W	Mean	SD
Strength of tie to contact (S_{TW})	—	−.403	−.230	1.210	.408
Occupational status of contact (O_{TW})	202	—	.645	46.015	24.826
Attained occupational status (W)	204	205	—	36.795	24.028

	Seeking Current Job				
	S_{TY}	O_{TY}	Y	Mean	SD
Strength of tie to contact (S_{TY})	—	−.292	−.305	1.339	.475
Occupational status of contact (O_{TY})	170	—	.679	53.428	21.942
Attained occupational status (Y)	171	173	—	45.421	25.497

NOTE: All correlations at $p < .01$. The pair-wise analyses were based on the Ns shown in the lower off-diagonal cells.

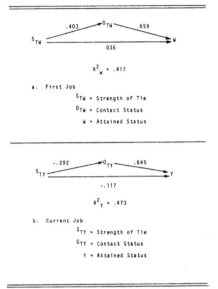

Figure 2. Effects of Strength of Tie and Contact Status on Attained Occupational Status

all three variables, suggesting the viability of both the strength-of-ties formulation and the social-resources formulation. The relative efficacy of the two formulations were examined by the extent to which the strength of the tie directly affected the attained occupational status. We simply regressed the attained occupational status on both the strength of tie and contact status variables and constructed path models. The results, in Figure 2, show that strength of tie has a weak (for the current job) or no (for the first job) direct effect on attained status. The social resources variable (contact status), on the other hand, retained its strong direct influence on attained status. The two independent variables explained 41% (for the first job) to 47% (for the current job) of the variation in attained status. The evidence suggests a concatenation in which the use of weak ties facilitates the reaching of higher status contacts, which in turn directly affects the attained occupational status.

The strength-of-ties perspective implies that weak ties lead to better social resources. From the social-resources perspective, however, the value of weak ties seems to depend on the job seeker's original position in the hierarchical structure. When his/her initial position in the structure is relatively low, only weak ties can provide access to social resources significantly higher up. But, when his/her initial position is relatively high, there is little reason to expect weak ties to have significantly greater advantage than strong ties. We hypothesize that the closer a job seeker's original position gets to the apex of the hierarchy, the more likely it is that strong ties will reach desirable social resources as well as weak ties. In fact, at the very top we should find strong ties to be more important, for weak ties will simply increase the likelihood of reaching downward in the structure.

We did not have the data to test the hypothesis regarding this limiting case; however, it was possible to test whether the weak tie became less significant as the job seeker's original status was higher in the hierarchical structure.

SOCIAL RESOURCES AND STRENGTH OF TIES   399

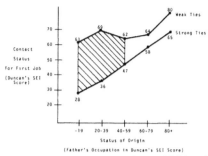

Figure 3. Relations Between the Status of Origin and the Contact Status Through Weak and Strong Ties (Shaded area indicates significant statistical differences.)

If we take father's occupational status to indicate the job seeker's original status, we can examine for each original status level whether a strong or a weak tie led to better social resources, as indexed by the status of the contact used for the first job. Figure 3 presents some data on this question. The benefit of using a weak tie seems constant; regardless of original status, the weak tie tends to lead to high-status contacts. When the original status is low, using a strong tie provided little benefit, but that benefit increases linearly as the original status goes up. In fact, toward the higher end of the original status level, the benefit of using a strong tie is almost as great as that of using a weak tie.[5] One must exercise caution in interpreting these trends, for the highest levels of original status may incur a ceiling effect. However, this caution itself is meaningful only if one adopts the social-resources perspective postulated earlier. Furthermore, what the data show is not that the use of weak ties declines in effectiveness, but

rather that the use of strong ties becomes more helpful.[6]

Strength of the Tie between the Contact and the Firm

The strength-of-ties literature focuses on the relationship between the ego and the contact. It says little about the relationship between the contact and the destination—in the case of job seeking, the relationship between the contact utilized and the employing firm. A superficial application of the strength-of-tie variable would suggest that a weak tie between the contact and the firm would be more advantageous for the job seeker. This, of course, is false. From Granovetter's discussion (1973) it should be clear that the weak tie is useful to the ego because it extends his or her reach by being close to the desired destination and thus possessing information about and influence with the destination—in this case the hiring firm. Thus, a more appropriate hypothesis states that a weak tie between the job seeker and his or her contact tends to be related to a strong tie between the contact and the firm, which in turn is related to attaining a higher status job.

Similarly, the social-resources literature has not spelled out how the relationship between the ultimate contact and the hiring firm brings about the job seeker's being hired for the job. Again, interpreting the intent of the conceptual formulation, our hypothesis states that better social resources are related to a strong tie between the contact and the firm, which in turn is related to attaining a higher status job.

In the Albany survey each respondent who used a personal contact in job seeking

---

[5] The interactive effect of the status of origin and the strength of ties on the contact status can also be seen in the zero-order correlation between the simple product term and the contact status $[r(O_F \cdot S_{TW})(O_{TW}) = .518]$. Much of this effect of course is due to the association between the status of origin and the contact status $(r = .497)$. This becomes apparent when the interaction term is expressed in terms of deviations from the means $(O_F - \overline{X}_{OF})(S_{TW} - \overline{X}_{STW})$. Its zero-order correlation with O_{TW} is .120. A regression analysis in which contact status is regressed on S_{TW}, O_F and $(O_F - \overline{X}_{OF})(S_{TW} - \overline{X}_{STW})$ reveals that the first two terms explained 34.5% of the variance and the interaction term contributed an additional 2.6%.

[6] It would be illuminating to use the attained status of the first job (W) as the ultimate dependent variable in the analysis presented in Figure 3. However, a four-way breakdown (W by O_F, S_{TW}, and O_{TW}) results in three empty cells and extremely small frequencies (between 2 and 22) in all except one remaining cell. Statistical tests could not be conducted. A similar plot for the current job was not done, because we could not justify using W as the status of origin and ignoring the job changes that had taken place between W and Y. A treatment of the model taking into account the individual's job history is beyond the scope of the paper.

was asked to characterize the relationship between his contact and the hiring company. Responses were put into two groups: (1) weak—the contact knew someone in the company or someone who had an acquaintance in the company—and (2) strong—the contact owned the company or worked for the company.[7] This variable is hereafter identified as F_{TW} relative to the first job, and F_{TY} relative to the current job.

While conceptually we can compare the strength of the tie between the respondent and the contact and between the contact and the firm, the measures we used for the two relations in this study differed. That is, we measured the strength of tie between respondent and contact by their relationship (i.e., whether they were relatives, friends, neighbors, acquaintances, etc.). We measured the strength of the tie between the contact and the firm by whether the contact owned the firm, was employed there, or was altogether unconnected with it. The latter measure is admittedly crude. We hope better measures will be devised in future studies.

Again, we constructed structural equations models for the occupational attainment process for the first and current jobs. These results are shown in Figure 4 as path models. The strength of the tie between the contact and the firm does not appear to be an important variable in finding a prestigious first job. It does not contribute significantly to the attained status of the first job, nor is it much affected, in a linear fashion, by the strength of the tie between the respondent and the contact or by the contact's status.

As for the current job, a strong tie between the contact and the firm shows a moderate direct effect on the attained status. The strength of the tie between the

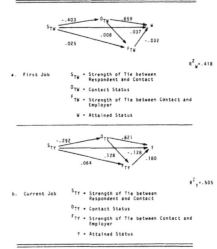

a. First Job S_{TW} = Strength of Tie between Respondent and Contact
O_{TW} = Contact Status
F_{TW} = Strength of Tie between Contact and Employer
W = Attained Status

b. Current Job S_{TY} = Strength of Tie between Respondent and Contact
O_{TY} = Contact Status
F_{TY} = Strength of Tie between Contact and Employer
Y = Attained Status

Figure 4.   Effects on Attained Occupational Status of Strength of Tie Between Respondent and Contact, Contact Status, and Strength of Tie Between Contact and Firm

contact and the firm is in turn directly affected by the contact's status, but not by the strength of the tie between the job seeker and the contact.

The anomalous finding that the strength of the tie between the contact and the firm does not contribute to explaining the attained status of the first job requires further deliberation and analysis.

We wondered whether the job seeker's personal resources (e.g., father's occupation and education, and job seeker's own education) at different phases of his occupational career affected the job-seeking process and the contacts and resources evoked. One speculation was that when entering the occupational structure (seeking the first job), the job seeker's personal resources would greatly affect the social relations he could utilize. Thus, parental characteristics should play an important role in reaching the "right" contacts and resources, not necessarily because these contacts and resources have direct links with possible employers, but because they represent the farthest that the job seeker can reach. Once a person begins working, he can make more of his own contacts, many of which are work-related. One ceases to rely largely

---

[7] For the STW group, 26.8% of the contacts knew an employee in the company or knew someone who had an acquaintance in the company; 67.3% were an employee in the company; and 5.9% owned the company. For the STY group, 21.5% knew an employee or had an acquaintance who knew an employee; 74.2% were employed by the company; and 4.3% owned the company.

A separate analysis showed no differential effects on status attainment whether the contacts were owners or employees, so we collapsed the two categories.

Table 2. Types of Contacts Used for First and Current Jobs

Nature of the Tie Between Respondent and Contact	First Job (N = 185) %	Current Job (N = 219) %
Strong ties		
Neighbor	2.8	2.8
Relative	41.1	26.1
Friend	35.5	37.2
Weak ties		
Acquaintances	15.4	32.8
Other indirect ties (relative's friend, friend's relative)	5.1	1.2

on prescribed (both consanguineous and affinial) relations and comes to rely on one's own constructed relations. As a person becomes more embedded in a network of constructed relations, contacts tied to a potential employer increase in significance.

Table 2 shows the relative frequency of various types of contacts used for obtaining first and current jobs. For the first job, 41% of the respondents using personal contacts went to relatives, 35% to friends, and 21% to acquaintances and indirect links (e.g., relative's friend or friend's relative). For the current job, only 26% used relatives, friends accounted for 37%—about the same as for first jobs—while use of acquaintances and indirect links increased to 34%. Thus, there is some evidence that constructed ties gradually replace prescribed ties (relatives) as one progresses in an occupational career. Granovetter (1974:42) obtained comparable data. The direct impact of personal background on one's status appears to decrease as one's occupational career develops.

To examine in detail such processes would require data beyond what was available to us. However, we were able to incorporate some personal resources variables into the models and explore their differential effects on the social resources factors as well as on the attained status of jobs.

Differential Impacts of Personal and Social Resources on Status Attainment

We examined the variables in the basic Blau-Duncan model, as well as the three

structural factors (the strength of the tie between the respondent and the contact, the contact's status, and the strength of the tie between the contact and the firm) for their effects on the job-seeking process. However, this is not exactly the same as expanding the Blau-Duncan model, since we analyzed only data from respondents who used personal contacts in seeking first and/or current jobs. We wanted to examine further certain hypotheses derived from the social-resources and strength-of-ties literature. Nonetheless, the analysis did allow us to determine after we had taken personal resources variables into account whether the effects of the structural factors on job seeking were spurious.

The analysis entered the variables in the following causal sequence: (1) the father's education (E_F) and occupational status (O_F) as the exogenous variables; (2) the job seeker's education (E); (3) the strength of the tie between the job seeker and the contact; (4) the contact's occupational status; (5) the strength of the tie between the contact and the firm; and (6) the job seeker's attained status. For the current job, we also entered the occupational status of the first job as an independent variable. Again, we conducted separate analyses relative to the first and current jobs. The results appear in Tables 3 and 4 respectively.

For the first job, personal resources (father's occupation and job seeker's education) have a significant effect on the status of the contact reached, but not on the strength of the tie evoked. The strength of the tie between the job seeker and the contact, however, affects contact's status as well. Personal resources and use of weak ties appear to have independent effects on reaching higher status contacts. However, neither the strength of the tie between the job seeker and the contact nor that between the contact and the firm directly affect the prestige of the first job. When the job seeker's personal resources are taken into account, the contact's status shows the strongest direct effect among all independent variables on getting a prestigious first job.

In gaining the current job, the status of

Table 3. Ordinary Least Squares Estimates for First-Job Status Attainment

Dependent Variable	E_F	O_F	E	S_{TW}	O_{TW}	F_{TW}	a	Error of Estimate
				Metric Coefficients				
Education	.321	.046						
(E)	(.063)	(.011)	—	—	—	—	7.76	2.58
Tie to respondent	.003	−.002	−.019					
(S_{TW})	(.010)	(.002)	(.011)	—	—	—	.92	.40
Contact status	.407	.255	2.05	−17.58				
(O_{TW})	(.507)	(.085)	(.558)	(3.57)	—	—	−14.45	19.36
Tie to firm	.001	−.001	.001	.027	.000			
(F_{TW})	(.001)	(.002)	(.001)	(.088)	(.002)	—	1.23	.45
First-job status	.495	.118	1.98	2.01	.411	−1.30		
(W)	(.437)	(.075)	(.497)	(3.27)	(.064)	(2.75)	−15.55	16.66
				Standardized Coefficients				R^2
(E)	.382	.320	—	—	—	—		.409
(S_{TW})	.033	.132	−.152	—	—	—		.053
(O_{TW})	.065	.240	.276	−.289	—	—		.405
(F_{TW})	.001	−.034	.001	.025	.026	—		.001
(W)	.082	.115	.276	.034	.425	−.024		.535

NOTE: Standard errors appear in parentheses below their corresponding metric coefficients.

the first job, rather than other personal resources, has the strongest direct effect on the strength of the tie between the job seeker and the contact and on the contact's status.

The job seeker's educational achievement and the status of his contact have a modest effect on the strength of the tie between the contact and the firm. The contact's status and his strong tie to the firm, as well as the seeker's education and first-job status, directly aid in acquiring a prestigious current job. These results further confirm that family background gradually ceases to affect directly the choice of contact or the outcome of the job search, while increasingly work status (as reflected in first-job status) does. The contact's status and his tie to the firm directly affect acquisition of a prestigious

Table 4. Ordinary Least Squares Estimates for Current-Job Status Attainment

Dependent Variable	E_F	O_F	E	W	S_{TY}	O_{TY}	F_{TY}	a	Error of Estimate
				Metric Coefficients					
Education	.254	.047							
(E)	(.065)	(.010)	—	—	—	—	—	8.59	2.44
First job	.362	.217	4.01						
(W)	(.505)	(.081)	(.588)	—	—	—	—	−25.01	18.19
Tie to respondent	.011	−.002	−.005	−.005					
(S_{TY})	(.013)	(.002)	(.017)	(.002)	—	—	—	1.14	.46
Contact status	.873	.088	.925	.244	−7.21				
(O_{TY})	(.499)	(.082)	(.657)	(.079)	(3.07)	—	—	10.65	17.56
Tie to firm	−.003	−.001	.024	−.002	.051	.002			
(F_{TY})	(.012)	(.002)	(.016)	(.002)	(.075)	(.002)	—	1.46	.41
Current job status	.001	−.007	3.35	.129	−4.78	.426	9.39		
(Y)	(.001)	(.063)	(.558)	(.070)	(2.67)	(.069)	(2.96)	−20.00	14.70
				Standardized Coefficients					R^2
(E)	.321	.372	—	—	—	—	—		.402
(W)	.058	.217	.502	—	—	—	—		.481
(S_{TY})	−.093	−.094	−.031	−.242	—	—	—		.079
(O_{TY})	.158	.100	.132	.278	−.156	—	—		.380
(F_{TY})	−.030	−.029	.185	−.112	.059	.123	—		.032
(Y)	.001	−.006	.412	.127	−.089	.366	.152		.681

NOTE: Standard errors appear in parentheses below their metric coefficients.

job, even after the personal resources variables have been taken into account. We should also note that both the structural factors and the personal resource variables explained 67% of the variation in the attained status.

While the analyses only involved job seekers who used contacts in seeking first and current jobs, the fact that the basic Blau-Duncan model was verified (see the relative direct contributions of job seeker's education and father's occupation on the first-job status in Table 3 and those of job seeker's education and first job on the current-job status in Table 4) increases our confidence that our three structural factors do contribute to the status attainment process.

DISCUSSION

The picture which emerges from these preliminary conceptual and empirical deliberations shows that the social resources an individual job seeker evokes have a significant association with the status of the job he attains. Whether the job seeker can utilize a high-status contact depends on both his personal resources (initially his family background but eventually his educational and occupational achievements) and his use of weak ties. As the job seeker progressively comes to rely on his constructed relations rather than his ascribed relations, his contact's strong tie with the hiring firm becomes increasingly important.

Of course, the strength of ties and social resources are not the only important structural factors in the status attainment process, nor are our measurements anything but rudimentary. But our data did permit us to measure social resources in terms of the contact's educational status. The zero-order correlation between the contact's educational status and respondent's first and current occupational status (.519 and .559, respectively) was comparable to that between the contact's occupational status and the respondent's first and current occupational status (.645 and .679, respectively). When we substituted the contact's educational status for his occupational attainment, the variables in the model explained almost 50% of the variance (47.8%) in first job and more than

60% (60.2%) of the variance in current job.

We collected data on both first-job income and current-job income. These could be used as alternate measures of job prestige. We did not have enough confidence in the first-job income data because it required overtime adjustments and because the respondents could not always remember the figures accurately. We decided to focus on the current-job income.

When we examined current-job income as the dependent variable, the analysis showed that both the strength of the respondent's tie to the contact and the contact's occupational status related significantly to current-job income (r = −.264 and .438, respectively). In addition, the mean income of respondents using weak ties was some $2,500 more than those using strong ties. When we entered the contact's occupational status and the strength of the tie between the respondent and the contact as well as the strength of the tie between the contact and the firm into the regression equation along with the basic status attainment variables, the model explained almost 31% of the variance in current income. Compared to other models of income attainment (Sewell and Hauser, 1975), this increases by more than 15% the variance explained in current-job income.

This, it appears that alternative measures of both the contact's characteristics and the job seeker's socioeconomic status demonstrated patterns similar to those discussed earlier.

Another explanation (the like-me principle, Laumann, 1966) suggests that a higher social position has advantage because it connects to many other positions on the same level. This should mean that a person's status would be similar, in general, to that of his contact—that the higher a person's status, the higher the status of his or her contact. But, we did not find this to be the case (see the differential contact and attained job statuses in Table 1).

An earlier discussion (Lin, Vaughn, and Ensel, 1981) pointed out that we need to determine whether the structural variables incorporated in the model could be proxy variables for the criterion variables. For example, we may ask whether the contact's occupational status merely reflects

404   AMERICAN SOCIOLOGICAL REVIEW

the occupational status the job seeker de-
sires (the dependent variable) or whether
it is a causal factor. This is a difficult task
empirically. However, we conducted a
preliminary examination of the proxy hypothesis with the available data and found
no evidence of its presence.

If a proxy variable is present (call it Y')
in terms of the finally achieved occupational status (current job, Y), Y' and Y
should have two empirical properties, at
least as far as internal validity of the attempted causal modelling is concerned:

(1) Y' and Y should have approximately the same status level. This is a
strong statement of the proxy hypothesis.
However, our data show the contact
status (O_{TY}) to be much higher than the
achieved status (Y). This can be seen in
Table 3 (the means are statistically different when the standard deviations are
used to compute the standard errors).

(2) Y' and Y should have similar causal
patterns in terms of their relationships
with the independent variables. Negation
of statement 1 does not necessarily reject
the proxy hypothesis, since the proxy
variable may involve a different type of
measure and be subject to a different
amount of error. Thus, a more definitive
test is to examine the patterns of relationships between the dependent variable and
its proxy and the independent variables.
In our case, we needed to examine the two
estimation equations.

On the right side of each equation the
first two terms are, of course, the father's
education and occupation; the third term
is the job seeker's education; and the last
term is the job seeker's first job—the usual
status attainment causal formation. The
proxy hypothesis does not insist that the
parallel Bs have similar magnitude, since
these independent variables should have
greater effect on Y than on its proxy variable Y'. However, the patterns among the
Bs must be similar to those among the B's.
The results of our data appear in Table 5.
The last two coefficients (for E and W) are
in reversed magnitudes as far as Y and Y'
are concerned.

Thus our data do not support the proxy
hypothesis as reflected in statements 1
and 2.

That the characteristics of one's contact

Table 5. Test of Proxy Status Hypothesis (Y = Current Occupational Status, Y' = Contact
Status)

Dependent Variable	Estimated Coefficients			
	E_F	O_F	E	W
Y	.048	.034	.494	.250
Y'	.144	.115	.137	.316

in an instrumental action are empirically
distinctive from the characteristics of
one's desired destination rather than their
proxies was also confirmed in a
smallworld study (Lin, Dayton, and
Greenwald, 1978). In chains which
eventually reached a target person, the
intermediaries tended to have weak-tie
relations with each other and to have
higher status and prestige than both the
starters and the target person. Since the
smallworld study involved actual individuals in an actual chain process, it further
validates the findings discussed in this
paper.

Within conceptual and measurement
confines discussed above, we have gained
some insight concerning certain linkages
between individuals and the social
structure. To the extent that the hierarchical structure of society dictates the networks in which individuals are embedded,
our discussion and analysis point to the
potential theoretical usefulness of social
resources and strength of ties as structural
factors. For a class of social actions iden-
tifiable as instrumental for the individual
involved (in this case, seeking a job), resources reached through his or her social
network probably have much to say about
the outcome of the action (in this case, the
job attained).

Nor does this emphasis deny the part
that personal resources contribute to instrumental actions. The preliminary evidence suggests an intricate interplay between personal resources and social resources. An individual's personal (especially prescribed) resources may greatly
affect, at least initially, what social resources are available to him or her. As
social resources are accumulated, however, these become more directly important than personal resources in further
elaborating social networks and, therefore, social resources. In time, the indi-

SOCIAL RESOURCES AND STRENGTH OF TIES   405

vidual's accumulated social resources become the personal (and prescribed) resources for the next generation of actors.

REFERENCES

Blau, Peter M. and O. D. Duncan
1967 The American Occupational Structure. New York: Wiley.
Boorman, Scott A.
1975 "A combinational optimization model for transmission of job information through contact networks." Bell Journal of Economics, 6:216–49.
Boorman, Scott A. and Harrison C. White
1976 "Social structure from multiple networks II: role structures." American Journal of Sociology 81:1384–446.
Breiger, Ronald L.
1980 "The social class structure of occupational mobility." Mimeographed paper.
Burt, Ronald S.
1977 "Positions in multiple network systems, part one: a general conception of stratification and prestige in a system of actors cast as a social typology." Social Forces 56: September.
1979 "Studying the status/role-set duality by mass survey: ersatz network positions and structural equivalence in large populations." Working Paper 27, Survey Research Center, University of California at Berkeley.
Duncan, Otis D., David L. Featherman, and Beverly Duncan
1972 Socioeconomic Background and Achievement. New York: Seminar Press.
Duncan, Otis D., A. O. Haller, and A. Portes
1968 "Peer influences on aspirations: a reinterpretation." American Journal of Sociology 74:119–37.
Edwards, Richard C., Michael Reich, and David M. Gordon
1975 Labor Market Segmentation. Lexington, Mass.: Heath.
Featherman, David and Robert Hauser
1978 Opportunity and Change. New York: Academic Press.
Goode, William
1978 The Celebration of Heroes. Berkeley: University of California Press.
Gordon, David M.
1972 Theories of Poverty and Underemployment. Lexington, Mass.: Heath.
Granovetter, Mark
1973 "The strength of weak ties." American Journal of Sociology 78:1360–80.
1974 Getting a Job. Cambridge, Mass.: Harvard University Press.
1979 "Toward a sociological theory of income differences." Paper read at the Annual Meetings of the American Sociological Association, Boston, Mass., August.
Homans, George C.
1950 The Human Group. New York: Harcourt, Brace, Jovanovich.

Jencks, Christopher, Marshall Smith, Henry Acland, Mary Jo Bane, David Cohen, Herbert Gintis, Barbara Heyns, and Stephen Michelson
1972 Inequality. New York: Harper and Row.
Jencks, Christopher and Lee Rainwater
1977 The Effects of Family Background, Test Scores, Personality Traits, and Education on Economic Success. Report prepared for the National Institute of Education and the Employment and Training Administration of the U.S. Department of Labor.
Laumann, Edward O.
1966 Prestige and Association in an Urban Community. Indianapolis: Bobbs Merrill.
Laumann, Edward O. and R. Senter
1976 "Subjective social distance, occupational stratification and forms of status and class consciousness: a cross-national replication and extension." American Journal of Sociology 81:1304–38.
Lin, Nan, Paul Dayton, and Peter Greenwald
1978 "Analyzing the instrumental uses of social relations in the context of social structure." Sociological Methods and Research 7:149–66.
Lin, Nan, John C. Vaughn, and Walter M. Ensel
1981 "Social resources and occupational status attainment." Social Forces (June).
Rees, A. and G. P. Schultz
1970 Workers and Wages in an Urban Labor Market. Chicago: University of Chicago Press.
Sewell, William and Robert M. Hauser
1975 Education, Occupation and Earnings: Achievement in the Early Career. New York: Academic Press.
Sorensen, Aage B.
1977 "The structure of inequality and the process of attainment." American Sociological Review 42:965–78.
Spilerman, Seymour
1977 "Careers, labor market structure, and socioeconomic achievement." American Journal of Sociology 83:551–83.
Stolzenberg, Ross M.
1978 "Bringing the boss back in." American Sociological Review 43:813–28.
U.S. Department of Labor
1975 Job Seeking Methods Used by American Workers. Bureau of Labor Statistics Bulletin, no. 1886.
Verbrugge, Lois
1979 "The structure of adult friendship choices." Social Forces 56:576–97.
Wellman, Barry
1979 "The community question: the intimate networks of East Yorkers." American Journal of Sociology 84:1201–32.
White, Harrison C.
1970 Chains of Opportunity. Cambridge, Mass.: Harvard University Press.
White, Harrison C., S. A. Boorman, and R. L. Breiger
1976 "Social structure from multiple networks I: blockmodels of roles and positions." American Journal of Sociology 81:730–80.

1

Building a Network Theory
of Social Capital

Nan Lin

In the past two decades, social capital in its various forms and contexts has emerged as one of the most salient concepts in social sciences. While much excitement has been generated, divergent views, perspectives, and expectations have also raised the serious question: is it a fad or does it have enduring qualities that will herald a new intellectual enterprise? The purpose of this chapter is to review social capital as discussed in the literature, identify controversies and debates, consider some critical issues, and propose conceptual and research strategies for building a theory. I argue that such a theory and the research enterprise must be based on the fundamental understanding that social capital is captured from embedded resources in social networks. Deviations from this understanding in conceptualization and measurement lead to confusion in analyzing causal mechanisms in the macro- and microprocesses. It is precisely these mechanisms and processes, essential for a theory about interactions between structure and action, to which social capital promises to make contributions.

I begin by exploring the nature of capital and various theories of capital, so that social capital can be properly perceived and located. I then identify certain controversies which, unless clarified or resolved, will hinder the development of a theory and the research enterprise. By considering social capital as assets in networks, I discuss some issues in conceptualization, measurement, and causal mechanism (the factors leading to inequality of social capital and the returns following investments in social capital). A proposed model identifies the exogenous factors leading to the acquisition (or the lack) of social capital as well as the expected returns of social capital.

WHAT IS CAPITAL?

To understand social capital, it is necessary to consider the family of capital theories and trace their historical and conceptual development. A more detailed explication of the concepts of capital and social capital is available elsewhere (Lin 2001). Suffice it here to present a summary of their historical development. The notion of capital can be traced to Marx (1933/1849, 1995/1867, 1885, 1894; Brewer 1984). In his conceptualization, capital is part of the surplus value captured by capitalists or the bourgeoisie, who control the means of production, in the circulation of commodities and monies between the production and consumption processes. In such circulation, laborers are paid for their labor (commodity) with a wage allowing them to purchase commodities (such as food, shelter, and clothing) to sustain their lives (exchange value). But the commodity processed and produced by the capitalists can be circulated to and sold in the consumption market at a higher price (user value). In this scheme of the capitalist society, capital represents two related but distinct elements. On the one hand, it is part of the *surplus value* generated and pocketed by the capitalists (and their "misers," presumably the traders and sellers). On the other hand, it represents an *investment* (in the production and circulation of commodities) on the part of the capitalists, with expected returns in a marketplace. Capital, as part of the surplus value, is a product of a process; capital is also an investment process in which the surplus value is produced and captured. It is also understood that the investment and its produced surplus value refer to a return/reproduction of the process of investment and of more surplus values. It is the dominant class that makes the investment and captures the surplus value. Thus, it is a theory based on the exploitative nature of social relations between two classes. I have called Marx's theory of capital the *classical theory of capital* (Lin 2001, Chapter 1).

Subsequent theoretical modifications and refinements have retained the basic elements of capital in the classical theory, as represented in Table 1. Fundamentally, capital remains a surplus value and represents an investment with expected returns. Human-capital theory (Johnson 1960; Schultz 1961; Becker 1964/1993), for example, also conceives of capital as investment (e.g., in education) with certain expected returns (earnings). Individual workers invest in technical skills and knowledge so that they can negotiate with those in control of the production process (firms and their agents) for payment of their labor-skill. This payment has value that may be more than what the purchase of subsisting commodities would require

Table 1. Theories of Capital[a]

	Explanation	Capital	Level of Analysis
The Classical Theory (Marx)	Social relations Exploitation by the capitalists (bourgeoise) of the proletariat	A. Part of surplus value between the use value (in consumption market) and the exchange value (in production-labor market) of the commodity B. Investment in the production and circulation of commodities	Structural (classes)
The Neocapital Theories			
Human Capital (Schultz, Becker)	Accumulation of surplus value by laborer	Investment in technical skills and knowledge	Individual
Cultural Capital (Bourdieu)	Reproduction of dominant symbols and meanings (values) Social relations	Internalization or misrecognition of dominant values	Individual/class
Social Capital (Lin, Burt, Marsden, Flap, Coleman)	Access to and use of resources embedded in social networks	Investment in social networks	Individual
(Bourdieu, Coleman, Putnam)	Solidarity and reproduction of group	Investment in mutual recognition and acknowledgment	Group/individual

[a]Summary of discussion from Lin (2001, Chapters 1 and 2).

6   Building a Network Theory of Social Capital

and, thus, contain surplus value that in part can be spent for leisure and lifestyle needs and turned into capital. Likewise, cultural capital, as described by Bourdieu (Bourdieu 1990; Bourdieu & Passeron 1977), represents investments on the part of the dominant class in reproducing a set of symbols and meanings, which are misrecognized and internalized by the dominated class as their own. The investment, in this theory, is in the pedagogic actions of the reproduction process, such as education, the purpose of which is to indoctrinate the masses to internalize the values of these symbols and meanings. Cultural-capital theory also acknowledges that the masses (the dominated class) can invest and acquire these symbols and meanings, even if they misrecognize them as their own. The inference is that while cultural capital is mostly captured by the dominant class through intergenerational transmissions, even the masses (or at least some of them) may generate returns from such investment and acquisition.

However, these theories break significantly from the classical theory— that is, because the laborers, workers or masses can now invest, and thus acquire certain capital of their own (be they skills and knowledge in the case of human capital, or "misrecognized" but nevertheless internalized symbols and meanings), they (or some of them) can now generate surplus value in trading their labor or work in the production and consumption markets. The social relations between classes (capitalists and noncapitalists) become blurred. The image of the social structure is modified from one of dichotomized antagonistic struggle to one of layered or stratified negotiating discourses. I have called these the *neocapitalist theories* (Lin 2001, Chapter 1). The distinctive feature of these theories resides in the potential investment and capture of surplus value by the laborers or masses. Social capital, I argue, is another form of the neocapital theories.[1]

WHY DOES SOCIAL CAPITAL WORK?[2]

The premise behind the notion of social capital is rather simple and straightforward: *investment in social relations with expected returns* (Lin 2001, Chapter 2). This general definition is consistent with various renditions by scholars who have contributed to the discussion (Bourdieu 1980, 1983/1986; Burt 1992; Coleman 1988, 1990; Erickson 1995, 1996; Flap 1991, 1994; Lin 1982, 1995; Portes 1998; Putnam 1993, 1995a). Individuals engage in interactions and networking in order to produce profits. Generally, four explanations can be offered as to why embedded resources in social networks will enhance the outcomes of actions (Lin 2001, Chapter 2). For one, it facilitates the flow of *information*. In the usual imperfect market situations, social ties located in certain strategic locations and/or hierarchical positions (and thus better informed about market needs and demands) can provide an individual with useful information about opportunities and choices otherwise not available. Likewise, these ties (or their ties) may alert an organization (be it in the production or consumption market) and its agents, or even a community, about the availability and interest of an otherwise unrecognized individual. Such information would reduce the transaction cost for the organization to recruit "better" (be it skill, or technical or cultural knowledge) individuals and for individuals to find "better" organizations that can use their capital and provide appropriate rewards. Second, these social ties may exert *influence* on the agents (e.g., recruiters or supervisors of the organizations) who play a critical role in decisions (e.g., hiring or promotion) involving the actor. Some social ties, due to their strategic locations (e.g., structural holes) and positions (e.g., authority or supervisory capacities), also carry more valued resources and exercise greater power (e.g., greater asymmetry in dependence by these agents), in organizational agents' decision making. Thus, "putting in a word" carries a certain weight in the decision-making process regarding an individual. Third, social-tie resources, and their acknowledged relationships to the individual, may be conceived by the organization or its agents as certifications of the individual's *social credentials*, some of which reflect the individual's accessibility to resources through social networks and relations—his/her social capital. "Standing behind" the individual by these ties reassures the organization (and its agents) that the individual can provide "added" resources beyond his/her personal capital, some of which may be useful to the organization. Finally, social relations are expected to reinforce identity and recognition. Being assured of one's worthiness as an individual and a member of a social group sharing similar interests and resources not only provides emotional support but also public acknowledgment of one's claim to certain resources. These *reinforcements* are essential for the maintenance of mental health and the entitlement to resources. These four elements—*information, influence, social credentials,* and *reinforcement*—may explain why social capital works in instrumental and expressive actions not accounted for by forms of personal capital such as economic capital or human capital.[3]

PERSPECTIVES AND CONTROVERSIES IN SOCIAL CAPITAL

While the fundamental definition of social capital is in general agreed on, two perspectives can be identified relative to the level at which return or profit is conceived—whether the profit is accrued for the group or for individuals. In one perspective, the focus is on the use of social capital by individuals—how individuals access and use resources embedded in social networks to gain returns in instrumental actions (e.g., finding better jobs) or preserve gains in expressive actions. Thus, at this relational level, social capital can be seen as similar to human capital in that it is assumed that such investments can be made by individuals with expected return, some benefit or profit, to the individual. Aggregation of individual returns also benefits the collective. Nonetheless, the focal points for analysis in this perspective are (1) how individuals invest in social relations, and (2) how individuals capture the emebedded resources in the relations to generate a return. Representative works (see review in Lin 1999) can be found in Lin (Lin & Bian 1991; Lin & Dumin 1986; Lin, Ensel, & Vaughn 1981), Burt (1992, 1998, 1997), Marsden (Marsden & Hurlbert 1988; Campbell, Marsden, & Hurlbert 1986), Flap (Boxman, De Graaf, & Flap 1991; De Graaf & Flap 1988; Flap & De Graaf 1988; Flap 1991; Sprengers, Tazelaar, & Flap, 1988; Volker & Flap 1996), and Portes (Portes & Sensenbrenner 1993) as well as in discussions of social capital by Coleman (1990) and Bourdieu (1983/1986).

Another perspective has its focus on social capital at the group level, with discussions dwelling on (1) how certain groups develop and maintain more or less social capital as a collective asset, and (2) how such a collective asset enhances group members' life chances. Bourdieu (1983/1986, 1980) and Coleman (1988, 1990) have discussed this perspective extensively and Putnam's empirical work (1993, 1995a, 2000) is exemplary. While acknowledging the need for individuals to interact and network to develop payoffs of social capital, the central interest of this perspective is to explore the elements and processes in the production and maintenance of the collective asset. For example, dense or closed networks are seen as the means by which collective capital can be maintained and reproduction of the group can be achieved. Another major interest is how norms and trust, as well as other properties (e.g., sanctions, authority) of a group are essential in the production and maintenance of the collective asset.

Whether social capital is seen from the societal-group level or the relational level, all scholars remain committed to the view that it is the interacting members who make the maintenance and reproduction of this social asset possible. This consensual view puts social capital firmly in the neo-capital-theory camp.[4]

However, the divergence in analyzing social capital at different levels has created some theoretical and measurement confusion (Lin 2001, Chapter 2). Further confusion arises from the fact that some discussions have flowed freely between levels. For example, Bourdieu provides a structural view in pointing to the reproduction of the dominant class and nobility groups as the principal explanation of social capital, which is represented by aggregating (1) the size of the group or network and (2) the volume of capital possessed by members (Bourdieu 1983/1986, p. 248). This representation makes sense only when it is assumed that all members maintain strong and reciprocal relations (a completely dense or institutionalized network), so that the strength of relations does not enter into the calculus. Yet, Bourdieu also describes how individuals interact and reinforce mutual recognition and acknowledgment as members of a network or group. Coleman (1990, Chapter 12), while emphasizing how individuals can use sociostructural resources to obtain better outcomes in their (individual) actions, devotes much discussion to the collective nature of social capital in stressing trust, norms, sanctions, authority, and closure as part or forms of social capital. It is important to identify and sort through these confusions and reach some understanding before we can proceed to build a coherent theory of social capital. I have identified some of these issues in Table 2.

One major controversy generated from macro- versus relational-level perspectives is whether social capital is a collective or an individual good (see Portes' critique, 1998). Most scholars agree that it is both collective and individual; that is, institutionalized social relations with embedded resources are expected to benefit both the collective and the individuals in the collective. At the group level, social capital represents some aggregation of valued resources (such as economic, political, cultural, or social, as in social connections) of members interacting as a network or networks. The difficulty arises when social capital is discussed as a collective or even a public good, along with trust, norms, and other "collective" or public goods. What has resulted in the literature is that the terms have become alternative or substitutable terms or measurements. Divorced from its roots in individual interactions and networking, social capital becomes merely another trendy term to employ or deploy in the broad context of improving or building social integration and solidarity. In the following, I argue

Table 2. Controversies in Social Capital[a]

Issue	Contention	Problem
Collective or individual asset (Coleman, Putnam)	Social capital or collective asset	Confounding with norms, trust
Closure or open networks (Bourdieu, Coleman, Putnam)	Group should be closed or dense	Vision of class society and absence of mobility
Functional (Coleman)	Social capital is indicated by its effect in particular action	Tautology (cause is determined by effect)
Measurement (Coleman)	Not quantifiable	Heuristic, not falsifiable

[a]Adapted from Lin (2001, Chapter 2, Table 2.1).

that social capital, as a relational asset, must be distinguished from collective assets and goods such as culture, norms, trust, etc. Causal propositions may be formulated (e.g., that collective assets, such as trust, promote the relations and networks and enhance the utility of embedded resources, or vice versa), but it should not be assumed that they are all alternative forms of social capital or are defined by one another (e.g., trust is capital).

Another controversy, related to the focus on the collective aspect of social capital, is the assumed or expected requirement that there is closure or density in social relations and social networks (Bourdieu 1986; Coleman 1990; Putnam 1993, 1995a,b, 2000). Bourdieu, from his class perspective, sees social capital as the investment of the members in the dominant class (as a group or network) engaging in mutual recognition and acknowledgment so as to maintain and reproduce group solidarity and preserve the group's dominant position. Membership in the group is based on a clear demarcation (e.g., nobility, title, family) excluding outsiders. Closure of the group and density within the group are required. Coleman, of course, does not assume such a class vision of society. Yet, he also sees network closure as a distinctive advantage of social capital, because it is closure that maintains and enhances trust, norms, authority, sanctions, etc. These solidifying forces may ensure that individuals can mobilize network resources.

I believe that the linkage between network density or closure to the utility of social capital is too narrow and partial. Research in social networks has stressed the importance of bridges in networks (Granovetter 1973; Burt 1992) in facilitating information and influence flows. To argue that closure or density is a requirement for social capital is to deny the significance of bridges, structural holes, or weaker ties. The root of preferring a dense or closed network lies, rather, in certain outcomes of interest (Lin 1992a, 1986, 1990). For *preserving or maintaining resources* (i.e., expressive actions), denser networks may have a relative advantage. Thus, for the privileged class, it would be better to have a closed network so that the resources can be preserved and reproduced (e.g., Bourdieu 1986); or for a mother to move to a cohesive community so that her children's security and safety can be assured (Coleman 1990). On the other hand, for *searching for and obtaining resources* (i.e., instrumental actions), such as looking for a job or better job (Lin 1999; Marsden & Hurlbert 1988; De Graaf & Flap 1988; Burt 1992), accessing and extending bridges in the network should be more useful. Rather than assert that closed or open networks are required, it would be theoretically more viable to (1) conceptualize for what outcomes and under what conditions a denser or more sparse network might generate a better return, and (2) postulate deduced hypotheses (e.g., a denser network would be more likely to promote the sharing of resources which, in turn, maintain group or individual resources; or, an open network would be more likely to access advantaged positions and resources, which in turn enhance the opportunity to obtain additional resources) for empirical examination.

A third controversy that requires clarification is Coleman's statement that social capital is any "social-structural resource" that generates returns for an individual in a specific action. He remarks that "social capital is defined by its function" and "it is not a single entity, but a variety of different entities having two characteristics: They all consist of some aspect of a social structure, and they facilitate certain actions of individuals who are within the structure" (1990, p. 302). This "functional" view may be a tautology: social capital is identified when and if it works; the potential causal explanation of social capital can be captured only by its effect, or whether it is an investment depends on the return for a specific individual in a specific action. Thus, the causal factor is defined by the effect. Clearly, it would be impossible to build a theory where causal and effectual factors are folded into a singular function. This is not to deny that a functional relationship may be hypothesized (e.g., resources embedded in social networks enhances obtaining better jobs). But the two concepts must be treated as separate entities with independent measurements (e.g., social capital is the investment in social relations and better jobs are represented by occupational status or supervisory position). It would be incorrect to allow the outcome variables to dictate the specification of the causal variable (e.g., for actor X, kin ties are social capital because these ties channel X to get a better job, and for actor Y, kin ties are not social capital because these ties do not channel Y to get a better job). The hypothesized causal relationship may be conditioned by other factors (e.g., family characteristics may affect differential opportunities for building human and social capital) which need be specified in a more elaborate theory. A theory would lose parsimony quickly if the conditional factors become part of the definitions of the primary concepts. In fact, one would question whether it remains a theory if it is required to make a good prediction for every individual case and individual situation.

Perhaps related to this view of social capital as indistinguishable from its outcome—and perhaps given his view that social capital, as a collective good, can also be seen in many different forms such as trust, norms, sanctions, authority, etc.—Coleman questions "whether social capital will come to be as useful a quantitative concept in social science as are the concepts of financial capital, physical capital, and human capital; its current value lies primarily in its usefulness for qualitative analyses of social systems and for those quantitative analyses that employ qualitative indicators" (1990, pp. 304–5). Again, the confusion can be seen as resulting from extending the notion of social capital beyond its theoretical roots in social relations and social networks and the unattainable theoretical position that prediction holds for every individual case. Once these issues are resolved, social capital should and must be measurable.

CONCEPTUALIZING AND MEASURING SOCIAL CAPITAL

These debates and clarifications lead to the suggestion that social capital, as a concept, is rooted in social networks and social relations, and must be measured relative to its root. Therefore, social capital can be defined as *resources embedded in a social structure which are accessed and/or mobilized in purposive actions* (Lin 2001, Chapter 3). By this definition, the notion of social capital contains three ingredients: resources embedded in a social structure; accessibility to such social resources by individuals; and use or mobilization of such social resources by individuals in purposive actions. Thus conceived, social capital contains three elements intersecting structure and action: the structural (embeddedness), opportunity (accessibility) and action-oriented (use) aspects.

These elements have been mentioned by most scholars working on social capital. The social resources theory (Lin 1982) has specifically proposed that access to and use of social resources (resources embedded in social networks) can lead to better socioeconomic status. Further, the theory proposes that access to and use of social resources are in part determined by positions in the hierarchical structure (the strength of position proposition) and by the use of weaker ties (the strength of tie proposition). Bourdieu defines the volume of social capital as a function of the size of the network and the volume of capital (economic, cultural and symbolic) possessed by networked individuals. Burt (1992) postulates that certain network positions (structural holes and structural constraints) have effects on individuals getting better positions or rewards in organizations. Flap (1994) defines social capital as a combination of network size, relationship strength, and resources possessed by those in the network. Portes (1998) also advocates focusing on social relations and networks in the analysis of social capital.

Embedded Resources and Network Locations

Given the significance of resources and relations in social capital, it is not surprising that scholarly research has shown differential focus on one of the two elements. Some have chosen to focus on the location of individuals in a network as the key of social capital. Burt's work (1992) typifies this approach. By identifying the locations of individual nodes, it is possible to assess how close or how far the node is from a strategic location, such as a bridge, where the occupant has the competitive advantage in possible access to more, diverse, and valued information. Strength of ties (Granovetter 1973, 1974) is also a well-known, conceptually argued, network-location measurement of a bridge's usefulness. Other location measures are readily available in the literature, such as density, size, closeness, betweenness, and eigenvector (see review of such location measures in Borgatti, Jones, and Everett (1998)). Implicit in this approach is the argument that network location is the key element of identifying social capital.

Another approach focuses on embedded resources. In social-resource theory, valued resources in most societies are represented by wealth, power, and status (Lin 1982). Thus, social capital is analyzed by the amount or variety of such characteristics in others with whom an individual has direct or indirect ties. Measurement of social resources can be further specified as network resources and contact resources. Network resources refer to those embedded in one's ego-networks, whereas contact resources refer to those embedded in contacts used as helpers in an instrumental action, such as job searches. Thus, network resources represent accessible resources and contact resources represent mobilized resources in instrumental actions. For contact resources, the measurement is straightforward— the contact's wealth, power and/or status characteristics, typically reflected in the contact's occupation, authority position, industrial sector, or income.

There is little dispute that embedded resources are valid measures for social capital. There is some debate as to whether network locations are measures of social capital or precursors to social capital. My view is that if it is assumed that social capital attempts to capture valued resources in social relations, network locations should facilitate, but not necessarily determine, access to better embedded resources. What types of network locations evoke resources in order to generate returns depend on the type of returns one expects. In the Modeling Section below, I argue that two types of outcomes are possible as returns to social capital: instrumental and expressive. In the former, the return is the gaining of added resources, resources not possessed by ego; whereas in the latter, the return is the maintaining of possessed resources. For example, if we assume that bridges link to different information, the utility of that information depends on whether it concerns resources valued by the individual but not yet attained. If it does not, then the bridge serves little utility. If it does, the bridge is very useful. That is, not all bridges (or network locations) lead to better information, influence, social credentials or reinforcement. A bridge linking an individual looking for a job in a corporation to people occupying influential positions in large corporations will likely be of significantly more utility to that individual than a bridge that leads to others who are members of a health club. On the other hand, a mother with young children would prefer to live in a dense, cohesive community rather than one with a mobile population and open access to the external world. Likewise, a person facing personal stresses such as divorce might benefit from access to and interaction with others who have had similar stress and understand its psychological effects, rather than someone who is happily married. These are expressive actions and we should expect the benefit of a dense network and homogenous partners.

These considerations suggest that network locations should be treated as exogenous variables rather than endogenous variables of social capital itself. I will return to this topic in the Modeling section. Suffice it to conclude here that social capital is more than mere social relations and networks; it evokes the resources embedded and accessed. Nevertheless, such embedded resources cannot possibly be captured without identifying network characteristics and relations. Network locations are necessary conditions of embedded resources. In a given study, it is advisable to incorporate measures for both network locations and embedded resources.

Measuring Social Capital as Assets in Networks

Paralleling these two conceptual elements of social capital have been two principal approaches in measuring social capital as assets captured by individuals in social networks, as depicted in Table 3. The first approach is to measure embedded resources. Here, resources embedded in the social networks are seen as social capital's core element. Thus, measurements focus on the valued resources (e.g., wealth, power, and status) of others accessed by individuals in their networks and ties. Such measurements can

Table 3.   Social Capital as Assets in Network

Focus	Mesurements	Indicators
Embedded resources	Network resources	Range of resources, best resource, variety of resources, composition (average resources); contact resources
	Contact statuses	Contact's occupation, authority, sector
Network locations	Bridge or access to bridge	Structural hole, structural constraint
	Strength of tie	Network bridge, or intimacy, intensity, interaction, and reciprocity

be made relative to two frameworks: (1) network resources and (2) contact resources. The former tap resources represented in the network an individual has access to. Typically, they include (1) the range of resources among ties (or the "distance" between the highest and lowest valued resources), (2) the best possible resources in the networks or among ties (or upper "reachability" in the resource hierarchy), (3) the variety or heterogeneity of resources in the networks, and (4) the composition of resources (average or typical resources). Research indicates that these measures are highly correlated and tend to form a single factor, with the highest loading usually on the range or upper-reachability measures. Contact resources indicate the valued resources represented by contacts or helpers in specific actions. These measures, usually the valued resources (wealth, power, and status) of the contact(s), are applied in the context of specific actions, such as job searches. There is consistent, strong evidence that both network and contact resources positively affect the outcome of instrumental actions, such as job searching and job advances (Lin 1999).

Another prevailing measurement strategy focuses on network locations as measurements of social capital. A major perspective is the argument that bridges or access to bridges facilitates returns in actions. Granovetter's notion of bridges as expressed in the strength of weak ties (1973) was a preview of this argument, which is elaborated and formalized by Burt in his notions of structural holes and constraints (1992). Other measures of bridges (e.g., betweenness) would also be candidates for social capital, even though they are used less in the social-capital context.

There are many other measures, such as size, density, cohesion, and closeness of social networks which are candidates as measures for social capital (Burt & Minor 1982; Burt 1984; Borgatti, Jones, & Everett 1998). However, research evidence is much less clear as to their viability in a social-capital theory. Unless clear theoretical arguments are presented along with the use of any specific measures, as both measures of social resources and network locations have been, it would be ill-advised simply to use any network measure as an indicator of social capital.

Sampling Techniques

Three sampling techniques have been employed to construct measures of social capital, as can be seen in Table 4. The saturation sampling technique is useful when it is possible to map a definable social network. In such networks, data from all nodes are gathered and their relationships identified, and measurements of network locations can be developed. The advantage of this technique is that it allows detailed and complete analyses of every network location as well as embedded resources in each node. Because of the requirement that the network have a defined and manageable bound-

Table 4.   Measurement Techniques

Technique	Advantages	Disadvantages
Saturation survey	Complete mapping of network	Limited to small networks
Name-generator	Customized content areas	Lack of sampling frame
	Ego-centered network mapping	Biased toward strong ties
Position-generator	Content free	Lack of specificity of
	Sampling of hierarchical	relations
	positions	
	Multiple "resources" mapped	
	Direct and indirect accesses	

ary, it is a technique most useful for studies of social capital within an organization or a small network among organizations.

For larger and less definable networks, ego-network sampling techniques are used. Typically, the name-generator (Laumann 1966; Wellman 1979; McCallister & Fischer 1978; Burt 1984; Marsden 1987) technique is employed. This measurement technique elicits a list of ties from ego, and the relationships between them as well as among them are identified. From these data, locations of ego as well as these ties, relative to one another, can be computed. Network resources can also be obtained from the name-generator technique. Measures such as composition (typical resource characteristics), heterogeneity (diversity of resources), and upper reachability (best possible resources) can be computed. The advantages of this approach include (1) the identification of specific content areas, relative to actions under investigations, as naming items, and (2) the mapping of ego-network locations and characteristics as well as social resources embedded in the ego-network. However, there are several serious shortcomings to this technique.

First, there is no theoretical or empirical framework that identifies the universe population from which the content areas to be studied can be sampled. While there may be a general understanding that certain instrumental and expressive dimensions might be involved (Lin 1986), no consensual knowledge is available as to what specific content areas under such dimensions constitute a set of elements in a content population for sampling. As a consequence, different content areas and wordings used make comparative analysis and validation impossible.

Second, the name-generator methodology tends to elicit stronger rather than weaker ties. Cognitively, names that come to mind first tend to be social ties with which ego is more intimate, more intensive in relations, more frequently interactive with, or more reciprocal in exchanges This bias may even be "beneficial" if the return or outcome concerns expressive or psychological consequences such as quality of life, health or mental health, as these returns are expected to be affected by strong-tie support or social integration (Lin 1986). If, however, the returns concern instrumental outcomes such as searching for better job or earnings, where theories have argued for the strength of weaker ties or bridges (Granovetter 1974; Lin 1982; Burt 1992), then the measure might miss the more critical social ties.

A third shortcoming of the name-generator methodology is that it identifies individual actors rather than social positions. When, as in many structural theories, the concerns focus on social positions (White, Boorman, & Breiger, 1976; White 1992; Cook 1982; Burt 1992), the name generator would not be appropriate.

While these shortcomings have been known, only recently has an alternative methodology emerged. The position-generator technique (Lin & Dumin 1986) samples positions in a given hierarchy representative of resources valued in the collective (e.g., occupational status or prestige, authority positions, sectors, etc.). In this technique, a sample of positions with identified valued resources (occupational status, authority positions, industrial sectors, etc.) is used and the respondent is asked to indicate if she / he knows anyone having that job or position. From the responses, it then becomes possible to construct network resource indexes such as extensity (number of positions accessed), range or heterogeneity (the "distance" between the "highest" and "lowest" positions accessed), and upper reachability ("highest" position accessed).

The position-generator methodology has several advantages: (1) it can be based on a representative sample of positions meaningful to a given society; (2) it can directly or indirectly identify linkages to such resource positions; and (3) it can be based on multiple resource criteria (e.g., occupation, authority, and industry). Studies in North America (Erickson 1996), as well as Europe (e.g., Flap & Boxman in the Netherlands: Boxman, De Graaf, & Flap 1988; Volker & Flap in East Germany:Volker & Flap 1996; Argelusz & Tardos in Hungary: Angelusz & Tardos 1991; Tardos 1996), have proven the utility of this theoretically derived methodology in the contact of social capital and instrumental action. It seems particularly useful if the valued resources are considered the core element of social capital. A sample of the position-generator instrument is presented in Table 5. A chapter in this volume (Lin, Fu, & Hsung) illustrates the utility of this methodology with data from Taiwan.

MODELING SOCIAL CAPITAL

To operationalize explicitly the critical elements, we may sharpen the definition of social capital to *investment in social relations by individuals through which they gain access to embedded resources to enhance expected returns of in-*

Table 5. Position Generator for Measuring Accessed Social Capital: An Example

Here is a list of jobs (show card). Would you please tell me if you happen to know someone (on a first-name basis) having each job?

Job	1. Do you know any-one having this job?[a] (If not, go to #7)	2. How long have you known this person (no. of years)	3. What is your relationship with this person?	4. How close are you with this person?	5. His/her gender	6. His/her job	7. Do you think you may find such a person through a person you know? (Person M)	8. Repeat #2–6 for Person M
Job A								
Job B								
Job C								
etc.								

[a]If you know more than one person, think of the one person whom you have known the longest (or the person who comes to mind first).

18

strumental or expressive actions. From this, three processes can be identified for modeling: (1) investment in social capital, (2) access to and mobilization of social capital, and (3) returns of social capital. While the above discussion clarifies social capital's definition, elements, and measurements, it is necessary to discuss briefly the types of outcomes that can be considered as expected returns. I propose two major types of outcomes: (1) returns to instrumental action, and (2) return to expressive action (Lin 1992, 1986, 1990). Instrumental action is taken to obtain resources not possessed by the actor, whereas expressive action is taken to maintain resources already possessed by the actor.

For instrumental action, we may identify three possible returns: economic, political, and social. Each can be seen as added capital. Economic return is straightforward. Political return is similarly straightforward, represented by hierarchical positions in a collective. Social gain needs some clarification. I have argued that reputation is an indication of social gain (Lin 2001, Chapter 9). Reputation can be defined as favorable/unfavorable opinions about an individual in a social network. A critical issue in social exchange where social capital is transacted is that the transaction may be asymmetric: a favor is given by the alter to ego. The ego's action is facilitated, but what is the gain for the alter, the giver of the favor? Unlike economic exchange, where reciprocal and symmetric transactions are expected in the short or long term, social exchange may not entail such expectation. What is expected is that the ego and the alter both acknowledge the asymmetric transactions that create the former's social debt to the latter, who accrues social credit. Social debt must be acknowledged in the public for the ego to maintain his/her relationship with the alter. Public recognition in the network spreads the reputation of the alter. The greater the debt, the larger the network, and the stronger the need for the ego and the alter to maintain the relationship; the greater the propensity to spread the word in the network and, thus, the greater the reputation gained by the alter. In this process, the alter is gratified by the reputation, which, along with material resources (such as wealth) and hierarchical positions (such as power) constitutes one of the three returns fundamental in instrumental actions. I have discussed this issue elsewhere (Lin 1998; 2001).

For expressive action, social capital is a means to consolidate resources and to defend against possible resource losses (Lin 1986, 1990). The principle is to access and mobilize others who share interest and control of similar resources so that embedded resources can be pooled and shared in order to preserve and protect existing resources. In this process, alters are willing to share their resources with egos because the preservation of the ego and its resources enhances and reinforce the legitimacy of alters' claim to like resources. Three types of return may be specified: physical health, mental health, and life satisfaction. Physical health involves maintenance of physical functional competence and freedom from diseases and injuries. Mental health reflects the capability to withstand stresses and the maintenance of cognitive and emotional balance. Life satisfaction indicates optimism and satisfaction with various life domains such as family, marriage, work, and community and neighborhood environments.

Oftentimes, returns to instrumental actions and expressive actions reinforce each other. Physical health offers the capacity to endure work load and may be responsible for attaining economic, political, and social status. Likewise, economic, political, or social status often offers resources to maintain physical health (exercise, diet, and health maintenance). Mental health and life satisfaction are likewise expected to have reciprocal effects on economic, political, and social gains. Factors leading to the instrumental and expressive returns, however, are expected to show differential patterns. As mentioned earlier, it may well be that open networks and relations are more likely to enable access to and use of bridges to reach to resources lacking in one's social circle and to enhance one's chances of gaining resources/instrumental returns. On the other hand, a denser network with more intimate and reciprocal relations among members may increase the likelihood of mobilizing others with shared interests and resources to defend and protect existing resources/expressive returns. Further, exogenous factors such as community and institutional arrangements and prescriptive versus competitive incentives may differentially contribute to the density and openness of networks and relations and the success of instrumental or expressive actions.

Having discussed the core elements of social capital, clarified some of the measurement and sampling issues, identified the types of returns, and briefly postulated differential patterns of causal effects, I would like to propose a model as an initial step of theorizing social capital. As can be seen in Figure 1, the model contains three blocks of variables in causal sequences. One block represents preconditions and precursors of social capital: the factors in the social structure and each individual's position in the social structure that facilitate or constrain the investment of social capital. Another block represents social capital elements, and a third block represents possible returns for social capital.

The process leading from the first to the second block describes the formation of the inequality of social capital: what structural and positional elements affect opportunities to construct and maintain social capital. It delineates patterns of differential distributions for social resources that are embedded, accessed, or mobilized. It should further demonstrate that there are social forces that determine such differential distributions. Thus, it is incumbent on a theory of social capital to delineate the patterns and determinants of the two ingredients of social capital or *the inequality of social capital* as accessible social resources and mobilized social resources (Lin

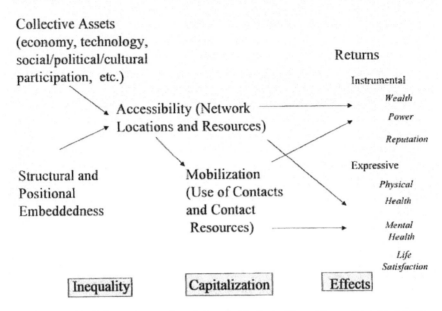

Figure 1.   Modeling a theory of social capital (adapted from Figure 13.1, Lin 2000).

2000, 2001, Chapter 7). Two types of causation forces are of special interest to scholars in the analysis of inequality of social capital: structural and positional variations. A structure may be characterized by many variations, such as economy, technology, and participation in the social, cultural, and political arenas. Within a structure, individuals may be described as occupying different positions in social, cultural, political, and economic strata. These variations may be hypothesized to affect the richness or poorness of various social ingredients.

Within the second block, there is a process linking two elements of social capital: access to and use of. The process linking the two elements represents social-capital mobilization—that is, given the unequal distributions of social capital how would an individual be enabled or disabled to mobilize such capital for specific actions? This is where the model, while recognizing structural contributions to social capital, as captured in the inequality process, also emphasizes possible choice action in mobilization.

Third, the theory needs to demonstrate that the three ingredients are interconnected. Thus, it needs to propose a causal sequence in which embedded resources constrain and enable individual choices and actions. The general expectation is that the better the accessible embedded resources, the more embedded resources can and will be mobilized in purposive actions by an individual. The more intriguing question is why, given the same level of accessible embedded resources, some individuals mobilize better resources than others. One contingency may be the network location. One could hypothesize that being a bridge or being closer to a bridge might make a difference: those at or near these locations are better able to mobilize embedded resources. Also, the cognitive recognition that there is a structural advantage to using better embedded resources may make a difference.

Finally, the process linking the second block (social capital) and the third block (outcomes) represents the process in which social capital produces returns or yields. Here, the theory should demonstrate how social capital is capital, or how it generates return or gain—that is, it should propose how one or more of the elements of social capital directly or indirectly impact an individual's economic, political, and social capital (resources), or her/his physical, mental, and life well-being.

These conceptualizations, as individual components and processes, are not new. This model, however, may be used to integrate rather diverse approaches and studies available in the literature. Research on social-resources theory (Lin 1999) has verified the proposition that social resources or social capital enhance an individual's attained status, such as occupational status, authority, and placement in certain industries. Through these attained positions, social capital enhances economic earnings as well. These relationships hold up after family background and education are taken into account. Burt (1997, 1998) and others (e.g., Podolny & Baron 1997) have shown that advances and economic rewards are also enhanced in organizations for individuals at strategic locations in the informal networks. Those closer to structural holes or bridges and, thus, under fewer structural constraints, seem to gain better returns, presumably because such locations give these individuals better opportunities to access certain capital in the organization. Research is progressing on how organizations use social capital to recruit and retain individuals. Fernandez and associates (Fernandez & Weinberg 1997) have shown that referrals increase applications, recruit better qualified candidates, and reduce costs in the screening process.

Some studies focus on collective assets. In Putnam's studies (1993, 1995a,b), this is indicated by participation in civic associations (e.g., churches, PTAs, Red Cross) and social groups (bowling leagues). Coleman (1990) provides examples of diffusion of information and mobilization through social circles among radical Korean students (i.e., network as capital), a mother moving from Detroit to Jerusalem in order to have her child walk to playground or school safely (norm as capital); and diamond traders in New York making trades through informal ties and informal agreements (network and trust as capital). Portes (1998) also specified "consummatory" and instrumental consequences of social capital (see Portes and Sensenbrenner 1993 for the consummatory consequences—solidarity and reciprocal support—of social capital for immigrant groups). While the primary focus for them is on the development, maintenance, or decline of collective assets, we need to be aware that not every member has an equal opportunity to access such assets. Thus, how these collective assets in conjunction with individuals' positions in these strata constitute precursors exogenous to the process of accessing or mobilizing social capital needs to be specified and demonstrated.

At the mesonetwork level, the focus shifts to how individuals have differential access to resources embedded in the collective. The question posed is why in a given collective certain individuals have better access to embedded resources than others. The nature of social networks and social ties becomes the focus of analysis. Granovetter (1973, 1974, 1982, 1985, 1995) proposes that bridges, usually reflected in weaker ties, provide better access to information. Burt (1992, 1997, 1998) sees that strategic locations in the networks, structural holes, or structural constraints imply better or worse access to information, influence, or control. Lin (1982, 1990, 1994a, 1995, 1999) has suggested that hierarchical positions as well as network locations facilitate or hinder access to embedded resources. Embedded resources are indicated by the wealth, status, and power of social ties.

At the microaction level, social capital is reflected in the actual linkage between the use of embedded resources in instrumental actions. For example, there is a substantial literature on how informal sources and their resources (contact resources) are mobilized in job searches and their effects on attained socioeconomic status (Lin, Ensel, & Vaughn 1981; De Graaf & Flap 1988; Marsden & Hurlbert 1988).

Research has also been extensive in the area of expressive actions' returns. Much is known about the indirect effects of networks on mental health and life satisfaction (Lin 1986; House et al. 1988; Berkman & Syme 1979; Berkman 1984; Hall & Wellman 1985; Wellman 1981; Kadushin 1983). In other words, network locations enhance the likelihood of accessing social support which, in turn, improves one's physical or mental well-being.

CONCLUDING REMARKS

Social networks scholarship has much to say about the development and future of social capital. Without anchoring the concept in social networks and embedded resources, chances are that social capital would fade away as an intellectual enterprise for the ever-broadening and -confounding definitions and almost utopian expectations of its practical applications. With ever-sharpening definitions and measurements, social-networks scholarship may have much to contribute to the sustained development of social capital as an intellectual enterprise.

NOTES

A portion of this chapter was presented as the Keynote Address at the XIX International Sunbelt Social Network Conference, Charleston, South Carolina, February 18–21, 1999, and appeared in *Connections*, 1999, 22–1: 28–51. I wish to thank Ronald S. Burt for reading and commenting on an earlier draft. I am, however, solely responsible for all the arguments presented here.

1. There is some ambiguity in Bourdieu's writings as to whether cultural capital should be seen as a structural theory or a theory that allows choice (Lin 2001, Chapter 1). He (Bourdieu 1990; Bourdieu & Passeron 1977) defines culture as a system of symbolism and meaning. The dominant class in the society imposes its culture by engaging in pedagogic action (e.g., education), which internalizes the dominant symbols and meanings in the next generation, thus, reproducing the salience of the dominant culture. The result is an internalized and durable training, *habitus*, in the reproduction of the culture. The masses are not cognitively aware of the imposition and take on the imposed culture as their own—misrecognition. This rendition of capital can trace its lineage to Marx. The social relations described by Marx are also assumed; there is a class, capitalists, who control the means of production—the process of pedagogic action or the educational institutions (in homes, schools, etc.). In the production (schooling) process, laborers (students or children) invest in the educational process and internalize the dominant class culture. Acquisition of this culture permits or licenses the laborers to enter the labor market, and earn money to support themselves. The capitalists, or the dominant class, gain cultural capital that supplements their economic capital and accumulate capital of both types in the circulation of the commodities (educated masses) and domination of the means of production (the educational institutions). However, there is a break from Marx, and it is important. Bourdieu does not assume perfect correspondence between the accumulation of economic and cultural capital. Some economic capitalists do not possess cultural capital and some cultural capitalists are not economically endowed. This less-than-perfect correspondence seems to open a possible path for some laborers, using their cultural habitus, to gain a foothold in the dominant class. It is conceivable that they become part of the educational institutions and gain returns in the labor market, due to their cultural capital. Bourdieu did not carry his analysis this far, but seems to leave open the process of social mobility and the possibility of agency.
2. This section is substantially extracted from Lin (2001, Chapter 2).
3. Another element, control, has also been mentioned for the usefulness of social capital. I consider control reflecting both the network location and the hierarchical position, central to the definition of social capital itself. Thus,

information, influence, social credentials, and reinforcement are all reasons why social capital works or controls.

4.   Two major and different theoretical positions distinguish scholars in the collective-asset camp. For Bourdieu, social capital represents a process by which individuals in the dominating class, by mutual recognition and acknowledgment, reinforce and reproduce a privileged group that holds various capital (economic, cultural and symbolic). Nobility and titles characterize such groups and their members. Thus, social capital is another way of maintaining and reproducing the dominant class. I would characterize this theoretical position as one that views social capital as class (privilege) goods. The other position on social capital as collective asset is represented by the works of Coleman and Putnam. Coleman, while defining social capital as consisting of any social-structural features or resources that are useful to individuals for specific actions, stresses social capital as a public good. These collective assets and features are available to all members of the group, be it a social group or community and regardless of which members actually promote, sustain, or contribute to such resources. Because social capital is a public good, it depends on the good will of the individual members to make such efforts and not to be free riders. Thus, norms, trust, sanctions, authority and other structural "features" become important in sustaining social capital. If one were forced to trace the theoretical lineage of these two explanatory schemes, one could argue that the privileged good view is principally an extension and elaboration of the social relations in the Marx' capital theory and that the public good view is primarily an extension and elaboration of the integrative or Durkheimian view of social relations.

REFERENCES

Angelusz, Robert, and Robert Tardos. 1991. "The Strength and Weakness of "Weak Ties." Pp. 7–23 in *Values, Networks and Cultural Reproduction in Hungary*, edited by P. Somlai. Budapest: The Coordinating Council of Programs.

Becker, Gary S. 1964/1993. *Human Capital*. Chicago, IL: University of Chicago Press.

Berkman, Lisa. 1984. "Assessing the Physical Health Effects of Social Networks and Social Support." *Annual Review of Public Health*. 5:413–32.

Berkman, Lisa F., and S. Leonard Syme. 1979. "Social Networks, Host Resistance, and Mortality: A Nine-Year Follow-Up Study of Alameda County Residents." *American Journal of Epidemiology* 109:186–284.

Borgatti, Stephen P., Candace Jones, and Martin G. Everett. 1998. "Network Measures of Social Capital." *Connections* 21(2):27–36, 2.

Bourdieu, Pierre. 1980. "Le Capital Social: Notes Provisoires." *Actes de la Recherche en Sciences Sociales* 3:2–3.

———. 1983/1986. "The Forms of Capital." Pp. 241–58 in *Handbook of Theory and Research for the Sociology of Education*, edited by John G. Richardson. Westport, CT: Greenwood Press.

————. 1990. *The Logic of Practice.* Cambridge, MA: Polity.

Bourdieu, Pierre, and Jean-Claude Passeron. 1977. *Reproduction in Education, Society, Culture.* Beverly Hills, CA: Sage.

Boxman, E. A. W., P. M. De Graaf, and Henk D. Flap. 1991. "The Impact of Social and Human Capital on the Income Attainment of Dutch Managers." *Social Networks* 13:51–73.

Breiger, Ronald L. 1981. "The Social Class Structure of Occupational Mobility." *American Journal of Sociology* 87(3):578–611.

Brewer, Anthony. 1984. *A Guide to Marx's Capital.* Cambridge, MA: Cambridge University Press.

Burt, Ronald S. 1984. "Network Items and the General Social Survey." *Social Networks* 6:293–339.

————. 1992. *Structural Holes: The Social Structure of Competition.* Cambridge, MA: Harvard University Press.

————. 1997. "The Contingent Value of Social Capital." *Administrative Science Quarterly* 42:339–65.

————. 1998. "The Gender of Social Capital." *Rationality and Society* 10(1):5–46, 1.

Burt, Ronald S., and M. J. Minor, eds. 1982. *Applied Network Analysis.* Beverly Hills, CA: Sage.

Campbell, Karen E., Peter V. Marsden, and Jeanne S. Hurlbert. 1986. "Social Resources and Socioeconomic Status." *Social Networks* 8(1), 1.

Coleman, James S. 1988. "Social Capital in the Creation of Human Capital." *American Journal of Sociology* 94:S95—S121.

————. 1990. *Foundations of Social Theory.* Cambridge, MA: Harvard University Press.

Cook, Karen S. 1982. "Network Structure from an Exchange Perspective." Pp. 177–99 in *Social Structure and Network Analysis,* edited by P. V. Marsden and N. Lin. Beverly Hills, CA: Sage.

De Graaf, Nan Dirk, and Hendrik Derk Flap. 1988. "With a Little Help from My Friends." *Social Forces* 67(2):452–72, 2.

Erickson, Bonnie H. 1995. "Networks, Success, and Class Structure: A Total View." Sunbelt Social Networks Conference. Charleston, SC, February.

————. 1996. "Culture, Class and Connections." *American Journal of Sociology* 102(1):217–51, 1.

Fernandez, Roberto M., and Nancy Weinberg. 1997. "Sifting and Sorting: Personal Contacts and Hiring in a Retail Bank." *American Sociological Review* 62:883–902.

Flap, Henk D. 1991. "Social Capital in the Reproduction of Inequality." *Comparative Sociology of Family, Health and Education* 20:6179–202.

————. 1994. "No Man Is An Island: The Research Program of a Social Capital Theory." World Congress of Sociology. Bielefeld, Germany, July.

Flap, Hendrik Derk, and Nan Dirk De Graaf. 1988. "Social Capital and Attained Occupational Status." *Netherlands Journal of Sociology.*

Granovetter, Mark. 1973. "The Strength of Weak Ties." *American Journal of Sociology* 78:1360–80.

————. 1974. *Getting a Job.* Cambridge, MA: Harvard University Press.

————. 1982. "The Strength of Weak Ties: A Network Theory Revisited." Pp. 105–

30 in *Social Structure and Network Analysis*, edited by Peter V. Marsden and Nan Lin. Beverly Hills, CA: Sage.

———. 1985. "Economic and Social Structure: The Problem of Embeddedness." *American Journal of Sociology* 91:481–510.

———. 1995. *Getting a Job (Revised Edition)*. Chicago, IL: University of Chicago Press.

Hall, Alan, and Barry Wellman. 1985. "Social Networks and Social Support." Pp. 23–42 in *Social Support and Health*, edited by S. Cohen and S. L. Syme. Orlando, FL: Academic Press.

House, James, Debra Umberson, and K. R. Landis. 1988. "Structures and Processes of Social Support." *Annual Review of Sociology* 14:293–318.

Johnson, Harry G. 1960. "The Political Economy of Opulence." *Canadian Journal of Economics and Political Science* 26:552–64.

Kadushin, Charles. 1983. "Mental Health and the Interpersonal Environment: A Re-Examination of Some Effects of Social Structure on Mental Health." *American Sociological Review* 48:188–98.

Laumann, Edward O. 1966. *Prestige and Association in an Urban Community*. Indianapolis, IN: Bobbs-Merrill.

Lin, Nan. 1982. "Social Resources and Instrumental Action." Pp. 131–45 in *Social Structure and Network Analysis*, edited by Peter V. Marsden and Nan Lin. Beverly Hills, CA: Sage.

———. 1986. "Conceptualizing Social Support." Pp. 17–30 in *Social Support, Life Events, and Depression*, edited by Nan Lin, Alfred Dean and Walter Ensel. Orlando, FL: Academic Press.

———. 1990. "Social Resources and Social Mobility: A Structural Theory of Status Attainment." Pp. 247–171 in *Social Mobility and Social Structure*, edited by Ronald L. Breiger. New York: Cambridge University Press.

———. 1992. "Social Resources Theory." Pp. 1936–42 in *Encyclopedia of Sociology, Volume 4*, edited by Edgar F. Borgatta and Marie L. Borgatta. New York: Macmillan.

———. 1994. "Action, Social Resources, and the Emergence of Social Structure: A Rational Choice Theory." *Advances in Group Processes* 11:67–85.

———. 1995. "Les Ressources Sociales: Une Theorie Du Capital Social." *Revue Francaise de Sociologie* XXXVI(4):685–704, 4.

———. 1998. "Social Exchange: Its Rational Basis." World Congress of Sociology. Montreal, August.

———. 1999. "Social Networks and Status Attainment." *Annual Review of Sociology* 23.

———. 2000. "Inequality in Social Capital." *Contemporary Sociology* 29–6 (November):785–95.

———. 2001. *Social Capital: A Theory of Social Structure and Action*. New York: Cambridge University Press.

Lin, Nan, and Yanjie Bian. 1991. "Getting Ahead in Urban China." *American Journal of Sociology* 97(3):657–88, 3.

Lin, Nan, and Mary Dumin. 1986. "Access to Occupations Through Social Ties." *Social Networks* 8:365–85.

Lin, Nan, Walter M. Ensel, and John C. Vaughn. 1981. "Social Resources and Strength of Ties: Structural Factors in Occupational Status Attainment." *American Sociological Review* 46(4):393–405, 4.

Lin, Nan, Yang-chih Fu, and Ray-may Hsung. 1998. "Position Generator: A Measurement for Social Capital." Social Networks and Social Capital. Duke University, November.

Marsden, Peter V. 1987. "Core Discussion Networks of Americans." *American Sociological Review* 52:122–31.

Marsden, Peter V., and Jeanne S. Hurlbert. 1988. "Social Resources and Mobility Outcomes: A Replication and Extension." *Social Forces* 66(4):1038–59, 4.

Marx, Karl (David McLellan, editor). 1995 (1867, 1885, 1894). *Capital: A New Abridgement.* Oxford: Oxford University Press.

Marx, Karl. 1933 (1849). *Wage-Labour and Capital.* New York: International Publishers Co.

McCallister, L., and Claude S. Fischer. 1978. "A Procedure for Surveying Personal Networks." *Sociological Methods and Research* 7:131–48.

Podolny, Joel M., and James N. Baron. 1997. "Social Networks and Mobility." *American Sociological Review* 62:673–93.

Portes, Alejandro, and Julia Sensenbrenner. 1993. "Embeddedness and Immigration: Notes on the Social Determinants of Economic Action." *American Journal of Sociology* 98(6):1320–50, 6.

Portes, Alex. 1998. "Social Capital: Its Origins and Applications in Modern Sociology." *Annual Review of Sociology* 22:1–24.

Putnam, Robert D. 1993. *Making Democracy Work: Civic Traditions in Modern Italy.* Princeton, NJ: Princeton University Press.

———. 1995a. "Bowling Alone, Revisited." *The Responsive Community,* Spring, 18–33.

———. 1995b. "Tuning In, Tuning Out: The Strange Disappearance of Social Capital in America." The 1995 Itheiel de Sola Pool Lecture. American Political Science Association. September.

———. 2000. *Bowling Alone: The Collapse and Revival of American Community.* New York: Simon & Schuster.

Schultz, Theodore W. 1961. "Investment in Human Capital." *The American Economic Review* LI(1):1–17, 1.

Sprengers, Maarten, Fritz Tazelaar, and Hendrik Derk Flap. 1988. "Social Resources, Situational Constraints, and Reemployment." *Netherlands Journal of Sociology* 24.

Tardos, Robert. 1996. "Some Remarks on the Interpretation and Possible Uses of the "Social Capital" Concept with Special Regard to the Hungarian Case." *Bulletin de Methodologie Sociologique* 53:52–62, 53.

Volker, Beate, and Henk Flap. 1996. "Getting Ahead in the GDR: Human Capital and Social Capital in the Status Attainment Process Under Communism." Universiteit Utrecht, the Netherlands.

Wellman, Barry. 1979. "The Community Question: The Intimate Networks of East Yorkers." *American Journal of Sociology* 84:1201–31.

Wellman, Barry. 1981. "Applying Network Analysis to the Study of Social Sup-

port." Pp. 171–200 in *Social Networks and Social Support*, edited by B. H. Gottlieb. Beverly Hills, CA: Sage.

White, Harrison C. 1992. *Identity and Control. A Structural Theory of Social Action.*
Princeton: Princeton University Press.

White, Harrison C., S. A. Boorman, and Ronald L. Breiger. 1976. "Social Structure
from Multiple Networks: I. Blockmodels of Roles and Positions." *American
Journal of Sociology* 81:730–80.

PART II

SOCIAL SUPPORT

Nan Lin and social support[*]

Lijun Song

A social network is a structure of social relationships linking actors, directly and indirectly (Lin et al. 1981b, 1981c; Mitchell 1969). Among various levels of complex social structures, social networks serve as a crucial mediating layer (Bian 1997; Burt 1992; Cook and Whitmeyer 1992; Lin 1990, 2001a; Song 2013b; Song and Pettis 2018). Traced back to the classic sociological work by Durkheim, Simmel, and Tönnies, the social network perspective has empowered researchers to identify various network properties and theorize and analyze their causes and consequences for thirteen decades. Among other network-based factors, the concept of social support has been given voluminous research attention especially for its diverse roles for health for more than four decades (for reviews see Barrera 2000; Berkman et al. 2000; Song et al. 2011; Thoits 2011; Turner and Brown 2010; Turner and Turner 2013; Uchino 2009; Umberson and Montez 2010). It has been claimed to be one possible fundamental social determinant of health (Link and Phelan 1995).

As a popular Chinese idiom says, "when you drink water, remember to think of its source." It is the pioneering efforts of several health scholars, including sociologist Nan Lin, in the mid and late 1970s that have stimulated the systematic development and rise of social support into a popular and powerful theoretical tool (Caplan 1974, 1976; Cassel 1974, 1976; Cobb 1974, 1976; Dean and Lin 1977; Henderson 1977; Kaplan et al. 1977; Lin et al. 1979, Chapter 6 in this book; Rabkin and Struening 1976; see Chapter 11 in this book for Lin's reflections on his research journey on social support). It has been overdue, however, to celebrate Lin's four-decade-long groundbreaking contributions to the social support literature. Lin is a theorist, methodologist, and empirical researcher. He perspicaciously foresaw the importance of social support and has been standing at the very forefront of its four-decade-long research tradition. He defines social support from the social network theoretical perspective, and distinguishes it from other network-based concepts. His social resources theory, one of the first and few theories on social support, advances the conceptualization, typologization, and operationalization of social support and the theoretical modeling of its structural causes and complicated functions. His original measurement efforts have encouraged generations of scholars to construct social support scales. His rigorous and advanced research designs, data collection, and analysis have laid the solid foundation for our causal and dynamic understanding of social support.

In this chapter, I first draw the trends of the social support research. Then I clarify the theoretical relationships between social support and another two related concepts – social

* Direct correspondence to Lijun Song, Department of Sociology, Vanderbilt University, PMB 351811, Nashville TN 37235-1811 (Lijun.song@vanderbilt.edu). The author is indebted to Nan Lin, Yanjie Bian, Ronald S. Burt, Gina Lai, and Chih-Jou Jay Chen for all their protective social support on this exciting and rewarding journey on social support.

resources and social capital – in Lin's social network research. Next, I focus on Lin's important and persistent five-stage research efforts on social support, and discuss his critical research impacts. Finally, I propose crucial future research directions enlightened by Lin's work. Note that many scholars have provided confusingly diverse definitions of social support. As reviewed below, I adhere to a recent, strict, network-based definition from Lin and colleagues: help or aid from social networks (Song and Lin 2009; Song et al. 2010, 2011).

Trends

Social support is a sociological phenomenon and concept by its nature. At least as old as the discipline of sociology, social support is rooted in classic sociological work. Comte (1875 [1852], p. 314), who coined the term sociology, states that "all mental action depends on social support." Another three forerunners of sociology – Durkheim, Simmel, and Tönnies – also mention the support or aid from social relationships in their seminal studies. Considering these sociological classics as well as thousands-year-old religions or philosophies such as Confucianism and Mohism emphasizing graded or universal love toward others (Fei 1992 [1947]), we concur with House (1981, p. 14) that "in some ways social support is really old wine in a new bottle" or with Turner (1981, p. 357) that social support "hardly reflects discovery of a new idea." Despite its long recognition, however, this old wine (or idea) was not handpicked with serious appreciation out of the gigantic wine cellar (or the enormous treasure of theoretical concepts) for explicit conceptualization and systematic analysis in social science until the mid-1970s (Caplan 1974, 1976, 1979; Cassel 1974, 1976; Cobb 1974, 1976; Dean and Lin 1977; Henderson 1977; Kaplan et al. 1977; Lin et al. 1979, Chapter 6 in this book; Rabkin and Struening 1976). Lin is one of these perspicacious scholars. He and colleagues foresee social support as "the most important concept for future study" (Dean and Lin 1977, p. 408).

We can picture the more than four-decade-long research tradition on "social support" and/ or "health" using two databases: the Social Sciences Citation Index (SSCI) in Web of Science and the China Knowledge Resource Integrated Database (CKRID). The SSCI can search articles published mainly in English since 1900 (see Figure 5.1), and the CKRID social scientific articles published in Chinese since 1915 (see Figure 5.2).

Two observations from the search results deserve some discussion. First, there is roughly a two-decade publication gap between articles in English and those in Chinese. The social support research took off in the mid-1970s in the English world and in the mid-1990s in China. This long publication gap may be in large part due to the shifting state policies in contemporary China. It is as early as the late 1940s that Fei Xiaotong, one of the founders of sociology in China, theorizes the importance of help from discrete social circles, even though not explicitly using the term "social support" (Fei 1992 [1947]). Sociology as a discipline, however, lost its political legitimacy and was abolished together with all its courses in 1952. It did not regain its legitimacy until 27 years later in 1979. Yanjie Bian applauds Lin's contributions to the rebirth of sociology in China in Chapter 8 in this book. Lin himself has not written in detail about his various forms of social support for the reestablishment of sociology in China. His own version will be crucial for us to understand the history of sociology in China and deal with current and future challenges the discipline of sociology faces in and beyond China.

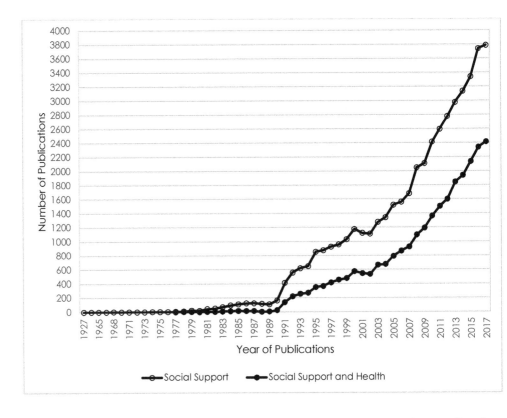

Figure 5.1   Journal articles in English with "social support," and "social support" and "health" in topic (Social Sciences Citation Index, 1900–2017)

The second observation can really disappoint sociologists. Sociology deserves but lacks visibility in the existing literature. The SSCI subsumes less than 3 percent of the social support literature under the category of sociology, and the CKRID groups about 20 percent of the social support studies under the category of sociology and statistics. Also, health and education studies respectively dominate the social support literature in English and Chinese. We must repeat the three-decade-old call from House and colleagues for sociologists to play a more central role in the advancement of future studies on social support (House et al. 1988). We also must bang the drum for the four-decade-old emphasis from Lin and colleagues on social support as "the most important concept for future study" (Dean and Lin 1977, p. 408).

Lin: one heart, two directions, and three concepts
Lin is first and foremost a seminal social network scholar. At the heart of his substantive work is the social network theoretical perspective. In his broad theoretical framework, he emphasizes meso-level social networks as the vital link mediating the reciprocal dynamic relationship between macrolevel social structures and micro-level individual actions (1983, 1990, 2001a). Also, from the very beginning, Lin's original passion for social network research takes two different directions: instrumental and expressive actions (Lin 1982, 1986a, 1999b, 2000,

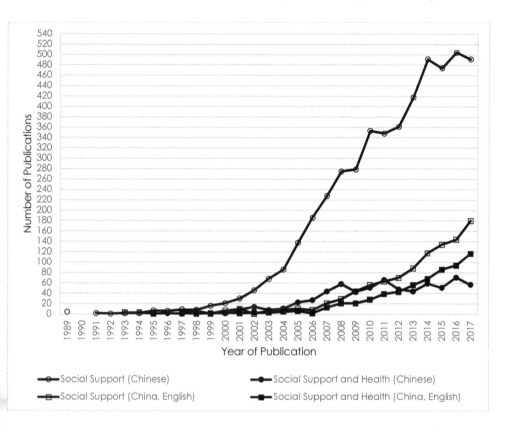

Figure 5.2   Journal articles with "social support," and "social support" and "health" in topic (China Integrated Knowledge Resources Database, Chinese Articles, 1915–2017; Social Sciences Citation Index, English Articles on China, 1900–2017)

2001a, 2008; Lin and Dean 1984; Lin and Ensel 1989; Lin et al. 1978, 1979, Chapter 6 in this book, 1985). These two actions will be introduced in detail later in the summary of his social resources theory. As his brief author biography in one of his earliest publications clearly states, Lin "is conducting research on the instrumental and expressive uses of social relationships as indicated in the process of status attainment, and in the buffering role of social support between stress and illness" (Lin et al. 1978, p. 166). Furthermore, in a chronological research order, Lin's social network research focuses on three network-based concepts: social resources, social support, and social capital (see Chapter 2 in this book for Ronald S. Burt's review of Lin's work on social capital).

The theoretical relationships among social support, social resources, and social capital have been dynamic in Lin's intellectual journey (see Figure 5.3). When commencing his two separate research paths respectively on the concepts of social resources and social support in the 1970s, Lin focused on the impact of social resources on instrumental actions (i.e., instrumental search and occupational status attainment) and that of social support on expressive

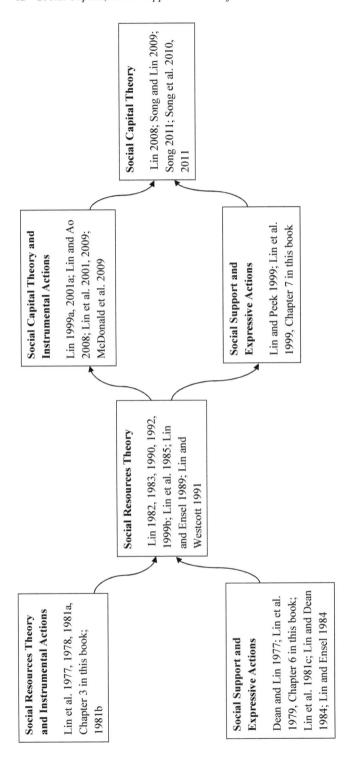

Figure 5.3   Lin's social network research: one heart, two directions and three concepts

actions (i.e., mental health) (Dean and Lin 1977; Lin and Ensel 1984; Lin et al. 1977, 1978, 1979, Chapter 6 in this book, 1981a, Chapter 3 in this book, 1981b, 1981c). Then, Lin subsumed social support as well as both instrumental and expressive actions under his social resources theory, and used social support to indicate social resources (Lin 1982, 1983, 1990, 1992, 1999b; Lin and Ensel 1989; Lin and Westcott 1991; Lin et al. 1985). He still reserved the concept of social support for expressive studies, and used general terms such as help, helpers, and resource borrowing for instrumental studies. Next, returning to the bifurcated beginning, these two concepts – social support and social resources – were employed separately again in expressive and instrumental studies (Lin 1999a, 2001a; Lin and Ao 2008; Lin and Peek 1999; Lin et al., 1999, Chapter 7 in this book, 2001, 2009).

Lin redeveloped social resources theory into social capital theory in the late 1990s (Lin 1999a). Social capital is constructed as a concept at the general theoretical level. Social resources change from a theoretical concept into a concept at the empirical and research levels. Although less visible in social capital theory, social support serves as a downstream mechanism. Lin defines social capital as resources embedded in social networks and specifies it mainly as accessed status and connections (network members' hierarchical status and social ties) and mobilized status and connections (hierarchical status and social ties of network members one contacts for help). In his monumental monograph, *Social Capital: A Theory of Social Structure and Action* (Lin 2001a), Lin chooses to focus on instrumental returns to social capital, and does include expressive returns into his theoretical model of social capital (Lin 2001a). One out of the six propositions on returns to social capital, the strength-of-strong-tie proposition, is related to expressive actions. As it states, social capital accessed from stronger ties can promote expressive actions more successfully. The book does not examine this proposition. But as reviewed below, this proposition is built upon Lin's prior work on social support and health, which demonstrates that social support from stronger ties is more protective of health. The book acknowledges "social support" explicitly once and relates that concept to expressive returns. As Lin explains why the book pays limited attention to expressive returns to social capital (2001a, p. 243):

> I chose to focus on the instrumental aspect of social capital and thus shortchanged its expressive aspect, not that my research efforts have ignored the latter. There is a substantial and thriving literature on the effects on mental health and the well-being of social support, social networks, and social resources. To do justice to the expressive aspect of social capital would require perhaps another monograph of comparable size.

In his book, Lin also mentions one form of social support – emotional support – once as one pathway for instrumental and expressive returns to social capital (Lin 2001a, p. 20). More recently, with his social capital theory extended to health outcomes, Lin and colleagues highlight social support as one main pathway for both instrumental and expressive returns to social capital (Lin 2008; Song 2011; Song and Lin 2009; Song et al. 2010, 2011).

In brief, the position of social support has been changing in Lin's network-based theoretical frameworks. It transfers from an indicator of social resources in his expressive or health studies to a pathway for the positive function of social resources in his social capital theory. Following Lin's steps, the following review of his work on social support will focus on his expressive or health studies, and draw upon his instrumental studies when relevant (see

Chapters 2 and 8 in this book for Ronald S. Burt and Yanjie Bian's focused reviews of Lin's instrumental studies). I roughly group his efforts on social support and health into five stages.

Five-stage work on social support and health

Stage one: a critical and fundamental review as a blueprint
Lin began his journey on social support 42 years ago. In spring 1976, he and colleagues from the Department of Sociology at the State University of New York at Albany and Albany Medical College had a series of meetings to discuss collaborative opportunities (see the preface in Lin et al. 1986). As they found out, what they had in common in terms of research interests was social determinants of mental health. After a thorough review of the relevant literature, they narrowed down their research interests into the concept of social support. "We felt that a concerted and systematic effort in teasing out the various components of social support and how they affected the stress process would be an invaluable contribution to the field" (Lin et al. 1986, p. xiii). Their feeling at that time has turned out to be true.

In December 1977, their first article on social support was published, titled "the stress-buffering role of social support" (Dean and Lin 1977). It is a critical and solid review of the two-decade-long literature on the established stress–illness relationship. It sharply pins social support into the stress–illness relationship. It discerns the "suggestive and useful" evidence for the emerging idea of social support as a mediator or buffer for the stress–illness relationship. It points out the theoretical, methodological, and empirical problems surrounding the concept of social support. It foresees the importance, urgency, and challenge of future research. It labels social support as "the most important concept for future study," draws our attention to the need for "more theoretical meaningful and penetrating" measures of social support, but also recognizes social support as "the most difficult task for instrumentation" (p. 408). In addition, it provides advanced research strategies to address these identified problems.

This review criticizes prior work for the neglect of social support, the absence of theoretical explanations for its role, and the lack of clear conceptualization. The review then conceptualizes social support and proposes hypotheses on its function. When conceptualizing social support, this review emphasizes social support as the principle functions of strong ties, that is, the primary group or primary relationships. It uses the family as the example of the primary group and operationalizes social support functions as the following features of the family: "a) emphasis on mutual responsibility, caring and concern; b) strong mutual identification; c) emphasis upon the person as a unique individual rather than upon his/her performance; d) face-to-face interaction and communication; e) intimacy; f) close association and bonds; and g) provision of support, affection, security and response" (p. 407). This review distinguishes two forms of functions the primary group fulfills: instrumental (i.e., "the fulfillment of tasks") and expressive functions ("the satisfaction of individual needs and the maintenance of solidarity") (p. 407). It emphasizes expressive functions as the main purpose of the primary group. It also encourages future efforts on the "mutual interaction" between the two functions (p. 407).

When theorizing the function of social support, this review proposes three principal hypotheses: 1) negative interaction with social stressors; 2) generalization of the interaction effect into different illness histories; and 3) social stressors as an antecedent of social support. The first hypothesis contains a moderating-effect subhypothesis: the moderating role of social support depends on the type or severity of social stressors. The third hypothesis has two competing subhypotheses: social stressors may decrease or increase social support.

This review recognizes methodological shortcomings in the existing studies: the lack of direct, reliable and valid instruments, and the lack of longitudinal designs and conclusive evidence. It warns against the indirect measurement of social support as social integration indicators such as marital status. It lists a couple of existing scales as the beginning, emphasizes the importance of a rigorous pretest of future scales, and suggests the necessity of employing clustering analysis in the exploration of the multidimensionality of social support. It criticizes existing studies for the lack of causal inferences and generalizability in their findings due to their case control designs and focus on patient population. It encourages future research to use longitudinal data from representative samples of normal population, conduct ideally three-wave cross-lagged path analysis to test the causal directions in the relationships among social stressors, social support, and illness, and compare the relative strength of all paths.

The 1977 review is at the forefront of the social support research tradition. It has three strengths in comparison with other forerunning work (Caplan 1974, 1976; Cassel 1974, 1976; Cobb 1974, 1976; Henderson 1977; Kaplan et al. 1977; Rabkin and Struening 1976). First, other forerunning work recognizes the main effect of social support but emphasizes more its negative moderating effect on the stress–illness relationship. As Cobb states, "social support facilitates coping with crisis and adaption to change. Therefore, one should not expect dramatic main effects from social support ... it is in moderating the effects of the major transitions in life and of the unexpected crises that the effects should be found" (Cobb 1976, p. 302). In other words, other forerunning work constrains social support to go after social stressors as a reliever of their detrimental impacts. In comparison, the 1977 review conceives of social support as "a dynamic variable" (Dean and Lin 1977, p. 411; see Gore 1981). Its proposed hypotheses and cross-lagged three-wave path analysis model draw a reciprocal line between social support and social stressors, and guide us to model not only the main and moderating effects of social support but also its three other effects: indirect effect through social stressors, and two mediating effect on the stress–illness relationship. Second, earlier work underscores emotional support more. The 1977 review discusses both expressive and instrumental support, and lists their interaction as a future research direction. The term "expressive" is similar to the term "emotional." Lin prefers the former term "in order to stress its social (interaction and confiding) rather than its psychological nature" (Lin 1986a, p. 20). In addition, the 1977 review offers a systematic methodological critique and an advanced future research design, which is missing in other forerunning work.

Stage two: the first systematic study, panel design, and instrumentation

In the second stage, using representative community data of normal population, the 1979 article is the first to systematically examine both the main and moderating effects of social support in the social dynamics of health and another three effects related to the reciprocal relationship between social support and social stressors (Lin et al. 1979, Chapter 6 in this book). Other empirical studies at that time are limited to the main and moderating effects of social support (Andrews et al. 1978; Gore 1978). Also, in this stage, Lin and colleagues make one of the first attempts to instrument social support and to design a longitudinal survey that addresses their objectives in the 1977 review.

In the 1979 article, social support is defined from a social network perspective as "support accessible to an individual through social ties to other individuals, groups, and the larger community" (Lin et al. 1979, p. 109, Chapter 6 in this book). Its structural sources extend beyond strong ties emphasized in the first stage to include multilayer relationships in social networks. Noticing the lower explanatory power of social stressors in existing work, this article proposes the independent effect hypothesis that social support should be negatively associated with illness net of social stressors. Two mechanisms are discussed: norms and reacting capabilities. Also, this article theorizes the reciprocal relationship between social support and social stressors in more detail than the 1977 review, and develops three hypotheses: stress prevention, support mobilization, and support deterioration. The stress prevention hypothesis expects social support to protect health through deterring the occurrence of social stressors. The support mobilization hypothesis states that social stressors have an indirect positive association with health through triggering the mobilization of social support. The support deterioration hypothesis maintains that social stressors have an indirect negative association with health through weakening available social support. Furthermore, the 1979 article offers some additional interaction-effect arguments for future research. The effects of social stressors on social support can vary by socioeconomic status. Social stressors may be more likely to trigger social support for higher-status people who possess more reacting capabilities, and to deteriorate social support for lower-status people. The functions of social support can further vary by its source (primary versus secondary group) and purpose (instrumental versus affective).

Using cross-sectional data from a representative community sample of the Chinese-American adult population in Washington, D.C., this 1979 study makes "a reasonable first scaling attempt" to measure social support using a scale of nine items (p. 113). These nine items capture people's social interactions and involvement with friends, neighbors, and the Chinese communities and their subjective feelings about the neighborhood, people nearby, and job. Multivariate and path analysis of psychiatric symptoms shows evidence for the stronger direct explanatory power of social support relative to that of social stressors, some inconclusive evidence for the support mobilization hypothesis, but no evidence for other hypotheses (support deterioration, stress prevention, and stressor-support interaction).

The inception of the four-wave Albany Area Health Survey project took place in fall 1977 (Lin et al. 1986). In August 1978, Lin and colleagues conducted a pretest to field test four different social support scales, including their own original 26-item and later revised 28-item instrumental-expressive support scale (Lin et al. 1981c). After the reliability and validity tests on these scales, the four waves of longitudinal survey data were collected respectively in 1979, 1980, 1982, and 1994 (Lin and Dean 1984; Lin and Ensel 1984, 1989; Lin et al. 1986, 1999, Chapter 7 in this book). Such a longitudinal initiative was really rare at that time (Henderson et al. 1981; Turner 1981).

Stage three: social resources theory, refined modeling, and longitudinal analysis
In the third stage, Lin builds fuller theoretical, methodological, and analytical frameworks on social support, in particularly as illustrated in the edited book, *Social Support, Life Events, and Depression* (Lin et al. 1986). He is one of the first to develop and apply a specific theory (i.e., social resources theory) to define, typologize, operationalize, and theorize social support (Lin 1982, 1983, 1986a; Lin and Dean 1984; Lin and Ensel 1989; Lin et al. 1981c, 1985). Also,

although the embeddedness of social support in social networks has been recognized in earlier work including Lin and colleagues' earlier work (Caplan 1974; Cobb 1976; Dean and Lin 1977; Gottlieb 1978; Henderson 1977; Kahn and Antonucci 1980; Kaplan et al. 1977; Lin et al. 1979, Chapter 6 in this book; Wellman 1981), Lin is the first to conceptualize the internal structure of social support from an interrelated, multilayer, social network perspective (Lin 1986a, 1986c). Furthermore, going beyond the 1979 study, Lin and colleagues contribute a richer list of theoretical models (Lin 1986b; Lin and Ensel 1989). In addition, they use first-hand longitudinal data from the Albany Area Health Survey, employ their instrumental-expressive social support scale as well as other scales, conduct advanced statistical analysis of diverse hypotheses, and achieve stronger causal inferences.

Lin began his construction of social resources theory in his small world experiment on packet forwarding in the late 1970s (Lin et al. 1977, 1978). Analyzing people's instrumental use of social ties in delivering packets and later in job search, Lin identified "relations as resources" and proposed the idea of social resources (Lin et al. 1977, 1978, p. 150, 1981a, Chapter 3 in this book, 1981b). As "resources embedded in one's social network," social resources are operationalized as "the wealth, status, power, as well as social ties, of those persons who are directly or indirectly linked to the individuals" (Lin 1982; Lin et al. 1981b, p. 1163). Identifying "the lack of an integrated theory" on the role of social support for health, Lin extends social resources theory to social support (Lin 1982, 1983, 1986a; Lin and Dean 1984; Lin and Ensel 1989; Lin et al. 1981c, 1985, p. 248). As Lin assumes, constrained by the hierarchical macrostructures of a society, most actions individuals take at the microstructural level are dichotomized into instrumental and expressive actions in terms of their purposes. Instrumental actions aim to "achieve an end" or search and obtain additional or new resources, while expressive actions intend to preserve and maintain existing resources and protect again resource loss (Lin 1982, 1983, 1986, 1990, 1992; Lin and Dean 1984; Lin and Dumin 1986; Lin et al. 1981a, Chapter 3 in this book, 1981b, 1981c, p. 76). Correspondingly, respectively on the instrumental and expressive dimensions, Lin distinguishes two types of interactions, relationships, and support functions (Dean and Lin 1977; Dean et al. 1981; Lin 1982; Lin et al. 1978, 1979, Chapter 6 in this book, 1981c). He further specifies three forms of returns to instrumental actions (economic, political, and social returns) and three forms of returns to expressive actions (physical health, mental health, and life satisfaction) (Lin 1999b, 2000, 2001a). He maintains that "the relative frequency and intensity of instrumental and expressive interactions in a society, I believe, hold the key in determining the dynamics of stability and change" (Lin 1982, p. 145).

Lin proposes two tie-purpose matching propositions: the strength of weak and heterophilous ties for instrumental actions, and the strength of strong and homophilous ties for expressive actions (Lin 1983). Successful instrumental actions need diverse and nonredundant social resources which are most available from weak and heterophilous ties. Successful expressive behaviors, however, require interaction with contacts sharing similar characteristics and resources, and such contacts are most reachable through strong and homophilous ties. Lin reminds us that the application of social resources theory to expressive actions was "not an exact mirror image" of its application to instrumental ones (Lin 1983, p. 14). Expressive actions are more complicated than instrumental ones for three reasons: the dependence of certain expressive actions on both instrumental and expressive support, strong ties sometimes as the sources of stress, and the dynamics of strong ties (Lin 1983, 1992). Lin also points out that instrumental actions are more costly as interactions with weak and heterophilous ties require more effort (Lin 2001a).

Assuming that the maintenance and promotion of health, in particular mental health, requires expressive actions, Lin later provides an operational definition of social support as "access to and use of strong and homophilous ties" (Lin 1986a; Lin and Dean 1984, p. 87; Lin et al. 1985). This definition overlaps with one statement in the first stage that emphasizes strong ties as the major sources of social support for expressive needs. Applying social resources theory, Lin states that social support thus conceived and operationalized should play an independent protective effect on health net of social stressors and other factors. Note that apart from the tie-purpose matching propositions, social resources theory contains one important proposition on the positive effect of accessed status on instrumental actions (Lin 1982, 1983, 1990). This proposition later becomes the social resources proposition in Lin's social capital theory (Lin 2001a). Lin and colleagues do not extend this proposition to expressive actions until the fifth stage.

Apart from his strong tie-based operational definition of social support, Lin reviews existing definitions and gives a synthetic conceptual definition, which, similar to the one in the second stage, is not limited to strong and homophilous ties. Social support is "the perceived or actual instrumental and/or expressive provisions supplied by the community, social networks, and confiding partners" (Lin 1986a, p. 18). This definition emphasizes certain forms of support differentiated on two dimensions: subjectivity or objectivity (actual or received versus perceived or cognitive support) (Caplan 1979), and content (instrumental versus expressive support).

From an interrelated, multilayer, social network perspective, Lin conceptualizes the internal structure of social support (Lin 1986a, 1986c). He decomposes social support into two components: the social (structural) component or support resources, and the support (processing) component or support processes. Support resources precede support processes, and involve three interrelated layers of social relations: belonging or community relations, bonding or network relations, and binding or intimate relations. The first layer bolsters the other two and the second one promotes the third one. The third layer in turn influences support processes, which contain social support on two dimensions: subjectivity or objectivity, and context (routine versus crisis). The two dimensions together generate four interconnected forms of social support. The content dimension is also integrable into the support processes. Using this conceptual framework, the Albany Area Health Survey collected information on social support in four ways: community support, network support, confident support, and instrumental-expressive support (Lin 1986b).

Furthermore, Lin considers all three possible temporal sequences of social support and social stressors, and constructs a list of twelve models using depression as the outcome (Lin 1986b). A previously ignored positive causal flow from social support to social stressors (i.e., stress induction) is added to the reciprocal relationship between social support and social stressors. When social support precedes social stressors, four models are possible: negative interaction or reduced protection of social support, stress prevention, stress induction, and independence. When social support and social stressors are measured simultaneously, four models are possible: contemporaneous negative interaction, contemporaneous mutual deterrence, contemporaneous mutual reinforcement, and contemporaneous independence.

When social support is subsequent to social stressors, four models are possible: negative interaction or reduced damage of social stressors, support deterioration, support mobilization, and independent compensation.

Using the longitudinal data from the Albany Area Health Survey, Lin and colleagues use advanced longitudinal analytical methods such as the path analysis models and structural equational models to extensively examine the role of social support in the stress–depression relationship. Most of their studies apply social resources theory and measure social support from strong and homophilous ties, and some of their studies employ diverse social support scales including the instrumental-expressive support scale (Dean and Ensel 1982; Ensel and Lin 1991, 1996, 2000, 2004; Lin 1986b; Lin and Dean 1984; Lin and Ensel 1984; Lin et al. 1985, 1986). In brief, they find strong evidence for the strength-of-strong-tie proposition, but mixed evidence for the strength-of-homophilous-tie proposition. Also, consistent with Lin's propositions on the integral structure of social support, strong tie support and instrumental-expressive support is more predictive than community and network support. Furthermore, they find strong evidence for the independence model and the support deterioration model, moderate evidence for the stress prevention model, but little evidence for the interaction model. The explanatory power of these models varies by other factors including age, gender, marital status, social class, and illness histories. In addition, the independence model and the support deterioration model are applicable when physical symptoms serve as the outcome and when both distal and proximal social stressors are examined. Finally, social support can mediate the effect of psychological resources.

In this stage, two more studies make theoretical and methodological contributions (Lin 1989; Lin and Ensel 1989). The study by Lin and Ensel (1989) expands the theoretical framework on the stress–illness relationship. It examines physical health, and treats depression, the primary outcome of interests in prior studies on the stress–illness relationship, as an antecedent of physical health. Theoretically, this study extends the six-model life stress process proposed by Dohrenwend and Dohrenwend (1981). From a temporal-causal perspective, it formulates the broadest conceptual model ever in the prediction of physical health, which involves both resources and stressors from all three environments: social, psychological, and physiological. This conceptual model allows the formulation of additional hypotheses beyond the original six models in the life stress process. Also, this study refines the definition of social support as "the process (e.g., perception and reception) by which resources in the social structure are brought to bear to meet the functional needs (e.g., instrumental and expressive) in routine and crisis situations" (Lin and Ensel 1989, p. 383). This definition uses the term social structure to imply the three-layer structural components of social support, and contains different forms of social support on three dimensions (subjectivity/objectivity, content, and context). Methodologically, this study measures strong tie support. Analysis of the three-wave data from the Albany Area Health Survey shows no evidence for the independent effect of social support as social resources but strong evidence for its interactive role. It interacts with both social stressors and depression, while psychological resources only with depression.

Although not directly related to social support, Lin's 1989 study is the first to construct a depressive symptom scale for the population in China. It lays a methodological foundation for future mental health research in China and future comparative research involving China. As Lin notices, prior studies on depression are limited to Chinese societies outside China, report different distributions of depression, and lack rigorous reliability and validity tests beyond the translation of the 20-item CES-D scale (the Center for Epidemiological Studies Depression Scale) established in the west. Collaborating with the Tianjin Academy of Social Sciences and the City Government of Tianjin, Lin collected representative adult data in Tianjin in 1986. His reliability and validity tests support a 22-item Chinese Depressive Symptom Scale (CDS-22). This scale removes the four positive items in CES-D and adds another six items on relational problems people experienced during the Cultural Revolution. Excluding these six items, a shorter version, CDS-16, can be used for comparative studies on China and other societies.

Stage four: structural or network embeddedness of social support
In the fourth stage, Lin and colleagues continue refining their social network perspective on social support, and extending our knowledge of the complicated "structural embeddedness" of social support or "a nested support system" (Lin and Peek 1999; Lin et al. 1999, pp. 344, 347, Chapter 7 in this book; Son et al. 2008). They are among the first to systematically examine the relationships among social network, social support, and health (Lin et al. 1999, Chapter 7 in this book).

Lin criticizes prior studies on social support for describing structure using sociodemographic factors, and advocates a social network perspective on our interpretation of structure. Lin and colleagues have long highlighted social networks as a structural antecedent of social support (Dean and Lin 1977; Lin et al. 1979, Chapter 6 in this book, 1981c). As in his 1986 conceptual framework on social support, Lin identifies two components of social support: a three-layer support structure and support functions. In their network theory on the relationship between marital status and health, Lin and Westcott (1991) emphasize social support as the crucial downstream explanatory mechanism. Lin and Peek (1999) later conduct a thorough review on the impact of social network properties on mental health, but find inconsistent results. They speculate that social network properties as upstream structural sources of social support affect mental health more indirectly and thus more inconsistently. Their speculation is consistent with results from their analysis of the three-wave data from the Albany Area Health Survey (Peek and Lin 1999). Strong-tie support affects depression more directly than social network compositions.

It is Lin et al. (1999, Chapter 7 in this book) that elaborate and systematically examine Lin's 1986 conceptual framework on social support (1986a, 1986c). Based on the belonging–bonding–binding formulation for the three layers of structural support, they hypothesize that each outer layer builds up each inner layer, and all three layers boost support functions with the inner layers exerting greater effects. Also, they expect support functions to decrease depressive symptoms more directly and strongly than structural support, and structural support to do so both directly and indirectly with the inner-most layer exerting the strongest effect. Methodologically, they integrate eight forms of support functions jointly classified on three dimensions emphasized in Lin's 1989 conceptual framework: subjectivity/objectivity, context, and content. Their structural equation modeling analysis of these support functions generates a three-level factor structure. They choose to examine the effects of perceived versus actual support in terms of instrumental versus expressive support. Results from their analysis of data from the 1993 Albany Area Health Survey support their hypotheses. Note that among four forms of social support, only perceived expressive support plays an independent protective role. Additional interaction effect analysis finds that the impacts of support structures and support functions do not vary by sociodemographic factors such as age, gender, and income. Nine years later, Son et al. (2008) replicate the structural analysis by Lin et al. (1999) using representative data from Taiwan, and report in general similar findings.

Although not involving social support, another study in this stage embeds the stress–illness model in broader social and cultural contexts, and demonstrates the varying detrimental impacts of social stressors across culture and society (Lin and Lai 1995). Lin and Lai investigate the stressor–depression relationship using the aforementioned Tianjin data as well as the 1982 Albany Area Health Survey data. Their results support the stress–illness model. But one work-related social stressor – work conflict – is detrimental only in the Tianjin sample. They attribute that finding to two institutional factors in urban China: the centrality of work units and the cultural norm of interpersonal harmony.

Stage five: distinction from and relationship with other network-based concepts
More recently, Lin and colleagues have taken on two challenges to address some critical and controversial issues on social capital and social support. One challenge is the lack of confidence in the explanatory power of social capital, and the other one the conceptual distinction and relationships between social support, social capital, and some other network-based concept. Lin and colleagues address these two challenges and clarify the conceptual distinction of social support from social capital and other network-based concepts, and their theoretical and empirical relationships with each other in the social dynamics of status attainment and health.

The first challenge appears when the explanatory power of Lin's social capital theory is questioned. The theory expects resources from social networks to advance status attainment. But its expectation is challenged by the puzzling facts that a big proportion of participants in the labor market reports no job search and a big percentage of job seekers uses no personal contacts. Facing this challenge, some lose confidence in the causal effect of social capital on job search and status attainment. Lin does not. He offers an intriguing proposition called the invisible hand of social capital (Lin 2000). He argues that individuals can receive useful information without actively seeking it if they access more social capital or live in resource-richer networks. In 2004, Lin and colleagues launched an unprecedented two-wave, three-society (the United States, urban China, and Taiwan) representative survey project, titled "Social Capital: Its Origins and Consequences" (Lin et al. 2014a). To my knowledge, this survey project is the first to collect longitudinal data on social capital simultaneously from multiple societies. It focuses on causes and consequences of social capital, and contains questions on the invisible hand of social capital, that is, unsolicited job leads (information on job possibilities, openings, or opportunities received without asking). Lin and colleagues analyze the U.S. sample and find strong evidence for the invisible hand proposition (Lin and Ao 2008). Accessed status is positively associated with the receipt of unsolicited job leads, which in turn is positively associated occupational status and income. Following this study, Lin and colleagues further demonstrate the unequal access to unsolicited job leads by gender and race/ethnicity (McDonald et al. 2009). White men are advantaged in receiving unsolicited job leads in comparison with women and minorities.

Lin and colleagues' work on causes and consequences of unsolicited job leads expand the theoretical frameworks not only on the stratified mechanisms linking social capital to status attainment but also on the structural causes of social support. Although not explicitly called as social support in their work, unsolicited job leads represent one specific form of unsolicited support, that is, help passively obtained without asking. On the solicitedness dimension (i.e., whether support is received with or without active seeking), health scholars have long classified received or actual support into two subtypes: solicited (sought and obtained) versus unsolicited support (Barrera 1986; Eckenrode and Wethington 1990; Kessler et al. 1985; Pearlin and McCall 1990; Thoits 1995). But health scholars do not take the causes of unsolicited support into much consideration. The three-society social capital survey project is the first to collect information on unsolicited support from nationally representative samples. Lin and colleagues' work on the invisible hand of social capital is the first to demonstrate accessed status as one crucial structural cause of unsolicited support, and further expands Lin's structural analysis of social support in the fourth stage.

The second challenge emerges when social resources theory and social capital theory are extended into health outcomes. As summarized earlier, Lin develops social resources theory originally for instrumental actions, and then he and colleagues extend social resources theory into health and indicate social resources using social support. Lin later builds his social capital theory upon his social resources theory, focuses on the application of that theory into instrumental actions, and reserves social support mainly for expressive studies. As a result, the relationship between social support and social capital is blurred. Also, social capital has become a burgeoning term in the past three decades, but its definitions are diverse and controversial (for reviews see Lin 2001a; Pevalin 2003; Song 2013a; Song et al. 2010, 2018; Webber and Huxley 2004). Some equalize social capital with social support and other related network-based concepts. Such an equalization is criticized for pouring old wine into new bottles (Kawachi et al. 2004). Note that a couple of praiseworthy studies take into consideration simultaneously the concepts of social resources, social capital, and social support, but they do not clearly articulate the distinction and relationship between these concepts (Acock and Hulburt 1993; Drentea and Moren-Cross 2005). Before social resources theory developing into social capital theory, one quantitative study is the first to extend the social resources proposition to expressive actions, and demonstrates the positive health effect of accessed status (Acock and Hulburt 1993). It also examines the tie-purpose matching propositions, treating the positive health effects of strong and homophilous ties as evidence for the flow of social support and those of weak and heterophilous ties as the demonstration of social resources theory. One qualitative study applies Lin's arguments on the rise of social capital in the form of networks in cyberspace to social support or communications at a mothering board on a parent's website (Drentea and Moren-Cross 2005; Lin 1999, 2001a).

Lin and colleagues urgently recognize the danger of such entangled conceptualizations in jeopardizing the unique heuristic utility of these network-based concepts and confounding their causal relationships with each other. They have made careful efforts to differentiate social support from other related network-based concepts (Lin 2008; Song and Lin 2009; Song et al. 2010, 2011). Aiming to clarify the theoretical relationships between these network-based concepts, Lin and colleagues choose to favor a strict, neutral, network-based definition of social support: help or aid from social networks (Song 2011; Song and Lin 2009; Song et al. 2010, 2011). This definition allows us to understand and realize the nature and potential of social support more clearly and fully than before. First, this definition anchors the sources of social support firmly within social networks, and narrows the "support" part down into a specific relational content. Thus defined, social support is separated from its preceding social structures, in particular more upstream network-based concepts. Also, this definition is not limited to certain forms and functions of support, and is not based on health effects. It leaves vast space and freedom for researchers to operationalize and investigate various and richer forms and functions of support and to examine non-health outcomes.

This strict definition overcomes two main shortcomings many previous conceptual attempts suffer from to different degrees: lack of precision and health-focused functionalist assumption (Caplan 1979; House 1981; Shinn et al. 1984; Shumaker and Brownell 1984; Song et al. 2011; Thoits 1982). Imprecise definitions can lead to broad and, even worse, inconsistent and invalid operationalizations and measurements, and further mixed and inconclusive findings. Some, for example, do not explain the meaning of support (Cassel 1974, 1976; Lin et al. 1979, Chapter 6 in this book). Some explain the meaning of support but use more abstract or upstream concepts (e.g., social interaction, integration, relations, ties, and bonds) of and/or downstream mechanisms (e.g., information, and meaning) for support (Caplan 1974; Cobb 1974, 1976; Kaplan et al. 1977; Henderson 1977; Lin and Ensel 1984; Pearlin et al. 1981; Thoits 1982, 2011; Turner and Brown 2010). Some constrain social support to involve only two types of actors, the provider and the recipient, or as a form of "interpersonal transaction" (House 1981; Kahn and Antonucci 1980; Shumaker and Brownell 1984). They ignore the possible complicated long chain in the mobilization of certain social support, which can involve both direct and indirect ties (C.J. Chen 2014; Bian 1997; Lin 2001c, 2004; Lin et al. 1977, 1978). Some nail down the nature of social support as an exchange (Shumaker and Brownell 1984), and neglect that social support is not always symmetric (Lin 2001a; Nahum-Shani et al. 2011). Some argue against social networks as the sources of social support in order to include strangers as support providers (Shumaker and Brownell 1984). But social networks contain both strong and weak ties, and strangers may exemplify extreme weak ties (Granovetter 1973). With the rise of information technologies, receiving support from strangers in the cyberspace has become normal (Lin 1999b, 2001a; Wellman et al. 1996; see Cotten et al. 2011; Drentea and Moren-Cross 2005; Song and Chang 2012; Yin et al. 2017). Finally, the strict definition is similar to that from Berkman (1984), but it does not list specific supportive contents as in hers in order to avoid the underestimation of the complexity in supportive contents.

The other shortcoming some prior definitions share is the health-focused functionalist assumption, based on which they define social support in terms of its protective health effect (e.g., Caplan 1974, 1976; Cobb 1974, 1976; Cohen et al. 2000a; Kaplan et al. 1977; Henderson 1977; Shumaker and Brownell 1984). Some scholars hold this assumption partly because social support emerged as a post-hoc speculative explanation for the salubrious effects of relational factors found in human and animal studies in the 1970s, and partly because health scholars are primarily interested in disease prevention and health promotion. Health-focused functionalist definitions, however, have three problems. First, they mix social support with its consequences, and fall into the trap of functionalist tautology. Tautological definitions make operationalization and measurement difficult and render hypothesis testing impossible (Lin 1999b, 2001a). Second, functionalist definitions simplify the complexity and variability of social support and weaken its theoretical breadth and depth by neglecting the existence of dysfunctional or harmful support. As we now know, the receipt of social support is not always supportive or effective, and sometimes can be null and even harmful to recipients' health (Barrera 1986, 2000; Bolger and Amarel 2007; Deelstra et al. 2003; Ross and Mirowsky 1989; Song 2014a; Song and Chen 2014; Wortman and Lehman 1985). In addition, health-focused functionalist definitions constrain the theoretical utility of social support for non-health research areas, and hinder us from more fully examining its causes and consequences. Social support tends to be reserved for health studies. An SSCI search for review articles on social support finds 125 results, 122 of which focus on health and well-being. Social support is one major pathway linking various more upstream network properties to not only expressive but also instrumental outcomes (Song and Lin 2009; Song et al. 2011). But the exact term of "social support" is missing in main network-based theories on social stratification and mobility (e.g., social capital theories by Bourdieu 1986 [1983] and Coleman 1990; structural hole theory by Burt 1992; weak ties theory by Granovetter 1974). We are in great need of the bridging efforts like Lin's to fully recognize the varying potential of social support for both instrumental and expressive outcomes.

Using the strict definition, Lin and colleagues have made efforts to distinguish social support from another four related but different network-based concepts: social networks, social cohesion, social integration, and social capital (Song 2011; Song and Lin 2009; Song et al. 2010, 2011). In brief, social networks represent not a theory but a theoretical perspective (Mitchell 1974). From this perspective, we identify various network-based concepts or theories such as social cohesion, social integration, social capital, and social support. Social cohesion is the degree of social bonds and social equality within social networks, indicated by trust, norms of reciprocity, and the lack of social conflict (Kawachi and Berkman 2000; Sampson et al. 1997). Social integration is the extent of participation in social networks, indicated by active engagement in social roles and social activities, and cognitive identification with network members (Berkman et al. 2000; Brissette et al. 2000; Moen et al. 1989). Social capital represents resources embedded in social networks, measured as network members' structural positions and social connections (Lin 2001a). Thus conceived, social cohesion as a norm is more upstream and can influence other network-based factors. Social integration affects the quality and quantity of social capital and social support. Social capital is a direct determinant of social support as it is network members' resources that can be drawn for various supportive purposes. Social support is a downstream factor subsequent to the operation of the other three network features. Certain indicators of social integration and social capital may act as proximate measures of social support. Note that the relationship between these network-based factors can be indeed reciprocal and dynamic from a longitudinal perspective.

Furthermore, Lin and colleagues integrate social support and social capital into their theoretical and empirical analysis. One study explicitly investigates the joint health effects of social support and social capital using representative data from the 1997 Taiwan Social Change Survey (Song and Lin 2009). Applying social capital theory, it extends the four mechanisms Lin proposes for instrumental returns to accessed status to hypothesize the independent protective effect of accessed status on health: information, influence, social credential, and reinforced identity. It also proposes two competing hypotheses – compensation effect and cumulative advantage – for the interaction effect between social and personal capital. It examines two health outcomes: depressive symptoms and self-reported health. It uses two network instruments (the position generator and the name generator) to measure social capital as accessed status (network members' occupational status) and social support as tie strength. Results replicate the protective independent effect of social support, as measured through the name generator, on both outcomes. Consistent with social capital theory, accessed status measured through the position generator has direct salubrious effects on both outcomes, while its effect size is smaller than that of social support. As the compensation effect hypothesis predicts, accessed status negatively interacts with education in the estimation of depression. These findings suggest that accessed status and social support are two independent network-based causes of disease and require different network instruments. Similar to the speculation in Lin and Peek (1999), the weaker explanatory power of accessed status relative to that of social support may reflect its more upstream position as a structural determinant of social support and its less direct health effects.

Research impacts
As a pioneer, Lin is one of the most highly recognized and cited contributors in the field of social support and health. The work of Lin and colleagues has stimulated this research field to transition from primitive and intuitive definitions and lack of theoretical explanations to clearly refined definitions and complicated theoretical models (containing reciprocal and competing hypotheses), and from lack of valid and reliable instruments, lack of panel and comparative survey designs on normal populations, and suggestive evidence to proliferating sophisticated measurement scales on multiple dimensions, longitudinal and multi-society representative surveys, and direct and longitudinal evidence with strong causal inferences. Lin's work has significant impacts, both theoretically and methodologically.

The theoretical impacts take six directions: the buffering effect of social support, the tie-purpose matching propositions, the multilayer network structure of social support, the competing propositions on the reciprocal relationship between social support and social stressors, the invisible hand or unsolicited support, and the relationship between social support and social capital. First, the work of Lin and colleagues sparks the debate over and substantial research on the buffering effect of social support (for reviews see Aneshensel 1992; Barrera 2000; Thoits 1982; Wheaton 1985). Some pioneers, including Lin and colleagues, use the term buffering or cushioning to refer to the speculative protective effect of social support in the face of social stressors (Cassel 1974, 1976; Dean and Lin 1977; Kaplan et al. 1977; Rabkin and Struening 1976). The metaphorical stress buffering model versus the independent main effect model has dominated the social support and health literature since then. Scholars, however, diverge on the theoretical meanings and statistical modeling of the buffering role of social support (for reviews see Barrera 2000; Cohen and Wills 1985; Gore 1981; House et al. 1988; Kessler and McLeod 1985; Lin 1986b; Wheaton 1985). Lin clarifies three interpretations in terms of the breadth of the meanings of buffering (Lin 1986b; Lin et al. 1985). In the most restrictive and also the most popular interpretation, the buffering effect refers to only the reduced damage model or the negative moderating effect of social support on the positive relationship between social stressors and illness (Andrews et al. 1978; Cohen and Wills 1985; Gore 1978; Kahn and Antonucci 1980; House 1981; Thoits 1982; Turner 1981). The stress process paradigm, one of the most applied conceptual frameworks for social causes and health consequences of stressors, includes social support into the stress process mainly as a moderating element (Pearlin et al. 1981). In the less liberal view, the buffering effect contains two models: reduced damage and support deterioration (Lin et al. 1979, Chapter 6 in this book; Wheaton 1985). In the most liberal view, the buffering effect includes three models: reduced damage, support deterioration, and support mobilization (Kessler and McLeod 1985; Lin 1986b; Lin and Dean 1984; Lin and Ensel 1984; Lin et al. 1985). As Lin suggests (1986b), in order to avoid confusion, we discuss each specific model separately instead of using the word buffering. Hundreds of empirical studies have provided strong evidence for the independent protective effect of social support (especially perceived or emotional support) on health, in particular mental health, mixed evidence for the moderating effect of social support, and some evidence for the varying effects of social support by other social factors such as gender, marital status, and socioeconomic status (for reviews see Cohen and Wills 1985; Kessler and McLeod 1985; House et al. 1988; Song et al. 2011; Thoits 2011; Turner and Brown 2010).

Second, Lin's social resources theory has "immeasurably" advanced our understanding of social support (Berkman and Glass 2000, p. 144). The social support literature used to be disappointingly deficient of theories. Pearlin is concerned that "social support should have the clearest and best established theoretical links to social theory. Somewhat surprisingly, however, this is not the case. Perhaps one reason is that sociologists who are interested in social networks tend not to be the same as those working in stress and social support" (Pearlin 1989, p. 251). He calls for "joining the study of social support more closely to the study of social networks." As Pearlin also approvingly recognizes (Pearlin 1989), Lin is one of these sociologists who firmly integrate the social network perspective into social support research. Apart from the stressor-support interaction model and the independent main effect model, Lin's social resources theory contains two tie-purpose matching propositions on expressive actions (the strength of strong and homophilous ties) and a series of propositions on the multilayer network structure of social support.

Consistent with the aforementioned findings from Lin and colleagues, there is more consistent evidence for the strength-of-strong-tie proposition but mixed evidence for the strength-of-homophilous-tie proposition (Acock and Hurlbert 1995; Burt 1987; Haines and Hurlbert 1992; Jackson 1992; Kana'Iaupuni et al. 2005; Thoits 1984, Zhao 2008; for reviews see Lin and Peek 1999; Song et al. 2011; Thoits 1995). As the review from Lin and Peek concludes, "the simplest and most powerful indicator of social support appears to be the presence of an intimate and confiding relationship" in the protection of mental health (Lin and Peek 1999, p. 243). There are another three matching models in the stressor-support literature. Similar to Lin's tie-purpose matching propositions, the source-type matching model takes a social network perspective and emphasizes the importance of strong and homophilous ties (Thoits 2011). But different from Lin's general focus on tie strength and homophily, the source-type matching model specifically centers on primary relationships and experiential homophily. As it argues, primary group members and secondary group members with similar prior experience are two main categories of supporters and they can provide different forms of support to meet the need of recipients. The other two matching models do not take a social network perspective, and emphasize the match between the types of support and the need of recipients (Cohen and McKay 1984; Cutrona 1990). Lin's propositions on the multilayer network structure of social support have inspired more application of the network-based structural perspective into social support (Pearlin 1989; Thoits 2011). Going beyond Lin's focus on three interrelated layers of social relations (belonging, bonding, and binding relations), network scholars have examined other network-based factors (e.g., role relationships, density, heterogeneity, heterophily, proximity, and multiplexity) as determinants of social stressors, social support, and health (Acock and Hurlbert 1993; Beggs et al. 1996; Burt 1987; Haines and Hurlbert 1992; Haines et al. 1996, 2011; Hurlbert et al. 2000; Wellman and Wortley 1990).

Third, Lin develops two pairs of competing propositions on the reciprocal relationship between social support and social stressors in the social dynamics of health: the impact of social support on social stressors (stress prevention versus stress induction), and the effect of social stressors on social support (support mobilization versus support deterioration) (for reviews see Aneshensel 1992; Barrera 1986, 2000; Gore 1981). Guided by these propositions, health scholars are able to break the assumption on the temporal subsequence of social support to social stressors, and conduct "processual rather than static analyses" (Gore 1981, p. 215). Despite its repeatedly recognized theoretical and practical importance (Aneshensel 1992; Barrera 2000; Gore 1981), the dynamic relationship between social support and social stressors has received less research attention. One methodological reason is that its examination requires longitudinal data, ideally three-wave longitudinal data as Lin and colleagues suggest (Dean and Lin 1977; Lin 1986b; Lin et al. 1979, Chapter 6 in this book). Existing results are mixed partly due to differences in samples and measurement (for reviews see Aneshensel 1992; Barrera 2000). Aneshensel and Frerichs (1982), for example, report evidence for the support mobilization model. Kaniasty and Norris (1993) find results consistent with the support deterioration model. Noh and Avison (1996), Russell and Cutrona (1991), and Snow et al. (2003) show findings supporting the stress prevention model. Turner and Noh (1988) find no significant results. Considering the aforementioned findings from Lin and colleagues, the stress prevention model seems more possible than others. The idea of social support as "a dynamic variable" should not be limited to the reciprocal relationship between social support and social stressors (Dean and Lin 1977, p. 411). The quantity and quality of social support can change over time. Such changes, positive or negative, can generate changes in health conditions. Among adolescents, for example, support growth protects mental health, while support decay does the opposite with an even greater effect size (Cornwell 2003). Note that there is a huge literature on the mobilization of formal help such as the utilization of health care from professionals, which is beyond the scope of this chapter (for a review see Pescosolido 2006). In the health literature, social support is traditionally and mainly used to refer to help from social network members, most (if not all) of whom are likely to provide informal nonprofessional assistance (Gottlieb 1978). Also note that instrumental actions such as the job search process or chain involve support mobilization but are also beyond the purpose of this chapter (see Chapters 2 and 8 in this book respectively for Ronald S. Burt and Yanjian Bian's reviews of Lin's relevant work).

In addition, Lin's invisible hand proposition has encouraged systematic research on health consequences of unsolicited support. Unsolicited support has long and repeatedly been recognized as a promising direction for us to understand and dissolve the persistent puzzle on the discrepant health effects of received support (Barrera 1986, 2000; Eckenrode and Wethington 1990; Kessler et al. 1985; Pearlin and McCall 1990; Thoits 1995). Despite its theoretical utility and its prevalence in ordinary social life, unsolicited support has been given limited theoretical and empirical attention for its health consequences. A couple of existing empirical studies find evidence for the destructive effect of unsolicited support (Bolger and Amarel 2007; Deelstra et al. 2003). But they are conducted in experimental settings, and their results have limited generalization. Privileged by their access to Lin's three-society survey data, Lin's students have made the first attempts to systematically examine the health consequences of unsolicited support indicated by unsolicited job leads (Song 2014a; Song and Chen 2014). They develop a series of hypotheses on the effect of unsolicited support on depressive symptoms: a pair of competing hypotheses – distress reducing versus distress inducing – on its direct effect, a need contingency hypothesis on its negative interaction effect with financial stressors, a pair of competing hypotheses – stress prevention versus comparative reference group – on its indirect effect, and one institutional hypothesis – reinforced collectivistic norm – on the variation of its effect between individualistic and collectivistic culture. Findings from the urban China sample demonstrate the distress inducing hypothesis, and the comparative reference group hypothesis on the positive indirect effect of unsolicited support through financial dissatisfaction (Song 2014a). Results from the U.S. sample support the distress inducing hypothesis on the positive association between unsolicited job leads and depression, and the need contingency hypothesis (Song and Chen 2014). These findings imply that, depending on societal contexts, unsolicited support can damage mental health, directly and indirectly, and can moderate the detrimental effect of social stressors. As Song and Chen (2014, p. 157) conclude, "to extend House's classic statement, the objective of social support research is to investigate 'who gives what' – solicited or unsolicited, needed or not, visible or invisible – 'to whom regarding which problems.'"

Furthermore, after the distinction and relationships between social support and social capital are clarified, a lot of studies across different societies have applied the social resources proposition in social capital theory to examine the associations between accessed status and various health outcomes, and used social support as one of the major mechanisms for those associations (see Figure 5.4; for reviews see Song 2013a; Song et al. 2010, 2018). Many studies demonstrate the social resources propositions (Moore et al. 2009b, 2011, 2014; Song 2011; Song and Chang 2012; Verhaeghe and Tampubolon 2012; Verhaeghe et al. 2012; Yang et al. 2013). Some studies find evidence for the double-edged – protective and detrimental – role of accessed status for health outcomes, and further the variation of that role by gender, life domain, culture, and society (Lee and Kawachi, 2017; Moore et al. 2009a; Song 2014b, 2015a, 2015b; Song and Pettis 2018; Song et al. 2017). Song proposes social cost theory in contrast with social capital theory to theorize that double-edged role (Song and Pettis 2018; Song et al. 2018). In contrast with social capital theory emphasizing the bright side of accessed status as a resource source, social cost theory highlights the dark side of accessed status as a source of detrimental social expenses. Social cost theory proposes three main mechanisms for the harmful effect of accessed status, including the receipt of detrimental resources such as unsolicited social support, negative social comparison, and networking expenses. Based on relevant institutional arguments including Lin's arguments on guanxi culture and structural parameters, Song further develops three institutional explanations – collectivistic advantage, collectivistic disadvantage, and inequality structure – to interpret the varying double-edged health effects of accessed status by culture and society (Lin 2001a, 2001c; Song 2014b, 2015a, 2015b; Song and Pettis 2018).

Among these studies on accessed status and health outcomes, two studies investigate and demonstrate the positive relationship between accessed status and social support. The first study analyzes the direct and indirect associations between accessed authority (knowing authoritative contacts in the workplace) and depression using the urban China sample from the three-society survey (Song 2015b). Consistent with social cost theory instead of social capital theory, accessed authority has indirect detrimental effects through unsolicited job leads and financial dissatisfaction. The other study examines accessed status as a structural source of social support mobilization using data from the 2004 General Social Survey (Song and Chang

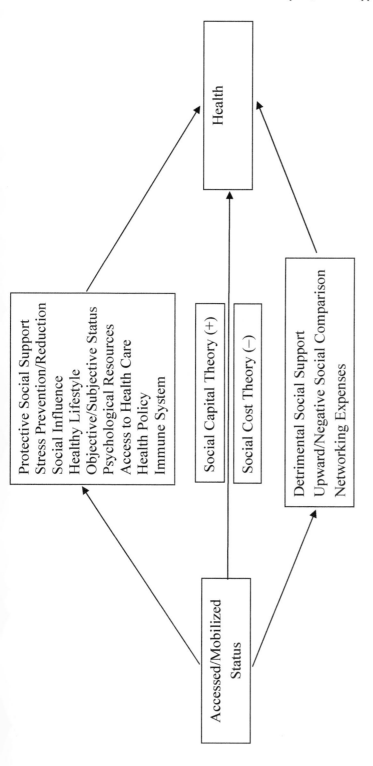

Note: Based on Song and Pettis (2018); Song et al. (2018).

Figure 5.4   A conceptual model for the double-edged role of accessed and mobilized status for health

2012). Consistent with social capital theory, accessed education is positively associated with the frequency of health information seeking, seekers' diversity of used sources, and seekers' frequency of use of three sources (friends or relatives, medical professionals, and the Internet).

Finally, the methodological impacts of Lin's work are manifested in three ways: social support typology and measurement, longitudinal research designs, and depression measurement. First, Lin and colleagues contribute to typologizing social support on two dimensions (instrumental versus expressive or emotional, routine versus nonroutine or crisis), drawing our attention to the lack of reliable and valid social support instruments, and constructing one of the earliest instruments, the instrumental-expressive support scale (for reviews see Barrera 1981, 1986, 2000; Gore 1981; Turner 1983). Instrumental and expressive support has been recognized as the "central" types of support, and the latter proves to be more protective of health (House 1981; Pearlin et al. 1990, p. 590; Turner and Brown 2010). In line with the concern of Lin and colleagues with people's different needs in routine versus crisis situations, for example, people with less educated network members are more likely to receive informal recovery support in a natural disaster as such network members possess more disaster-relevant occupational skills (Beggs et al. 1996). Responding to Lin and colleagues' urgent call for instrumentation efforts, Gottlieb (1978) publishes a classification scheme of 26 informal helping behaviors. Wellman (1981) derives five forms of social support from 21 interactional strands. Henderson and colleagues construct a 52-item Interview Schedule for Social Interaction scale (Henderson et al. 1981). Barrera and colleagues develop three scales: the six-category Arizona Social Support Interview Schedule, the 40-item Inventory of Socially Supportive Behaviors, and the six-item Barrera Social Support Scale (Barrera 1981; Barrera et al. 1993). Sarason and colleagues offer a 27-item Social Support Questionnaire (Sarason et al. 1983). These scales are just a few examples. Various social support scales have been developed and reviewed elsewhere (for reviews see Barrera 2000; Cohen et al. 2000b). Second, after Lin and colleagues' cry for longitudinal research designs for the purpose of stronger causal inferences, diverse longitudinal data sets have been collected and many longitudinal studies on social support and health have appeared (e.g., Aneshensel and Frerichs 1982; Blazer 1982; Henderson et al. 1981; Noh and Avison 1996; Thoits 1982, 1984; Turner 1981; Turner and Noh 1988; Williams et al. 1981). In addition, Lin's work on the measurement of depression in China has continued to bolster mental health research among and beyond Chinese populations (Lai 1995; Noh and Avison 1996; Ren and Treiman 2015; Wu et al. 2003; Xi et al. 2013).

Future research directions

Lin's work will continue to enlighten future research. Due to limited space, I discuss three promising future research directions here: the reciprocal relationship between social support and social stressors, the invisible hand or unsolicited support, and the integration of social support back into social capital theory.

First, based on the above literature review, we echo the need for more future longitudinal research on the reciprocal relationship between social support and social stressors (Aneshensel 1992; Barrera 1986, 2000; Gore 1981). This reciprocal relationship is theoretically intriguing. It involves two pairs of competing propositions: support mobilization versus support deterioration, and stress prevention versus stress induction. The existing limited studies report mixed results, and cannot help generate conclusive evidence yet. Related to this reciprocal relationship, an interaction effect proposition in Lin's earlier work has been given little attention (Lin et al. 1979, Chapter 6 in this book; Gore 1981). As it argues, stress is more likely to trigger support mobilization among high-status people but more likely to lead to support deterioration for low-status people. As Gore (1981, p. 219) recognizes, "further analyses of this kind are warranted to examine the tenuousness or conditional nature of support." Future research on this proposition can further advance our understanding of the social dynamics of and social inequality in the stress process (Pearlin et al. 1981). Low-status people may face a triple jeopardy. They may be more likely to encounter social stressors, experience difficulty in mobilizing social support, and lose social support in the face of social stressors.

Second, future research needs to make the invisible hand more visible and salient, and pay more systematic research attention to unsolicited support as well as solicited support. As mentioned earlier, solicited versus unsolicited support has long and repeatedly been discussed as one promising research direction for us to extricate the puzzling mixed health effects of received support (for reviews see Barrera 1986, 2000; Eckenrode and Wethington 1990; Thoits 2011; Turner and Turner 2013; Uchino 2009). Only a few experimental and survey studies have directly examined and demonstrated the detrimental health consequences of unsolicited support (Bolger and Amarel 2007; Deelstra et al. 2003; Song 2014a; Song and Chen 2014). These empirical studies focus on unsolicited instrumental or informational support. Future research should investigate and compare different content areas of unsolicited support. Unsolicited job leads, for example, represent only one salient form of informational support. In comparison with other forms of support (e.g., instrumental, emotional, and appraisal), informational support has a less direct relationship with health because it is "not in and of itself helpful" but "helps people to help themselves" (House 1981, p. 25). Unsolicited recommendations on medical services may be more protective by directing recipients to better health care (Pescosolido 2006). Unasked-for provision of food and shelter in non-routine situations such as natural disasters can be lifesaving (Hurlbert et al. 2000). Unsolicited expression of "I love you" may be heartwarming for all recipients regardless of their need (Eckenrode and Wethington 1990). Also, future comparative research is needed to investigate the generalizability of existing findings to other societies and cultures. Inconsistent with the reinforced collectivistic proposition that unsolicited support is more likely to be experienced positively in collectivistic versus individualistic culture, the receipt of unsolicited job leads is negatively associated with mental health in both the United States and urban China, and moderates the stress–depression relationship only in the United States (Song 2014a; Song and Chen 2014). Whether the reinforced collectivistic proposition apply more to other content areas of social support remains an interesting research question. Furthermore, future research needs to analyze and compare instrumental and expressive returns to unsolicited support. Existing findings suggest that unsolicited job leads can advance status attainment but hurt mental health (Bolger and Amarel 2007; Deelstra et al. 2003; Lin and Ao 2008; Song 2014a; Song and Chen 2014). The opposite roles of unsolicited support for instrumental and expressive actions are consistent with Lin's earlier statement that expressive actions are more complicated than instrumental ones. In addition, the existing empirical studies examine the health and social consequences of receiving versus not receiving unsolicited support. In order to achieve fuller comprehension of how solicitedness affects the health and social impacts of received support, future research needs to investigate and compare the impacts of solicited versus unsolicited support. Finally, note that visibility versus invisibility has been used in two different ways in the existing social support literature. Scholars like Lin uses the visible and invisible hands to refer to solicited versus unsolicited support. Some other scholars distinguish visible and invisible support based on whether recipients are aware or unaware of received support (Bolger and Amarel 2007). Future research on social support needs to further explore the interplay between these two different dimensions of visibility.

Third, future research needs to make the concept of social support more visible and prominent in network-based theories that have been applied mainly to instrumental actions (e.g., Bourdieu 1986 [1983]; Burt 1992; Coleman 1990; Granovetter 1974). One fruitful line of future research will be to integrate the concept of social support more closely and systematically back into Lin's social capital theory. As introduced earlier, Lin used to subsume social support under his social resources theory, upon which he builds his social capital theory. The integration of social support back into social capital theory will be a win–win not only for both social support research and social capital research but also for both expressive and instrumental research. In the case of social support, this integration can embed it firmly within social capital theory, one of the most popular theories in the social networks literature, enrich the theoretical explanations on its causes and consequences, expand its structural analysis, remove its limitation to expressive or health outcomes, extend its application to instrumental or status attainment outcomes, and eventually achieve its potential more completely than before. In the case of social capital theory, this integration can help elaborate its theoretical arguments, refine its assumptions, and extend it to health outcomes. Social capital is a relatively more upstream network-based concept, and social support a more downstream one. Being at a relative downstream position in the theoretical chain does not render social support any less important. It is quite the opposite. The coherent formulation and continuous development and refinement of social capital theory requires and relies upon clear and rigorous conceptualization, measurement, and empirical examination of social support. Social support is one of the fundamental pathways in Lin's theoretical framework on social capital. On the one hand, protective social support can link accessed and mobilized status to positive health outcomes. On the other hand, detrimental social support can link accessed and mobilized status to negative health outcomes. The double-edged role of social support cautions us the generalizability of the social resources assumption in social capital theory into health outcomes. The social resources assumption states that accessed and mobilized status indicates valuable protective resources. With the growing evidence for the detrimental health effect of accessed status, social cost theory is a possible rival theory for social capital theory (see Figure 5.4; Song and Pettis 2018; Song et al. 2017).

Bringing social support back to social capital theory can help bridge expressive and instrumental research. Scholars rarely pursue research on both instrumental and expressive actions simultaneously. But Lin does. He carefully distinguishes these two actions, and proposes separate propositions on the success of these two actions. With an extensive scope of vision, Lin develops broader network-based theoretical frameworks (social resources and social capital theories) that bridge a few main research traditions in sociology: social stratification and mobility (corresponding to instrumental returns) and medical sociology and mental health (related to expressive returns). As a proverb puts it, "he who chases two rabbits will catch neither." But this proverb does not apply here. Lin's broad theoretical view can help not only defend medical sociology and sociology of mental health against the charge of being atheoretical but also integrate them with other sociological subdisciplines and even non-sociological disciplines (Pearlin 1992; Pescosolido 2006). Demonstrating Lin's earlier statement that expressive actions are more complicated than instrumental ones, existing relevant studies suggest that social support and accessed status tend to exert both protective and detrimental effects on health but mainly positive impact on status attainment and social mobility. These findings necessitate future research on the "complementarity as well as tension" between instrumental and expressive actions (Lin 1982, p. 145).

Lin's existing work on social resources, social support, and social capital has actually laid the solid foundation for us to welcome social support and its positive function back into social capital theory. Despite its lack of explicit use in Lin's work on social capital, the term of social support has always been used obviously but implicitly in Lin's theoretical arguments on social capital. Based on Figure 13.1 in Lin's social capital book (2001a, p. 246; also see Figure 1 in Lin 1999b), we may draw Figure 5.5 to tentatively conceptualize the simplified, mainly unidirectional relationship between accessed and mobilized status and social support with various factors at the micro, meso, and macro-levels serving as social antecedents and moderators (for studies on the three levels of antecedents and moderators, see Lin 2001a, 2001c; Song et al. 2018). In brief, seeking and soliciting social support mediates the relationship between accessed and mobilized status; providing social support, perceiving social support, and receiving unsolicited social support intervenes the relationships of accessed and mobilized status with instrumental and expressive outcomes; and receiving solicited social support links mobilized status with instrumental and expressive outcomes. Due to limited space here, Figure 5.5 takes into consideration only two reciprocal relationships. Mobilized status and solicited social support can be convertible into accessed status over time. Due to limited space, I include social support only as one mechanism linking accessed and mobilized status to outcomes. Other mechanisms are beyond the scope of this chapter (see Figure 5.4). In his work, Lin highlights four major mechanisms through which accessed and mobilized status can advance instrumental and expressive returns: information, influence, social credentials, and reinforced identity (Lin 2001a). Information from network members represents one form of social support: informational social support (House 1981; Song 2014a; Song and Chen 2014). Also, influence, social credentials, and reinforced identity can all operate to directly trigger seeking social support and elevate perceived social support. Guided by Figure 5.5, future research can explore the diverse roles social support can play for both expressive and instrumental outcomes through its various forms of interplay with accessed and mobilized status.

The integration of social support back into Lin's social capital theory can also help us identify more dimensions of social support: the spacial dimension, the directedness dimension, and the resource source dimension. First, with the rise of the information technology, Lin has a high hope for the rise of social capital in the cyberspace (Lin 1999b, 2001a; Wellman 2001). The contrast between online support (support from social networks in the digital space) versus offline support (support from social networks in the real world) has become a burgeoning dimension to categorize social support (Cotten et al. 2011; Drentea and Moren-Cross 2005; Song and Chang 2012; Yin et al. 2017). The operationalization and measurement of social capital (as well as social costs) in the cyberspace is now one challenge we need to overcome in order to clearly differentiate social capital from and coherently integrate it with the concept of online support. It is difficult, for example, to directly capture cybernetwork members' resources or accessed status in usually anonymous online forums. Second, as Lin's small world studies on packet delivery and his studies on job search chains imply (C.J. Chen 2014;

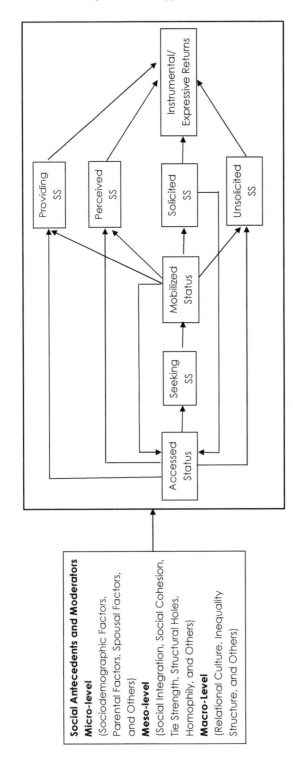

Figure 5.5   A simplified conceptual framework linking social support (SS) with accessed and mobilized status

Lin 2001c, 2004; Lin et al. 1977, 1978, 2014b), the process of seeking social support can be a complicated long chain. How social support from direct versus indirect ties and from short versus long chains can affect health similarly or differently deserves future research. Third, the resource source dimension focuses on the support providers' side. In his social capital theory (Lin 2001a), Lin distinguishes two components of social capital: network members' personal resources that are under their direct and absolute control, and their positional resources that they can control and are entitled to only through their positions in their organizations. In other words, people will lose their positional resources the moment they leave their positions. Empirically, it will be challenging to distinguish personal from positional resources. But theoretically, it will be intriguing and important to examine whether providers give support using their personal or positional resources and how these two different forms of support may affect expressive as well as instrumental actions, similarly or differently.

Lin's theoretical arguments on the costs in access to and use of social capital or network resources can guide future research to investigate various forms of costs involved in the mobilization and receipt of social support, and to achieve deeper understanding of the detrimental effect of social support. They can further help the development of social cost theory. Lin's theoretical arguments on access to and use of network resources contain two possible reasons for the detrimental side of receiving social support: investment beforehand and "commitments to reciprocity" afterwards (Lin 1983, 1992, 2001a, p. 51). As Lin argues, borrowing resources from social networks entails the investment of various forms of necessary parental and personal resources (e.g., time and efforts) in social relationships in advance. The investment can cost more if the targeted social relationships are weaker and heterophilous. Such relational investment is a precondition for seeking and receiving social support. Also, Lin reminds us that the use of network resources can burden users with the obligation and indebtedness to repay the help and create upsetting over-reciprocating exchange (support received exceeds support given), in particular for those who possess less resources than their network members. Such a stressful burden is applicable to recipients of social support (Nahum-Shani et al. 2011; Shumaker and Brownell 1984; Song and Chen 2014). These two possible reasons for the harmful side of receiving social support serve as arguments for the dark side of accessed status in social cost theory (Song et al. 2018; Song and Pettis 2018).

At the very end, as one of Lin's students, I would like to end this chapter with a personal note. Lin exemplifies the unity of knowing and doing. He is not only a researcher on social support but also a generous and thoughtful provider of various forms of valuable social support to so many people, inside or outside his social networks, which are deeply and warmly appreciated but beyond the scope of this chapter. Lin does not hesitate to help others stand upon his shoulders and get them to reach higher in their intellectual endeavors. As an age-old motivational saying in Chinese states, "the master initiates the apprentices, but their training depends upon their own efforts." This saying does not apply to the life long relationship between Lin and his students (see Chapter 8 in this book for a short list of Lin's students). Lin's warm and encouraging support is always there for his students and does not decrease or cease after his students graduate. As Lin states in the very last three sentences in the 1986 book Lin 1986c, p. 342):

[T]here is a long list of items on the research agenda ahead. The tasks will be both exciting and difficult. Hopefully, stimulation, encouragement, and challenges provided by our colleagues in the research community, and by the users of the research literature constitute the essential social support for those choosing to undertake these tasks.

[6]

Social Support, Stressful Life Events, and Illness: A Model and an Empirical Test

NAN LIN
State University of New York at Albany

WALTER M. ENSEL
State University of New York at Albany

RONALD S. SIMEONE
State University of New York at Albany

WEN KUO
University of Utah

Journal of Health and Social Behavior 1979, Vol. 20 (June):108–119

The effects of social support and stressors (stressful life events) on illness (psychiatric symptoms) are examined in a model with data from a representative sample of the Chinese-American adult population in Washington, D.C. The analysis shows that, as expected, stressors are positively related to the incidence of psychiatric symptoms, and social support is negatively related to psychiatric symptoms. Further, the contribution of social support to predicting symptoms is greater in magnitude than that of stressful life events. When marital status and occupational prestige are incorporated into the model, the significant (negative) contribution of social support to symptoms is not reduced. Implications for the theoretical development of a sociomedical theory of illness are discussed.

This paper examines the potential role of social support in relation to stressful life events and subsequent illness. Two of these parameters of epidemiology, stressful life events and illness, have been amply explored in recent epidemiological literature. The third, social support, while being considered in numerous discussions to be related to the incidence of illness, has not been systematically linked to the stressor-illness model.

An earlier version was presented at the 73rd Annual Meeting of the American Sociological Association, San Francisco, California, September 4–8, 1978. The study was supported in part by a Ford Foundation grant and by a NIMH grant (1R01 MH 30301–01).

After a brief review of the literature relating stressful life events to illness, we shall discuss the potential theoretical significance of social support in the study of the etiology of illness. A proposed model is then tested using data gathered from a Chinese-American population.

In the last 15 years, one important thrust in the study of the etiology of illness has been the examination of the potential causal effect of life changes on illness. The pioneering work in this area by Meyer (Lief, 1948), Holmes, Rahe, and their associates (Holmes and Masuda, 1974; Holmes and Rahe, 1967; Rahe, 1975; Rahe et al., 1964) led to the development of life-events scales. High scores on life-events scales (from either the number of events or the sum of weighted events) have been related to psychiatric symptoms, physical indices of undifferentiated psychiatric illnesses, depression, and suicide attempts, as well as to heart disease, leukemia, and other physiological symptoms and illnesses (see a recent summary of these findings in Dean and Lin, 1977).

It is evident that there is a substantial and growing body of literature linking stressors (especially as indicated by stressful life events) to illness. However, several important theoretical and measurement problems have prevented this body of literature from progressing toward a more rigorous paradigm that could form the basis for a sociomedical theory of illness.

The statistical and methodological issues at hand in relating stressful life events to illness have been pointed out by a number of researchers (Brown, 1974; Brown, Sklair, et al., 1973; Brown, Harris, et al.; 1973; Dohrenwend and Dohrenwend, 1976; Gunderson and Rahe, 1974; Myers, 1976; Rahe et al., 1971; Ruch and Holmes, 1971). Perhaps the most significant statistical issue concerns the precise relationship between life events and illness. In a recent review of the literature, Rabkin and Struening (1976) pointed out that the vast majority of studies on life events until recently have employed rather crude analytic techniques. Percentage differences or tests of differences between means have dominated the analysis. Studies using correlational analysis are rather rare; when such analysis is used, the coefficients produced are rather small (usually between .20 and .29) and account for very little of the variance in illness (Bieliavaskas and Webbs, 1974; Gersten et al., 1974; Markush and Favero, 1974; Rahe, 1975; Wershow and Reinhart, 1974). In general, scores on Rahe SRRS-type scales have been consistently related to illness; however, their predictive power is rather limited.

Conceptually, there is a need to explore other variables that, along with stressful life events, may figure in the explanation of illness (Dohrenwend and Dohrenwend, 1976; Myers, 1976). If, indeed, stressful life events account for only about 3%–4% of the explained variance in illness, then it is important to consider other potential causal factors relating to illness. The model to be presented and examined in this paper represents one such attempt.

One set of variables frequently associated with illness in discussions and studies concerns aspects of what can be identified as the social support system. *Social support may be defined as support accessible to an individual through social ties to other individuals, groups, and the larger community.* The general assumption is that social support is negatively related to illness. The greater social support that an individual receives, in the form of closer relationships with family members, kin, friends, acquaintances, co-workers, and the larger community, the less likely that the individual will experience illness.

Surprisingly, while the research interest in social support has been substantial, the literature provides almost no theoretical explanation as to *why* social support should play a (negative) role in the etiology of illness. We may, nevertheless, draw some inferences from several related areas of discussion. Langlie (1977), for example, posited two hypotheses as to why social group characteristics would affect an individual's preventive health behavior: (1) Social groups differ in their *norms* regarding preventive health behavior and in their ability to exert pressure to conform to these norms, and (2) interaction patterns may provide *information* of practical utility, such as how to prevent disease (e.g., where to go for preventive services). Inferentially, we may postulate that social support possibly acts as a preceding factor reducing the likelihood of the onset of illness, in providing normative pressure against the likelihood of certain events occurring (e.g., divorce). Or, alternatively, it serves as a "buffer" against the exacerbation of response to life changes by providing the information needed to reduce or eliminate drastic psychological or physical consequences of life changes (e.g., how to locate a marriage counselor, where to find a job).

If social support is considered as serving a coping function (Gore, 1978), then discussion of the functions of coping behavior may also shed light on the issue at hand. Pearlin and Schooler (1978), for example, pointed out that the protective function of coping behavior can be exercised in three ways: "by eliminating or modifying conditions giving rise to problems; by perceptually controlling the meaning of experience in a manner that neutralizes its problematic character; and by keeping the emotional consequences of problems within manageable bounds" (p. 2). Again, we may infer that social support copes with the potential stressor-illness relationship by acting either as an *antecedent* factor that reduces the likelihood of (undesirable) life changes occurring, or as a *buffering* factor, following the occurrence of life changes, that controls interpretations of the events and emotional responses to them.

The theoretical issues involved concerning the role of social support in the stressor-illness model, therefore, are significant and varied and need systematic explication in the future, such explication being amply warranted by the discussions on the potential significance of social support in the stressor-illness model (Cobb, 1976; Dean and Lin, 1977; Pinneau, 1976; Rabkin and Struening, 1976) and by the rich empirical evidence that aspects of social support are negatively related to aspects of illness. Familial support obviously plays an important role in reducing the likelihood of stress and the onset of illness. However, research evidence suggests that such support may be effectively provided through a person's ties to extrafamilial individuals and groups as well. Nuckolls et al. (1972) showed, for example, that the pregnancy complication rate was much higher for those women who experienced many life events but had low support scores (as measured by quality of marital relationship, interactions with the extended family, and adjustment within the community) than for those who also experienced many life events but scored high on the social support scale. Gore's study of unemployed men (1978) indicated that strain in the form of elevated cholesterol levels, increased depression, and more frequent illness was considerably lessened among those with supportive marital relations and ties to the extended family and to peer groups. Langlie (1977) provided some evidence that social networks (especially non-kin interactions), along with health beliefs, positively affected certain indirect risk-reducing preventive health behavior (e.g., dental care, medical checkups). The structural characteristics of social support, as reflected in ties to the community and homogeneity of community characteristics, have often been mentioned as contributing negatively to the rates of illness and death (e.g., Antonovsky, 1974; Leighton, 1959;

Leighton et al., 1963; Murphy, 1973; Stout et al., 1964).

Myers and his associates (1975) have presented provocative findings regarding the role of social integration in the stressor-illness model. They noted that, for most persons, there is a direct relationship between the number of life events experienced and the extent of symptomatology. Some people do not fit this pattern, however. Among such individuals, those who display a number of symptoms, but experience few stressful life events, are found to be less well integrated than those who experience few symptoms but many events. These investigators interpreted this finding in terms of the individual's integration into the larger social stratification system, as measured by sociodemographic variables, and of the individual's expressive and instrumental role performance, as measured by marital and employment status, job satisfaction, and organizational membership. While social integration cannot be equated with social support, the implication that social support may play a mediating role in the stressor-illness model is apparent.

Interestingly, while the mediating role of social support has been extensively suggested, the research evidence for such a relation has so far been partial at best. In most of the studies where the mediating role of social support was examined, only selected values of the variables were involved. For example, Nuckolls et al. (1972) compared the high-life-events/low-support group with the high-life-events/high-support group. Gore's study (1978) focused on the high-life-event group (the unemployed). Myers et al. (1975) contrasted the high-life-events/low-symptoms group and the low-life-events/high-symptoms group. These results were meaningful but partial, since their generalizability to the relationships covering the entire range of values for the variables is unknown. In fact, several investigators (Andrews et al., 1978; Pinneau, 1976) found no significant stress-buffering effect of social support on physiological or psychological strain.

These findings thus fail to provide direct evidence for incorporating the social support system in the stressor-illness model. What is needed is an explicit model specifying the joint effects of social support and stressors (e.g., stressful life events) on illness. Such a model is presented and subjected to empirical evaluation in the following sections.

The Theoretical Model

The foregoing research findings and discussions lead to some straightforward propositions, as pointed out by Dean and Lin (1977); namely:

1. Stressful life events (SLE) are positively related to illness. General research evidence on the etiology of illness provides the rationale for this expected relationship.

2. Social support (SS) is negatively related to illness. Following sociological theories on social integration and indirect research evidence, it seems reasonable to expect that the stronger social support an individual can amass, the less likely he/she would be to experience illness. This negative relationship should remain even if the individual is confronted with stressful life events.

The model, in its simplest form, provides an explicit structure for examining the relative magnitudes of stressful life events and social support in the prediction and explanation (in the statistical sense) of illness.

If the model is a credible one, then we would expect the total variance of illness to be statistically explained to a much greater degree by both social support and stressful life events than by stressful life events alone. In other words, we expect social support to substantially improve the explanatory power in terms of the variance explained in illness.

The relationship between SLE and SS, however, is a complicated one. At this point of theoretical development, several alternative hypotheses are plausible. One research direction suggests viewing social support as a structural factor in the alleviation or reduction of illness-producing stressors. Discussions of the effects of community ties and characteristics (Antonovsky, 1974; Leighton, 1959; Leighton et al., 1963; Murphy, 1973; Stout et al., 1964) lend support to such a causal formulation. The derivation, then, proposes that there should be a negative correlation between social support and stressors and that social support causally precedes stressors. Symbolically expressed,

the proposition states: SS (social support) $\overset{-}{\rightarrow}$ SLE (stressful life events).

Another theoretical formulation, probably supported by the great majority of researchers working in this area, sees social support as a reactive mechanism to stressors (e.g., Dohrenwend, 1973; Gore, 1978; Langner and Michael, 1963; Myers et al., 1975). It posits differential reacting capabilities of individuals following the occurrence of life changes. The derivation from this perspective is more complex. The direction of the relationship between stressors and social support becomes contingent upon differential reacting capabilities, which are probably related to the social standing of the individuals (class, status, etc.). For individuals of higher social standing and, therefore, with greater reacting capabilities, stressors and social support would be positively related; symbolically, SLE $\overset{+}{\rightarrow}$ SS. That is, life events trigger the mobilization of social support, which is abundantly available. One may postulate, however, that for individuals of lower social standing and, therefore, with lesser reacting capabilities, stressors and social support would be negatively related; symbolically, SLE $\overset{-}{\rightarrow}$ SS. In other words, the occurrence of life changes brings about a further weakening of initially meager social support.

To examine these hypotheses properly and lend credibility to one or the other theoretical formulations requires longitudinal data from a panel design. Our data are of a limited nature and not longitudinal in nature. However, we will explore these alternatives as far as our data allow.

To submit this model to any empirical test, other variables, especially basic demographic variables, must be taken into account for several reasons. First, as the past literature has shown, the socioeconomic status of the individual affects the degree of his or her vulnerability to illness. Some researchers have, in fact, argued that the SES variables indicate the degree of an individual's "social integration" (Langner and Michael, 1963; Myers et al., 1975). For our model to gain credibility, it must be demonstrated that the contribution of social support to the explained variation of illness is substantially independent of socioeconomic status. Second, socioeconomic status is used as an indicator of social standing, which, as previously discussed, may play a role in the relationship between stressors and social support.

METHOD

The Data

The model was tested utilizing a sample of Chinese-Americans interviewed in a survey in the District of Columbia in the summer of 1972. The present study data were collected as a part of a larger study that was concerned with several characteristics, including Chinese-Americans' assimilation, social stress, and political attitudes (Kuo and Lin, 1977).

The sample was selected systematically from a nonrepeated, alphabetically ordered, master list of Chinese-American households. The sampling frame consisted of 550 names and was compiled from several sources, including Chinese community associations, merchant associations, surname associations, the local telephone directory, and Chinese-Americans whose names were provided by persons being interviewed. A comparison of the final sampling frame with the 1970 census indicated that the final sampling frame was adequate in regard to representativeness.

The sample comprised 121 males and 49 females: 59% married, 36% unmarried, and 5% either widowed, divorced, or separated. Twenty-four percent of the sample were American-born, 38% were born in Hong Kong or Canton, 9% in Taiwan, and 28% in other Chinese communities or other countries. Among the American-born Chinese, 70% reported that their families had been in the United States for two generations. Approximately 72% of the sample had a high school education or higher, which was close to the overall Chinese population average in the metropolitan area of Washington, D.C. (70.9%).

The instrument used in this study was prepared both in English and in Chinese. Interviewers were instructed to interview the household heads, if he or she were available. Interviews were carried out in the native language or Chinese dialects of the respondents to ensure respondent accuracy.

Measurement of Variables

The Holmes and Rahe Social Readjustment Rating Scale (SRRS) has been a significant stimulus, as well as measure of stressors, in

life-events research (Holmes and Rahe, 1967). This instrument in both its original and modified forms has been used in a variety of studies, thus providing for comparability between studies. In testing our model, we utilized a modified version of the Holmes-Rahe SRRS scale. The comparability between the original and our reduced version appears in the Appendix.[1] Each event in the scale has a score indicating the relative magnitude of stress produced (Holmes and Rahe, 1967). The weighted items were subsequently summated to produce our measure of stressful life events.[2]

To measure illness symptomatology, a scale was developed relating to psychiatric symptoms that had occurred within the last six months before the survey. The question used stated: "Below is a list of the ways you might have felt or behaved. Please indicate how often you have felt this in the last six months." A list of 24 items followed and four response categories were provided ("no time," "little time," "moderate time," and "most or all the time"). The item scores were then summated. The psychiatric symptom scale, consisting of 24 items (see Table 1),[3] indicated item-total cor-

TABLE 1. Item-Total Correlations of Psychiatric Symptoms

Items	Correlation with Summated Scale
Things bother me*	.616
Not hungry	.388
Have the blues	.704
Just as good as other people	.502
Can't keep my mind on things*	.586
Depressed	.778
Hopeful	.472
Life is a failure	.587
Fearful	.649
Sleep is restless*	.648
Happy	.584
Talked less	.590
Lonely	.669
People are unfriendly	.582
Sad	.733
People dislike me	.664
Can't "get going"*	.599
Tense*	.581
Overeat	.435
Take pills	.398
Smoke heavily	.131
Drink more wine*	.280
Take "bets"	.234
Lose temper	.596

Note: $\alpha = .88$; all coefficients were significant at the .001 level.

* Comparable to items utilized in Gurin scale.

relations ranging from .13 to .78. All coefficients were significant at the .001 level with an alpha of .88.

Social support, the crucial variable in the study, was measured utilizing a scale of nine items (see Table 2).[4] The items tapped the respondent's interactions and involvement with friends, neighbors, people nearby, and the subcultural community (Chinese activities and associations), as well as social adjustment components (feelings about the neighborhood, community, and workplace). Adjustment to one's environment is considered a major dimension for the assessment of social support (Nuckolls et al., 1972). The scale focuses on non-kin support, because, according to recent literature, weak ties serve useful functions (Granovetter, 1973, 1974; Lin et al., 1977, 1978), and non-kin interactions are important in health-related behavior (Langlie, 1977). It would seem desirable, however, to incorporate family dimensions into the scale in the future. We were somewhat concerned that the items measuring involvement in the Chinese subculture might play a major role in the scale, thus limiting its generalizability to other populations. As it turned out, the subcultural items were less important than some of the other items. The items were summated to create a scale of social support. The item-total correlations ranged from .36 to .74, with all correlations being significant at the .001 level. The alpha (.52) was not as strong as it ideally should be. However, it was a reasonable first scaling attempt to measure the variable.

Occupational prestige was measured using the two-digit Hodge, Siegel, and Rossi scale

TABLE 2. Item-Total Correlations of Social Support Items

Items	Correlation with Summated Scale
Feelings about the neighborhood	.40
Feelings about people nearby	.43
Frequency of talking with neighbors	.64
Close friends in D.C. area	.60
Get together with friends from old country	.74
Involved in Chinese activities	.50
Involved in Chinese association	.49
Officer in Chinese association	.43
Satisfied with job	.36

Note: $\alpha=.52$; all coefficients significant at the .001 level.

(1964) of prestige scores, ranging from 00 to 89. Marital status was reduced to a dichotomous variable; the category of being married was coded as 2, the category of not being married as 1.

Multiple regression was then performed for psychiatric symptoms on marital status, occupational prestige, stressful life events (SLE), and social support (SS).

FINDINGS

Correlations, means, and standard deviations for all variables to be considered in the analysis appear in Table 3. Subsequent regression analyses were performed using this correlation matrix.

The results of the analysis, presented in Table 4, indicate that, as expected, stressful life events (b = .21) and social support (b = −.36) are important factors in explaining psychiatric symptoms, even when the marital status (b = −.11) and the occupational prestige (b = −.15) of the individual are taken into account in the regression model. The analysis also indicates that social support contributes significantly to the explained variance (R^2) in psychiatric symptoms. Marital status, occupational prestige, and stressful life events combine to explain about 8% of the variance, consistent with past findings. The variance explained in the dependent variable increases to 21% when social support is incorporated into the model. Thus the unique contribution of social support, independent of marital status, occupational prestige, and stressful life events, accounts for approximately 13% of the variation in psychiatric symptoms (or 62% of the explained variance).

We further explored any partial effects that SS and SLE might jointly have on the dependent variable. First, SS and SLE were trichotomized into three groups (high, medium, and low). A cross tabulation of the two variables resulted in a 3×3 table in which the mean psychiatric symptoms score was computed for each cell, as shown in Table 5. We then tested for significant differences between the two extreme mean scores in each row or column. In effect, we examined, for each social support level (each row), whether or not different levels of stressors would have significantly different effects on symptoms, and, likewise, for each stressor level (each column), whether

TABLE 3. Intercorrelations of Variables Specified in the Complete Recursive Models

	Marital Status	Occupational Prestige	Stressful Life Events (SLE)	Social Support (SS)	Psychiatric Symptoms	X̄	S.D.
Marital status	1.000	.123	.048	−.072	−.091	1.412	.494
	—	(.055)	(.269)	(.204)	(.121)		
Occupational prestige	170	1.000	.019	.130	−.206	39.177	21.223
		—	(.405)	(.067)	(.004)		
Stressful life events (SLE)	170	170	1.000	.049	.186	25.937	32.399
			—	(.286)	(.008)		
Social support (SS)	134	134	134	1.000	−.364	23.545	4.530
				—	(.001)		
Psychiatric symptoms	167	167	167	132	1.000	34.485	8.597
					—		

Note: The zero-order correlation coefficients are shown on the first line of the upper diagonal, the level of significance on the second. The number of cases is indicated in the lower diagonal.

different levels of social support would have differential impacts on symptoms.

A series of t-tests showed that when the social support level was low (the first row), the high stressor group experienced greater symptoms than the medium stressor group, and that when the social support levels were medium or high (the second and third rows), levels of stressors had no significant effect on symptoms. Further, when the stressor level was high (the last column), the low social support group experienced greater symptoms than the high social support group, and when the stressor level was low (the first column), the low social support group experienced greater symptoms than the medium social support group. Social support levels had no significant effect on symptoms when the stressor level was medium. In general, then, the findings suggest that social support performs more of a mediating role between stressors and psychiatric symptoms than stressors do between social support and psychiatric symptoms, but the evidence is inconclusive.

As we pointed out earlier, the structural perspective would predict that a negative relationship exists between the two variables or that

some mediating effect of stressors between social support and illness exists. Our data (see Tables 3 and 5) provide no support for the structural explanation—at least not in the general manner portrayed and discussed in the literature. On the other hand, the results do not rule out the reactive perspective, for the derivations allow for canceling out of both positive and negative relations due to some confounding factors. Also, Table 5 shows some partial mediating effect of social support between stressors and illness.

One of the potential confounding factors, as discussed earlier, is the individual's social standing. Therefore, we proceeded to examine our data further to ascertain the extent to which controlling for the individual's social standing might reveal clearer relations between SS and SLE.

We used occupational prestige as an indicator of social standing. We examined marital status also, since the literature has extensively used it in either a direct or indirect manner in studying the etiology of illness. Respondents' occupations were classified into four groups: high white-collar (professional and managerial), low white-collar (clerical and sales), high

TABLE 4. Regression of Psychiatric Symptoms on Marital Status, Occupational Prestige, Stressful Life Events, Social Support, and the Interaction of Social Support and Stressful Life Events

Independent Variables	Standardized Regression Coefficients	Standard Error	Cumulative R^2
Marital status	−.1089	.0799	.0116
Occupational prestige	−.1488	.0802	.0378
Stressful life events	.2115	.0791	.0794
Social support	−.3631	.0799	.2120

TABLE 5. Mean Symptom Scores by Levels of Social Support and Stressors

Social Support		Stressors		
		Low	Medium	High
		A	B	C
Low	Mean symptom score	38.31	34.60	41.35
	N	16	15	14
		D	E	F
Medium	Mean symptom score	31.0	31.70	36.07
	N	13	17	15
		G	H	I
High	Mean symptom score	33.13	30.87	32.00
	N	16	15	13

$t_{(B-C)} \leq .033$; $t_{(D-F)} \leq .094$; $t_{(G-H)} \leq .466$.
$t_{(A-D)} \leq .016$; $t_{(B-H)} \leq .172$; $t_{(C-I)} \leq .010$.

TABLE 6. Analysis of Covariance for Effects of Occupational Status, Marital Status, Social Support, and Stressors on Psychiatric Symptoms

Sources of Variation	Sum of Squares	DF	F	Level of Significance
Covariates	262.572	2	2.035	.133
Marital status	26.746	1	.415	.999
Occupational status	197.929	1	3.069	.079
Factors	1151.484	4	4.463	.002
Social support (SS)	846.594	2	6.563	.002
Stressors (SLE)	315.206	2	2.443	.089
SS x SLE	274.474	4	1.064	.378

blue-collar (craftspersons and skilled), and low blue-collar (operatives and unskilled) workers. SLE was broken down into three score categories (high, medium, and low) by trichotomizing the frequency of the weighted scores. A cross-tabulation of the four categories of occupation and three categories of SLE allowed us to examine the mean of the social-support-scale score for each of the 12 cells. If the reactive explanation involving social class is valid, we would expect a positive trend between the stress level and social support scores for the high white-collar workers and a negative trend between the stress level and social support scores for the low blue-collar workers. However, there were no discernible differences in the social support scores for these cells. Similarly, the mean social support scores were similar in all cells in a cross-tabulation between marital status (married vs. not married) and stress level.

Finally, we performed an analysis of covariance employing marital status and occupational prestige as covariates and SS and SLE as independent variables for the dependent variable, psychiatric symptoms. Again, we did not obtain any interaction effect between SS and SLE on psychiatric symptoms, nor any independent effects of marital status and occupational prestige on the symptoms (see Table 6). Thus, if the reactive perspective explanation anticipates confounding factors in the relationship between SS and SLE, the case made earlier to consider occupational prestige and

marital status as such factors has been weakened by our data.

In summary, the data support a simple model indicating joint effects of social support and stressors on illness (psychiatric symptoms), as shown in the path analytic diagram in Figure 1. This set of relationships is not significantly affected by the demographic variables of occupational prestige and marital status. There is some inconclusive evidence that social support mediates between stressors and illness (psychiatric symptoms).

DISCUSSION

The findings of this study are twofold: (1) The expected relationship between stressful life events and illness measures was observed. The zero-order coefficient was consistent with estimates found in previous studies, utilizing different populations (approximately .20). (2) *Social support contributes significantly and negatively to illness symptoms.* Compared to stressors (SLE), the social support measure was much more significantly (and negatively) related to psychiatric symptoms. The unex-

FIGURE 1. Psychiatric symptoms as a function of stressful life events and social support ($R^2 = .174$).

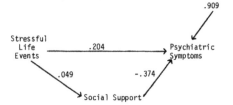

plained variance of the illness measure was significantly reduced by the incorporation of the social support scale in the model. In fact, the social support scale explained more than twice as much of the illness variance as the stressful life events and the demographic variables combined.

These findings, while preliminary, strongly suggest that social support may be just as important as stressful life events, if not more important, in exercising an influence on illness symptoms. Future research in the etiology of illness may well be incomplete unless social support is taken into account.

The data, however, failed to show any relationship between stressors and social support and did not provide support for a structural explanation (social support precedes and negatively affects stressors). Nor was there any strong support for a reactive (buffering) explanation (stressors differentially trigger social support). Further conceptual and methodological considerations must be proposed before such alternative explanations can be properly tested.

Pragmatically, the findings and the model have an important bearing on public health policy and services. Stressful life events are in most cases extremely unmanipulatable. They are difficult, and sometimes impossible (as in the case of death), to reverse by external forces. However, social support, when future research can further delineate separate effects for primary and secondary groups, may be susceptible to manipulation through services and policies. Such a demonstration would have significant implications for effective intervention in the improvement of the general health level of the public.

While we are encouraged by these findings, the data were of a limited nature and caveats must be mentioned. First, the study population, consisting of Chinese-Americans, represents only a segment of the general population. While there is research evidence (Rahe, 1969) to suggest that Chinese-Americans may not be significantly different from other populations in their perceptions of life events, the particular linkage between social support (as herein defined) and illness demonstrated here needs confirmation in studies of other populations (Dohrenwend et al., 1978). We adduce as evi-

dence for our conclusion that the relationship is a stable one the fact that we found the social support items having strongest correlation with the illness symptoms to be "feelings about the neighborhood," "feelings about people nearby," "frequency of talking with neighbors," and "satisfied with job" rather than the ethnically associated items (see Table 2 for all the items).

Second, the social support scale must be further refined for general research use. While we are encouraged by its usefulness in our model, it is clear that the scaling (i.e., the alpha coefficient) must be improved. If, for example, different types of social support are utilized by different types of individuals to buffer illness, an adequate scale must attempt to cover a wide range of social groups (primary and secondary) as well as purposes (instrumental and affective).

Finally, the interactive effect of social support and stressors on illness needs further exploration. Our data lend no support to the thesis that stressors mediate between social support and illness (i.e., that, given a support level, different levels of stressors impact symptoms differentially). We did find some, but very weak, mediating effect of social support between stressors and illness (i.e., given a stressor level, different levels of support impact symptoms differently). Marital status and occupational status did not help clarify the relations. In this regard, longitudinal data from a panel design would provide the necessary rigor for disentangling the complex mediating effects, if there are any, of these variables.

Currently, work incorporating these refinements to verify the model is under way.

NOTES

1. Specific wordings and response categories of all scales used in the study are available upon request from the first author.
2. Several studies have recently examined the nature (desirable, undesirable, and ambiguous) of the events and measurement procedures (simple additive, weighted, and effect-proportional) relative to the criterion variable (Mueller et al., 1977; Ross and Mirowsky, 1979; Vinokur and Selzer, 1975). These authors found that the simple addition of undesirable events predicts psychiatric symptoms as well as the weighted summation of

all events. This finding does not substantially change the validity of the procedure used here nor the results (see a similar position in Dohrenwend, 1973). The best predictive index found by Ross and Mirowsky (the effect-proportional method) is sample- and population-specific. Future research involving large populations should consider the use of such an index in place of additive or subjective weighting procedures.

3. Crandell and Dohrenwend (1967) subdivided the Midtown Psychiatric Impairment Index (Srole et al., 1962) into four subscales: psychophysiological symptom index, psychological index, physiological index, and ambiguous index. We purposely excluded all the items belonging to the last two subscales in the questionnaire except one scale item dealing with acid stomach, since we wanted to focus on the respondent's psychological state.

4. Originally, 13 items were used in the scaling. After item analysis, four items were deleted because of their many negative correlations with the other items. The remaining nine items were all positively correlated with one another. The eliminated items tapped (1) having relatives in the neighborhood, (2) keeping in touch with relatives, (3) having close friends outside Washington, D.C., and (4) keeping in touch with friends outside Washington, D.C.

REFERENCES

Andrews, G., C. Tennant, D. M. Hewson, and G. E. Vaillant
1978 "Life event stress, social support, coping style, and risk of psychological impairment." Journal of Nervous and Mental Disease 166:307–16.

Antonovsky, A.
1974 "Conceptual and methodological problems in the study of resistance resources and stressful life events." Pp. 245–58 in Barbara S. Dohrenwend and Bruce P. Dohrenwend (eds.), Stressful Life Events: Their Nature and Effects. New York: Wiley.

Bieliavaskas, L., and J. Webbs
1974 "The social readjustment rating scale: Validity in a college population." Journal of Psychosomatic Research 18:115.

Brown, G. W.
1974 "Meaning, measurement, and stress of life events." Pp. 217–43 in Barbara S. Dohrenwend, and Bruce P. Dohrenwend (eds.), Stressful Life Events: Their Nature and Effects. New York: Wiley.

Brown, G. W., F. Sklair, T. O. Harris, and J. L. T. Birley
1973 "Life events and psychiatric disorders—part 1: Some methodological issues." Psychological Medicine 3:74–87.

Brown, G. W., T. O. Harris, and J. Peto
1973 "Life events and psychiatric disorders—part 2: Nature of causal link." Psychological Medicine 3:159–76.

Cobb, S.
1976 "Social support as a moderator of life stress." Psychosomatic Medicine 38:300–314.

Crandell, D. L., and B. P. Dohrenwend
1967 "Some relationships among psychiatric symptoms, organic illness and social class." American Journal of Psychiatry 123:1611–31.

Dean, A., and N. Lin
1977 "The stress-buffering role of social support: Problems and prospects for systematic investigation." Journal of Nervous and Mental Disease 165:403–17.

Dohrenwend, B. S.
1973 "Social status and stressful life events." Journal of Personality and Social Psychology 28:225–35.

Dohrenwend, B. S., and B. P. Dohrenwend
1976 "Future research in stress related disorder." Paper presented at the annual convention of the American Sociological Association, New York.

Dohrenwend, B. S., L. Krasnoff, A. R. Askenasy, and B. P. Dohrenwend
1978 "Exemplification of a method for scaling life events: The PERI Life Events Scale." Journal of Health and Social Behavior 19:205–29.

Gersten, J. C., T. S. Langner, J. G. Eisenberg, and L. Orzeck
1974 "Child behavior and life events: Undesirable change or change per se?" Pp. 159–70 in Barbara S. Dohrenwend and Bruce P. Dohrenwend (eds.), Stressful Life Events: Their Nature and Effects. New York: Wiley.

Gore, S.
1978 "The effect of social support in moderating the health consequences of unemployment." Journal of Health and Social Behavior 19:157–65.

Granovetter, Mark S.
1973 "The strength of weak ties." American Journal of Sociology 78:1360–80.
1974 Getting a Job. Cambridge: Harvard University Press.

Gunderson, Eric K., and Richard Rahe
1974 Life Stress and Illness. Springfield, Ill.: Charles C Thomas.

Hodge, R. W., P. M. Siegel, and P. H. Rossi
1964 "Occupational prestige in the United States, 1925–63." American Journal of Sociology 70:286–302.

Holmes, T. H., and M. Masuda
1974 "Life change and illness susceptibility." Pp. 45–72 in Barbara S. Dohrenwend and Bruce P. Dohrenwend (eds.), Stressful Life Events: Their Nature and Effects. New York: Wiley.

Holmes, T., and R. Rahe
  1967   "The social readjustment rating scale."
         Journal of Psychosomatic Research
         11:213–18.
Kuo, W. H., and N. Lin
  1977   "Assimilation of Chinese-Americans in
         Washington, D.C." Sociological Quarterly
         18:340–52.
Langlie, J. K.
  1977   "Social networks, health beliefs, and pre-
         ventive health behavior." Journal of Health
         and Social Behavior 18:244–60.
Langner, Thomas S., and Stanley T. Michael
  1963   Life Stress and Mental Health. New York:
         Free Press.
Leighton, Alexander
  1959   My Name Is Legion. New York: Basic
         Books.
Leighton, Dorothea, John Harding, David Macklin,
  Allister Macmillan, and Alexander Leighton
  1963   The Character of Danger. New York: Basic
         Books.
Lief, Alfred (ed.)
  1948   The Common Sense Psychiatry of Dr.
         Adolf Meyer. New York: McGraw-Hill.
Lin, N., P. W. Dayton, and P. Greenwald
  1977   "The urban communication network and
         social stratification." Pp. 107–19 in Brent
         Ruben (ed.), Communication Yearbook I.
         New Brunswick, N.J.: Transaction Books.
  1978   "Analyzing the instrumental uses of rela-
         tions in the context of social structure."
         Sociological Methods and Research 7:
         149–66.
Markush, R., and R. Favero
  1974   "Epidemiologic assessment of stressful
         life events, depressed mood, and
         psychophysiological symptoms—A pre-
         liminary report." Pp. 171–90 in Barbara S.
         Dohrenwend and Bruce P. Dohrenwend
         (eds.), Stressful Life Events: Their Nature
         and Effects. New York: Wiley.
Mueller, D. P., D. W. Edwards, and R. M. Yarvis
  1977   "Stressful life events and psychiatric symp-
         tomatology: Change or undesirability?"
         Journal of Health and Social Behavior
         18:307–17.
Murphy, J.
  1973   "Social networks in a study of community
         integration." Community Mental Health
         Epidemiology Working Paper, No. 55,
         Nashville.
Myers, J.
  1976   "Future research in mental disease." Paper
         presented at the annual convention of the
         American Sociological Association, New
         York.
Myers, J., J. Lindenthal, and M. Pepper
  1975   "Life events, social integration and psychi-
         atric symptomatology." Journal of Health
         and Social Behavior 16:421–29.

Nuckolls, C. G., J. Cassel, and B. H. Kaplan
  1972   "Psycho-social assets, life crises and the
         prognosis of pregnancy." American Journal
         of Epidemiology 95:431–41.
Pearlin, L. I., and C. Schooler
  1978   "The structure of coping." Journal of
         Health and Social Behavior 19:2–21.
Pinneau, S. R., Jr.
  1976   "Effects of social support on occupational
         stress and strains." Paper presented at the
         annual convention of the American Psycho-
         logical Association, Washington, D.C.,
         September.
Rabkin, J. G., and E. Struening
  1976   "Life events, stress, and illness." Science,
         Dec. 3, pp. 1013–20.
Rahe, R. H.
  1969   "Multi-cultural correlations of life changes
         scaling: America, Denmark, and Sweden."
         Journal of Psychosomatic Research
         13:191–95.
  1975   "Epidemiological studies of life change and
         illness." International Journal of Psychiatry
         and Medicine 6:133–46.
Rahe, R. H., U. Lundberg, L. Bennett, and T.
  Theorell
  1971   "The social readjustment rating scale: A
         comparative study of Swedes and Ameri-
         cans." Journal of Psychosomatic Research
         15:241–49.
Rahe, R. H., M. Meyer, M. Smith, G. Kjaer, and T.
  H. Holmes
  1964   "Social stress and illness onset." Journal of
         Psychosomatic Research 8:35–44.
Ross, C. E., and J. Mirowsky II
  1979   "A comparison of life-event-weighting
         schemes: Change, undesirability, and
         effect-proportional indices." Journal of
         Health and Social Behavior 20:166–77.
Ruch, L. O., and T. H. Holmes
  1971   "Scaling life change: Comparison of direct
         and indirect methods." Journal of
         Psychosomatic Research 15:221–27.
Srole, Leo, Thomas S. Langner, Stanley T. Michael,
  Marvin K. Opler, and Thomas A. C. Rennie
  1962   The Midtown Manhattan Study. New York:
         McGraw-Hill.
Stout, C., J. Morrow, N. Brandt, and S. Wolf
  1964   "Unusually low incidence of death from
         myocardial infarction." Journal of the
         American Medical Association 188:845–55.
Vinokur, A., and M. L. Selzer
  1975   "Desirable versus undesirable life events:
         Their relationship to stress and mental dis-
         tress." Journal of Personality and Social
         Psychology 32:329–37.
Wershow, H., and G. Reinhart
  1974   "Life changes and hospitalization—A heret-
         ical view." Journal of Psychosomatic Re-
         search 18:393.

APPENDIX

Comparability and Weights of Stressful-Life-Event Scales

Holmes and Rahe Scale Item	Weight	Chinese-American Item	Weight
1. Death of spouse	100	—	—
2. Divorce	73	Widowed, divorced, or	
3. Marital separation	65	separated	79.33
4. Jail term	63	Arrested, indicted, or convicted	63
5. Death of close family member	63	Death of loved one	63
6. Personal injury or illness	53	Illness or injury	53
7. Marriage	50	Married	50
8. Fired at work	47	Laid off, fired, business failed	47
9. Marital reconciliation	45	—	—
10. Retirement	45	Retired	45
11. Change in health of family member	44	—	—
12. Pregnancy	40	Pregnancy	40
13. Sex difficulties	39	—	—
14. Gain of new family member	39	Relative came to live with family from U.S.	39
—	—	Relative came to live with family from outside of U.S.	39
15. Business readjustment	39	—	—
16. Change of financial state	38	—	—
17. Death of close friend	37	—	—
18. Change in line of work	36	—	—
19. Change in number of arguments with spouse	35	—	—
20. Mortgage over $10,000	31	—	—
21. Change in responsibilities at work	29	—	—
22. Son or daughter leaving home	29	—	—
23. Trouble with in-laws	29	—	—
24. Outstanding personal achievement	28	Promotion or business achievement	28
25. Wife begins or stops work	26	—	—
26. Beginning or end of school	26	—	—
27. Change in living conditions	25	—	—
28. Revision of personal habits	24	—	—
29. Trouble with boss	23	Demotion	23
30. Change in work hours	20	—	—
31. Change in residence	20	Changed residence	20
32. Change in schools	20	—	—
33. Change in recreation	19	—	—
34. Change in church activities	19	—	—
35. Change in social activities	18	—	—
36. Mortgage $10,000	17	—	—
37. Change in sleeping habits	16	—	—
38. Change in eating habits	16	—	—
39. Vacation	13	Vacation	13
40. Christmas	12	—	—
41. Minor violation of law	11	—	—

[7]

Social Support and Depressed Mood: A Structural Analysis*

NAN LIN
XIAOLAN YE
Duke University

WALTER M. ENSEL
University at Albany, State University of New York

Journal of Health and Social Behavior 1999, Vol 40 (December) 344–359

Current literature on social support identifies social structure as a source of distress. However, past efforts tend to operationalize structure in terms of demographic characteristics. The present paper argues that structure should be conceived of as participation and involvement in community and social relations. Structure may include community ties, social networks and intimate ties. We hypothesize that the three elements represent the outer layer (belongingness), the intermediary layer (bonding), and the inner layer (binding) of social relations and should exhibit differentiated effects on mental health. We further hypothesize that these structural elements, in sequence, provide functional (i.e., instrumental-expressive, perceived-received, and routine-non-routine) supports which, in turn, prevent or protect against distress. Using data from the 1993–1994 Albany survey, we construct measures for elements of structural and functional support to test the relationship between the two as well as their effects on depression. Results confirm that elements of structural support, as predicted, differentially affect functional supports, and that the elements of both structural and functional supports exert direct effects on depression. Further, structural supports also exert indirect effects on depression, mediated by functional supports.

In the past two decades, social support has gained salience in the research literature on the stress process. Yet our understanding of this concept remains general and diverse. Social support can be seen as a structural property (e.g., being part of a community, a social network, or having interpersonal ties) or as a functional property (e.g., being instrumental or expressive). Research has proceeded without resolving whether these properties are alternative measures of social support or two distinctive components of social support. The purpose of the present paper is an attempt to clarify these conceptual issues.

In principle, we argue that social support contains two major components: its structural bases and its functional elements. A person's locations in different layers of the structure (e.g., the community, the social networks, and interpersonal ties) constitute the structural bases on which certain support functions (e.g., instrumental and expressive support) may be elicited. We hypothesize that the layers of the structure form a nested support system: the outer layer (being part of a community) enhances the likelihood of a person's better location in an inner layer (e.g., social networks or interpersonal ties). Further, these structural layers promote functional elements in sequence. The inner layers, rather than outer layers, better enhance the likelihood of an individual's having more satisfactory support

* The study reported here has been supported by a grant from the National Institute of Mental Health (MH48167). Please direct correspondence to Nan Lin, Department of Sociology, Box 90088, Duke University, Durham, NC 27708; email at nanlin@duke.edu.

functions. Finally, we hypothesize that support functions directly affect mental health, where effects of structural supports tend to be indirect, mediated through support functions.

The present study attempts to integrate these structural and functional elements and formulate possible causal processes among these elements. We then subject this integrated model to an empirical examination. Subsequently, we explore the differential benefits of structural and functional supports for individuals with different socioeconomic standings. Since it is well documented that gender, age, and income are differentially associated with psychological well-being (e.g. Turner 1994; Williams and Collins 1995), we will take these socioeconomic variables into consideration in the analysis.

We begin with discussions of the structural and functional elements of support and we follow with a formulation of their linkages and sequential effects on distress.

STRUCTURAL AND FUNCTIONAL SUPPORT

The Structural Elements of Support

Sociological analysis has traditionally given attention to the protective functions served by being part of a community or social group (Durkheim 1897). The notion that an individual's position in the social structure impacts on well-being is recognized in the stress literature (Aneshensel 1992; Pearlin 1989) and well documented in community studies (Hall and Wellman 1985; Leighton 1959; Wellman 1981). Yet recent studies illustrating structural effects tend to operationalize structural elements with demographic or social group characteristics (Aneshensel 1992). In this perspective, structure is understood in terms of socioeconomic statuses indicating class and social standing. This perspective is different from the perspective of structure based on social participation and social relations. While acknowledging the significance of social standings on distress (see, e.g., Turner, Wheaton, and Lloyd 1995), we argue that a structural analysis based on social participation and social relations offers a more cohesive theoretical development of the social etiology of health and illness.

Yet how the structural elements bring about protection against distress remains unclear in

the literature (Lin and Peek 1999). One formulation suggests that structural positions trigger a cognitive capability to manage stress (e.g., self-efficacy, self-esteem, self-competence, etc.). It is assumed that this cognitive capability provides both a buffer to stress and a protection against distress. We argue that an alternative explanation can be found in an integration of the structural effects and the notion of social support. That is, locations in the social structure (e.g., participation in community organizations, involvement in social networks, and immersion in intimate relationships) enhance the likelihood of accessing support which in turn provides the protective function against distress.

Scholars have long argued that social participation, reflecting both community and interpersonal linkages, is a protective factor for psychological well-being. It has been shown that individuals in different positions or locations may be differentially exposed to or vulnerable to stressful life experiences (Berkman and Syme 1979; House, Robbins, and Metzner 1982; Hughes and Gove 1981; Lin, Woelfel, and Dumin 1986).

Human relations consist of multiple layers extending out from the ego. Typically, these layers extend from the community to social networks and intimate relations. The outer layer, the community, reflects the broad range in which individuals are engaged with others. In this layer, participation and involvement are reflected in involvement with community and voluntary organizations. Such participation does not require or impose actual person-to-person interactions; rather, it provides a sense of *belongingness* and general social identity. Sociological theorists have argued that social participation and identification promote psychological well-being and reduce potential distress (Durhkeim 1897; Faris and Dunham 1939; Leighton 1959). Researchers focusing on group membership find either positive effects or insignificant effects of social participation on mental health (Kessler and Essex 1982; Thoits 1982; Williams, Ware, and Donald 1981).

Within this layer, social networks are constructed from interactions between ego and others. In a sub-layer within the outer layer are social linkages that require interpersonal interactions, and these form an individual's social networks. Social networks are maintained by interactions among the ties, either directly or indirectly. Without such interactions, social networks break down. These relations require a greater effort than mere participation, in that ego and alters must invest in maintaining the relations with a reasonable frequency of and commitment to interactions. Such interactions reflect a *bonding* relationship. The most often examined network characteristics are size of the network and frequency of contact. Studies focusing on size of network in relation to mental health have reported mixed findings. Many studies have found positive effects of the size of network on mental health (Bowling and Browne 1991; Cohen, Teresi, and Holmes 1985; Lin et al. 1979; Wilcox 1981; Williams et al. 1981). However, others have found negative effects (George et al. 1989) or no significant effects (Acock and Hurlbert 1993; Israel and Antonucci 1987; Schaefer, Coyne, and Lazarus 1981). Other studies have focused on frequency of contact, which is typically measured as how often ego is in contact with specific network members. The general conclusion is that higher frequency of contact is either associated with better mental health or with no significant effects (Kessler and Essex 1982; Roberts, Dunkle, and Haug 1994).

In the inner-most layer, a small number of alters (sometimes even a single alter) and the ego, through intimate and intense interactions, construct strong ties with the mutual sharing of confiding information and an implied obligation to reciprocate the confiding aspect of the relationship. These constitute *binding* relations.

The belongingness-bonding-binding formulation of social participation allows us to formulate a number of hypotheses linking these structural elements. The general proposal is that each inner layer is contingent upon the outer layers. That is, each outer layer of linkages affords the opportunity to construct inner-layer linkages. Thus, we hypothesize that (1) belongingness promotes bonding (i.e., community participation increases the likelihood of constructing and maintaining interactive ties in social networks), and (2) that bonding provides opportunities for finding binding relations (i.e., social networks increase the likelihood of finding and maintaining intimate ties).

The Functional Elements of Support

The functional elements of support include communication and transaction activities serving a variety of needs. From early on, researchers have proposed various functional dimensions of support (for a review, see House, Umberson, and Landis 1988; Lin 1986). For example, Cobb (1976) suggested that support provided emotional, esteem, and informational functions. Dean and Lin (1977) focused on the distinction between instrumental and expressive support. Caplan (1979) suggested three dimensions: (1) objective versus subjective, (2) tangible, and (3) psychological. Kahn and Antonucci (1980) proposed aid and affect (or affirmation) as the main functions of support. House (1981) summarized previous proposals and identified instrumental, expressive, community, network, confidant, appraisal, and information support. Schaefer et al. (1981) discussed perceived support, tangible support, emotional support, network support, and informational support. Numerous other variations have appeared in the literature (e.g., Johnson 1992).

We suggest that a synthesis of these various concepts results in three major dimensions: (1) *perceived versus actual support*, (2) *instrumental versus emotional support*, and (3) *routine versus crisis (or non-routine) support* (Lin, Dean, and Ensel 1986). While there is a large body of literature on one or more of these dimensions, a brief summary of their nature and principal findings is appropriate here.

Perceived versus actual support focuses on the subjective versus objective continuum of support (Cohen and Wills 1985; Turner and Marino 1994; Wethington and Kessler 1986). Perceived support refers to the perceptions of the availability of support when it is needed, the appraisal of its adequacy, and the quality of such support. Actual support refers to the nature and frequency of specific support transactions. Research evidence reveals a somewhat controversial relationship between perceived and actual support. There is substantial agreement that the two dimensions of support are not highly correlated and show different patterns of association with distress (Barrera 1986; George 1987; Wethington and Kessler 1986). In general, findings have shown that perceived support is more effective in resisting distress.

Support can also be classified into expressive (emotional) and instrumental types (George 1989; Wethington and Kessler 1986.[1] Expressive support involves the use of social relations to share sentiments, seek understandings, vent frustration, and build up self-esteem (Lai 1995). Instrumental support refers to tangible assistance, for example, helping with household chores, taking care of children, or lending money. Most scholars suggest that expressive support should be more effective against distress, since both phenomena deal with psychological states—that psychological discomfort should be resolved with psychological support. However, research findings (Ensel and Woelfel 1986) have also shown that instrumental support may be effective in meeting certain material needs (e.g., financial needs, child care, etc.).

A third distinction, somewhat less apparent in the literature, is between routine and crisis (or non-routine) support (Lin et al. 1986). Routine support is the process by which support is received or perceived relative to routine, day-to-day activities (e.g., child care, carpooling, grocery shopping), whereas crisis support reflects the process by which support is perceived or received when the ego is confronted with a crisis situation and event (e.g., a divorce or a car accident). Research is rather scarce in actual examination of whether support meeting these needs. However, many measures of support contain both types of situations. For example, one study (Lin, Woelfel, and Light 1986) examined support following experience with a most-important life event. They found that both actual support (e.g., frequency of contact with the helper, reciprocal discussion of problems with the helper, and the accessibility of the helper) and perceived support (importance of the helper) were both effective in reducing subsequent distress. Thus, there is some evidence that both actual and perceived supports are important in crisis situations.

While these concepts have all appeared in the social support literature, seldom have investigators incorporated multiple dimensions and measures into a single study. A typical approach has been to examine one dimension, say between perceived and actual support, and to demonstrate, for example, that perceived support is more significantly associated with reduced distress. Even when multiple dimensions have been incorporated in a study, they are usually treated as separate support factors predicting distress, either as independent or mediating variables (George 1989; Thoits 1995).

The present paper will attempt to incorporate and integrate the three dimensions into a single model. Several hypotheses guide this integration. First, since these dimensions are assumed to be subconcepts of support functions, they should be correlated. However, we need to examine the extent to which they are related. Further, it is conceivable that these indicators converge on the latent concept of support functions in a hierarchical order through multiple steps. They may first form lower-level latent concepts that in turn converge into a single latent concept: support functions. However, there is no theoretical basis for expecting perceived-versus-actual support to first converge with instrumental-versus-expressive support or crisis-versus-routine support. Thus, the structure should be allowed to emerge in analysis.

Structural Effects Mediated Through Support Functions

Having identified the structural and functional elements of support and specified the internal dynamics of the various dimensions in each group, we may now hypothesize the relationships among the elements of structural and functional support as well as their relationships to distress (Figure 1). We argue that the structural elements constitute the structural environment in which support functions may be located, constructed, and sustained. Thus, we hypothesize that structural embeddedness promotes better support functions. That is, community participation, social networks, and intimate ties enhance various dimensions of support functions, namely, instrumental-expressive, routine-crisis, and perceived-actual support dimensions. Given the fact that the extent of structural embeddedness is characterized by three layers, we further hypothesize that the relative effects on support functions would be least significant for community participation and more significant for social networks and intimate ties.

Finally, we hypothesize that these structural and support functions negatively affect distress. Further, these relationships should remain significant, even when stressors (undesirable life events), age, gender, and income

FIGURE 1. The Conceptual Model

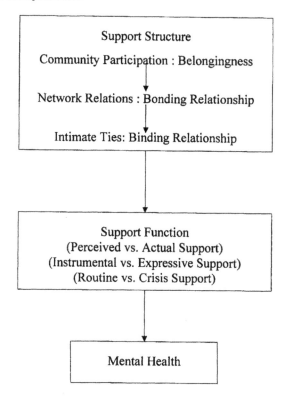

are taken into account. More specifically, we postulate that the inner-most layer of the structure (intimate ties) has the greatest effect on distress of all the structural elements. It is not clear which of the functional elements will be more significant in deterring distress. This question needs to be resolved empirically. In the remainder of the paper we present a formulation of an integrative model of social support, and we attempt to validate the formulation empirically.

Inequality of Supports: Gender, Age and Income

In examining an integrative model of social support, we shall also examine the plausibility that social supports are differentially beneficial to different social groups. The literature has consistently demonstrated that certain social groups tend to have higher levels of psychological well-being; for example, males, younger persons and persons of higher income tend to have better psychological well-being (House et al. 1994; Turner 1994; Williams and Collins 1995). We are interested in whether these advantages are due to differential access to support structures and support functions. That is, do the effects of support on mental health vary across social groups? Are the effects of support on mental health stronger for males, younger persons, and persons with higher income? There is no consistent theoretical basis to suspect that such support-inequality exists across social groups. Nevertheless, by incorporating gender, age, and income as additional exogenous variables in the analyses, we will attempt to uncover any potential clues that may help direct future research.

METHODS

Data

The data come from a personal-interview survey of a representative community sample conducted in 1993 in upstate New York. It is part of a continuing community study conducted in this metropolitan area (the Albany-Schenectady-Troy area) since 1979. The total sample, representative of the adult population in the area, consists of 1,261 individuals. A majority of the respondents (94 percent) are white. The mean household size is 2.9 individuals.

Measurement of Control Variables

Undesirable life events. We use a shortened list of 118 life events compiled from previous work (Tausig 1986). Each respondent was asked if he or she has experienced each event in the past 12 months. When a response was positive, the respondent was asked to indicate if the event is "good," "uncertain," or "bad." We summate the number of "bad" life events experienced into a single measure of undesirable life events. Each respondent has experienced about 1.5 undesirable events during the past 12 months.

Income. We use an ordinal household income, a measure containing 26 categories ranging from $999 to $95,000 or more. Smaller numbers represent lower levels of income. From income level 1 to level 8 (i.e., between $999 and $9,999), there is a $1,000 increase between each level. From level 9 to level 25 (i.e., between $10,000 to $94,999), the increment between each interval is $5,000. Level 26 signifies household income of $95,000 or more. The mean income is around level 15, which represents $40,000 to $45,000.

Age. We measure age in years. The sample's mean age is about 47.

Gender. Gender is a dummy variable with male equal to 0 and female equal to 1. For clarity and easy understanding, we use female as the variable name in all tables. Male respondents account for 48 percent of the total sample, and females account for 52 percent.

Measure of Support Structure

Community ties. We measure community ties by *participation in community organizations.* To a large extent, this measure reflects one's involvement in community activities. Therefore, to measure community ties, we asked each respondent to report the number of social clubs and organizations with which he or she was associated. These clubs and organizations extend into many life domains, including church-related groups, job-related associations, recreational groups, fraternal services, civic and political groups, and senior citizenship groups. Respondents were asked to report the number of organizations that they were involved with in each category. The total number of affiliated social clubs and organizations is used to capture the overall participation in organizations, indicating the strength of community ties (Appendix A for details). Most people are involved in one or two organizations, with an average of 1.72.

Social networks. For network relations, we use *number of weekly contacts* as the measure of network size. Respondents were asked to estimate how many people they came in contact with each week. The number of people mentioned is used as the measurement (Appendix A for details). On average, respondents make about 38 contacts each week.

Intimate ties. We use one measure to assess *presence of an intimate relationship*: whether a respondent currently has a spouse or an intimate partner. First, we determined whether a respondent was married or not. For those currently not married, we asked, "are you currently living with another adult as a partner in an intimate relationship?" We constructed a dummy variable where 1 represents either currently married or living with an intimate partner and 0 represents the absence of both conditions. Sixty-seven percent of the people live with a partner.

Measure of Depressed Mood

We use the Center for Epidemiological Studies Depression Scale (CES-D) as our measure of depressive symptoms, the dependent variable. The 20-item instrument has been used widely in community sample surveys and is recognized as possessing acceptable levels of validity and reliability (Radloff 1977). The total score ranges from 0 to 60, with higher scores indicating more depressive symptoms.

In our sample, the mean score of CES-D is 11.01. The reliability test of the total CES-D scale yields an alpha coefficient of .88, indicating high internal consistency. To further insure that no single item significantly reduces the reliability of the total scale, we calculated alpha coefficients with each item deleted. The alphas range from .88 to .90, again indicating that the items are consistent in their patterns of variations.

Measure of Support Functions

We have devised measures corresponding to various dimensions of support functions and designed items for perceived crisis support, actual crisis support, perceived routine support and actual routine support. For each dimension, we have also incorporated instrumental as well as expressive items.

Perceived crisis support. We use a ten-item list to measure perceived crisis support. Respondents were asked if they could get any help in ten hypothetical situations of crisis and emergency (Appendix B). The perception of support availability is measured on a three point scale: 3 = "yes," 2 = "yes but with difficulty," and 1 = "no." A factor analysis reveals that the ten items yield two factors: the first is instrumental in nature, the second expressive. In the analysis, we use two summated measures of perceived crisis support, one for instrumental perceived crisis support ($PCRISIS_I$) and one for expressive perceived crisis support ($PCRISIS_E$). Each corresponds to the summation of the five items embedded in each factor.

Actual crisis (non-routine) support. To measure actual crisis support, we use the same ten-item list as the one used to measure perceived crisis support (Appendix B). However, in this scenario, the situations were actual instead of hypothetical. The ten items have five original response categories: 1 = "yes," 2 = "yes but with difficulty," 3 = "no," 4 = "never faced with the situation," and 5 = "never needed help when faced with the situation." Some preliminary analysis on this support led to a rescaling of the response categories: 3 = "yes," 2 = "yes but with difficulty," and 1 = "no."[2] The ten items are of two types: instrumental and expressive. A factor analysis of the ten items

confirms the conceptual design with a two-factor solution. Accordingly, we create two summated scores of instrumental ($ACRISIS_I$) and expressive actual crisis support ($ACRISIS_E$).

Perceived routine support. Perceived routine support is measured in the same manner as perceived crisis support (Appendix B). Respondents were given ten hypothetical situations of routine needs and were asked if they could get help when they needed it. We use a three-point scale to measure the availability of the routine support: 3 = "yes," 2 = "yes but with difficulty," and 1 = "no." Again the ten items yield instrumental and expressive factors, and we thus construct measures of instrumental ($PROUTINE_I$) and expressive perceived routine support ($PROUTINE_E$).

Actual routine support. We assess actual routine support with ten items depicting real situations where regular support might be sought (Appendix B). Following the procedure applied to actual crisis support, we obtain three response categories: 3 = "yes," 2 = "yes but with difficulty," and 1 = "no." The factor analysis confirms a two factor design embedded in the ten items, instrumental and expressive, and we thus construct two summated measures of instrumental ($AROUTINE_I$) and expressive actual routine support ($AROUTINE_E$).

We performed a reliability test on each of the four scales. The alpha coefficients for the scales measuring perceived crisis support, actual crisis support, perceived routine support and actual routine support are .85, .85, .82, and .84, respectively; these coefficients suggest reasonable internal consistency for each of the scales. For each individual scale, to further insure that no single item significantly reduces the reliability of the scale, we calculated alpha coefficients with each response item deleted. The alphas all range from .81 to .85, indicating the consistency of variation patterns of the items.

Integration of Support Functions

To integrate the three dimensions of support functions, we used the structural equation modeling approach to explore a hierarchical factor structure. Details of an analysis of similar nature are available elsewhere (Lin, Ye, and Ensel 1999). As shown in Figure 2, the analysis results in three levels of a factor structure. At the initial level, all eight support dimensions are entered into an exploratory factor analysis. At the second level, there are four factors and at the third level, there are two factors. Thus, the eight factors of the first level converge into four second-level factors that can be identified as perceived-instrumental, actual-instrumental, perceived-expressive, and actual-expressive. These four factors further converge into the instrumental and expressive factors at the third level.

These analyses suggest a structurally integrated measurement of support functions. The two ultimate functional dimensions can be expressed in a two-stage estimation procedure utilizing information in Figure 2. At the first stage, four equations can be constructed for perceived or actual support as functions of routine and crisis support:

$$\text{Perceived Instrumental} =$$
$$1.00 \; PCRISIS_I + .87 \; PROUTINE_I$$

$$\text{Actual Instrumental} =$$
$$.85 \; ACRISIS_I + 1.00 \; AROUTINE_I$$

$$\text{Perceived Expressive} =$$
$$1.00 \; PCRISIS_E + .99 \; PROUTINE_E$$

$$\text{Actual Expressive} =$$
$$.94 \; ACRISIS_E + 1.00 \; AROUTINE_E$$

At the second stage, in accordance with the structural equation model in Figure 2, it is possible to further consolidate these four equations into two equations for instrumental and expressive support as functions of received and actual support:

$$\text{Instrumental Support} =$$
$$1.00 \; Perceived \; Instrumental +$$
$$.86 \; Actual \; Instrumental$$

$$\text{Expressive Support} =$$
$$1.00 \; Perceived \; Expressive +$$
$$.96 \; Actual \; Expressive$$

However, the research literature has consistently shown differential effects between perceived and actual support, even though such measurements have no instrumental versus expressive support components. Our analyses

FIGURE 2. Integration of Support Functions

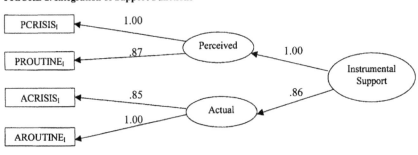

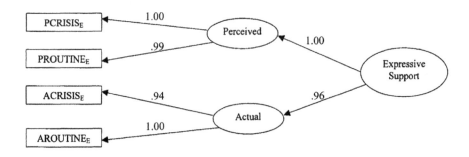

suggest an opportunity, then, to examine the differential effects of perceived versus actual support *in terms of instrumental versus expressive support*. Thus, our final decision is to use the resulting four measures from stage 1 as the measures of support functions: (1) perceived instrumental support, (2) actual instrumental support, (3) perceived expressive support, and (4) actual expressive support.[3] The means of the four integrated support functions are all around 28 (which is at the high end of support) and indicate that most people in this sample can receive a significant amount of social support when in need, either in perception or in reality.

ANALYSES AND RESULTS

The first set of analyses examines the hypotheses concerning the sequential relationships among the support elements. A set of regressions were conducted, and the results appear in Table 1. Each column represents a dependent variable, and the row variables are the independent variables. Gender, age, and income are used as control variables in all equations. The first dependent variable, number of weekly contacts, was regressed on participation in community organizations and the control variables. As can be seen, the two variables are highly associated (the metric regression coefficient is 4.52, significant at .001 level), confirming the hypothesis that belongingness increases the likelihood of bonding. In the next column, the presence of an intimate tie is shown to be affected by participation in community organizations, but not by the number of weekly contacts. Thus, the hypothesis that bonding leads to binding support does not receive support. Instead, binding seems also to have been affected by belongingness.[4] We suspect that the item tapping bonding was relatively poor. Number of weekly contacts cannot reflect adequately the extensity and range of social ties in a typical social network. We shall return to this issue in the discussion and conclusions section.

In columns 3 through 6 of Table 1, the four support function variables, perceived instrumental support, actual instrumental support, perceived expressive support, and actual expressive support, are regressed on participation in community organizations, number of weekly contacts, presence of an intimate rela-

tionship, and the control variables. As can be seen, participation in community organizations shows little direct effect on any of the support functions (the only significant effect is on actual instrumental support). Number of weekly contacts, however, shows significant relations with all four support functions, especially the two expressive support variables (see the last two columns). The presence of an intimate relationship has strong effects on the two instrumental supports but not on the expressive supports. The results partially confirm the hypotheses that support networks enhance support functions. However, the effect of support networks on different support functions appears to be different.

There is little discussion in the literature addressing whether the presence of an intimate relationship should result in more instrumental or expressive support, although the general assumption is that expressive support is more important for psychological well-being. Our finding that the presence of an intimate tie affects instrumental support rather than expressive support is interesting. One possible explanation is that intimate ties may provide instrumental support to both males and females, but serve expressive functions only for females. Thus, this general finding might have camouflaged such differential effects. We explored this explanation by conducting separate analyses for males and females (while excluding gender from the equations) and found that the patterns are essentially the same for both groups. A further check of the zero-order correlations confirms the significant associations between the presence of an intimate relationship and instrumental supports, but not between intimate relationship and expressive supports. Thus, the finding, that intimate ties is associated with instrumental supports but not with expressive supports, is not spurious.

In the second stage of the analyses we regressed psychological distress on support structures and support functions. Table 2 shows the results of five nested regression models examining the sequential effects of support structures and functions on depressed mood. All models incorporate age, gender, income, and undesirable life events as control variables. The initial model (model 1) incorporates the factor representing the outer layer of the structural elements of support: participation in community organizations. The metric

TABLE 1. The Sequential Effects of Outer Layer Support on Inner Layer Support and Support Functions[a]

	Number of Network Contacts	Presence of an Intimate Relationship	Perceived Instrumental Support	Actual Instrumental Support	Perceived Expressive Support	Actual Expressive Support
Female	2.20 (.03)	-.06 (-.07)*	.19 (.03)	.02 (.01)	.54 (.11)***	.31 (.06)
Age	-.31 (-.13)***	.01 (.05)	-.01 (-.03)	-.01 (-.03)	-.01 (-.03)	-.01 (-.02)
Income	1.16 (.14)***	.01 (.09)**	.04 (.06)	.01 (.01)	-.01 (-.02)	-.04 (-.07)
Participation in community organizations	4.52 (.22)***	.01 (.04)*	.07 (.05)	.10 (.07)*	.03 (.03)	.04 (.03)
Number of weekly contacts		.01 (.01)	.01 (.07)*	.01 (.07)*	.01 (.08)**	.01 (.11)***
Presence of an intimate relationship			.90 (.15)***	.77 (.13)***	.07 (.01)	.22 (.04)

* p < .05 **; p < .01 ***; p < .001 (two-tailed test)
[a]Metric coefficients are presented with standardized coefficients in parentheses.

TABLE 2. Regression of Depressed Mood on Social Factors[a]

Independent Variables	Model 1	Model 2	Model 3	Model 4	Model 5
Female	1.50 (.08)**	1.56 (.09)**	1.35 (.07)**	1.32 (.07)*	1.28 (.07)*
Age	-.01 (-.01)	-.01 (-.02)	-.01 (-.01)	-.01 (-.01)	-.04 (-.08)
Income	-.18 (-.10)**	-.16 (-.08)**	-.14 (-.07)*	-.14 (-.07)*	-.08 (-.05)
Undesirable life events	1.41 (.30)***	1.43 (.30)***	1.38 (.29)***	1.36 (.29)***	1.22 (.27)***
Participation in community organizations	-.43 (-.10)**	-.33 (-.08)*	-.30 (-.07)*	-.32 (-.07)*	-.16 (-.04)
Number of weekly contacts		-.04 (-.10)***	-.03 (-.09)***	-.02 (-.08)***	-.01 (-.07)*
Presence of an intimate relationship			-2.85 (-.15)***	-2.91 (-.15)***	-2.63 (-.14)*
Instrumental needs				.03 (.06)	.42 (.08)
Expressive needs				.06 (.01)	.11 (.02)
Perceived instrumental support					.03 (.01)
Actual instrumental support					-.35 (-.10)
Perceived expressive support					-.63 (-.17)**
Actual expressive support					-.10 (-.03)
Intercept	11.10	11.79	13.36	10.14	39.19
R^2	.13	.14	.16	.16	.22

* p < .05; ** p < .01; *** p < .001 (two-tailed test)
[a]Metric coefficients are presented, with standard coefficients in parentheses.

regression coefficient for community partici-pation is significantly related to depressed mood (–.43), supporting the hypothesis that belonging to community and voluntary organi-zations reduces the likelihood of becoming depressed. The model explains 13 percent of the variance of the dependent variable.

The next model (model 2) adds the inner layer of the structural elements, the network factor (i.e., number of weekly contacts). Results show, as expected, that the network variable makes a modest but significant contri-bution to explaining depressed mood; the explained variance slightly increases to .14. Further, the direct effect of participation in community organizations is reduced in magni-tude from –.43 to –.33, indicating that the net-work measure does, to a modest extent, serve a mediating role between the outer layer (com-munity participation) and depressed mood. That is, as expected, belonging to community and voluntary organizations affects the likeli-hood of involvement in bonding relations.

Model 3 incorporates the variable represent-ing the inner-most layer of structural elements: intimate ties. This variable is significantly related to depressed mood, and its addition sig-nificantly increases the explained variance of depressed mood from .14 to .16. Further, the contributions of participation in community organizations and network relations are corre-spondingly reduced somewhat, suggesting that portions of their effects are now mediated by the intimate relationship variable, as hypothe-sized. That is, belonging to community and voluntary organizations and network relations affects the likelihood of constructing an inti-mate relationship which in turn affects depressed mood.

Before we proceed to add the four support function variables to the equation, we must address the possibility that a respondent might not have faced a situation in which he or she needed support. It is necessary to verify that the effects of the support functions are not due to the absence of needs for support. Thus, the next model (model 4) incorporates two need-for-support variables: the extent to which a respondent faces a situation in which he or she needs (1) instrumental or (2) expressive sup-ports. Each variable is constructed by subtract-ing from 10 the number of items to which the respondent answered "never faced with the sit-uation," a larger score reflecting more situa-tions in which each support is needed. As can

be seen in model 4, neither the need for instru-mental support nor the need for expressive support contributes to the explanation of depressed mood.

Finally, model 5 adds the four support func-tion variables. The addition of the four vari-ables significantly increases the explained variance of depressed mood (from .16 to .22). Correspondingly, the direct effects from par-ticipation in community organizations, num-ber of weekly contacts, and presence of an inti-mate relationship have been reduced. That is, the support function variables mediate between the structural elements and depressed mood, as expected. In the equation, two of the four support function variables remain signifi-cant: actual instrumental support and per-ceived expressive support. Because all four support functions show significant correla-tions with depressed mood, the significance of the two variables may merely reflect the differ-ential statistical effects of the covariances among the four variables. Nonetheless, it is interesting that actual instrumental support seems more important than perceived instru-mental support whereas perceived expressive support seems more important than actual expressive support. These findings lend sup-port to the general hypothesis in the literature that perception of expressive support is more important than actual expressive support expe-rienced.

It should also be noted that the presence of an intimate relationship continues to exert a direct significant effect on depressed mood, even when support functions are entered in model 5. That is, the mediating roles of sup-port functions cannot account for all of the effects from the inner layer of the structural elements.

In summary, the results largely confirm the hypothesized sequential effects of structural and functional elements of support. Among the structural elements, as predicted, the inner most layer, (i.e., the presence of an intimate relationship), incrementally adds significant effects to explaining depressed mood (note that the explained variance increases from .14 in model 2 to .16 in model 3). As hypothesized, the effects of intimate ties on distress are the greatest among the three structural elements. To a modest extent, effects of the support structure are mediated by those from the sup-port functions. Nevertheless, both the inner layer of support structures and support functions exert direct effects on depressed mood.

Effects of Gender, Age, and Income: Testing the Inequality Hypotheses

From Table 2, we observe that across the five sequential models, being female has a persistent negative effect on depressed mood. This finding is consistent with what has been documented in the literature: women are more depressed than men. Although being young seems to have some beneficial effects on depressed mood, its effects are not statistically significant. People from high socioeconomic class are less depressed than those from lower class.

However, these direct associations between gender, age, and income and depressed mood do not address the critical issue: whether the effects of structural support and functional support on depressed mood are contingent on gender, age, or income. To examine these contingent arguments, we need to analyze the interaction effects between these group variables and support variables on depressed mood. We carry out this analysis by constructing and incorporating interaction terms (centered) between the inequality variables (gender, age, and income) and the support variables (support structures and support functions). None of the interaction terms makes a significant contribution to explaining the variance in depressed mood. We therefore conclude that there is no substantial evidence in support of the inequality argument that the effects of the structural and functional elements of support on mental health vary by gender, age, and income.

DISCUSSION AND CONCLUSION

The present paper attempts to differentiate social support into two components: the structural elements and the functional elements. For the structural elements, we identified three potentially nested layers (participation in community organizations, number of weekly contacts, and the presence of an intimate relationship) reflecting belongingness, bonding, and binding. For the functions, we examined three dimensions of support: instrumental-expressive, perceived-actual, and routine-crisis. We

hypothesized that the three layers of support structure have sequential effects, each inner layer mediating the effects of the outer layers on depressed mood. Further, we expected that support functions would mediate the effects of the support structure on depressed mood. Data from a large-scale survey of a metropolitan area in upstate New York largely confirm these expectations. Thus, the present study advances the structural perspective in understanding the stress-process by demonstrating the significance of social participation, network contacts, intimate relations, and functional supports (especially instrumental and expressive supports) for mental health.

Three particular findings deserve further discussion. First, binding relations (intimate ties) are not significantly associated with bonding relations (social networks) as hypothesized. We suspect that it might be due to the fact that the general estimate of the number of weekly contacts does not adequately reflect essential characteristics of network contacts such as the extent or range of social ties, heterogeneity of social ties, and the strength of ties (intensity, frequency of interactions, and reciprocity of services). With improved measures, we remain confident that the theoretical hypothesis should stay viable.

Second, we find that the presence of an intimate relationship affects instrumental supports but not expressive supports. One possible explanation may be that most studies measure intimate ties with emphasis on the degree of intimacy, thus overlapping with expressive or emotional support. In contrast, our measurement is a direct measure of the presence or absence of a spouse or partner, more in line with a structural interpretation. If this distinction is indeed crucial, then further research is needed to verify that expressive support depends on a network of interpersonal ties while instrumental support requires the presence of intimate and strong ties. Consistent findings of this sort would lead to a major revision of a theory linking support structure to support functions.

Third, effects of structural and functional supports on psychological well-being did not differ across age, gender and income levels. We did find age is related to structural support (younger respondents had greater structural support) and gender is related to expressive support (females received more expressive support) (see Table 1). We also found that females and older and lower-income respondents tend to be more depressed (see Table 2). However, there is no evidence to support the argument that the effects of structural supports and functional supports on mental health do not vary by age, gender, or income. This latter finding does not preclude the possibility that other measures of social standings (occupational and work characteristics, for example) might better reflect differential social participation by various socioeconomic groups, thus allowing them to receive the benefits of structural and functional supports. Further research is needed to substantiate the validity or invalidity of the inequality argument.

Nevertheless, the results of the current study justify the conceptual utility of conceiving "structure" in terms of social relations. The specification of the types or layers of social relations helps clarify the "structural" etiology of supports. These supports—be they actual or perceived, instrumental or expressive, and routine or non-routine—help individuals maintain their mental health, even when they experience stressful life events. Future refinements in measurement and conceptual specification promise further advances in linking social structure to support functions and mental health.

APPENDIX A.
Measurement of Support Structures

Community Ties
Do you belong to one or more of the following clubs or organizations?
1. Church-related group, such as board/standing committee, men's/women's group, voluntary service (choir, usher)?
2. Job-related association, such as business/professional organization, labor union?
3. Recreational groups, such as bowling league, women's club, card club, golf club?
4. Fraternal services, such as Mason's or Eastern Star Service Club (Lions or Rotary), Hospital Auxiliary?
5. Civic-political groups, such as Parent-Teachers Association, Political Party Club, Chamber of Commerce?
6. Senior citizens group, please specify?
7. Other groups, please specify?

Social Networks
In a typical week, how many of the following people do you come in contact with? By contact, we mean either face to face or by phone. Give us your best guess.
1. Brother/sister
2. In-laws
3. Other relatives
4. Close friends
5. Neighbors
6. Co-workers
7. Boss/supervisor
8. Other acquaintances
9. Helping professionals
10. Member of same group or club

APPENDIX B.
Measurement of Support Functions

Perceived Crisis Support
I would like to present you with some hypothetical situations. I want to know if you could get help or assistance with the following emergencies if you needed it. Remember these are hypothetical situations. Please use the following response categories:
3. Yes
2. Yes, with difficulty
1. No

If you needed it, could you get:
1. Someone to lend you money to pay an important bill that was past due?
2. Someone to help you with a minor emergency around the house (i.e., broken water pipe/clogged drain)?
3. Someone to lend you a car for an emergency situation?
4. Someone to help you deal with a medical emergency like an injury to a child or spouse?
5. Someone to watch the house or kids if you got called away for an emergency?
6. Someone to talk to about a serious problem you were having at work?
7. Someone to talk to about the death of a someone close to you?

8. Someone to talk to about serious problems you were having with your husband/wife or closest friend?
9. Someone to talk to about a serious problem you were having with your health?
10. Someone to talk to about something that was seriously affecting your life?

Actual Crisis Support
I would like to look at some real situations with you. I want to know if you ACTUALLY got help or assistance with the following emergency situations the last time you needed it. Remember these are real situations. Please use the following response categories;
1. Yes
2. Yes, with difficulty
3. No
4. Never faced with the situation
5. Never needed help when faced with the situation
Note: Items are the same as those for measuring perceived crisis support.

Perceived Routine Support
I would like to present you with some hypothetical situations. I want to know if you could get help or assistance in the following areas on a regular basis if you needed it. By regular, I mean at least 2–3 times a week. Remember, these are hypothetical situations. Please use the following response categories:
3. Yes
2. Yes, with difficulty
1. No
1. Someone to lend you money to pay bills or help you get along?
2. Someone to help in doing things around the house (i.e., cooking, cleaning)?
3. Someone to give you a ride to someplace you had to go (shopping, post office, airport)?
4. Someone to help with your daily routine if you were not feeling well?
5. Someone to watch your house (care for plants/pets) while you were away?
6. Someone to talk to about something that was bothering you?
7. Company when you felt lonely or just wanted to talk?
8. Someone to talk to about a small argument you had with your husband/wife or closest friend?
9. Someone to make you feel good, loved, or cared for?
10. Someone to talk to about a series of disappointments or bad days?

Actual Routine Support
I would like to look at some real situations with you. I want to know if you ACTUALLY got help or assistance in the following areas the last time you needed it. Remember these are real situations. Please use the following response categories to give me your answer:
1. Yes
2. Yes, with difficulty
3. No
4. Never faced with the situation
5. Never needed help when faced with the situation
Note: Items are the same as those used to measure perceived routine support.

NOTES

1. There is a third category, informational support, which means providing a person with information that he or she can use in coping with personal and environmental problems. In contrast to expressive and instrumental support, informational support has been less discussed in the literature. In essence, such information is helpful only when people utilize it to help themselves. We do not explore support dimension in this paper.
2. People who answer "never faced with the situation" are assigned the mean values of the items. Further, we find that the "never needed help when faced with the situation" group is difficult to interpret and the num-

ber is relatively small (n = 19), which renders them rather unstable. Therefore, we decided to eliminate this category. The scaling of actual routine support is coded in the same way.
3. We acknowledge an anonymous reviewer for suggesting this approach.
4. The zero-order correlation between number of network contacts and intimate ties is .02.

REFERENCES

Acock, Alan C. and Jeanne S. Hurlbert. 1993. "Social Networks, Marital Status, and Well-being." *Social Networks* 15:309–34.

Aneshensel, Carol S. 1992. "Social Stress: Theory and Research." *Annual Review of Sociology* 18:15–38.

Berkman, Lisa, and S. Leonard Syme. 1979. "Social Network, Host Resistance, and Mortality: A Nine-year Follow-up Study of Alameda County Residents." *American Journal of Epidemiology* 109:186–204.

Barrera, Manuel, Jr. 1986. "Distinctions Between Social Support Concepts, Measures, and Models." *American Journal of Community Psychology* 14:413–45.

Bowling, Ann and Peter Browne. 1991. "Social Networks, Health, and Emotional Well-Being among the Oldest Old in London." *Journal of Gerontology* 46:20–32.

Caplan, Robert D. 1979. "Social Support, Person-environment Fit, and Coping." Pp. 89–138 in *Mental Health and the Economy,* edited by L. A. Ferman and J. P. Gordus. Michigan: W. E. Upjohn Institute for Employment Research.

Cobb, Sidney. 1976. "Social Support as a Moderator of Life Stress." *Psychosomatic Medicine* 38:300–14.

Cohen, Carl, Jeanne Teresi, and Douglas Holmes. 1985. "Social Networks, Stress, Adaptation, and Health." *Research on Aging* 7:409–31.

Cohen, Sheldon and Thomas A. Wills. 1985. "Stress, Social Support and the Buffering Hypothesis." *Psychological Bulletin* 98:310–57.

Dean, Alfred and Nan Lin. 1977. "The Stress Buffering Role of Social Support." *Journal of Nervous and Mental Disease* 165(2):403–13.

Durkheim, Emile. [1897]1966. *Suicide.* New York: Free Press.

Ensel, Walter M. and Mary Woelfel. 1986. "Measuring the Instrumental and Expressive Functions of Social Support." Pp. 129–50 in *Social Support, Life Events and Depression,* edited by N. Lin, A. Dean and W. M. Ensel. Orlando, FL: Academic Press.

Faris, Robert E. L. and H. Warren Dunham. 1939. *Mental Disorders in Urban Areas.* New York: Hafner.

George, Linda K. 1987. "Easing Caregiver Burden: the Role of Informal and Formal Supports." Pp. 112–43 in *Health in Aging: Sociological Issues and Policy Directions,* edited by R. A. Ward and S. S. Tobin. New York: Springer.

George, Linda K. 1989. "Stress, Social Support, and Depression." Pp. 241–67 in *Aging, Stress, and Health,* edited by K. S. Markides and C. L. Cooper. New York: John Wiley & Sons.

George, Linda K., Dan Blazer, Dana Hughes, and Nancy Fowler. 1989. "Social Support and the Major Outcome of Depression." *British Journal of Psychiatry* 154:478–85.

Hall, Alan and Barry Wellman. 1985. "Social Networks and Social Support." Pp. 23–42 in *Social Support and Health,* edited by Cohen Sheldon and Syme Leonard. Orlando, FL: Academic Press.

House, James S. 1981. *Work Stress and Social Support.* Reading MA: Addison-Wesley.

House, Jame S., James M. Leprowski, Ann M. Kinney, Richard P. Mero, Ronald C. Kessler, and A. Regula Herzog. 1994. "The Social Stratification of Aging and Health." *Journal of Health and Social Behavior* 35:213–34.

House, James S., Cynthia Robbins, and Helen L. Metzner. 1982. "The Association of Social Relationships and Activities with Mortality: Prospective Evidence from the Tecumseh Community Health Study." *American Journal of Epidemiology* 116:123–40.

House, James, S., Debra Umberson, and Karl R. Landis. 1988. "Structures and Processes of Social Support." *Annual Review of Sociology* 14:293–318.

Hughes, Michael, and Walter R. Gove. 1981. "Living Along, Social Integration, and Mental Health." *American Journal of Sociology* 87:48–74.

Israel, Barbara A. and Toni C. Antonucci. 1987. "Social Network Characteristics and Psychological Well-Being: a Replication and Extension." *Health Education Quarterly* 14: 461–81.

Johnson, J. Randal. 1992. "Social Support." Pp. 1976–78 in *Encyclopedia of Sociology,* edited by Edgar Borgatta. New York: MacMillan.

Kahn, Robert L. and Toni C. Antonucci. 1980. "Convoys over the Life Course: Attachment, Roles, and Social Support." Pp. 253–86 in *Life Span Development and Behavior, Vol. 3,* edited by P. B. Bales and O. G. Brim. New York, NY: Academic Press.

Kessler, Ronald C. and Marilyn Essex. 1982. "Marital Status and Depression: The Role of Coping Resources." *Social Forces* 61:484–507.

Lai, Gina. 1995. "The Work and Family Context of Stress and Distress: a Study in Urban China." Ph.D. dissertation, Department of Sociology, State University of New York, Albany, NY.

Leighton, Alexander Hamilton. 1959. *My Name is Legion.* New York: Basic Books.

Lin, Nan. 1986. "Conceptualizing Social Support." Pp. 17–30 in *Social Support, Life Events and Depression,* edited by N. Lin, A. Dean, and W. M. Ensel. Orlando, FL: Academic Press.

Lin, Nan, Alfred Dean, and Walter M. Ensel, eds. 1986. *Social Support, Life Events and Depression.* Orlando, FL: Academic Press.

Lin, Nan and M. Kristen Peek. 1999. "Social Networks and Mental Health." Pp. 241–58 in *A Handbook for the Study of Mental Health,* edited by A. Horwitz and T. L. Scheid. New York, NY: Cambridge University Press.

Lin, Nan, Ronald S. Simeone, Walter M. Ensel, and Wen H. Kuo. 1979. "Social Support, Stressful Life Events, and Illness: a Model and an Empirical Test." *Journal of Health and Social Behavior* 20:108–19.

Lin, Nan, Mary Woelfel, and Mary Dumin. 1986. "Gender of the Confidant and Depression." Pp.

283–306 in *Social Support, Life Events and Depression,* edited by N. Lin, A. Dean, and W.M. Ensel. Orlando, FL: Academic Press.

Lin, Nan, Mary Woelfel, and Stephen Light. 1986. "Buffering the Impact of the Most Important Life Event." Pp. 307–32 in *Social Support, Life Events and Depression,* edited by N. Lin, A. Dean, and W. M. Ensel. Orlando, FL: Academic Press.

Lin, Nan, Xiaolan Ye, and Walter M. Ensel. 1999. Forthcoming. "Revisiting Social Support: Integration of its Dimensions." *The Chinese Journal of Mental Health.*

Pearlin, Leonard I. 1989. "The Sociological Study of Stress." *Journal of Health and Social Behavior* 30:241–56.

Radloff, Lenore. 1977. "The CES-D Scale: A Self-Report Depression Scale for Research in the General Population." *Applied Psychological Measurement* 1:385–401.

Roberts, Beverly L., Ruth Dunkle, and Marie Haug. 1994. "Physical, Psychological, and Social Resources as Moderators of the Relationship of Stress to Mental Health of the Very Old." *Journal of Gerontology* 49:35–43.

Schaefer, Catherine, James C. Coyne, and Richard. S. Lazarus. 1981. "The Health-related Functions of Social Support." *Journal of Behavior Medicine* 4:381–406.

Tausig, Mark. 1986. "Measuring Life Events." Pp. 267–79 in *Social Support, Life Events and Depression,* edited by N. Lin, A. Dean, and W. M. Ensel. Orlando, FL: Academic Press.

Thoits, Peggy A. 1982. "Life Stress, Social Support, and Psychological Vulnerability: Epidemio-

logical Considerations." *Journal of Community Psychology* 10:341–62.

Thoits, Peggy. A. 1995. "Stress, Coping, and Social Support Processes: Where Are We? What Next?" *Journal of Health and Social Behavior* 36(Extra Issue):53–79.

Turner, Heather. 1994. "Gender and Social Support." *Sex Roles* 30:521–41.

Turner, R. Jay. and Franco Marino. 1994. "Social Support and Social Structure." *Journal of Health and Social Behavior* 35:193–212.

Turner, R. Jay, Blair Wheaton, and Donald Lloyd. 1995. "The Epidemiology of Social Stress." *American Sociological Review* 60:104–25.

Wellman, Barry. 1981. "Applying Network Analysis to the Study of Social Support." Pp. 171–200 in *Social Networks and Social Support,* edited by Benjamin Gottlieb. Beverly Hills, CA: Sage.

Wethington, Elaine and Ronald C. Kessler. 1986. "Perceived Support, Received Support and Adjustment to Stressful Life Events." *Journal of Health and Social Behavior* 27:78–89.

Wilcox, Brian L. 1981. "Social Support in Adjusting to Marital Disruption: a Network Analysis." Pp. 97–116 in *Social Networks and Social Support,* edited by Benjamin Gottlieb. Beverly Hills, CA: Sage.

Williams, Ann W., John W. Ware, and Cathy A. Donald. 1981. "A Model of Mental Health, Life Events, and Social Support Applicable to General Populations." *Journal of Health and Social Behavior* 22:324–36.

Williams, David R. and Chiquita Collins. 1995. "U.S. Socioeconomic and Racial Differences in Health: Patterns and Explanations." *Annual Review of Sociology* 21:349–86.

Nan Lin is Professor of Sociology and Director of the Asian/Pacific Institute at Duke University. His areas of research interests include: stress and coping, social capital, social networks, social stratification and mobility, and social transformation in China and Taiwan.

Xiaolan Ye is a doctoral candidate in the Department of Sociology at Duke University. Her major interests are the life course of stress process, social support and coping, social stratification, urban and rural life in China, and research methodologies.

Walter M. Ensel is a research Sociologist in the Department of Sociology and a senior Research Associate in the Center for Social and Demographic Analysis at the University of Albany. His current research focuses on the relationship between distal stressors and psychological well-being and the role played by psychosocial factors in the stress process.

PART III

STRATIFICATION IN CHINA

Nan Lin and the sociology of China

Yanjie Bian

The sociological imagination we all have learned from C. Wright Mills (1959) situates an individual biography in the historical process of a larger social context. In this chapter, I describe the post-1978 history in which sociology in China came to its rebirth and sociological research of Chinese society rose to global significance. Within this changing, larger social context, I offer a close observation on Nan Lin's timely and unique contributions to the reestablishment of Chinese sociology and the sociology of reform-era China. On his research contributions, I pay special attention to Chinese social stratification and Chinese social networks, the two areas of research in which Lin's creative scholarship has had the greatest impact.

The revival and development of Chinese sociology

Overview

Sociology was brought to China from Europe at the turn of the nineteenth to the twentieth century, and it quickly grew to be one of the main social sciences long before the 1949 Communist revolution (Bian 2009). In educational restructuring in 1952, however, Mao Zedong's new government terminated sociology being criticized as a "bourgeois" subject of study. Consequently, Chinese sociologists became a target of political tortures during the Anti-Rightists Movement of 1957 and the Cultural Revolution of 1966–76. A dramatic change occurred to Chinese sociology after the death of Mao in 1976; a few months following the announcement of a "reform-and-opening up" policy at the end of 1978, China's new paramount leader Deng Xiaoping called for the revival of sociology, along with political science, law study, and world politics, as the discipline was believed to be a useful, rather than disastrous, social science field for modernizing China (Deng 1994, pp. 180–81). The reestablishment of the Chinese Sociological Association (CSA) in March 1979 benchmarked the rebirth of Chinese sociology (Cheng and So 1983).

An elaboration of the term "Chinese sociology" is in order. For many career sociologists, sociology is the scientific study of society. To them, "Chinese" sociology is nonsense or fantasy; instead, "sociology in China" is the correct and preferable term used to address the discipline. That is an unfortunate arrogance. Sociology was born in Europe in 1839 and flourished in the United States after 1895. Over the twentieth century, American influence was felt in every sociological corner of the globe, even though there was political resistance as in the former Soviet Union shortly after the 1917 Russian revolution and in Mao's China. Nevertheless, the legacy of the American influence has caused reactions from non-Communist regimes as well, calling for the indigenization of sociology in their respective societies;

consequently, expressions like Canadian sociology, Japanese sociology, Taiwanese sociology – to name just a few, appeared in the titles of sociological journals.

This history has had a strong impact in China. China suffered from a series of post-1840 foreign military invasions, and the political-economic independence of the People's Republic of China has been a central ideology of the ruling Communist Party since 1949. Therefore, for many reasons the indigenization of sociology was a research topic of central attention at the very start of the reestablishment of CSA (Fei 1994), and continues to appear in the headline articles of leading Chinese sociology journals even today (Liang 2018; Xie 2018; Zhai 2018). Despite all these complications, for practical reasons here I use the term "Chinese sociology" to refer to the sociological discipline and community within China, and I use the term "sociology of China" to refer to sociological research on Chinese society in and outside the country.

Early initiatives

Fei Xiaotong was a key figure in the remaking of Chinese sociology. A sociology major in Beijing in the early 1930s, Fei enjoyed the lectures of, among others, Robert Park, a visiting professor from Chicago, and studied for his doctorate with Bronislaw Malinowski at the London School of Economics before a home return in 1939. With his field studies of rural villages and insightful analysis of Chinese society under transition from agriculture to industry, and for his popular essays combined with active political participation, Fei soon reached his national and international prominence as a leading Chinese sociologist and anthropologist. Unfortunately, due to a "rightist element" directly appointed by Mao in 1957, Fei was among the 300,000 intellectuals removed from their academic or leadership positions. During the Cultural Revolution of 1966–76, Fei lost his personal freedom, was forced to clean toilets as a daily duty in his school, was eventually sent to labor camps for years, and once contemplated suicide (Bian and Zhang 2008). By 1979, having survived all political tortures and personal persecution since 1957, Fei, at the age of 69, still held high his scholarly spirit to seek truth through science and was determined to devote the rest of his life to the revival and redevelopment of Chinese sociology.

Fei (1994, 1999) designed early initiatives which he vividly described as "five key institutions and six foundational courses" (五脏六腑, *wuzangliufu*). The five key institutions to be established were (1) professional associations for sociologists, (2) institutes through which to develop frontier research, (3) academic departments where sociology teaching and degrees are offered, (4) libraries and references centers, and (5) publishers to serve the discipline of sociology. While there was fear of the Maoist legacy that sociology was a bourgeois subject of study, Fei traveled around the country to mobilize interests to establish these institutions at national and provincial levels. Beijing, Tianjin, Shanghai, Guangdong, Jiangsu, Hubei, Liaoning, and Sichuan were among the very first provinces and municipalities to resume sociology research institutes, and Fudan, Zhongshan, Nankai, Peking, Renmin, and Nanjing universities were in the first wave to reestablish departments of sociology to offer undergraduate and graduate degrees in sociology. For teaching programs, Fei firmly believed that six foundational courses were essential: Introduction to Sociology, Social Research Methods, Social Psychology, Rural and Urban Sociology, Comparative Sociology, and Western Sociological Theories. Like others in his generation, Fei had lost track of nearly 30 years of intellectual progress outside China, and he thus felt the urgency of educating young students and nurturing young scholars, a top priority on the agenda of disciplinary revival and reconstruction.

As Fei's judgment was that no one within China could teach sociology at the time, his strategy was to invite established sociologists from around the globe to help train a new generation of Chinese sociologists. In the period of 1980–85, a score of leading sociologists and anthropologists were invited to China to teach full courses, offer public seminars, and conduct collaborative research in China. They include, to name just a few, Peter Blau (Columbia University), Peter Burgher (Boston University), Ken'ichi Fukunaga (Waseda University, Japan), Alex Inkeles (Stanford University), Chefu Lee (Catholic University of America), Nan Lin (SUNY Albany), William Parish (University of Chicago), Burton Pasternak (anthropologist, City University of New York), Alice Rossi (University of Massachusetts at Amherst), and C.K. Yang (University of Pittsburgh).

Two training programs were of historical significance. The first was a two-month summer school in Beijing in 1980 and 1981 (Li, 2000), to which some 100 middle-aged teachers and researchers from China's major universities and research institutes were invited to take sociology courses offered by C.K. Yang, Fei's college classmate and lifetime friend, his former Chinese students Rance Lee and C.K. Lau, then on the sociology faculty at the Chinese University of Hong Kong, and his University of Pittsburgh colleagues. From this summer school emerged a score of scholars immediately active in sociological research and education in China in the 1980s and 1990s.

The second training program was a yearlong coursework offered to a group of 40-plus college seniors selected from China's leading comprehensive universities, housed at Nankai University in Tianjin in the calendar year of 1981. Peter Blau (theory), Nan Lin (methods), and Chefu Lee (social statistics) were invited to teach this selected group, which was later known as the "1981 Nankai Class" (see Zhang [2016] for a detailed review), or the first cohort of post-Mao college graduates in sociology. From this class grew a large number of career sociologists, many became influential academics or public intellectuals, and about half took a department chair or school dean position to lead sociology programs throughout China. A few went abroad for doctoral studies and have since been active in sociological research and teaching around the world. The author of this article was one of the students in the 1981 Nankai Class, and he later became a doctoral advisee of Nan Lin's in the United States.

Nan Lin's timely contributions
Nan Lin was a perfect fit for helping to rebuild Chinese sociology. Born in the Chinese Mainland in 1938, Lin grew up in Taiwan, studied for his doctorate in the United States in the 1960s, and subsequently stayed in the country to develop a distinguished sociological career (Lin, Chapter 11 in this book). In light of changes in post-Mao China, Lin paid a private visit to his relatives in Beijing during the summer of 1979, only a few months after the reestablishment of the CSA. His identity as an American sociologist of Chinese origin was mysteriously made known to Fei Xiaotong and his colleagues, and almost immediately he was approached for an interview in his hotel room. In love with his motherland and having a passion for spreading sociological knowledge, Lin agreed to the request. The two-hour taped conversation in Mandarin Chinese went very well, even if it was with a total stranger who was full of primitive questions about sociology. How many career sociologists are there in the United States? What are the main topics of their theoretical and empirical studies? What are

the leading schools of thought in American sociology today? What are the required courses a sociology major must take before getting a degree? What jobs are available for college graduates with a sociology degree in the U.S.? How many years are required for the completion of a higher degree in sociology? And, after all, what are your suggestions for Chinese sociology? Combing Chinese politeness and American candidness, Lin's informed answers to these questions were obviously appreciated as a meeting with Fei was subsequently arranged, and Lin was warmly invited to contribute to the rebuilding of Chinese sociology in multiple ways.

One of the consequences of Lin's contact with Fei was his successful delivery of an introductory course on social research methods to the 1981 Nankai Class. The course was taught from mid-May to mid-June, five days a week, and the students were thirsty for every drop of juice from totally fresh lectures by Peter Blau on theory (in the mornings) and those by Nan Lin on methodology (afternoons). Keep in mind that the students in the class were majored in philosophy, economics, history, international politics, Chinese linguistics, or English literature, and they previously had taken no sociology course at all. Peter Blau, a master classroom lecturer on Marx, Durkheim, and Weber, was unfortunately frustrated by his first Chinese interpreter, who could handle no sociological vocabularies or phrases delivered in a strong Austrian accent. Happily, his second interpreter, a son of a pre-revolution landlord who studied English by memorizing entries of a few old dictionaries during the Cultural Revolution decade, did a terrific job and won the respect of Blau as well as all students. Nan Lin, as expected, lectured in Mandarin Chinese, and his clear instructions were immediately favored by the entire class. After nearly every lecture, Lin was surrounded by a crowd of his students asking questions about lectured contents. His lecture notes were compiled into a textbook-type manuscript, informally circulated beyond the 1981 Nankai Class, and quickly became a standard reading on social research methods throughout China.

Lin was not only a great classroom instructor, but he was an effective communicator and a forward-looking program initiator as well. The following is a list of some of the activities and programs Lin initiated with continuous and successful efforts of resource mobilization:

- August 1981, the North American Chinese Sociologists Association (NACSA) was established and Lin became the founding president. This association became a timely bridge of scholarly exchange with Chinese universities and research institutes. NACSA was renamed to ICSA (International Chinese Sociological Association) in 2018 and its annual mini-conferences prior to the annual meetings of the American Sociological Association continue to serve as a forum for scholarly exchange of frontier research on China.
- Summer 1982, Lin returned to Nankai University to offer a three-week seminar on advanced topics of social survey research to post-Mao China's first M.A. program in sociology; the fifteen students admitted to the program all came from the 1981 Nankai Class. Subsequently, most of the students pursued their doctoral degrees in the United States and China and became career sociologists.
- Summer 1983, he led a select group of NACSA members to offer a series of courses on sociology to one hundred of mid-age scholars invited to a second summer school of sociology in Wuhan (the first was in Beijing, 1980–81, organized by Fei Xiaotong). A

great majority of the students from this summer school became career sociologists to lead degree programs and research institutes throughout China.

- Summer 1984, through Lin's communicative efforts, Alice Rossi, the 1983–84 president of the American Sociological Association, led a formal delegation of American anthropologists and sociologists to China, paying visits to a handful sociology programs in Beijing, Tianjin, and Shanghai. Nan Lin, Victor Nee, William Parish, and Elena Yu were the China-studies experts on the delegation. At the universities and research academies to which they visited, the delegates delivered public talks and gave seminars. Consequently, Chinese sociology acquired an identity, Chinese sociologists began attending the annual meetings of the American Sociological Association, and Chinese institutions opened more channels through which to send their top students to the U.S. for degree programs in sociology.
- 1984, with Lin being the liaison, a scholarly exchange program between SUNY-Albany and Nankai University was signed into a formal agreement, through which the two campuses began to send each other young scholars and students for non-degree academic studies. This program was expanded in 1987 to allow for a select group of sociology graduate students at Nankai University to study for doctoral degrees at SUNY-Albany.
- 1985, Lin was in collaboration with the Tianjin Academy of Social Sciences to conduct the very first international collaborative survey project on "quality of life" in post-Mao Tianjin, the third largest city of China. This set up a model for a series of collaborative research projects between foreign sociologists and Chinese institutions to follow.
- Summer 1985 in conjunction with the annual meeting of the American Sociological Association in Washington D.C., through Lin's initiative and organization a special workshop was offered to Chinese doctoral students studying in the United States. The instructors included William Bielby, Judith Blake, Peter Blau, Donald Bogue, Lucie Cheng, Deborah Davis, Glen Elder, Burkart Holzner, Joan Huber, Alex Inkeles, Thomas Gold, Marshall Johnson, Wen Kuo, Che-Fu Lee, Nan Lin, William Parish, Alejandro Portes, Alice S. Rossi, Peter Rossi, H.Y. Tien, Donald Treiman, Yung-Mei Tsai, and Martin Whyte.
- 1986, with Lin's assistance, Peter Blau and Andrew Walder conducted their collaborative survey project with the Tianjin Academy of Social Sciences on "Social Networks and Work Life in Tianjin."
- 1988, Lin and Wen Xie, a former student from the 1981 Nankai Class and a doctoral student at Columbia University at the time, published an article "Occupational prestige in urban China" in the *American Journal of Sociology*, which kicked off a stream of publications on reform-era China in leading sociology journals in the United States (Bian 2000).
- 1988, through Lin's initiation and negotiation, the Ford Foundation implemented a research and training program in support of young Chinese sociologists, which Nan Lin and Deborah Davis served as co-directors in the first term and Richard Madsen and Jersey Liang in the second and last term. For over ten years, the program mounted annual training workshops and sponsored empirical studies in China. A good number of empirical sociologists were trained and retrained through this workshop series, and they were the initial core of China's quantitative sociologists in the 1980s and 1990s (see "The development of sociology in China: a delegation report" by Lin et al. 1992).

Four decades of fruitful development

All of these activities and programs were of tremendous help to the reestablishment and fast growth of Chinese sociology in the first decade of its redevelopment (see Rossi 1985; Lin et al. 1992). As of 2018, Chinese sociology is a fully-developed social science discipline, with 148 sociology departments to offer B.A. and M.A. degrees, more than 20 doctoral programs, the annual meeting of the CSA attended by more than 2,000 participants, and the annual number of graduates estimated at 4,000 with a sociology degree and 14,000 with a social work degree (Bian and Yang 2018). Meanwhile, sociology is a big grant category in the annual budget of China's Social Science Foundation, reaching 300 funded projects with 60 million *RMB* (roughly 10 million USD) allocated in 2017. Four public data archives (Chinese General Social Survey 2003–, Chinese Social Survey 2004–, Chinese Family Panel Study 2010–, and Chinese Labor Dynamic Survey 2012–) have been established by Chinese sociologists and these databases have sponsored more than 20,000 scholarly users around the world. Three sociology journals in Chinese language (社会学研究、人口研究、社会) are rated among the highest, each with an impact factor of more than 4.00, and three English-language sociology journals have each reached its international recognition (*Chinese Sociological Review*, *Chinese Journal of Sociology*, and *Journal of Chinese Sociology*).

The post-1979 development of sociological research within China has been impressive. Annual reviews of Chinese sociology have been a good resource to help us assess the growth of sociological research within China, and several most recent reviews of 40 years' development of Chinese sociology are timely available (Bian and Yang 2018; Li 2018). In English language, we have seen several periodical reviews of China-based sociological research by Cheng and So (1983), Rossi (1985), Lin et al. (1992), Zhou and Pei (1997), Bian (2003), and Bian and Zhang (2008). These reviews indicate that Chinese sociology had successfully made three transitions in the first three decades after its reestablishment. The first was the transition from ideological propaganda to studies of social issues and problems; studies of small towns, marriage and family, and rural–urban developments were of national influence to the making of state policies and laws (Fei 1999). The second was the transition from issue-oriented studies to theoretically-informed, evidence-based research programs; exemplary research programs included those on social stratification, socioeconomic transition, social networks, women and gender, and migration (Bian 2003). The third was the transition toward the institutionalization of creative scholarship by international standards. This includes the institutionalization of scholarly journals through the use of a double-blinded peer review system, the creation and dissimilation of public data archives, the annual review of sociology undergraduate teaching programs, and the periodic reviews of M.A. and Ph.D. degree programs in sociology (Li 2016).

The most recent decade has witnessed the development of sociological research in several directions. One direction is the emergence of critical sociology; some public intellectuals, including career and non-career sociologists, use sociological perspectives to discuss institutional problems sensitive to regime change. Sun Liping (2000), a former student from the 1981 Nankai Class, is among the very few to do this kind of critical sociology. Another direction is the officialization of academic sociology; salaried sociologists are mobilized to engage in government-sponsored research programs designed to help implement state and local policies, such as anti-poverty, social construction, and one-belt one-road strategy. Here, many of these research projects are under the umbrellas of social governance and social construction (Li 2016). Still another direction is the new orientation toward creating a sociological discourse to enhance China's self-confidence in its development path, institution building, theoretical construction, and cultural heritage. As stated by the current president of the CSA Li Youmei (2018), another former student from the 1981 Nankai Class, this sociological discourage is part of a bigger campaign to realize China's dreams for becoming a world power under Xi Jinping's leadership.

Sociological research of Chinese social stratification
The rise of the sociology of China in Western countries has been remarkable (Bian 2003). Four comprehensive reviews of English-language publications on China have appeared in the *Annual Review of Sociology* (Whyte et al. 1977; Walder 1989; Nee and Matthews 1996; Bian 2002), and a most recent review on China's inequality and social stratification is forthcoming in the same journal (Wu 2019). As evaluated in these authoritative reviews, Chinese social stratification is one of the most accomplished areas of research. Based on my earlier reviews (Bian 2002) and the most recent review by Wu (2019), I summarize several topics of research before discussing Nan Lin's pioneering contributions in this area.

Occupational prestige
Occupational prestige is an important angle to study social stratification in modern society (Treiman 1977). Maoism, nonetheless, totally rejected the notion of occupational prestige and its egalitarian ideology reached a historical momentum during the Cultural Revolution decade (Kraus 1981). But hard reality is an enlightening lesson for any conscious individuals. Shanghai high school seniors in the early 1980s, for example, held strong preferences for nonmanual jobs over manual jobs (Lan and Zhang 1982). Working adults, whether in China's capital Beijing (Lin and Xie 1988) or an industrial city Tianjin (Bian 1996), had no problem rating job titles into a prestige scale, even when income variation among occupations was small. When income variation grew substantially in the 1990s and thereafter, a quasi-national sample showed similar scaling results (Zhe and Chen 1995; Li 2005). As compared to the U.S. and most advanced countries (Blau and Duncan 1967; Treiman 1977), between-job variations in constructed prestige scales were attributable more to variation in education than in income (Lin and Xie 1988), a pattern that was also observed in the more industrialized, more globalized, capitalist Taiwan (Tsai and Chiu 1991). One consistent finding different from the U.S. was that nonmanual jobs required higher levels of education from job holders than manual jobs, and the former tended to be rated higher in prestige scales than the latter even if they might have been paid lower (Bian 1996). Another finding different from the U.S. was that occupational prestige was sensitive to economic sectors in which specific jobs are located; as of the first decade of the twenty-first century, more than two decades into market reforms, state sector jobs are still rated significantly higher than nonstate jobs even if these are on the same codes in the occupational classification (Li 2005).

Constructed prestige scales from these studies provided helpful measurement tools for examining Chinese occupational hierarchies, making it possible for comparative analysis with the United States (Blau and Ruan 1990) and elsewhere. Chinese prestige scales are comparable to those from the United States and to an international scale (Treiman 1977), seemingly confirming theories of modernization and societal convergence (Treiman 1970; Treiman and Yip 1989). These interpretations, however, may have overlooked an important Chinese characteristic: state allocation of resources led to the identification of work units, rather than occupations, as the primary measure of social status (Lin and Bian 1991). Because prestige scales are stable cross-nationally and over time, they are insensitive to the political dimensions of social mobility peculiar to Communism (Walder 1992, 1995) and to changes brought about by shifting state polices (Whyte and Parish 1984; Zhou et al. 1996, 1997). In current research, both prestige scales and occupational categories are utilized in empirical studies of Chinese social stratification and social mobility (see reviews by Bian 2002; Wu 2019).

Status attainment
Early efforts from urban-China surveys made modifications to standard status attainment models originated in the United States (Blau and Duncan 1967). These efforts suggest the existence of Communist regime-relevant measures of inheritance (family class origin), achievement (Communist party membership in addition to education), and socioeconomic status (work unit sector and rank in addition to the occupation of a wage job) (Parish 1981, 1984; Whyte and Parish 1984; Walder 1986, 1992; Lin and Bian 1991; Bian 1994). Later efforts with event history data found that the Cultural Revolution policies had reduced middle-class reproduction, that a "distrusted" family class origin significantly lowered one's chance of getting a state-sector job from 1949 to 1993, and that a superior education and Communist party membership increased one's chance of working in state organizations in which desirable jobs were located in post-1949 urban China (Zhou et al. 1996, 1997).

Walder (1995) argues that Communist party membership and education are qualitatively different credentials. His 1986 Tianjin survey with Peter Blau shows that individuals with superior education often become professional elite with high social prestige, while individuals with both educational credentials and party membership tend to enter an administrative elite enjoying high levels of social prestige, authority, and material privileges. A 1996 national survey shows that professional and administrative careers have been separated from Mao's era onward, party membership has never been a criterion for the attainment of professional positions, and a college education did not become a criterion for an administrative position until the post-Mao period (Walder et al. 2000). Party organization preferentially sponsors young members for adult education and eventually promotes them into leadership positions (Li and Walder 2001).

A few other studies have pointed to both stability and change in China's politicized social mobility regime. Zang (2001), compiling scattered sources into a unique profile of 757 (in 1988) and 906 (in 1994) central and local government officials, shows that college education allows cadres to climb upwardly in both party and state job tracks, but party seniority gives them the advantage of holding positions of political authority. Bian et al. (2001) argue that membership loyalty is both an organizational imperative and a survival strategy for any communist party and show that in Tianjin and Shanghai political screening led, from 1949 to 1993, to attainment of party membership and promotion into positions of political and managerial authority. Zhou (2001) argues that the political dynamics induced by shifting state policies cause bureaucratic career patterns to vary over time, and his 1994 multicity survey shows that Chinese bureaucrats in the Mao and post-Mao periods have distinctive characteristics. Cao's (2001) comparative analysis of Shanghai and Guangzhou has found a pattern of change within the state sector: the effects of human capital on career mobility are constant between profit-oriented firms and nonprofit organizations in less marketized

Shanghai, yet increased market competition in Guangzhou leads to a finding that human capital is a stronger determinant of the success of career mobility in profit-oriented firms than in nonprofit organizations.

Increased inequalities

China produced an average 8 percent annual growth of gross domestic product (GDP) from 1978 to 2017, and in the same period its per capita disposable income jumped from an extremely low level to 58 percent of the world average (World Bank 2018). In the meantime, China's income inequality increased from 0.24 on the Gini index in the late 1970s to a sustainable level of around 0.50 in the twenty-first century (Bian et al. 2018b). A significant portion of income inequality was due to "categorical differences" measured by regions, rural–urban localities, and industrial sectors (Wang 2008), and the rural–urban gap only began to decline around 2014 when the household registration system (*hukou*) was reformed to relax residential restrictions (Wu 2015).

Housing inequality has significantly increased since rapid privatization implemented in the 1988–98 decade. While public housing rent in towns and cities was 1 or 2 percent of household income in Mao's regime (Logan and Bian 1993), in 2000 a home of 100 square meters in an apartment building in Shanghai, for example, could cost 600,000 to 800,000 RMB, or 30 to 40 years of average income (Fraser 2000). Housing prices in frontier cities continued to increase in the first and second decades of the twenty-first century, although homes in city outskirts, smaller cities, and less developed inland cities are considerably less expensive (Logan 2018). Buyers with no cash ability can take mortgage loans from a designated state bank to pay for a new home, but a prerequisite is that their work units or private employers have deposited a proportion of employee income as housing reserve funds in the bank on behalf of their employees. While government offices and nonprofit organizations (containing 10 percent of state jobs) can secure such funds in state budgetary allocations, many state-owned enterprises, most private firms, and virtually all household businesses do not do so (Davis 1999). This enhanced housing inequality by work sector and created the new urban and rural poor, an area for targeted poverty reduction under Xi Jinping's administration (Bian et al. 2018b).

Research on gender inequality has generated mixed and inconclusive results (Entwisle and Henderson 2000). Significant improvements in rural and urban women's employment and income were observed in Mao's era (Whyte 1984), especially women's gains in basic education (Hannum and Xie 1994), and the growth of market economies after reforms created off-farm employment opportunities for rural women, narrowing the gender gap in pay as well as household status (Matthews and Nee 2000). However, the rising market gradually eroded the power of the state both as employer and as advocate for women's rights and led to labor market discrimination against female workers in hiring and layoffs, job placement, and wage determination in state and especially the booming private sector, thus lowering the status of women relative to men both in the workplace and domestic sphere (Honig and Hershatter 1988; Shu et al. 2013). To address these conflicting results, Whyte (2000) suggests that future researchers must carefully identify a realm of research, must utilize a well-defined set of indicators and measures, and must rely on comparable and systematic data.

Efforts of explanation

How market reforms have reshaped the pattern of inequality and social stratification has been a hotly debated issue in the sociological research of reform-era China (see reviews by Nee and Matthews 1996; Bian 2002; Keister and Borelli 2012; Wu 2019). Nee's (1989) "market transition theory" argues for the declining significance of political power and the increasing significance of human capital in income distribution. The theory gains empirical support from a 1985 Fujian survey of rural households (also see Nee 1991, 1996; Nee and Cao 1999; Matthews and Nee 2000). However, city-based and nationally representative surveys show increasing income returns to both education and political power over time, indicating the coexistence and coevolution of market and political forces in maintaining and increasing income inequalities (Bian and Logan 1996; Parish and Michelson 1996; Xie and Hannum 1996; Zhou 2000). Even in rural areas political power is a significant source of inequality since the growing nonagricultural industry gives village cadres the control over economic resources that generate higher income for themselves (Walder 2002).

Going beyond the theoretical framework of the market transition debate, most recent research in the field has advanced by paying attention to two socialist institutions still influential in reform-era social stratification, namely the household registration (*hukou*) and urban work unit (*danwei*) systems. Several findings are reviewed here. First, returns to education did not monotonically increase in the state-sector work units when bonuses, an increasingly significant portion of work compensation in more marketized firms, were more equally distributed up to the early 1990s (Xie and Hannum 1996; Wu 2002). Second, rapid privatization through the "grab the big, release the small" policy in the late 1990s had restructured the work unit system into the state monopoly sector (along with government agencies and nonprofit state organizations) and the market competitive sector, but inequality persisted between them favoring the former over the latter (Wu 2002, 2013). Third, not only are opportunities for attaining higher education and Communist party membership in favor of urbanites over rural residents (Wu and Treiman 2004, 2007), returns to education and Communist party membership differ significantly between rural and urban *hukou* holders (Xiao and Bian 2018). Finally, as rural migrant workers became a large proportion of urban labor force, many local governments continue to employ *hukou* status as the explicit basis for providing subsidies, welfare and public service, thus causing systematic "institutional discrimination" against migrants without local hukou in sectorial placement and job assignment (Wu and Song 2014). An urban *hukou* premium is found between rural-to-urban *hukou* converters and non-convertors (Wu and Zheng 2018).

Another line of analysis is the process of finding employment between a small privileged state sector and the expanding yet diversified private sector. While early entrants into the private sector had neither higher earnings nor higher returns to education than those who remained in the state sector, later entrants showed both higher earnings premium and higher returns to education when they were voluntary rather than forced to leave the state sector (Wu and Xie 2003). This implies that market alone generates no higher earnings nor higher return to education, but the macro-level market forces are contingent upon both worker characteristics and labor market structure to make a difference. Quantitatively, nearly half of the growth in earnings inequality from 1996 to 2010 was due to increased returns to education, with the other half due to the shrinkage of the public sector and a surge in rural-to-urban migration (Zhou 2014).

The availability of nationally representative household surveys has been behind the new advancement just described. The market transition debate in the 1980s and 1990s was generated among researchers who relied on local or regional sample surveys, whose limited sampling scope and varying research designs were partly the reason for producing conflicting results. Starting in the second part of the 1990s throughout the first two decades of the twenty-first century, China-based researchers began working closely with leading scholars in the area of social stratification and inequality around the world in generating public data archives made available internationally, providing several solid, variable-rich data sets to allow for an innovative and systematic analysis of relevant issues. These public data archives include the Life Histories and Social Change in Contemporary China project (LHSCC), completed in 1996 (Treiman and Walder 1996); the Chinese Household Income Project (CHIP), launched 1988 and conducted every four to five years (Li et al. 2013), the Chinese General Social Survey (CGSS), launched in 2003 and modelled after the U.S. General Social Survey (Bian and Li 2012), the China Family Panel Studies (CFPS), launched in 2010, which represents the burgeoning interest in collecting panel data in China (Xie and Hu 2014); and China's Labor Dynamics Survey, launched in 2012, which is another panel study design targeting wage earners and their household members (Liang et al. 2015).

Lin's pioneering contributions
In China in the 1980s, social stratification was a topic of popular discourses concerning whether market reforms might generate new forms of inequality as observed in capitalist societies. To the rising sociological research of Chinese social stratification, Lin has made three pioneering contributions, each having an eye-opening and lasting impact on later researchers. The first is his pioneering study of Chinese occupational prestige based on a probability sample survey (Lin and Xie 1988). Although a Chinese-language paper on the topic was published a few years earlier (Lan and Zhang 1982), it was a descriptive report about high school students' aspirations toward desirable jobs. In sharp contrast, the article by Lin and Xie was an analytical piece, delivering the first statistically-rigorous study of occupational prestige in reform-era urban China. Inspired by Lin's lectures on the topic in the 1981 Nankai Class, two students from the class (Wen Xie and Zhaokai Xuan) conducted the Beijing survey on occupational prestige in 1983. Lin was in a position to advise the design of the Beijing survey by modeling after the standard occupational prestige study originated in the United States. First, 50 job titles were selected through a probability procedure by using the Occupational Classification of the 1982 Chinese census. Second, on the questionnaire a five-level rating scale was used to evaluate each job title from "very good" to "not good at all." Third, raters were adults randomly selected from the Beijing residential population. Finally, using this well-designed survey Lin and Xie (1988) presented a systematic analysis of Chinese occupational prestige, providing not only the results on ranked job titles but also explanations of why certain jobs were rated higher than others as compared to the ratings from advanced industrial societies. The authors also generated the very first equation of Chinese socioeconomic status, which was used to calculate ranking scores for all jobs in China. The work presented in the Lin-Xie article has since been followed up by later researchers of Chinese occupational prestige (Zhe and Chen 1995; Bian 1996; Li 2005).

The second is Lin's pioneering research of status attainment in urban China (Lin and Bian 1991). Before Lin's study on China, status attainment research followed Blau and Duncan's

(1967) classic model on how factors of ascription and achievement affect an individual's status attainment, with the attention paid to such status indicators as education and occupation as observed in the United States and other advanced capitalist countries. Lin and Bian point to the structural differences in resource allocation between advanced capitalism and state socialism. They argue that structural segmentation is a universal phenomenon in all complex societies and across political economies. But each political economy uses specific criteria in delineating segments of its economic organizations. In China, state-tailored resources are vertically allocated through work-unit organizations, and consequently work-unit sectors become a critical socioeconomic status for individuals to achieve under state socialism. Lin's 1985 Tianjin survey is analyzed to show that entrance into the core sectors (state agencies and enterprises), rather than the job per se, constitutes the primary goal of status attainment. Mobility from the peripheral to the core sector, moreover, is an important pathway for one's job change from a lower occupational status to a higher one. Finally, gender inequality is not just measured by job placement but more affected by a differential process into the core sectors. These are pathbreaking arguments and empirical findings, which have encouraged numerous studies of work-unit segmentation as an underlying logic of social stratification and mobility under traditional (Walder 1992; Logan and Bian 1993; Bian 1994; Davis 1995; Zhou et al. 1996, 1997) and reforming state socialism (Bian and Logan 1996; Bian and Zhang 2002; Wu 2002, 2013; Wu and Xie 2003; Xie and Wu 2008; Lin et al. 2014a).

Finally, the third is his pioneering effort for opening up the channels through which to conduct representative sample surveys in China. In the 1980s and 1990s, foreign scholars were not permitted to conduct survey research anywhere in China, and entering the twenty-first century a statistical law was made and enforced to prohibit and, if any, punish the "illegal" implementation of social surveys by overseas involvements without official approval. But such approval is always hard, if not impossible, to obtain. Lin's 1985 Tianjin survey was a collaborative project with the Tianjin Academy of Social Sciences. In an officially approved operation, Lin constructed the questionnaire, designed the sampling procedure, and financed the data collection, and his collaborator was granted the total responsibility for implementing the survey and invited to work with Lin on the data set. Since this operational procedure worked for both sides, it became the standard model for many later researchers to follow. Lin had timely raised his voice for a GSS-type of national sample survey to be implemented in China (Lin et al. 1992), and he made efforts for conducting a series of multiple-wave, topic-focused national representative surveys on comparative social capital in the United States, China, and Taiwan (Lin et al. 2014a). All of these pioneering efforts paved the way for later researchers to conduct nationally representative surveys, and he lent his hands, in roles as a connector, a consultant, or a formal advisor, to several of these surveys, such as the Tianjin-Shanghai survey in 1993 (Bian and Logan 1996), the 17-city survey in 1994 (Zhou et al. 1996), the LHSCC project in 1996 (Treiman and Walder 1996), the Health and Family Life Survey in 1999–2000 (Parish et al. 2004), the CGSS in 2003 (Bian and Li 2012), and the CLDS project in 2012 (Liang et al. 2015). Looking at today's availability of public survey data archives which make it possible and convenient for conducting quantitative analysis of reform-era China, we owe a big thank-you to Lin for his direct and indirect contributions one way or another.

Sociological research of Chinese social networks

Social networks are of central importance to Chinese society. On the eve of 1949 Communist Revolution, Morton Fried (1953) observed that the networks of kinship and social relationships were the "fabric" of Chinese society, in which valued resources and collective actions were organized and mobilized through the network channels of kinships, friendships, neighbors, and villagers. The centrality of the networks of kinship and social relationships was found to have continued in China after 1949 (Yang 1959; Walder 1986; Yang 1994; Yan 1996; Bian 1997; Lin 2001c). In reform-era China, networks of ongoing relationships play an influential role in job allocation, business founding and development, the legal sphere, and local and national politics (Bian 2019).

Fei Xiaotong (1947) developed a theory of the "mode of differential associations" to explain the centrality of *guanxi*, or personalized social relations, to Chinese culture and society, and the influence of this theory is widespread in the social sciences in general and sociology in particular as of today. A decade earlier, American sociologist Sutherland (1939) developed a differential association theory to explain the ways in which criminal behavior is learned from others with whom a subject is associated through intimate ties. These two theories of differential association were developed independently from one another, although in their respective countries both were part of the scholarly roots of social network analysis (SNA) which rose as a new analytical paradigm in the U.S. in the 1970s. It is Nan Lin, a world authority in the SNA field, who both introduced the SNA knowledge system to reform-era China and pioneered a SNA approach to the sociological research of social and institutional change of Chinese society (Bian and Ikeda 2014). The flourishment of *guanxi* and SNA studies in China today are due, to a significant extent, to the original contributions of Fei's and Lin's, and my review in this section starts with them.

The mode of differential associations: Fei's network theory

"The mode of differential associations" is my translation of Fei's original Chinese phrase "差序格局" (*cha xugeju*). Elsewhere, the phrase was translated as "the differential mode of association" (Fei 1992) or "the configuration of differentiated associations" (Yan 1996). None of these translations, including my own, can be understood without elaboration because an equivalent phrase is unavailable in the English-language literature in sociology or anthropology. To me, what Fei meant by the phrase is what we describe in today's SNA terminology as a system or structure emerging from "the overlapping of egocentric networks."

Fei's original vision was brilliant and pathbreaking. In the 1930s, Fei learned much from his American and British teachers about a positional approach to defining social structure as groups of interest-oriented individuals, or in his words "团体格局" (the mode of grouped individuals). In this group-based social structure, argued Fei, individuals are recognized for their equal citizen-rights as well as their private interests as the primary order of social organization, and individuals with similar interests are socially grouped together to exercise their rights and realize their interests, structurally leading to the emergence of individualism as a moral system in society at large. While this group-based social structure matched Fei's observation on Western societies such as the U.K. and the U.S., it did not at all fit his image of Chinese social structure. For him, social structure in rural China was fundamentally different; it had never been group-based, but instead it had since before the Qin dynasty been based on the overlapping of egocentric networks of family, kinship, and extended particular ties.

Writing originally in a popular essay for a newspaper, Fei used a metaphor to describe his ideas. When a rock (the ego) is thrown into a lake (society), circles (networks) of water ripples (relationships with significant others) will be made and pushed by the rock from the center to the periphery, with the magnitudes of water ripples changing from thick (stronger ties closer to the ego) to thin (weaker ties distant from the ego). The circles of water ripples as a whole look like a cobweb, elaborated by Fei, and this cobweb is like the web of social relations for all villagers. In a village community, Fei argued, each individual makes his own network of stronger and weaker ties through which to learn about how to perform in social roles, to mobilize resources via favor exchanges with closer and distant others of social relevance, and thus to realize their private interests and satisfy private needs. The descriptions in parentheses above are mine to help readers understand what Fei implied in his metaphorical analysis.

Fei maintained that this egocentric network had a fundamental implication for how a village community or the entire traditional Chinese society was structured. For him, the ego and his/her alters are not aware of "citizen rights" but know each other very well in terms of family, kinship, and extended particular ties that connect them. Structurally, the underlying logic of a village community as a social system does not lie in the patterned arrangements of social positions occupied by villagers, but instead is in the overlapping of egocentric networks of villagers. At this point, Fei coined the phrase "the mode of differential associations" to define Chinese social structure.

Fei forcefully argued that the social structure of differential associations has no way of generating a Westernized version of "individualism" (个人主义, *gerenzhuyi*). A moral system of individualism recognizes citizens' private rights and interests as the underlying logic of social structure. In sharp contrast, what emerges from the social structure of differential associations is a moral system of "egoism" (个体主义, *getizhuyi*) in which selfishness drives the dynamics of egocentric networks of particular ties. For Fei, egoists are totally different from individualists because egoists have no "society" in mind but care only about the personally networked communities around them. These personal communities are adjustable in size and composition depending on the ego's needs to keep alters of social relevance in his network. In Fei's view, a universal notion of public morality never has existed in Chinese society, which has been full of relational morality of particularism.

The contemporary significance of Fei's network theory

To be sure, Chinese society today is full of the personally networked communities of Fei's characterization. There are many examples that can be cited here to qualify this proposition. Villages that were studied by Yang (1959), Jacobs (1979), Yan (1996), Kipnis (1997), Michelson (2007), and Chang (2010) are all a rich source of evidence on how *guanxi* networks of villager ties rule in socioeconomic exchanges, political governance, and legal processes in rural communities. Mao's factories studied by Walder (1986), on the other hand, show how Communist cadres formed patron–client networks of trust–loyalty bonds with political activists through which to allocate economic incentives and exercise political control on the shop floor. For China under reform today, Bian (2019) presents systematic evidence on how *guanxi* networks of particular ties have become the effective informal structures through which to obtain desirable jobs (Chapter 3 in Bian 2019), start businesses (Chapter 4), govern and develop organizations (Chapter 5), and secure opportunities of career advancement in various domains of society (Chapter 6).

There is a structural reason why China today, rural and urban, is still a *guanxi* society. The reason is, I argue, that any larger society of interest-oriented, rational strangers is ruled through personally networked communities of governing elites. Giddens (2001) defines governing elites as the uniform elites holding hegemonic power or the established elites holding democratic power. China's Communist cadres fit Giddens's first type of governing elites, as they are missioned to govern a village, a school, a university, a company, a corporation, or a certain level of government by following the uniform rules of the central government under the hegemonic Communist party-state. Yet governing elites in various domains of Chinese society and at different levels of the government hierarchy cannot perform their jobs without densely networked communities around them. A local official wanting to win a promotion competition, for example, forms a canvassing net consisting of his or her deputies, superiors, relatives, close subordinates, and equal-ranking colleagues to work for him or her. This canvassing net is also the personally networked community through which any Communist cadre performs his or her governing job every day (Feng 2010). In fact, governing a society of citizens or managing a sizable organization of employees is always done through the personally networked communities of governing elites, whether the society or organization in question is a public entity or a private venture. Consequently, Fei's image of the overlapping of egocentric networks of particular ties is of contemporary significance in every corner of Chinese society today.

Research conducted by China-based sociologists has presented systematic evidence in support of my argument. Sun (1996) observed that when resources were allocated through the bureaucratic system of work units in Mao's era, an ordinary worker could obtain these resources through two channels: the "vertical" channel of trust–loyalty relations with superiors within one's own work unit, and the "horizontal" channel of direct or indirect ties to redistributors of other work units. Sun argued that this overlapping of the vertical and horizontal channels is the basic social structure through which to obtain vertically allocated resources in all post-Mao regimes. Lin and Chen (1999) observed that in Chinese villages and townships under reform, particular ties of high intimacy were the basic social structures through which to realize the private interests of individuals, who then made efforts to construct and reconstruct their *guanxi* networks of particular ties. One explanation of why Fei's mode of differential associations still rules village communities under reform is that villages are not only interpersonally networked communities but also the power structures through which to allocate lands and other basic rural resources (He 2007). Even in a larger society of urbanites, *guanxi* networks are extended from personal worlds to invade the "small" publics within which to satisfy people's basic needs (Xiao 2014) under the ethics of affection, sharing, and reciprocity (Zhou 2017).

Social network analysis as a sociological paradigm: Lin's influence

Fei's "mode of differential associations" was an indigenous network theory, but it had nothing to do with such standard SNA terms as network ties, density, centrality, closure, and brokerage, which were nonexistent in Chinese sociology in the 1980s. Nan Lin is both the very first to teach social network analysis in China and the very first to conduct social network studies in the country. These studies include the 1985 Tianjin survey, the observational study of

Daqiuzhuang village, and the China–Taiwan–America survey of social networks and social capital (Lin 2001a; Lin and Ao 2008). Among several significant achievements is the development of a role-relation measurement and its application to the research of job-search networks and status attainment. His 1985 Tianjin survey shows that while kinship and friendship ties were more frequently used to help Chinese youths secure jobs than were acquaintance ties, it was acquaintance ties through which they obtained desirable jobs in the resource-richer state sector in the 1980s (Lin and Bian 1991). While this result confirms the American findings about the strength of weak ties in channeling labor market information and mobilizing broadly defined social resources, it has encouraged future researchers to conduct a series of follow-up studies, in which strong ties proved to be more effective in providing jobs as a substantive favor to those in need (Bian 1997, 2018; Bian and Huang 2009).

A score of Lin's former Chinese students have followed in his footsteps to specialize in the SNA research of Chinese social networks, and there is also a good number of established social network researchers who have been well-connected with him. For a couple of decades now, these SNA researchers have all conducted empirical studies about Chinese social networks whether they are based in North America (Bian 1997, 2019; Chen 2015; Chen et al. 2017; Fu and Lin 2013, 2014; McDonald et al. 2015; Song 2015b; Song et al. 2017), China (Dan Ao, see Lin and Ao 2008; Tian and Lin 2016; Zhang and Lin 2016), Hong Kong (Lai et al. 2015; Ruan 1998), Singapore (Son 2013, forthcoming), or Taiwan (Jay Chih-jou Chen in collaboration with Lin and Fu, as in Fu 2005, 2009; Hsung and Breiger 2013; Lin et al. 2014a). The scholarship achievements of these researchers are a marker of Lin's fruitful influence, continuous mentorship, and close collaboration.

Lin's conceptualization of guanxi

Guanxi is a colloquial term that has generated multiple understandings. Before Lin's (2001c) conceptualization, two "schools of thought" (Bian 2001) were influential in China area studies. The first school of thought argues that the family is the core of social structure and the original source of social relations in Chinese society. Consequently, *guanxi* is understood as the web of extended familial ties, familial sentiments, and familial obligations. When social relationships share familial sentiments and obligations, they transform into "pseudo familial relationships." Proponents of this conception include, in the Chinese-language literature, such influential scholars as Fei Xiaotong (1947), Liang Shuming (1949), and Ambrose King (1985, 1994), and, in English, Morton H. Fried (1953) and C.K. Yang (1959).

The second school of thought considers *guanxi* as exchange networks of instrumental particular-ties (Walder 1986; Hwang 1987; Yang 1994). This view does not automatically reject the idea that *guanxi* is a web of extended familial sentiments and obligations; here, instead, the defining character of *guanxi* is the instrumentality of particular ties (familial ties included) that facilitate favor exchanges. The shift in emphasis on instrumental particular ties points to a different set of implications: the relational bases of *guanxi* include a broad range of durable connections, reciprocity for favor exchanges becomes a primary rule of *guanxi* networks (Hwang 1987), and the goals of networking have shifted from extending ties of familial sentiments and obligations to cultivating ties of diverse resources for mutual favor exchanges (Yang 1994).

Lin's (2001c) conceptualization represents the third school of thought about *guanxi*. In "*Guanxi*: a conceptual analysis" Lin takes a SNA perspective and defines *guanxi* as social exchange networks of asymmetric transaction. According to him, economic and social exchanges differ in one significant distinction: whereas the former is symmetric, the latter asymmetric. In a social exchange, resources flow from a favor-giver to a favor-receiver, but the favor-giver gains the recognition of being resourceful and increasing his/her network centrality. "It is the relationship that is valued and must be maintained, not the value of the favor transacted per se"; thus, "instrumental action becomes the means and *guanxi* [building] becomes the end" (Lin 2001c, p. 122). In this conceptualization, the relational bases of *guanxi* become very broad, including all kinds of kin and non-kin relations. The key source of *guanxi* capital is neither the reputation of fulfilling moral obligations to family and pseudo-families, nor the reputation for keeping promises in favor exchanges; after all, resource transactions in social exchanges are asymmetric. Instead, *guanxi* capital lies in one's reputation as a generous favor-giver and a network bridge to resourceful ties. In this context, face – the Chinese version of social capital – can be reinterpreted: Face giving means lending access to connections, and face receiving means getting access to connections. Expectedly, granting favors (access to connections) is the best strategy to maintain one's networks and enhance one's capacity of accumulating *guanxi* capital.

Lin's (2017) most recent effort is to extend from his earlier work and develop a sentiment-based theoretical framework on *guanxi*. This framework is centered on the notion of *guanxi* as a sentimental relationship through which favor seeker and favor granter are involved in a social exchange process. Sentiment is the fundamental element in a *guanxi* relationship, and without sentiment the relationship either is nonexistent or becomes dissolved. The centrality of sentiment to a *guanxi* relationship helps explain the pattern and manifestations of *guanxi* practices in Chinese society, such as the art of *guanxi* in the case of "pulling *guanxi*" (Yang 1994) and resource mobilization via the overlapped egocentric networks as described in the theory about the "mode of differential associations" (Fei 1992 [1947]).

Lin's model on local market socialism

Rural industrialization has played a significant role in China's economic takeoff. Township and village enterprises (TVEs), a central element of China's rural industrialization, experienced tremendous development during the early reforms in the 1980s, growing from 1.5 million in 1978 to 12 million in 1985. Their economic outputs increased from 37 percent of agricultural GDP in 1978 to 104 percent in 1987. As of 2006, TVEs hired 29 percent of the rural labor force, made 69 percent of rural economic value, and accounted for 29 percent of China's total GDP (Naughton 2006). How do we explain the social mechanisms through which TVEs emerged, operated, and grew?

Seeking empirical clues to these questions, Lin (1995) conducted an in-depth study of one of China's most successful TVEs, the corporation of *Daqiuzhuang* village (大邱庄). It is located in north China, 80 kilometers south of Tianjin. The village head and Party secretary Yu Zuomin had been the chairman of the corporation, with one of his sons serving as the CEO and president. Other members of the Board of Trustees were vice presidents of the corporation and CEOs of the five component companies of the corporation, all of them being Yu's other sons, sons-in-law, cousins, grandsons, or close confidants. Clearly kinship networks function as the governance structure of Daqiuzhuang corporation, exemplifying Boisot and Child's (1996) clan model of network capitalism.

Lin's emphasis on kinship networks as governance structure of TVEs was reinterpreted by Peng (2004) who studied a large number of TVEs. In the absence of property rights laws, argues Peng, TVEs rely on kinship networks in producing and enforcing informal norms and asset protection. In villages where rural industrialization take place, kin solidarity and kin trust played an important role in protecting the property rights of private entrepreneurs and reducing transaction costs during the early stages of market reform, when formal property rights laws were ineffective and market institutions underdeveloped. An analysis of 366 villages throughout China shows two pieces of supportive evidence. First, in villages where a large lineage becomes dominant, private enterprises are likely to emerge and survive. Second, in these villages, private enterprises are highly likely to grow in size and maintain a stable market position. These effects are insignificant for collective enterprises.

Lin's theory of centrally-managed capitalism
How do we explain the pattern of market economy with Chinese characteristics? To be certain, we have learned diverse perspectives from a score of influential sociologists. Nee's (1989, 1991, 1996) market transition theory points to the shift of dominant stratification mechanisms from political power to human capital during market reforms. Walder (1992, 1995, 2002) examines Chinese social stratification from the perspectives of property rights and regime change in Communist cadre's power over public property. Bian and Logan (1996) emphasize the stability of China's political institutions and its resulted implications of power persistence. Zhou (2000) argues for the coexistence of interest politics and market growth and calls for attention to their interactive effects on stratification dynamics. Wu and Xie (2003) have considered the self-selective nature of people going into the private sector and demonstrated that market generates differential returns for education between earlier and later goers. Finally, the network capitalism perspective (Boisot and Child 1996) acknowledges the roles of government and networks of patronage ties between state officials and economic actors. Recognizing China's strong party-state is the point of departure for Lin's (2011) "centrally-managed capitalism" perspective.

For Lin, there is no doubt that China has developed capitalistic capacities (private property rights, international joint ventures, banking system, labor markets, etc.). Along with market growth, however, the party-state has, he argues, increasingly tightened control of the economy and synchronized political and economic stratification. Two elements are key to this centrally-managed capitalism (CMC) perspective. First, the party-state itself acts as a capitalist. The party-state "commands the economy by controlling personnel, organizations, and capital in both political and economic arenas. At the same time, it delegates fiscal and administrative authorities to multiple and diversely formed corporations to compete in the marketplace" (Lin 2011, p. 63). Second, economic activities are heavily embedded in *guanxi* networks. Ties to government officials at all levels, for example, are the key channels through which to acquire economic resources (Li et al. 2011), operate business groups (Keister 2000), and govern relational contracts (Zhou et al. 2003). "The combination of state guidance with informal *guanxi* enables Chinese businesses to connect with each other and with officialdom at various levels and build trust and harmony for long-term mutual benefit and stability in both business and social aspects" (Wang and Rowley 2016, p. 110).

Lin's tri-society project on social capital

In studying China, Lin has never deviated himself from an empiricism-oriented theorist position. This position gives him the vantage point of conducting comparative analysis of his social capital theory, and his study sites are the United States, China, and Taiwan. Sponsored by Taiwan's Academia Sinica, Lin led a group effort to conduct the tri-society project on a comparative analysis of social capital with the first wave survey in 2004–2005. Based on a refined position generator and a probability sample design, the project collected data about the origins and consequences of social capital in Taiwan, China, and the United States. This valuable data set is publicly available (www.soc.duke.edu/socialcapital) and has been analyzed in a series of scholarly publications, providing an insightful analysis into relation-specific social capital among the three societies (Hsung and Breiger 2013; Lin and Ao 2008; Lin et al. 2010, 2014a). A summary of the three most significant achievements from the tri-society project is as follows.

The first is an occupational position generator of social capital across the three societies. The key idea about the position generator, originated in Lin's earlier U.S. study, is that the ongoing networks of social relations allow people to access a variety of social positions through which to mobilize social resources or social capital from connected others. For the tri-society project, Lin and his colleagues selected 22 job titles, which cover a whole range of the occupational hierarchies across the three societies. Each job title is assumed to represent a distinctive social position, thus the social capital that is embedded in that position. In addition, they identified 18 relations common to the people of the three societies, and each relation is assumed to have the potential to access and mobilize social capital that is embedded in the occupations of connected others. The survey respondents were asked whether or not they had known someone ("social contact" so to speak) in each of the 22 job titles, and when a positive answer was given, the respondents were further asked to identify their relation with the social contact and his/her personal attributes. For each respondent, this results in an occupation by relation matrix. This matrix data allows for an analysis of cross-society variation in relational access to occupation-embedded social capital.

The second is a systematic analysis of cross-society variations in prominent relational types. East Asian social networks are thought to be centered on the family and close kin ties. This proposition implies that the family and close kin ties may produce a greater amount of occupation-embedded social capital than other types of social relations in Taiwan and China than in the United States. Lin and his colleagues presented a clear set of empirical results which, unexpectedly, do not lend support to this hypothesis. Individuals in the United States produce greater social capital through spouses, children, and close kin ties than those in Taiwan and China, and the same is also true about social capital production through friends. That is, the production of social capital through spouses, children, close kin, and friends follows the order of U.S.>Taiwan>China. This is just opposite to a long-standing hypothesis about the instrumental values of the family and close kin in Chinese societies. Following the same analytic strategies, Lin and his colleagues also reported that social capital production through coworkers, neighbors, and distant kin follow the rank order of Taiwan>China>U.S. Finally, associational relations produce the greatest social capital for Taiwanese people, followed by the Chinese and Americans, and school relations produce the great social capital for Chinese people, followed by the Taiwanese and Americans.

The third is a theoretical account of cross-society variation in social capital production. Three explanations have been offered by Lin and his associates to make sense about the cross-society variations in social capital production just reviewed. These explanations point to cross-societal variations in economic structures (industrialization and marketization), socio-cultural institutions (Confucianism and Christianity), and political-economic regimes (capitalism and post-socialism). In the U.S., kin ties, friends, work ties, and other ties are distinctive types of social relations, and friends and other ties, rather than kin ties or work ties, exert stronger effects on social capital production. In China, kin ties, friends, and other ties are interrelated, and share effects on social capital production. In Taiwan, kin ties, friends, and other ties still overlap but to a lesser extent than they exhibit in China, and the relative effect of kin ties on social capital has eased up relative to the effects of work ties, friends, and other ties. Cultural and institutional context has the potential to moderate life course patterns of social interaction and network connectivity, yet few have attempted to empirically assess this claim. Analyzing this tri-society data set, McDonald et al. (2015) show that social capital accumulation varies significantly across institutional contexts: in individualistic societies social capital accumulation is facilitated by employment and civic institutions, whereas family institutions form the basis for social capital accumulation in collectivist societies.

The growth of social network analysis of China
Under Lin's influence, SNA studies on China have grown tremendously and fruitfully. Minded about space constraint, I briefly enlist the most significant achievements gained by Lin's former students and those influenced by him.

On measuring devices of Chinese social networks, Danching Ruan (a student from the 1981 Nankai Class), in collaboration with Peter Blau, Lin Freeman, and others, is among the very first to have replicated the American GSS name generator question in their 1986 and 1993 Tianjin city surveys and produced a number of publications (Blau et al. 1991; Ruan 1998, 2001). On networks of job-search contacts, which Lin included in his 1985 Tianjin survey, and his tri-society project, has been further developed in a series of job-search surveys (JSNET) by Yanjie Bian (from the 1981 Nankai Class and Lin's former doctoral advisee) and produce a large number of publications both in English (Bian 1994, 1997, 1999, 2002, 2018, 2019; Bian and Ang 1997; Bian and Huang 2009, 2015a, 2015b; Bian and Zhang 2014; Bian et al. 2015a, 2015b) and in Chinese (Bian and Zhang 2001; Bian et al. 2012, 2018a; Sun and Bian 2017). The Chinese New-Year greeting network is an innovative measurement device extended from Lin's (Lin and Dumin 1986) position generator approach, and its Chinese version rests its measure on an event of cultural significance (Chinese New Year) and combines work-unit sectors with occupations in the revised position generator. This measurement device has led to numerous publications in English (Bian 2001, 2008; Bian et al. 2005) and Chinese (see Sun and Bian 2017). Finally, a completely new measurement device is social eating networks, in which frequency and composition of social eating partners are measured (Bian 2001; Liu et al. 2017). This network measure has been incorporated into East Asian Social Survey program (2012 module) and International Social Survey Programme (2017 module).

To what extent do social networks matter for behavioral outcomes? One line of analysis is how social networks affect job search outcomes. We have seen studies about how job search channels matter for an analysis of causal role of social contacts (Shen and Bian 2018), about relative efficacies of strong and weak ties (Bian 1997; Lin and Ao 2008; Tian and Lin 2016), about differential effects of informational and influence network resources that flow through the networks of social contacts (Bian et al. 2015a), and about advantages of boundary-spanning networks in mobilizing social and institutional resources (Bian et al. 2015a). Another line of analysis is how social networks matter for rural migrants into the cities. A large-scale study of Shanghai shows that migrants not only suffer severe network social capital deficits but also capital return deficits, providing a structural explanation of social exclusion of migrants in Chinese cities (Lu et al. 2013); still another line of analysis about health outcomes as a result of social network influence. Here, Lijun Song (a Lin's doctoral advisee at Duke) has taken a leading role in examining how one's depression and financial dissatisfaction are associated with one's resource-richer network alters, and how authority–subordinate relations at work increases one's depression (Song 2015b). Fourth, Wenhong Chen (a postdoctoral researcher with Lin at Duke) has conducted numerous studies on online social networks, paying attention to the gender gap network mobilization of business opportunities on the Internet (Chen et al. 2015). Finally, under Lin's supervision, Qiang Fu (another doctoral advisee of Lin's at Duke) and other collaborators conducted a survey of 39 urban residential communities in Guangzhou, which shows that neighborhood ties and neighborly interactions are positively associated with neighborhood attachment and cohesion, whereas uneven power relations between grassroots governments and civic homeowners associations are negatively associated with these two measures (Fu et al. 2015).

Most recently, Ronald Burt (a former M.A. student of Lin's in the 1970s) and Sonja Opper conducted a sample survey of 700 entrepreneurs randomly selected in the Yangtze River Delta region in 2012, using a "network name generator" module to collect information about business events and contacts valuable to the entrepreneurs on the events. This valuable data set has led to a stream of publications (Burt and Burzynska 2017; Burt and Opper 2017; Burt et al. 2018), producing three impressive set of results. First, core social contacts involved in business founding are *guanxi* contacts because their mutual-trust level is high and relatively independent of third parties. Second, the most successful entrepreneur has the right *guanxi* contact at founding, whose help wins immediate success for the new establishment, but in the next business event this entrepreneur must mobilize new *guanxi* contacts who are either from the family or are someone close to the founding contacts. This positive move can enlarge and diversify the entrepreneur network, but at the same time also maintains closeness and high trust among event contacts within the network. Finally, the later success of a Chinese business is a result of high trust among *guanxi* contacts significant in business events and a low network constraint due to diverse and nonredundant *guanxi* contacts. These research findings are in support of Lin's (2001c) distinction between *guanxi* and pseudo-*guanxi* ties.

Conclusion

"History calls those men the greatest who have ennobled themselves by working for the common good" (Marx 1835). In the sociological community surrounding China over the past four decades, I've found Nan Lin to qualify Karl Marx's characterization of "the greatest" so far as Chinese sociology and the sociology of reform-era China are concerned. Lin, in my close observation, was never trained to be a China specialist, nor was he consciously prepared to make any contribution to Chinese sociology in his early career development. When he was on his way to become a sociologist in the late 1960s and early 1970s, a politized China's doors were still closed to the West. Post-Mao reforms and the revival of Chinese sociology, however, brought him to a new historical destiny. For the common good to which sociology as a scientific study of society can possibly contribute, he welcomed the opportunity, took the challenge, and performed marvelously in the following four roles: Nan Lin has been a respected and successful educator in helping train and nurture the new generation of Chinese sociologists, he has been an innovative and pioneering researcher in the research of Chinese social stratification, he has been an influential leader and fruitful mentor in the research of Chinese social networks, and he has been an empiricism-oriented theorist of China's institutional change.

Acknowledgements

I'm grateful to Nan Lin for his endorsement of and help with my effort in developing this chapter, to Ron Burt for his helpful comments on an earlier draft, to Danching Ruan for her assistance with a number of historical events described in this chapter, and to Wenhong Chen, Qiang Fu, Yang-chih Fu, Gina Lai, Steve McDonald, Danching Ruan (again), Joonmo Son, Lijun Song, and Felicia F. Tian for providing specific information related to their sociological growth under Nan Lin's mentorship and scholarly influence. Yang Yang assisted with the references.

[9]

Getting Ahead in Urban China[1]

Nan Lin
Duke University

Yanjie Bian
University of Minnesota

This article argues that structural segmentation is a universal phenomenon in all complex societies and across political economies.
Each political economy uses specific criteria in delineating segments
of its economic and work organizations. Furthermore, it is argued
that segmentation identification constitutes a critical destination
status for individuals engaged in the status-attainment process. A
representative sample of the working population in Tianjin, China,
is analyzed to show that entrance into the core sectors (state agencies and enterprises), rather than the job per se, constitutes the
primary goal of status attainment. Entering into a more desirable
work-unit sector in China takes on differential significance and process for males and females. For males, the direct effect of intergenerational factors (i.e., the effect of father's work-unit sector) is evident. For females, such an effect is only indirect; instead, to a
great extent, their status attainment depends directly on their own
educational attainment. Also, upward occupational mobility across
sectors (from the peripheral to the core) between first and current
jobs is substantially greater among male workers (over 60%) than
among female workers (20%). Likewise, males benefit more from
social resources (the use of social contacts and their resources) in
the job search than females. These findings shed light on the significance of political economy in defining statuses and the viability
of the industrialization-attainment thesis. They also point to other
operating processes that transcend the effects of political economy
or industrialization. Specifically, these explanatory schemes do not
yet prove adequate in accounting for gender differences and the use
of social resources in the status-attainment process.

INTRODUCTION

The study of social stratification and social mobility has benefited greatly
from the conceptual and empirical developments concerned with segmentation in society. Conceptually, it has been shown that in a market econ-

[1] Data for the paper were drawn from a collaborative study by the first author, the
Tianjin Academy of Social Sciences, and the municipal government of Tianjin. We

American Journal of Sociology

omy, firms competing for advantageous positions attempt to maximize concentration, capital intensity, state-sponsored production, size, and economic scale (Kalleberg, Wallace, and Althauser 1981; Hodson and Kaufman 1982). Advantaged firms show distinctive features in recruitment, internal labor markets, and reward structures (Wallace and Kalleberg 1981; Althauser and Kalleberg 1981; Baron and Bielby 1984), which, in turn, attract the best qualified laborers, which further strengthens these firms' relative advantages in the market (Edwards 1975; Gordon, Edwards, and Reich 1982). Empirically, segmentation theory has led to fruitful examinations of the segmented labor market, the dynamics of the internal labor markets, and differential reward systems (Bibb and Form 1977; Beck, Horan, and Tolbert 1978; Baron and Bielby 1980; Kalleberg, Wallace, and Althauser 1981; Hodson 1983).

Interestingly, the development of the segmentation theory and the research on it have been closely identified with the market economy or the capitalist society. Both conceptual arguments and empirical attention have focused on the societies in North America, Western Europe, and other capitalist states such as Japan (see Kalleberg [1988] for a review). To many, the development has even been seen as an extension of the Marxist or neo-Marxist conceptualization with the intent of establishing a theory of capitalist development (Gordon et al. 1982; Nolan and Edwards 1984). The implication is, therefore, that segmentation is a conceptualization and phenomenon associated primarily, if not solely, with the capitalist society and its associated market economy.

We argue that segmentation is a universal phenomenon associated with all complex societies and all political economies. It is true that each political economy evokes a set of criteria that produces the development of a particular segmentation structure. In the market economy, free competition compels firms to make certain choices in order to maximize their advantages and their relative dominant positions in the market (Edwards 1975; Gordon et al. 1982). While such market competitiveness may not exist in a nonmarket economy, that does not imply that segmentation either does not or need not exist. On the contrary, another political econ-

express gratitude to Hui Wang and Yun-kang Pan of the Tianjin Academy and Hanzhang Yang and Kuo-hua Yuan of the Tianjin municipal government for their cooperation in the study. The study was in part supported by a travel grant to the first author from the Committee for Scholarly Communication with the People's Republic of China. Previous versions of the manuscript were presented at the 1988 annual meeting of the American Sociological Association, Atlanta. The paper has benefited from comments on the various versions kindly provided by Peter Blau, Chris Bose, Deborah Davis, Mark Granovetter, Alan Kerckhoff, John Logan, Joel Smith, Kenneth Spenner, Glenna Spitze, Wen Xie, Andrew Walder, and the anonymous reviewers of *AJS*.

omy may well exercise another set of choices and promote segmentation of its economic and labor structures in order to maximize its internal and external advantages (for different but compatible analyses, see Burawoy and Lukacs 1985; Stark 1986). If this argument is valid, then one should expect to find segmentation in every complex society. The issue becomes not whether segmentation exists, but, rather, what criteria a political economy chooses in implementing it.

Take the state socialist societies as the alternative political economy. Rather than arguing that because these societies lack market economies segmentation would not exist in them, it would be more fruitful to examine how such societies are segmented and what consequences such segmentation has for the labor market.

We argue that, in a state socialist society, social organizations are conceived and structured so as to maximize the centralized process relative to allocation, production, and distribution of labor, material, and financial resources. Therefore, institutions and enterprises of certain industries and administrative functions are given priorities in allocation of labor, material, and financial resources, elaboration and size of the structure, differential rewards, closeness to the central planning process, and power over other parts of the society (Domanski 1988). These priorities form the basis for segmentation of social organizations in the society. A most explicit implementation of this segmentation, for example, is the degree to which the central government exercises direct control of a particular organization. High-priority organizations are "owned" by the state, while low-priority organizations tend to be decentralized as collectives sponsored by local governments or communities (Whyte and Parish 1984; Walder 1986; Bian 1990).

Furthermore, such segmentation not only dictates interorganizational dynamics, but also has profound implications for individual workers (Szelenyi 1978; Domanski 1988). It offers a differential opportunity structure for rewards such as promotion opportunities, financial benefits, quality of housing, quality of schooling for children, and so forth. More important, it confers unequal socioeconomic status on workers. Social mobility becomes a matter not of getting a better job or making more money (although such consequences may well follow) but rather of getting into the right work units—work units in the advantaged sectors.

If this argument is valid, study of social mobility, especially of the process of status attainment, across political economies must similarly redirect its focus to segments of the labor structure as well as to occupations or wages. For example, Tremain's (1970) thesis that the criteria of status attainment tend to shift from ascribed factors to achieved ones as a society becomes more industrialized needs to be examined relative to the work-unit status as well as to the occupational status and earnings

659

American Journal of Sociology

of an individual. Yet, so far, the research program concerned with the industrialization-attainment thesis has mainly focused on occupation and income, excluding status criteria associated with segmentation identification or those criteria meaningful in political economies other than the capitalist state. Proper segmentation identification for each type of political economy and its inclusion as status criterion may, to a large degree, help resolve controversies in this literature.

A case in point is the study of the status-attainment process in China, a state socialist society. Since the mid-1970s, several large-scale survey studies have been conducted on status attainment in China. The major finding is that parental status does not directly affect one's own occupational status. Rather, its effect is mediated through education. For example, Parish (1984) and Whyte and Parish (1984), using informant data collected in the mid-1970s, found that effects of parental status on a child's educational and occupational attainment have been waning since 1966. More recent studies conducted in Beijing (Xie and Lin 1986) and Tianjin (Blau and Ruan 1989; Lin and Bian 1990) have further confirmed that parental status had no direct effect on the attained status of both first and current jobs. These data seem consistent with the findings conducted in Eastern Europe. Data from Hungary and Poland also show little direct effect of parental status on occupational attainment (Meyer, Tuma, and Zagorski 1979; Zagorski 1984; Treiman and Yip 1989).

According to the industrialization-attainment thesis, these findings can be interpreted as suggesting that these state socialist societies, having attained a certain level of industrialization, show a reducing effect of ascription. However, data from the United States (Blau and Duncan 1967; Duncan, Featherman, and Duncan 1972) and other industrialized countries (Treiman and Yip 1989) show that the direct effects of parental status on one's own job status (both first and current jobs) are at least as strong, and perhaps stronger compared with those found in China, Hungary, and Poland. The industrialization-attainment thesis would certainly have anticipated a somewhat different pattern; that is, the parental status effects should be somewhat stronger in China, Hungary, and Poland than in the United States.

An alternative explanation for the waning effect of parental status in China was offered by Parish (1984) and Whyte and Parish (1984). They suggested that, since 1949, the Chinese society has undergone a transformation in which intergenerational inheritance of status has been significantly reduced. Thus, the reduction of the parental status effect is seen as a consequence of political economy and its policies rather than as derived from the industrialization process.

Getting Ahead in China

We argue that the resolution of this controversy depends, first of all, on identifying the status criteria meaningful to each society. Once the status criteria are identified, it would then be possible to assess appropriately the relative contributions of ascribed and achieved characteristics and to shed light on the relative merits of the industrialization and the political economy arguments.

The contention here is that for the Chinese society, the status-attainment process should be more focused on attainment in the "right" work units than on attainment in occupational status. Locations in the segmented labor structure confer relative status and become appropriate "destinations" of status attainment. In the following section, we will explain why the work unit takes on such significance and why status attainment in China is more geared to work units than to occupations per se. Then, we will test models of status attainment containing both occupation and work-unit sector as status criteria to (1) examine the relative merits of these status criteria, and (2) ascertain the relative contributions of ascribed and achieved characteristics to these criteria.

SIGNIFICANCE OF WORK-UNIT SECTORS IN STATUS ATTAINMENT IN CHINA

Private, Collective, and State Sectors

For China, allocation and distribution of resources and their effects on the workers are differentiated between state and collective sectors (Whyte 1984). In general, the ownership of most social organizations and industries is divided into four major groupings: (1) the private sector, (2) the collective sector, (3) state enterprises, and (4) state institutes and agencies.

The private sector is made up of self-employed laborers and family-based enterprises (i.e., bicycle repairers, carpenters, barbers, and small restaurants). It was practically eliminated during late 1960s and early 1970s but has reemerged following the Cultural Revolution. The number and sizes of private enterprises, while increasing significantly in the 1980s, especially in the rural areas, remain small. By 1987, about 4% of the labor force in cities and towns were employed in the private sector (State Statistical Bureau of China 1988, p. 123).

The remaining labor force is employed in either state enterprises and institutes/agencies (about 70% of the labor force in 1987) or the collectives (about 25% of the labor force in 1987). Generally, the state takes control of all major and vital agencies, institutions, and enterprises, while the remaining units are collectives under the jurisdiction of city, district, and town governments. The state work units, because they are owned by all the people (*quan-min suo-you*) and are chiefly responsible for the well-

American Journal of Sociology

being of all the people and the nation, claim priority in resource allocations. The material, financial, and labor needs of the state work units
greater resources and benefits, for both the work units themselves and
their workers, than the collectives, but also exercise much control over
resource allocations for collective enterprises. The state employees receive
benefits that are substantially higher and more extensive in both quantity
and quality than those available to their counterparts in the collectives.
Such benefits extend to the families of the workers in terms of better
housing, better schools, and better services (access to groceries, hospitals,
bathhouse privileges, and top-brand appliances) and pensions (Whyte
and Parish 1984; Walder 1986; Davis 1988).

The state agencies and institutes (to be referred to as state agencies
from this point on), employing almost exclusively white-collar (mental
labor) workers (along with a minor service and custodian staff) administer, manage, and conduct office and research work, whereas the state
enterprises, employing a mixture of white-collar and blue-collar (manual
labor) workers, are mainly engaged in manufacturing. The collectives,
on the other hand, employ primarily blue-collar workers with a relatively
small administrative staff and engage in smaller scale manufacturing and
services (Whyte 1984).

Labor Allocation

This stratification differentiation also applies to labor-allocation practices. Two distinguishing features can be identified. First, new laborers
are assigned to work units instead of to jobs. Second, the state-sector
work units are given priority over the collectives in labor allocations
(Whyte and Parish 1984; Walder 1986; Bian 1990).

The labor-allocation process begins at the central government agency,
the National Planning Commission, which sets up principles of recruitment for all work units. Furthermore, in consultation with various industries and ministries and with a projection of worker needs, the Commission identifies annual quotas for all state agencies, institutes, and
enterprises. The state work units are given priority in the assignment of
new workers. Then, the planning commissions at local levels (provinces,
cities, and towns), using the same consultative procedures, identify quotas for all regional and local agencies, institutes, and enterprises. The
local labor bureaus use these guidelines to assign the required numbers
of workers for each unit to subdistrict offices and schools. Eligible youths
and school graduates are screened, evaluated, and assigned by the screening committees in the subdistricts and schools, which submit specific
recommendations to the labor bureaus. The bureaus then formally notify

each youth of his or her assigned work unit.[2] The assignment process matches the recruiting work unit and the new worker. Little attention is given to the specificity of the job to the worker.[3]

State work units are given priority in this labor-allocation process in two ways. First, when quotas at the national and local levels are set up, labor demands from the state work units are worked into the plans first. Second, when eligible laborers are matched with work units, attention is always given first to the allocations available in the state work units.

These structural properties and relationships strongly indicate that the relationship of the state work units and the remaining units in the collectives and the private sector is one of core to periphery. Individuals are identified with their work units. Such identification lends differential status to the individual workers, not only in terms of visible benefits such as wages, bonuses, housing, nurseries and schools, medical care, and even bathhouses, but also, and just as important, access to social, economic, and political services (e.g., sports and cultural events, trains, flights, and hotels, better quality food and goods, etc.; see Whyte and Parish 1984; Walder 1986).

In contrast, the distribution of resources and rewards relative to occupations are much less differentiated. In most cases, rewards and benefits to workers are graded according to seniority, and, to a lesser extent, work and political performances, rather than occupations (Korzec and Whyte 1975). Such distributional and recruitment characteristics further reinforce status identification, primarily, with work-unit sector, and, secondarily, with occupation.

FORMULATION OF RESEARCH HYPOTHESES

Now that we have established that work-unit sector is a significant status criterion, we can reformulate for examination the controversy we discussed earlier. That is, the issue becomes one of assessing how the introduction of the work-unit sector as a status criterion affects the analysis of intergenerational transmission of status relative to work-unit sector. The controversy can be respecified as two alternative hypotheses. If the industrialization-attainment thesis is credible—and because China is a

---

[2] Since 1988, a new policy has been implemented whereby college and vocational school graduates can either wait for assignments, as they previously did, or seek out work units. In the latter case, when a satisfactory match is obtained by both sides, the work unit informs the labor bureau, which then formally approves the employment.

[3] Again, some attention is given to job assignments to college and technical school graduates.

American Journal of Sociology

developing country—data should show that parental characteristics retain some direct effect on one's entering and moving into the core (state) work units. In particular, status of father's work unit should exert a direct effect on the status of one's first work unit. On the other hand, if the political economy argument is credible—and because China is a state socialist society—the data should show that such direct parental influence is minimal.

An earlier study has explored the significance of work-unit sector in status attainment in China. In 1983, a study was conducted in Beijing with a representative sample ($N = 1,774$) of the employed adults (Xie and Lin 1986). This study replicated the Blau-Duncan model in which the effects of parental characteristics and education on occupational status were assessed. The study also examined the sector in which jobs were located. The state agencies and enterprises were found to offer many benefits and securities unmatched by the collectives and the small private sector. They also provided greater opportunity for internal mobility.

While the Xie-Lin study provided some evidence that the work-unit sector was an important variable as a measure of current occupational status, it did not gather data for father's work-unit sector or the work-unit sector of the first job. Thus, it was impossible to examine the relative merit of status inheritance.

In the remainder of the article, we will use recent empirical data from an urban area in China to examine the specified hypothesis. In order to demonstrate the value of work-unit sector as a status, the examination will incorporate work-unit sector along with occupation as an indicator of status destination.[4]

In addition, the analysis will be conducted separately for males and females. Past research (Andors 1983; Whyte 1984; Honig and Hershatter 1988) showed that Chinese women remain burdened with household and family. Furthermore, while they have largely participated in the labor force, women, as compared with men, tend to concentrate on certain

---

[4] Income constitutes yet another important status indicator. Presently, income differences for the majority of the Chinese work force are relatively small (Parish 1984; Whyte and Parish 1984) and may, in fact, be decreasing in urban areas (Walder 1990). Sensational reports of a few rich peasants and entrepreneurs aside, the overwhelming majority of urban workers in China draw regular salaries and bonuses from their work units. The latest estimate from Tianjin, for example, was that in 1988 only 1.8% of the work force were in the private sector. A significant portion of these workers are transients from neighboring rural areas. If the current tightening policy on the private sector, an aftermath of the Tiananmen Incident, persists for a period of time, the development of the private sector and, therefore, income differentiation will be further delayed.

jobs, work units, and industries, receive fewer wage increases, and are less likely to become party members. For the present study, it is important to explore the extent to which status attainment relative to work-unit sector as well as to occupation differs between males and females.

THE STUDY DESIGN AND MEASURES

The survey was conducted in the urbanized area of Tianjin, China, in November 1985. A stratified random-sampling procedure was used to obtain 1,000 employed adults in the urbanized districts of Tianjin.[5] The respondents sampled are, on the whole, quite representative of the adult population in the urbanized area, as defined by the census.

Since our focus here is on the status-attainment process, this study will only incorporate those respondents within the standard employment age ranges. In China, men generally retire when they are 65 (white-collar workers) or 60 (blue-collar workers) years old and women when they are 55 or 50. However, much flexibility is involved. Depending on the needs of units, individuals may be retained beyond the official retirement ages. Also, individuals may be able to continue work in another work unit. Thus, the study includes only the currently employed men of 65 years or younger and women of 60 years or younger. The sampled respondents within these ranges consist of 87.1% of the total sample. The characteristics of the 469 men and 402 women in the study group were similar to those for the total sample, with the sole exception of the average earnings. The mean earnings of respondents in the study sample is somewhat lower than that of the total sample (75.20 yuan vs. 86.55 yuan). The difference is due to the exclusion from the study sample of retired workers whose pensions were significantly higher than the average wage of those currently employed.

Our measurement for education consists of the following categories: (1) no schooling, (2) elementary school, (3) junior high, (4) senior high, (5) up to three years of college, and (6) four or more years of college. It is assumed to be an ordinal scale.

Assessment of the occupational prestige for father's job and the respondent's first job presents some problems. The prestige equation (Lin and Xie 1988) used to calculate such scores requires information on education and income. An effort was made to standardize incomes, so that such scores could be computed. However, it was impossible to estimate stan-

---

[5] Detailed description of the sampling procedure and the sample representativeness of the population can be obtained from the authors upon request.

American Journal of Sociology

dardized incomes prior to 1949, since, with the establishment of the present regime, price and wage information from previous decades that was relative to the 1949 standards was not available. Thus, the occupation variables (for the father's and the respondent's first and current jobs) were measured with the classifications: (1) farming, (2) sales, (3) manufacturing and transportation, (4) service, (5) office work, (6) administrative and managerial, and (7) professional and technical. The rank ordering of these categories was validated by examining their prestige scores for the current jobs. The higher the value, the higher the occupational status.[6]

Ownership of the work unit is used as a measure of the work-unit sector. We identified four segments: (1) private or family enterprise, (2) collective enterprise, (3) state enterprise, and (4) state agencies. The higher the value, the higher the presumed sector status.

It is important to validate differences between the major sectors. A cross tabulation, presented in table 1, shows that, in general, respondents in the state sectors consistently showed higher education, job occupation and prestige, and personal earnings. Thus, the data confirmed and validated the characterization of the state work units as the core sector and the collectives as the peripheral sector in the research literature (Whyte and Parish 1984, pp. 25–26, 30–33; Walder 1986, pp. 39–48).

MODELS

The initial model we use to assess the status-attainment process in Tianjin, China, is the basic Blau-Duncan model, in which the ultimate exogenous variables are father's socioeconomic characteristics (education and occupation) and the intervening variable is the attained education.

In the causal sequence, work-unit sector precedes occupational status. This proposition is stated in probabilistic rather than deterministic terms. Since the core sectors contain more white-collar jobs, entering a core sector increases the likelihood that an individual will attain a "better" occupation. The reverse cannot be true (that finding a better occupation increases one's likelihood of entering into a core sector).[7] The alternative strategy is to consider both sector status and occupational status as indi-

---

[6] Also eliminated from further analysis are military jobs (mostly as first jobs) and "other" jobs, which tend to be jobs acquired before 1949. It is difficult to place them in the rank ordering and there were few of them.

[7] The only exception is professionals who are likely to find themselves in the state-agency sector.

TABLE 1

CHARACTERISTICS BY WORK-UNIT SECTOR FOR RESPONDENTS' CURRENT JOBS

CHARACTERISTIC	STATE AGENCY		STATE ENTERPRISE		COLLECTIVE ENTERPRISE		PRIVATE AND FAMILY ENTERPRISES	
	Male	Female	Male	Female	Male	Female	Male	Female
Education*	4.0	3.8	3.1	3.0	2.9	2.6	2.0	2.0
Nonmanual (%)	80.0	77.0	23.0	21.0	22.8	15.4	.0	.0
Prestige score	75.6	69.2	58.9	53.8	54.1	44.6	49.8	33.0
Monthly salary (yuan)	96.0	81.2	78.0	64.4	70.4	52.8	104.0	40.0
Monthly bonus (yuan)	6.3	3.6	13.1	9.0	8.3	7.1	5.0	.0
Party member (%)	32.6	22.2	16.7	8.3	19.3	6.8	.0	.0
N's	95	81	310	194	57	117	1	2

NOTE.—Except for sample size, all entries are means.

* Education: 1 = no schooling, 2 = elementary school, 3 = junior high, 4 = senior high, 5 = up to three years of college, and 6 = four or more years of college.

American Journal of Sociology

cators of work status. Subsequent examination of this alternative found less consistency with the data.[8]

Party membership, another significant factor, will also be examined. In China, joining the Communist party customarily takes place following entrance into a work unit. Relatively few candidates are admitted into the party. It is usually a reward for personal loyalty to the ideology as well as for work achievements. Thus, in that context, it can be considered as a measure of achieved status. Once such a status is acquired, it then becomes a resource for further mobility—especially for moving from a worker status to a cadre status and from a regular cadre status to a decision-making cadre status—both within and, less frequently, across work units. Thus, in the process of status attainment, party membership holds a position somewhat similar to educational attainment in the United States. That is, it acts as both an endogenous variable (attainment variable) and an exogenous variable (resource variable). It is incorporated as an intervening variable, which places it between the first- and current-job measures in the causal status-attainment process. We will analyze factors leading to party membership to ascertain whether achieved or ascribed status is more likely to influence one's obtaining party membership. Then, we will examine the role of party membership in subsequent status attainments.

Age will be controlled for in all models. Age is considered an indicator of seniority and also reflects cohorts. While these subjects are not of central concern here, age has been known to affect education and work-unit sectors and occupational statuses of the first and current jobs. Thus, relative contributions of the key variables in the status-attainment process will be assessed with age being taken into account.

Throughout this article, comparisons will be made, where appropriate, between this study and several other studies. These are: (1) the Blau-Duncan data from American males (1967), (2) the Albany study of males (Lin, Ensel, and Vaughn 1981), (3) the New York State study of males and females (Ensel 1979), (4) the Whyte-Parish neighbors study (Whyte and Parish 1984), (5) the Beijing study of Chinese males and females (Xie and Lin 1986), and (6) the Blau-Ruan study in Tianjin (1989). None of

---

[8] The alternative conceptualization of two indicators and a single concept was put to test in a structural equation model in which a latent variable, work status, was constructed for father's first job and current job, each with two indicators; sector status and occupational status. The results show that such a model did not fit well with the data ($\chi^2 = 293$, $df = 19$ for males and $\chi^2 = 219$ for females; the adjusted goodness-of-fit index was .71 for males and .77 for females). Even when the error terms of each pair of indicators were correlated, the fit did not show significant improvement. Thus, we conclude that such an alternative conceptual formulation has received little support from our data.

Getting Ahead in China

these studies contain all the variables examined here; each, however, has certain important features. The Blau-Duncan study is considered the basic American data set for males in the 1950–60 period. The Albany study was a study of status attainment for males in an American urban community. The New York State study contains measures for status attainment of both males and females. The Whyte-Parish data were the earliest systematic study of status attainment in China and they, for the 1972–78 period, provide a critical reference to a period when the stratification and mobility processes underwent changes. The Beijing study of 1983 used the basic Blau-Duncan model variables as well as party membership and sector information pertaining to current job for both males and females. The Blau-Ruan study was conducted two years later, in Tianjin, the same city as the present study. They offer an opportunity to validate part of the results.

Zero-order correlations among the variables are presented in the Appendix table A1 for males and females separately. To assess the status-attainment data, we conduct a series of equations for several endogenous variables. The endogenous variables, in causal sequence, are: education (E), first-job sector (U_W) and occupation (O_W), party membership (P), and current-job sector (U_Y) and occupation (O_Y). In order to make comparisons with results from the United States, we construct separate estimation equations, wherever appropriate, for exogenous variables contained in the Western model and for the full complement of exogenous variables. These equations and estimations (unstandardized and standardized coefficients) are presented for males and females, respectively, in table 2. For a visual comparison of the results for males and females, we present path diagrams for the full-complement equations and the standardized path coefficients in figures 1 and 2.

ESTIMATIONS

Attaining Education

The first endogenous variable in the model is education. In equation (1) in table 2, education (E) is regressed on father's education (E_F) and father's occupation (O_F), as in the Western model. As expected, father's education rather than father's occupation exerts greater effect on the educational attainment of the respondent. This intergenerational model accounts for 7% of the variance in education for males and 11% for females.

Using the zero-order correlation and path coefficients from Blau and Duncan's U.S. study (1967, pp. 169–70), we calculated that about a quarter (26%) of the variance of educational attainment for males was

TABLE 2

UNSTANDARDIZED AND STANDARDIZED (IN PARENTHESES) REGRESSION COEFFICIENTS OF ATTAINMENTS OF EDUCATION, WORK-UNIT SECTOR, OCCUPATION, AND PARTY MEMBERSHIP ON FATHER'S AND ONE'S OWN STATUS, BY SEX

Dependent Variables	Independent Variables									Constant	R^2	N
	Age	E_F	O_F	U_F	E	U_W	O_W	P	U_Y			
(1) Education (E):												
Male	−.01 (−.05)	.19 (.20)**	.04 (.06)							2.98	.07	325
Female	−.02 (−.18)**	.15 (.16)*	.12 (.20)**							3.22	.16	296
Difference	−.01	.04	−.08*									
(2) Education (E):												
Male	−.00 (−.00)	.17 (.18)**	.01 (.01)	.20 (.14)*						2.41	.08	322
Female	−.02 (−.15)**	.10 (.11)	.04 (.07)	.38 (.26)**						2.35	.20	290
Difference	.02*	.07	−.03	−.18*								
(3) First work sector (U_W):												
Male	−.00 (−.00)	−.05 (−.07)	.01 (.02)	.32 (.32)**	.17 (.24)**					1.43	.18	290
Female	.02 (.23)**	.03 (.05)	...	.02 (.02)	.27 (.40)**					1.11	.18	290
Difference	.02*	−.08	...	.30**	−.10							
(4) First job status (O_W):												
Male	.03 (.22)**	...	...	...	.60 (.43)**					.07	.22	423
Female	.05 (.28)**	.00 (.00)	...	...	.66 (.44)**					−.64	.21	324
Difference	−.02	...	...	...	−.06							

(Continued overleaf)

(Continued)

	C1	C2	C3	C4	C5	C6	C7	C8	Constant	R^2	N
(5) First job status (O_W):											
Male	.04 (.29)**	...	...	.43 (.31)**	.82 (.44)**				−2.03	.39	394
Female	.03 (.17)**	−.03 (−.02)	...	.36 (.24)**	1.07 (.49)**				−1.88	.41	320
Difference	.01	−.02	.05	.08	−.22*						
(6) Party membership (P):											
Male	.01 (.13)*	−.02 (−.04)	−.03 (−.11)	...	.04 (.15)*	...	.03 (.15)*		.10	.05	326
Female	.01 (.14)**	...	...	...	.02 (.04)	...	...		−.39	.09	386
Difference	.00	...	...	...		...	...				
(7) Current work sector (U_Y):											
Male	.01 (.20)**	...	...	.11 (.20)**	.36 (.48)**	.00 (.00)	.17 (.12)**		.120	.34	394
Female	...	.02 (.03)	−.00 (−.01)	.13 (.19)**	.64 (.63)**	...	.00 (.00)		.64	.53	296
Difference	...	...	...	−.02	−.28*	...	.17*				
(8) Current job status (O_Y):											
Male	.03 (.18)**	...	...	.60 (.43)**		.32 (.31)**			−.18	.43	423
Female	...	.07 (.05)	.00 (.00)	.48 (.31)**		.48 (.45)**			.70	.42	296
Difference	...	...	...	.12		−.16					
(9) Current job status (O_Y):											
Male	.02 (.13)**	...	...	.52 (.37)**		.29 (.29)**	.54 (.15)**	.48 (.19)**	−1.06	.48	421
Female	...	.04 (.03)	.04 (.04)	.37 (.23)**		.39 (.37)**	.69 (.13)**	.43 (.19)**	.15	.46	290
Difference	...	...	−.08 (−.03)	.15		−.10	−.15	.05			

NOTE.—E_F, O_F and U_F are father's education, father's occupation, and father's work-unit sector, respectively. Ellipses indicate that the variable was eliminated from the equation because of the multicollinearity problem or because correlation with the dependent variable was less than .10. Equation numbers are given in parentheses before each dependent variable.

* $p < .05$.
** $p < .01$.

American Journal of Sociology

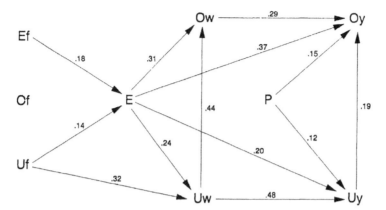

Fig. 1.—The status-attainment model and the estimates for males (after age has been controlled for).

accounted for by father's education and occupational status. Thus, compared with Western data, the explained variance is relatively low for China.

One explanation for this Chinese–U.S. difference could be that the measurement of occupation in our study differs from that used in the Blau and Duncan study. Further examination failed to confirm this explanation.[9] Instead, we felt that the difference might be due to the failure of the model to take into account the meaningful status measures in the Chinese context.

Equation (2) takes into account the sector in which the father's work unit (U_F) is located as an additional exogenous variable. Now, the explained variance for education increases to 8% for males and 20% for females. Thus, once the appropriate status measure (work-unit status) is incorporated into the Chinese model, the intergenerational effect on education is evident.

For males, the effects of father's education and sector of work unit are similar in magnitude (.18 and .14 in standard coefficients, respectively). For females, on the other hand, the coefficient for father's work-unit

---

[9] We computed occupational prestige scores for father's occupation, according to the Lin-Xie index (Lin and Xie 1988), which is a formula similar to the Duncan SEI index but based on Chinese data and individual rather than cohort information. The analysis was done only for those who entered into the work force after 1949, since earnings before 1949 could not be standardized. The results showed that father's occupational prestige did not have a significant effect on sons' and daughters' educational attainment. The effects of father's work-unit sector and father's education (in the case of males) retained their magnitudes of significance.

Getting Ahead in China

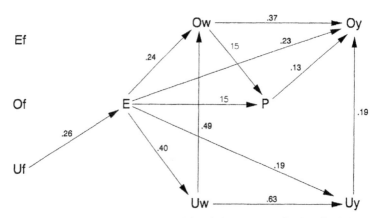

FIG. 2.—The status-attainment model and the estimates for females (after age has been controlled for).

sector is about two and one-half times higher than that for father's education (.26 and .11, respectively). For both men and women, father's occupation does not have any significant effect on educational attainment.

Why, then, should father's work-unit sector be so much more important in explaining females' education? One plausible explanation is that the sectors differentially represent structural resources. Housing is either directly provided from the work unit or obtained through it (Whyte and Parish 1984; Walder 1986). In either case, better work units tend to provide better housing and this housing tends to be located in districts where better schools are located (Bian 1990). Furthermore, such segregated housing arrangements provide differential neighborhood environments and interactional opportunities for the children. In this resource-rich environment, both sons and daughters were able to receive adequate educations. On the other hand, in the peripheral sectors, quality and facilities in both schools and housing environments are limited and restrained. In this resource-poor environment, a choice must be made in the investment of children's education. Under this condition, the traditional prejudice in favor of male offspring weighs heavily.

If this analysis is correct, the gender differences in education should occur primarily in the peripheral sectors and not in the core sectors. Analysis of average educational levels for males and females by father's work-unit sector indeed shows that the male/female ratios are the greatest in the private (1.48) and collective sectors (1.20) and virtually disappear in the state enterprises (1.08) and agencies (1.01).

Table 3 summarizes findings from various studies regarding parental effects on educational attainment in China. It is apparent that the find-

TABLE 3

EDUCATIONAL ATTAINMENT IN CHINA

STUDY	INDEPENDENT VARIABLE IN EQUATION						
	Father's Education	Father's Work-Unit Sector	Father's Occupation	Father's Class Label	Age	Gender	R^2
Whyte-Parish (1972–77) neighbors sample:							
Pre-1966 cohort	*		*	†	†	*	.38
1966–77 cohort	†		†	†	*	†	.10
Xie-Lin (1983) Beijing sample:							
Males	*		†				.11
Females	*		†				.20
Blau-Ruan (1987) Tianjin sample	*		†				.09
Lin-Bian (1985) Tianjin sample:							
Basic model:							
Males	*		†				.06
Females	*		*				.13
Extended model:							
Males	*	*	†				.08
Females	†	*	†				.18

NOTE.—Father's occupation is measured by (1) the 32 categories ranked by income status in the Whyte-Parish study; (2) occupational status in the Xie-Lin study and the Blau-Ruan study; and (3) the eight ranked categories in the Lin-Bian study.

* Partial regression coefficient significant at the .05 level.

† Variable in equation, but coefficient not significant at the .05 level.

ings are quite consistent, especially in the discrepancy for males and females of such effects.

Entering the Labor Structure

The next endogenous variable is the sector of the work unit in which the respondent found his or her first job. We used the four-category measure in table 2 to represent the sectors. The measure, while consisting of four categories reflecting the four segments, is also considered as an indicator of a dual-segment system with state agencies and enterprises as the core segment and the collectives and private enterprises as the peripheral.

As expressed in equation (3) in table 2 there is a difference between males and females. For males, both father's work-unit sector and his own educational attainment are significant predictors (unstandardized coefficients of .32 and .17, respectively). For females, on the other hand, only their own educational attainment is a significant contributor (.27). Their father's work-unit sector has no effect (.02).

We can more precisely decompose the relative effects of the ascribed (father's education, E_F, and father's work-unit sector, U_F) versus the achieved (own education, E) factor on one's probability of entering into a state agency/enterprise rather than a collective or private one (U_W).

For males, the total effects on first-job work-unit sector (U_W) can be decomposed, from figure 1, into the following components: (1) direct effect of father's work-unit sector (U_F) = .32; (2) indirect effect of U_F through education (E) (.14 × .24) = .03; (3) indirect effect of father's education (E_F) through education (E) (.18 × .24) = .04; and (4) the pure effect of education (.24 − .03 − .04) = .17. From these decomposed effects relative to their total effects on first-job work-unit sector (U_W) (.32 + .24 = .56), the estimated likelihood of a Chinese male entering into a particular sector is 70% due to intergenerational effects [(.32 + .03 + .04)/.56] and about 30% due to his own educational attainment.

We can conclude, therefore, that, in Tianjin, a Chinese male's likelihood of entering into the state rather than the other sectors is in large part due to the father's influence and much of that influence is due to the father's position in the segmented labor structure.

The picture for females is significantly different. As can be seen in figure 2, the total effect on first-job work-unit sector (U_W) can be decomposed into two parts: (1) the indirect effect of father's work-unit sector (U_F) through education (.26 × .40) = .10 and (2) the pure effect of education (.40 − .10) = .30. In other words, entering into a more desirable work-unit sector, for Chinese females, depends much more on her own educational attainment (75% of the effect, .30/.40) than intergenerational transmission of ascribed and achieved status. The intergenera-

675

American Journal of Sociology

tional transmission of ascribed status (U_F) only accounts for the remaining 25% of the effect on first-job work-unit sector (U_W), and all of
this effect is indirectly through education.

In summary, entering into a more desirable work-unit sector in China
takes on differential significance and process for the males and females.
For males, a substantial intergenerational effect involving direct parental
intervention is evident. For females, it depends to a great extent on their
own educational attainment.

For finding an occupation we construct two equations. Equation (4) in
table 2 regresses first-job occupation (O_W) on father's education (E_F),
father's occupation (O_F), and education (E), those factors used as predictors in the Western model. For both males and females, education is
the most important determinant and very little direct influence of intergenerational effect is evident. The effect of education is quite similar
for both males and females (unstandardized coefficients of .60 and .66,
respectively). The explained variance for O_W is about .22 for males and
.21 for females.

The effect of education on first-job occupation for males and females
in China, therefore, is very similar to that found in the United States.
Blau and Duncan's (1967) data showed a path coefficient of .44 from
education to first-job occupational status for males. However, the U.S.
data also showed a significant direct contribution from father's occupational status to son's first-job status. Thus, these two variables accounted
for 29% of the variance for first-job status for U.S. males.

Equation (5) in table 2 then incorporates work-unit sector for both the
father (U_F) and the respondent (U_W) as additional exogenous variables.
As can be seen, U_W exerts direct and strong effects on O_W, especially for
females. The R^2 is significantly increased, from .22 to .39 for males and
.21 to .41 for females. No direct intergenerational effects are evident for
either males or females.

The data suggest that there is a stronger correspondence of work-unit
sector and first-job occupation for females than for males. That is, when
the females entered into state agencies or enterprises, they also tended to
get better (white-collar) jobs than those other females who entered into
collectives. For males, such a correspondence is not as strong, suggesting
that even entering into collectives may not rule out their securing more
desirable occupations. Obviously, then, the work-unit sector represents
a stronger segmented occupational structure for females. Entering into
the core sector means not only receiving better resources but also having
the opportunity to attain better jobs.[10]

---

[10] That the females tend to do better in the core sectors than in the peripheral sectors
in the Chinese labor structure is different from the trends observed in Japan (Brinton

Getting Ahead in China

Becoming a Party Member

Party membership is the next endogenous variable in the causal model. As shown in table 2, regression of party membership, equation (6), on exogenous variables has no significant predictors, among the male respondents. For females, however, it is significantly affected by education and occupation at the first job.[11]

Party membership probably represents an achieved status resulting from loyalty and achievement. The data confirm a causal effect of achievement (education and first job) on party membership for females, but they do not confirm such an effect for males. These data suggest that perhaps future research should explore such other dimensions as a worker's ideological presentations and interpersonal skills for a better explanation of party membership, especially for males.

When party membership is regressed on the set of independent variables in equation (6) for both males and females and with gender added as the additional independent variable, we find that gender significantly affects party membership in favor of males.[12] That is, males are more likely to become party members than females, even when they have similar parental characteristics, educational background, and first-job occupational and sector statuses. This result reinforces the speculation that males are favored to become party members.

Changing Work-Unit Sectors

When each respondent was asked whether there was a job change from the first job or the first work unit, about 40% (42.9% of the males and 38.0% of the females) of the respondents reported that there was. In other words, about 60% of the respondents still worked at their first jobs in their original work units at the time of this study.

About 22% of both male and female respondents (21.8% of males and

---

1989) where gender difference remained strong in the core sectors. Few females in the Japanese core sectors could obtain permanent occupations. We suspect that in the Chinese political economy, occupation is not as important a status criterion as in most capitalist societies, since it is permanent for every occupant and occupational mobility is mostly based on seniority. Gender differentiation is focused instead on other status criteria such as party membership and cadre status,. We shall analyze party membership later in this article. The issue of cadre status, however, is beyond our scope here.

[11] The percentage of the party membership was 21% among males and 11% among females. Thus, the regression analysis probably would not induce any biased estimates for males. However, because of the skewedness of the female distribution, the estimates for female data are much less reliable.

[12] The partial regression metric coefficient is .09 and the standardized coefficient is .12, significant at the .01 level.

American Journal of Sociology

TABLE 4

WORK-UNIT SECTOR MOBILITY FROM FIRST TO CURRENT JOBS

	WORK-UNIT SECTOR FOR CURRENT JOB			
WORK-UNIT SECTOR FOR FIRST JOB	State Agency (%)	State Enterprise (%)	Collective (%)	Private (%)
Males:				
State agency (57)	70.2	29.8	0	0.0
State enterprise (218)	9.2	88.2	2.3	0.0
Collective (94)	19.2	34.0	46.8	0.0
Private (31)	6.5	87.1	6.5	0.0
Females:				
State agency (65)	76.9	21.5	1.5	0.0
State enterprise (176)	9.7	82.4	8.0	0.0
Collective (116)	9.5	12.1	78.5	0.0
Private (2)	0.0	0.0	50.0	50.0

NOTE.—Cases of "don't know" or "no answer" in either first or current work-unit sector are excluded. *N*'s of valid cases are in parentheses.

23.2% of females) reported job changes within the same sector. We do not know how many of these changes occurred across work units within the same sector and how many occurred within the same work units. In any event, a large portion of those, about 14%, did not change occupational categories, another 7% changed to better occupations, and less than 2% reported changing to worse occupations.

Because our primary interest here is in mobility across sectors, we combine those with job changes within the same sector with those who did not change jobs. We construct a mobility-across-sector table for the first and current jobs and present the results separately for males and females in table 4.

Slightly over 20% of male respondents (21.1%) and about 15% of female respondents (14.9%) changed jobs across sectors (i.e., from a state unit to a collective unit or vice versa). The likelihood of moving into a better sector differed for males and females. As can be seen in table 4, cross-sector movements for those males who began in the high-status sectors (i.e., state agencies or enterprises) were almost exclusively to the other state sector. A surprisingly large percentage of those who began their careers in the collective or private sectors, on the other hand, now worked in the state sectors. Over 60% (63.2%) of those males originating in the collective and private sectors had moved to the state agencies or enterprises.

The same trends held for the females. However, the extent of such

Getting Ahead in China

TABLE 5

Log-Linear Analysis of Gender Differences in Work-Unit Sector Mobility
from First to Current Work-Unit Sectors, $N = 782*$

Model (Null Hypothesis)	χ^2_{LR}	df
A. Full mobility matrix (4 $\times$ 4 $\times$ 2):		
1. $[U_c][U_1][S]$	652.52	24
2. $[U_cU_1][S]$	493.74	21
3. $[U_cU_1][U_1S]$	473.88	19
4. $[U_cU_1][U_cS]$	454.76	19
5. $[U_cU_1][U_cS][U_1S]$	422.34	16
A2 vs. A1	158.78	3
A3 vs. A2	19.86	2
A4 vs. A2	38.98	2
A5 vs. A4	32.42	3
B. Main diagonal blocked (movers):†		
1. $[U_c][U_1][S]$	197.79	17
2. $[U_cU_1][S]$	74.78	16
3. $[U_cU_1][U_1S]$	60.18	14
4. $[U_cU_1][U_cS]$	59.71	15
5. $[U_cU_1][U_cS][U_1S]$	35.23	12
B2 vs. B1	123.01	1
B3 vs. B2	14.60	2
B4 vs. B2	15.07	1
B5 vs. B4	24.48	3

Note.—All results for χ^2_{LR} and *df* are significant at less than .001.
* There were 90 cases excluded from the analysis because of the missing values of these cases.
† This analysis was based on a 3 $\times$ 4 $\times$ 2 matrix, rather than a 4 $\times$ 4 $\times$ 2 one. There was no
private worker left in the current sector after the main diagonal was blocked. The category of the private
worker in the current sector was therefore deleted in order to conduct the analysis.

upward movements was much less. There were, for example, some who
began careers in the state sectors but moved to current jobs in the collectives (1.5% of those from the state agencies and 8% from the state enterprises) and only 21% of those females who began careers in the peripheral
(collective and private) sector had moved up to the core sector (state
agencies and enterprises).

In table 5, we present estimates from log-linear models to verify the
significance of sex on first-to-current job mobility patterns. Both full-
mobility data (including immobility) and mobility-only data (excluding
immobility) are analyzed. The results clearly show that the interaction
between sex and the mobility patterns is significant.

We also examine various characteristics of respondents with different
mobility statuses. The data demonstrate that moving up to the core sectors promotes one's socioeconomic status in terms of occupational prestige and earnings. One interesting note is that those males who moved

American Journal of Sociology

"downward" from the state sectors to the collectives tended to be those who had a reasonably high education and maintained job prestige and earnings. No such retention effects were found for females. We suspect that these males tended to be cadres sent down to manage and administer the collectives, who were only willing to go to the collectives if such advantages were maintained. No such considerations were evident for females who moved from the state to the collective sectors.

These data provide substantial confirmation of the earlier speculation that the state sector constitutes the core sector, since the movements, if they occur, are systematically asymmetric: from the collectives to the state sectors and from the state enterprises to state agencies. Furthermore, the likelihood of such upward movements significantly differs for males and females and such movements result in increased socioeconomic status.

Attaining Current Sectors and Jobs

Equation (7) in table 2 shows that the sector of current work unit (U_Y) has differential causes for males and females. For males, the first job's work-unit sector (U_W) has the largest effect (standardized coefficient of .48), followed by education (.20), and party membership (.12). The effect of U_W represents to a large extent the immobility (or stability) within a segment of the occupational structure (state vs. collectives). The extent to which a male can move from one sector to another (after we account for those who stayed in the same sectors) reflects upward mobility and a move into the state sectors. And such movement is aided by age, education, and party membership.

For females, current job's work-unit sector (U_Y) is primarily determined by the work-unit sector at the time of entering into the labor structure (standardized coefficient of .63), and moderately by education (.19). Thus, there is strong evidence that immobility (stability) within work-unit sectors is much stronger for females than for males and that moving from collectives to the state sector is relatively rare for females. To the extent it is accomplished, it is affected by education. No discernible effects from age, occupation at the first job, or party membership, parallel to those for males, are evident for females.

It is quite clear, then, that cross-sector and upward mobility is much stronger for males than for females. This mobility, for males, is accomplished by bringing to bear both education and party membership. For females, such mobility is much less likely to occur and, when it does occur, education seems to be the sole determinant.

Finally, equations are computed for the occupation of the current job (O_Y). Equation (8) expresses it as a function of exogenous variables used

Getting Ahead in China

in the Western model (E_F, O_F, E, and O_W), and equation (9) adds the work-unit sector of the first and current jobs (U_W and U_Y). As in the Western model, the current job status (O_Y) is primarily determined by first job (O_W) and education (E). This is true for both males and females. For the Chinese, however, work-unit sector and party membership also contribute to the current job status. These exogenous variables explain about 48% and 46% of the current job variances for males and females respectively.

FURTHER ANALYSIS: USE OF SOCIAL RESOURCES

Once the intergenerational effect has been found, we need to explore the actual mechanisms by which such an effect is transmitted. Furthermore, it is important to ascertain whether such mechanisms also differ for males and females, since father's statuses directly affect sons' work-unit sectors but not daughters'.

In the study of the job-search process in Western capitalist states, research has found that use of social ties and, specifically, ties with better resources has increased the chance of entering or moving to better occupations (Granovetter 1974; Lin, Ensel, and Vaughn 1981; Marsden and Hurlbert 1988; DeGraaf and Flap 1988). In China, the importance of interpersonal ties (*guanxi*) in the functioning of individuals has long been noted (Whyte 1984; Gold 1985; Walder 1986; Yang 1986). Thus, we suspect that the use of such *guanxi* or their resources might provide one mechanism by which parental resources can promote children's finding the right work units. It would also be interesting to explore whether the use of *guanxi* and their social resources generated different results for sons and daughters.

We conducted an examination, therefore, to determine the extent to which the respondents used personal contacts in entering the work force and whether this use was affected differentially by father's statuses. In the survey, each respondent was asked whether anyone helped when they entered the labor force or moved to the current job, and, if so, what statuses (work-unit sector and occupation) the helper possessed. It was found that, for males, father's status characteristics were positively related to the likelihood of accessing contacts located in the state work units. Furthermore, these contacts increased the likelihood of one's entering into the state work units. Such relationships were absent for females. What these results suggest is that parental resources are employed in finding the right *guanxi* which, in turn, promotes the opportunity for the son to enter into the desirable work units. Details of this analysis are available elsewhere (Lin and Bian 1989).

Why the process did not work for females poses a further conceptual

American Journal of Sociology

issue. Three possible explanations can be postulated. One cause might be that fathers selectively choose social contacts and, for sons, make a maximal effort to get the right contact, whereas for daughters, their effort is less than maximal. A second possibility is that the contact exercises different efforts. Still a third possibility is that the target work unit recruits selectively by gender. There is some strong evidence that the third practice pervasively exists in China today (Honig and Hershatter 1988, chap. 7). These practices deserve further research attention in China as well as elsewhere, in order to explicate the actual dynamics of intergenerational influence in status attainment.

DISCUSSION

In concluding, we wish to highlight four important issues. The first issue derives from the argument that political economy determines the social stratification system. Segmentation of the economic and labor structures, therefore, is not unique to the market-economy system. Each political economy sets criteria in segmenting the structures, and priority is assigned to each segment accordingly. The data from urban China clearly demonstrate that segmentation based on the work-unit ownership criterion is both conceptually meaningful according to the political-economic ideology and empirically significant relative to the distribution of social (education and occupation), economic (wages and bonuses) and political (party membership) resources (see table 1). These arguments and findings challenge the theoretical assumption that segmentation is uniquely associated with the development of the capitalist economy. Reassessment and reformulation of the theoretical foundation for the structural segmentation phenomenon are clearly in order.

Second, it was argued that the segmentation phenomenon should not only be treated as a structural feature but also as an important identification for the individual workers striving for attainment in the labor structure. The inequality of allocation, processing, and production of material and of labor resources that is embedded in the segmented structure makes the seeking and landing in the "right" location in the structure a paramount consideration in job search and job mobility. Thus, segmentation identification becomes a status criterion and destination in the process of status attainment. Our data confirm the significance of work-sector status as a destination variable in the status-attainment process in urban China. Future studies of social mobility in all political economies, including those in the market economy, must incorporate segmentation identification as a status-destination variable.

Third, a further implication of the political economy and segmentation thesis advanced here concerns the controversy over the industrialization-attainment issue. To conduct appropriate empirical tests of the thesis requires incorporation of proper status criteria and destinations for each society. Ambiguity of results in past research may be due in large part to (1) the lack of attention given to segmentation identification as an appropriate status-destination variable and (2) the uniformed application across societies of status criteria (such as occupational status and income) uniquely suited to a particular political economy (such as the market economy). The fact that segmentation, appropriately specified according to each political economy, is seen as a meaningful status destination suggests that the industrialization-achievement controversy can be clarified only if segmentation identification is incorporated as a status variable. It may well be true that, for certain political economies, such as the market economy or the capitalist state, criteria such as occupation and income remain significant. It, nevertheless, becomes critical that segmentation identification, meaningfully constructed according to the political economy associated with each society, be adopted as a status variable. Only when appropriately specified status variables are taken into account, can a proper assessment of the relative effects across societies of ascribed versus achieved characteristics in the status-attainment process be made.

While we have identified political economy (and, therefore, structural segmentation) and industrialization as potentially useful explanatory schemes in understanding social mobility, our data also suggest their potential limits. This study offers evidence that at least two social phenomena seem to transcend levels of industrialization or types of political economy: gender difference and use of social networks and social resources.

Data clearly showed that females entering and moving into the core work-unit sectors are primarily affected by education rather than by family background. The industrialization thesis has no explicit provision to anticipate this gender difference. Because China is not considered an advanced industrial state, the industrialization thesis would predict that ascribed effect, as reflected in intergenerational effects, should remain. However, our data show that this effect operates primarily for males and not for females. Similarly, the persistence of the gender effect across different political economies (the state-socialist society and the capitalist society) also suggests that this effect has yet to be overcome by the current state of any particular political economy. [13]

---

[13] However, much of the data brought to bear on the industrialization-attainment thesis had come from male samples (Treiman and Yip 1989). Also, we lack mother's socioeconomic variables for examination of possible mother-daughter intergenerational effects. Thus, the thesis needs substantial further empirical verification.

683

American Journal of Sociology

Also, exploratory analysis showed the utility of using social contacts to enter and move into the core sectors. This is true for males but not for females. Studies in North America and Western Europe have also confirmed effects of social resources on occupational attainment. Again, these preliminary results suggest that differential access to and use of social resources persist across industrial levels and types of political economy. Further detailed studies are needed to confirm the differential effects of social resources for males and females in China.

One may argue that the present state of industrialization and political economy as seen in any society remains far from the ideal advanced state necessary to overcome such differential effects of gender and social resources. However, it is striking to find that even across differential levels of industrialization and types of political economy as represented in existing societies, little variation in such differential effects has been detected. It may well be fruitful to begin exploring social forces other than industrialization and political economy in accounting for these phenomena.

APPENDIX

TABLE A1

ZERO-ORDER CORRELATIONS, MEANS, AND STANDARD DEVIATIONS OF VARIABLES USED IN TABLE 2

	Age	E_F	U_F	O_F	E	U_W	O_W	P	U_Y	O_Y	Mean	SD
Age	…	-.18	-.47	.39	-.11	-.18	.17	.18	.12	.19	42.35	10.26
E_F	-.13	…	.40	.56	.24	.12	.01	-.13	.05	.04	2.16	1.08
U_F	-.27	.50	…	.55	.23	.35	.05	-.15	.02	-.05	2.70	.77
O_F	-.28	.59	.63	…	.20	.20	-.03	-.18	-.03	-.03	2.74	1.68
E	-.26	.30	.40	.34	…	.29	.41	.05	.33	.53	3.30	1.05
U_W	.12	.15	.14	.09	.36	…	.48	-.10	.49	.25	2.78	.77
O_W	.17	.10	.09	.07	.37	.60	…	.01	.35	.52	2.72	1.68
P	.13	.05	-.08	-.03	.18	.20	.25	…	.12	.22	.21	.40
U_Y	.04	.17	.16	.13	.42	.70	.39	.30	…	.44	3.08	.57
O_Y	.09	.19	.16	.17	.49	.44	.57	.11	.46	…	3.43	1.89
Mean	39.74	2.29	2.83	2.93	3.05	2.84	2.80	.11	2.90	3.44	…	…
SD	8.28	1.15	.70	1.83	1.03	.70	1.76	.31	.72	1.99	…	…

NOTE.—Entries in the upper diagonal are correlations, means, and standard deviations (SD) for males and entries in the lower diagonal for females. Symbols used are: E_F = father's education; U_F = father's work-unit sector; O_F = father's occupation; E = respondent's education; U_W = respondent's first work-unit sector; O_W = respondent's current work-unit sector; P = respondent's party membership; U_Y = respondent's current work-unit sector; and O_Y = respondent's current occupation.

American Journal of Sociology

REFERENCES

Althauser, Robert P., and Arne L. Kalleberg. 1981. "Firms, Occupations, and the Structure of Labor Markets: A Conceptual Analysis." Pp. 119–49 in *Sociological Perspectives on Labor Markets,* edited by Ivar Berg. New York: Academic Press.
Andors, Phyllis. 1983. *The Unfinished Liberation of Chinese Women: 1949–1980.* Bloomington: Indiana University Press.
Baron, James N., and William T. Bielby. 1980. "Bringing the Firms Back In: Stratification Segmentation and the Organization of Work." *American Sociological Review* 45:737–65.
———. 1984. "The Organization of Work in a Segmented Economy." *American Sociological Review* 49:454–73.
Beck, E. M., Patrick M. Horan, and Charles M. Tolbert II. 1978. "Stratification in a Dual Economy: A Sectoral Model of Earnings Determination." *American Sociological Review* 43:704–20.
Bian, Yanjie. 1990. "Work-Unit Structure and Status Attainment: A Study of Work-Unit Status in Urban China." Ph.D. dissertation. State University of New York at Albany, Department of Sociology.
Bibb, Robert, and William H. Form. 1977. "The Effects of Industrial, Occupational, and Sex Stratification on Wages in Blue-Collar Markets." *Social Forces* 55:974–96.
Blau, Peter M., and Otis Dudley Duncan. 1967. *The American Occupational Structure.* New York: Wiley.
Blau, Peter M., and Danqing Ruan. 1989. "Social Mobility in Urban China and America." Paper presented at the annual meeting of the American Sociological Association, San Francisco, August.
Brinton, Mary C. 1989. "Gender Stratification in Contemporary Urban Japan." *American Sociological Review* 54:549–64.
Burawoy, M., and J. Lukacs. 1985. "Mythologies of Work: A Comparison of Firms in State Socialism and Advanced Capitalism." *American Sociological Review* 50:723–37.
Davis, Deborah. 1988. "Unequal Chances, Unequal Outcomes: Pension Reform and Urban Inequality." *China Quarterly* 114:221–42.
DeGraaf, Nan Dirk, and Hendrik Derk Flap. 1988. "With a Little Help from My Friends: Social Resources as an Explanation of Occupational Status and Income in West Germany, The Netherlands, and the United States." *Social Forces* 67:452–72.
Domanski, H. 1988. "Labor Market Segmentation and Income Determination in Poland." *Sociological Quarterly* 29:47–62.
Duncan, Otis Dudley, David L. Featherman, and Beverly Duncan. 1972. *Socioeconomic Background and Achievement.* New York: Seminar.
Edwards, Richard C. 1975. "The Social Relations of Production in the Firm and Labor Market Structure." Pp. 3–26 in *Labor Market Segmentation,* edited by Richard C. Edwards, Michael Reich, and David M. Gordon. Lexington, Mass.: Heath.
Ensel, Walter M. 1979. "Sex, Social Ties, and Status Attainment." Ph.D. dissertation. State University of New York at Albany, Department of Sociology.
Gold, Thomas. 1985. "After Comradeship: Personal Relations in China since the Cultural Revolution." *China Quarterly* 104:657–75.
Gordon, David M., Richard C. Edwards, and Michael Reich. 1982. *Segmented Work, Divided Workers.* New York: Cambridge University Press.
Granovetter, Mark. 1974. *Getting a Job: A Study of Contacts and Careers.* Cambridge, Mass.: Harvard University Press.
Hodson, Randy D. 1983. *Workers' Earnings and Corporate Economic Structure.* New York: Academic Press.

Hodson, Randy D., and Robert L. Kaufman. 1982. "Economic Dualism: A Critical Review." *American Sociological Review* 47:727–39.

Honig, Emily, and Gail Hershatter. 1988. *Personal Voices: Chinese Women in the 1980s*. Stanford, Calif.: Stanford University Press.

Kalleberg, Arne F. 1988. "Comparative Perspectives on Work Structures and Inequality." *Annual Review of Sociology* 14:203–25.

Kalleberg, Arne F., Michael Wallace, and Robert Althauser. 1981. "Economic Segmentation, Worker Power, and Income Inequality." *American Journal of Sociology* 87:651–83.

Korzec, Michael, and Martin King Whyte. 1975. "Reading Notes: The Chinese Wage System." *China Quarterly* 86 (June): 248–73.

Lin, Nan, Walter M. Ensel, and John C. Vaughn. 1981. "Social Resources and Strength of Ties: Structural Factors in Occupational Status Attainment." *American Sociological Review* 46:393–405.

Lin, Nan, and Wen Xie. 1988. "Occupational Prestige in Urban China." *American Journal of Sociology* 93:793–832.

Lin, Nan, and Yanjie Bian. 1989. "Social Resources and Status Attainment: Evidence from Urban China." Paper presented at the annual meeting of the Sunbelt Conference of Social Networks, Tampa, Florida.

———. 1990. "Status Inheritance in Urban China." Paper presented at the annual meeting of the American Sociological Association, Washington, D.C., August.

Marsden, Peter V., and Jeanne S. Hurlbert. 1988. "Social Resources and Mobility Outcomes: A Replication and Extension." *Social Forces* 66:1038–59.

Meyer, John W., Nancy Brandon Tuma, and Krzysztof Zagorski. 1979. "Education and Occupational Mobility: A Comparison of Polish and American Men." *American Journal of Sociology* 84:978–86.

Nolan, P., and P. K. Edwards. 1984. "Review Essay on Gordon, Edwards, and Reich." *Cambridge Journal of Economics* 8:197–215.

Parish, William L. 1984. "Destratification in China." Pp. 84–120 in *Class and Social Stratification in Post-revolution China*, edited by J. Watson. New York: Cambridge University Press.

Stark, David. 1986. "Rethinking Internal Labor Markets: New Insights from a Comparative Perspective." *American Sociological Review* 51:492–504.

State Statistical Bureau of China. 1988. *Statistical Yearbook of China: 1988*. Beijing: State Statistical Press.

Szelenyi, Ivan. 1978. "Social Inequalities in State Socialist Redistributive Economies." *International Journal of Comparative Sociology* 19:63–87.

Treiman, Donald J. 1970. "Industrialization and Social Stratification." Pp. 207–34 in *Social Stratification: Research and Theory for the 1970s*, edited by Edward O. Laumann. Indianapolis: Bobbs-Merrill.

Treiman, Donald J., and Kam-Bor Yip. 1989. "Educational and Occupational Attainment in 21 Countries." Pp. 373–94 in *Cross-national Research in Sociology*, edited by Melvin L. Kohn. Newbury Park, Calif.: Sage.

Walder, Andrew. 1986. *Communist Neo-traditionalism: Work and Authority in Chinese Industry*. Berkeley and Los Angeles: University of California Press.

———. 1990. "Economic Reform and Income Distribution in Tianjin, 1976–1986." Pp. 135–56 in *Chinese Society on the Eve of Tiananmen*, edited by Deborah Davis and Ezra F. Vogel. Cambridge, Mass.: Harvard University Press.

Wallace, Michael, and Arne F. Kalleberg. 1981. "Economic Organization of Firms and Labor Market Consequences: Toward a Specification of Dual Economy Theory." Pp. 77–118 in *Sociological Perspectives on Labor Markets*, edited by Ivar Berg. New York: Academic Press.

Whyte, Martin King. 1984. "Sexual Inequality under Socialism: The Chinese Case

American Journal of Sociology

in Perspective." Pp. 198–238 in *Class and Social Stratification in Post-revolution China,* edited by James L. Watson. Cambridge: Cambridge University Press.

Whyte, Martin King, and William L. Parish. 1984. *Urban Life in Contemporary China.* Chicago: University of Chicago Press.

Xie, Wen, and Nan Lin. 1986. "The Process of Status Attainment in Urban China." Paper presented at the annual meeting of the American Sociological Association, New York.

Yang, Mayfair Mei-hui. 1986. "The Art of Social Relationships and Exchange in China." Ph.D. dissertation. University of California, Berkeley, Department of Anthropology.

Zagorski, Krzysztof. 1984. "Comparisons of Social Mobility in Different Socio-economic Systems." Pp. 13–41 in *International Comparative Research: Social Structures and Public Institutions in Eastern and Western Europe,* edited by Manfred Niessen, Jules Peschar, and Chartal Kourilsky. Oxford: Pergamon.

[10]

Occupational Prestige in Urban China[1]

Nan Lin
State University of New York at Albany

Wen Xie
Columbia University

The paper reports ratings of occupational prestige by urban residents in Beijing, China. Using a representative sample ($N = 1,632$) of adults aged 20–64 and a selected group of 50 occupations, we found that their rankings are remarkably consistent with those found in other countries. Within the general patterns of rankings, however, specific differences are found, and these reflect not only the specific skills required and resources valued at a particular historical moment in development but also the social effects of recent political events. These findings suggest a general correspondence of prestige rankings among major occupations across societies and that attention should be paid to the society's geopolitical characteristics and its recent historical experiences. Finally, a series of predictive equations are constructed to estimate prestige scores for all occupations in urban China.

The relative prestige associated with various occupations has been much studied. Since the early 1940s, when North and Hatt devised a judge-rated scale of occupational prestige in the United States, the concept of occupational prestige has become accepted in the literature of social stratification and mobility as a measure of socioeconomic achievement (North and Hatt 1947; Siegel 1971; Treiman 1977; Bose and Rossi 1983; Bose 1985; Nam and Powers 1983). The understanding and measurement of occupational prestige have also spurred the development of measures of socioeconomic status, authority and power, and other relevant dimensions of occupations (Duncan 1961; Goldthorpe and Hope 1972; Robinson

[1] An earlier version was presented at the annual meeting of the American Sociological Association, August 1985, Washington, D.C. The paper benefited from comments provided by Donald Treiman, Chris Bose, and three *AJS* reviewers on earlier drafts. The work was supported by a grant from the Research Foundation of the State University of New York. Requests for reprints should be sent to Nan Lin, Department of Sociology, State University of New York at Albany, Albany, New York 12222.

American Journal of Sociology

and Kelley 1979; Wright 1979). They have also played a role in the understanding of mobility processes (Blau and Duncan 1967; Hauser and Featherman 1977). The concept of occupational prestige is a primary focus of sociological theory and analysis and an essential ingredient in much significant work by sociologists in the past four decades.

Development of standardized measures, such as Treiman's Standard International Occupational Prestige Scale, has allowed the gathering and comparing of data from many different cultures and societies, including Eastern Europe and the Soviet Union. The evidence is that prestige rank ordering among major occupational groupings is generally similar across cultures and societies (Treiman 1977). Such similarities can be understood from the social differentiation perspective.

The division of labor in the process of industrialization, especially patterned after that initially developed in Europe, has achieved a universal influence. Therefore, in any society where industrialization has proceeded, the same pattern of division of labor becomes inevitable, and various occupations gradually acquire similar meanings and significance. This explanation is probably best reflected in the adaptation of Durkheim's theory to social development. Likewise, Weber ([1922] 1957) provides extensive conceptual analysis of social differentiation and gives special attention to status differentiation as reflected in occupations.

Yet such theoretical anticipations and the empirical evidence of general similarity in the rank ordering of prestige among occupations could grossly miss cross-societal differences between specific occupations because of distinct historical and cultural experiences. For example, it is important to evaluate whether setbacks and interruptions in the industrialization process owing to noneconomic factors (e.g., political and ideological) could alter the process of convergence in job prestige rankings.

The issue of interest, then, is in what happens to rankings of job prestige in an industrializing society whose cultural heritage and strong ideological bent conflict with the values associated with job rankings in industrialized and industrializing societies. The duality of industrialization and cultural/political forces allows us to extend our knowledge about the universal and particularistic features of occupational prestige rankings. China is one society ideally suited to such an analysis.

For thousands of years, China has built and maintained a social system based on strong indigenous ideologies and philosophies. It is one of the core cultures that have exerted considerable influence on neighboring and other regions (Chang 1986). Chinese society had maintained a strong sense of equilibrium and perception of itself as central until the 18th century, when Western culture, backed by dramatic technological and industrial superiority and its own philosophical and structural imperatives, overpowered the feeling of preeminence of Chinese culture not only

Occupational Prestige

in other societies but also in Chinese society itself. Indeed, in the last century, many Chinese intellectuals deemed Chinese culture, which was embedded in the feudal past, the antithesis of and, therefore, the barrier to modernization.

Such a barrier was presumably finally swept away when the communists triumphed in the civil war and brought in the new era in 1949. Since then, the country has continued, with some interruptions, to put great emphasis on industrialization. The achievements have been quite impressive, as judged by most statistics on industrial construction and output. The theoretical association between industrialization and the convergence in occupational differentiation and interpretations would lead one to speculate that, by now, three decades later, occupations and jobs in China would take on meanings quite similar to those in other industrialized or industrializing societies.

Yet, time and again, equalization of job prestige and rewards has been given a deliberate ideological focus and been subject to political and structural manipulation. For more than two decades, there have been campaigns to downgrade the status of intellectuals, upgrade the status of manual workers, shift urban and rural populations, and, in general, ensure equal or similar pay for all workers in urban areas. Frequent ideological campaigns to eliminate capitalist ideas and influences focus on the "proper" meanings and rewards associated with jobs. Even in the past 10 years, when such manipulation has been relaxed somewhat, the ideological struggle against the "capitalist" notion of occupational differentiation remains firm.

Therefore, we see China as a unique society in which industrialization and historical/cultural forces together have influenced the process of internalizing the meanings of jobs and occupations. Has the attention given to modernization in the past decade overshadowed both the cultural past and structural disruptions so that rankings of jobs now show convergence with those in other industrial and industrializing societies? Or have the cultural past and the ideological campaigns left distinct marks on the internalization of significance given to certain jobs?

To underscore these currents and undercurrents, a brief review of the occupational structure and mobility in contemporary China is in order. Special attention will be given to deliberate efforts to eliminate inequalities in occupational statuses and opportunities.

OCCUPATIONAL STRUCTURE AND MOBILITY IN
CONTEMPORARY CHINA

The traditional occupational structure in China before the 1949 revolution can be described as being divided into urban and rural sectors. The rural social structure was characterized by the dominance of the gentry and landowners over the peasants. In the urban areas, the top echelon of the structure consisted of merchants, government officials, army officers, and professionals. In the civil wars after 1910 and in the war with Japan (1937–45), the patterns of social mobility became unstable and uncertain. Many of the young revolutionaries in fact came from well-to-do families in the urban areas and dissociated themselves from the existing social and political order.

The 1949 revolution presumably brought about a new occupational structure in which the Soviet model of social and economic organization was adopted. Coupled with the determination to industrialize the nation (one slogan, e.g., was "to surpass Great Britain and to chase the United States") was the concerted effort to eliminate what was perceived as capitalist society's privileging of white-collar and "brain-power" professions over blue-collar and manual labor jobs. Much income differentiation between white-collar and blue-collar jobs and between mental and manual labor was eliminated or at least reduced to a minimum (Parish 1984).

Also significant were the extensive migrations of urban and rural populations. Because of the efforts in industrializing the country, the need for workers in urban areas brought about substantial population migrations from the rural to the urban areas in the early 1950s. The proportion of the urban population in China increased from 10.6% in 1949 to 18.4% in 1959. Urban laborers, who constituted only 8.5% of all laborers in 1949, made up 20.6% of such workers in 1959. At the same time, the number of university students in colleges increased sevenfold from 1949 to 1959. Thus, the period 1949–59 can be characterized by the rise of the urban working class and the rapid increase in cadres and professionals (Statistical Bureau of China 1984*b*).

After substantial and often violent struggle in the rural areas to eliminate the class of landlords and gentry, the antirightist campaign, initiated in 1957, had as its primary targets the intellectuals, academicians, and writers in the urban areas. Millions of intellectuals were engulfed by the campaign, and its effect on perceptions of job prestige, especially among the intellectual and academic professions, cannot be retrospectively estimated with any degree of certainty.

The Great Leap Forward campaign and the communalization movement, started in 1958, drastically pulled resources from the urban areas and disrupted the system of agricultural production. The immediate consequence was the difficult period of 1960–62, when significant shortages of food accounted for millions of deaths. Over 20 million workers were sent back from the urban centers to rural areas.

After a brief period of "recovery" (1963–65), the 1966 Cultural Revolu-

Occupational Prestige

tion brought about the greatest political, economic, and social upheaval
since 1949. The "establishment," including cadres and professionals,
were "pulled down" from their places and replaced with new cadres
(workers, peasants, and soldiers) who lacked the education, professional
training, and know-how to manage the specific tasks at hand. The educational system was completely disrupted. For four years (1966–69), no new
students were admitted to universities. From 1970 to 1977, universities
recruited students who were recommended by their units solely on the
basis of their political positions, family backgrounds, and at least two
years of work experience. Significant urban-to-rural migration occurred
because large numbers of urban young were sent away for "re-
education." Over 20 million university, high school, and junior high
school students were sent to rural and border regions. In the meantime,
the need for factory workers and military support in cities generated a
counter rural-to-urban migration. Over 16 million rural residents and
military dependents came into the cities. These dramatic crossovers in
social stratification and mobility resulted in significant disjunctions in the
normal mechanism of status attainment. For example, during 1966–76,
there was little correlation between education and occupational attainment (Xie and Lin 1986).

The year 1977 marked the end of social chaos and the beginning of a
new social order in China. Attention was given to the so-called Four
Modernizations (industry, defense, agriculture, and science and technology), which became the new battle cry, proclaimed by Zhou En-lai at the
National Assembly meeting of 1975. The pace of socioeconomic reform
has quickened further in recent years. First, the self-responsibility system
in the rural areas has decentralized responsibility for production as far
down as the family and individual levels, and the separation of administrative and production functions has to a large extent restored the authority structure of county and local governments in place of the commune
leadership. More recently, parallel reforms have been taking place in
urban areas and industries, where production and management responsibilities have been delegated to production units. Indeed, Deng Xiaoping has termed the current reforms another revolution (*Beijing Review*
1984). At the same time, nongovernment industries and services (collective or individual) have grown apace, and peasants and other rural people
now have limited opportunity to live and work in towns and cities, away
from their rural homes and registration.

A major consequence of this decentralization process and its physical
and occupational mobility is the rapid differentiation of occupations in
terms of compensation. It used to be that urban youth waiting for jobs in
state or collectively owned enterprises took jobs in privately owned enterprises as a stopgap, and, as soon as a job with a state or collectively

797

American Journal of Sociology

owned enterprise became available, the job in the privately owned enterprise was gladly abandoned.[2] The ultimate goal for people was to obtain a job in the state or collectively owned sectors. While the majority of those in the labor market remain committed to this ideology, many enterprises owned by individuals or local collectives (groups of individuals, districts, or cities or towns) are now well entrenched and can compete for qualified workers with state- and province-owned firms and industries. It is not unusual to hear of workers preferring to switch from state-run enterprises to nonstate-run firms. Even in state-run industries and factories, job changes are becoming possible and even probable, as each production unit is given responsibility for hiring and firing according to its need for workers. To be sure, such mobility remains limited and subject to employer-employee agreement. But the process espoused by the central government no doubt will encourage the movement of workers as each unit gears up for greater productivity and profitability.

As China undergoes such dramatic change and occupational differentiation in the 1980s, it is useful to examine occupational prestige as it is understood by the population. What prestige is accorded to occupations that have been downgraded time and again, such as intellectuals, academicians, and writers, for example? Are blue-collar and manual labor jobs on equal footing with the white-collar and mental labor jobs? Or is the pace of modernization and industrialization such that the inevitable convergence of job rankings has already occurred? At a minimum, it is important to establish a baseline for comparative analysis in the future. The fact that such information has never been available from China in any systematic form adds to the need to gather such information.

STUDY OF OCCUPATIONAL PRESTIGE IN CHINA

Relatively little is known about occupational prestige as measured in community-based samples in the People's Republic of China. It is of particular interest to both sociologists in general and stratification and mobility specialists alike. In China, which has been cut off from Western sociology since World War II and bound by a political ideology of the proletarian masses, socioeconomic classifications of occupations were deemed irrelevant—in fact, taboo. In the 1950s, much of the Chinese

---

[2] In China, enterprises are generally divided into (1) the state-owned (*guo-ying*) enterprises, (2) the collective enterprises (*ji-ti*) that are owned and managed by provincial or local agencies and factories, and (3) the individually owned (*ge-ti*) enterprises. Recent years have seen further blurring and gradation between the *ji-ti* and the *ge-ti*, as more variations of the *ji-ti* have emerged. Nowadays, collectives encompass enterprises owned by a province, a city or town, a district, or a group of individuals.

Occupational Prestige

attitude toward social sciences was copied from the Soviet Union. Sociology, in fact, was abolished as a recognized discipline in 1952, on the premise that Marxist theory should be the guiding sociological theory, providing all the theoretical materials necessary to explain and implement empirical social action and research. This position hardened further during the 1966–76 Cultural Revolution, when its "purification" campaign turned into a disastrous social and economic upheaval. Only after the death of Mao could the campaign be halted and the Marxist conceptualization of society and sociology be moderated.

The gradual liberalization of ideology, coupled with China's concerted effort at modernization, has now made it possible for sociology to regain its disciplinary status (for recent and current developments in sociology in China, see Cheng and So [1983]; Rossi [1985]; Lin [1986]). Large-scale sociological investigations exploring basic social stratification and social mobility issues have only now become possible.

So far as we can determine, the only available information about occupational prestige in China was a study conducted among high school students in Shanghai (Lan and Chang) in 1982. In that study, 150 high school students were asked to rate their preferences among 38 occupations, which were listed and rank-ordered by the students; descriptive data were reported.

The present paper reports a first effort at measuring and analyzing occupational prestige in a major Chinese city. A study of occupational prestige as rated by a representative sample of residents ($N = 1,774$) in the central city districts of Beijing was conducted in 1983.[3] Fifty occupations were selected for the ratings.

Since this data set is a historical first, we will provide as much detail as possible so that future comparisons and analyses have access to the descriptive statistics as well as the analytic results.

The primary purpose of this paper is to construct a prestige scale for the selected sample of occupations and to explore the sensitivity of the rankings in terms of societal and cultural features as well as demographic effects (e.g., sex, age cohort, and occupational groupings). To the extent possible, the scores obtained will be compared with those from various occupational prestige scales in Western and non-Western societies. A series of socioeconomic status indices of occupational prestige will be constructed so that prestige scores can be computed for all occupations in China. We hope that this effort will allow the establishment of baseline information on rankings of occupational prestige in China that is useful

---

[3] The study was conducted by Wen Xie, in cooperation with Zhao-kai Xuan. A preliminary report, extracting data from 100 respondents, was recently published (Xuan, Chang, and Xie 1984) in China.

American Journal of Sociology

for further studies of social stratification and mobility in China and for cross-national analyses of the universal and particularistic features of occupational prestige rankings.

The fact that the data came from the central city districts of Beijing presents both advantages and disadvantages. Beijing, as the capital of China and one of its largest metropolitan centers, provides many of the social and economic elements familiar to most urban dwellers in China. On the other hand, because of the city's especially close association with the central government, professionals and administrators are overrepresented among its residents. For example, about 47% of the respondents in our sample were professionals, managers, and administrators, compared with 23% for the nonfarm populations in Beijing and other cities in China (see table 1). Their attitudes and judgments regarding occupations may tend to be less economically oriented than those of residents of, say, Shanghai or Guangzhou, where commerce and trade are much more dominant. Nevertheless, given the opportunity, we were delighted to examine data from this important metropolis.

SAMPLE AND DATA

The data came from a survey conducted in Beijing in June 1983 by the second author, a member of the Institute of Sociology at the Chinese Academy of Social Sciences. The sampling area was the urban area of Beijing.[4] The sampling was a two-stage process. In the first phase, households were selected according to a systematic stratified method, and, in the second phase, one adult in the sampled household was selected.

From each central city district (which on the average has from eight to 10 subdistricts), a subdistrict was randomly selected. Within each selected subdistrict, one neighborhood (of about eight to 10 neighborhoods, each having roughly 600 households) was chosen randomly. Within each selected neighborhood, about 50% of all households were included in the sample—essentially, every other household. A total of 1,800 households were included in the sample. There were 985,060 urban households in

---

[4] The Beijing urban area includes the four districts in the central city and the nonfarm areas of the Chao-yiang and Hai-dian districts. This area represents the central city districts of the Beijing administrative area. But the Beijing metropolitan area also contains other suburban and "distant suburban" districts and counties. Therefore, compared with the entire metropolitan area, the city districts sampled contain more professionals, managers, and administrators and fewer heavy-industry workers (several major steel, petroleum, and chemical and mining plants are located in inner and more distant suburban districts). Similarly, there will be relatively fewer male employees in the central city districts than there are in the outlying suburban districts and counties.

TABLE 1
COMPARISON BETWEEN URBAN CHINA AND BEIJING OF MEAN AND PERCENTAGE OF THE RESPONDENTS' CHARACTERISTICS

CHARACTERISTIC	MALES (N = 1,121)			FEMALES (N = 653)			TOTAL (N = 1,774)		
	Sample	Beijing	Urban China	Sample	Beijing	Urban China	Sample	Beijing	Urban China
Sex (percentage)	63.2	58.4*	63.7	36.8	41.6*	36.3	100.0	100.0	100.0
Age (mean)	46.5	...	37.5	42.2	...	33.6	44.9	...	36.1
Education (mean)‡	4.48	...	...	4.51	...	...	4.49	...	2.92
Years of schooling (mean)	9.6	...	...	9.8	...	...	9.6	...	...
Annual income (mean) (in yuan)	986.2	...	...	828.0	...	...	928.1	935.0*	798.0†
Annual salary (mean) (in yuan)	835.7	...	...	689.8	...	...	781.9	...	716.5†
Occupations (percentage):§									
1. Professionals (0, 1)	29.9	15.1	17.5	40.3	21.8	19.4	33.7	18.0	18.2
2. Administrators (2)	15.7	7.5	7.7	8.8	2.4	1.6	13.2	5.4	5.5
3. Clerical workers (3)	6.6	6.0	5.5	7.2	5.2	3.2	6.8	5.7	4.6
4. Manufacturing, transportation, and kindred workers (4)	40.1	59.2	57.5	32.0	50.6	56.8	37.1	55.6	57.0
5. Sales workers (5)	2.8	3.8	5.4	4.0	6.9	8.4	3.2	5.2	6.5
6. Service workers (6)	4.9	7.2	6.4	7.7	12.5	10.6	5.9	9.8	7.9
7. Others (7)	...	1.2	...	...	.6	...	...	.3	...

Source.—Statistics from Statistical Bureau of China (1984a).

* From Statistical Bureau of China (1984c).

† From Statistical Bureau of China (1984b).

‡ Education: 1 = no formal school; 2 = lower elementary school; 3 = higher elementary school; 4 = junior high school; 5 = high school; 6 = associate/junior college; 7 = four or more years of university.

§ Actual census coding identifications are in parentheses.

American Journal of Sociology

Beijing's central city districts in 1982. Thus, the sample represents .18% (or 18 of every 10,000) households in the sampled districts.[5] Within each sampled household, one employed or formerly employed adult (20 or older) was interviewed.[6] If more than one adult qualified, then a random procedure was used to choose the respondent. The face-to-face interviews were conducted by 15 trained interviewers, most of them fourth-year university students. Three university faculty members served as field supervisors. The final sample consists of 1,774 interviews, representing a completion rate of 99%.[7] Our analyses, concerning occupational prestige, will only include those respondents between the ages of 20 and 64 (N = 1,632).

We attempted to make some comparisons for the demographic characteristics of the sampled respondents and employed adults in Beijing and in urban China as reported in the census. However, strict comparisons proved impossible, since the available census data are not all for 1983 (the year of the survey) and vary in age brackets used. Also, since the sample included only the urbanized portions of the six districts, certain characteristics of the sampled respondents do not match the available population statistics for the Beijing metropolitan area (which includes farm populations in the area as well). Thus, only general comparisons are possible and are reported in table 1. In the following discussion, different years or age brackets used in the census data will be mentioned.

As can be seen in table 1, the sample is 63.2% male, with a mean age of 44.9 and a mean of 9.6 years of education. The gender distribution of the respondents (63.2% male) approximated the 1982 national census data, which showed that 63.7% of the employed and nonfarm adults (20 and older) in the nation were males. But only 58.6% of the employed adults in the Beijing metropolitan area were males. The difference may be accounted for by the sampled area (the central city districts). In China, a greater percentage of female participation is found in the manufacturing

---

[5] No control was exercised in terms of the number of employed persons in each household. In urban China, household size is relatively small, and variations, not significant. E.g., in the urban area of Beijing in 1982, the average household size was 3.76, and the average of employed persons per household was 2.30. There was no reason to suspect there were any systematic differences across districts.

[6] It should be noted that, at the time of the survey, in China, most urban males retired at the age of 55 (workers) or 60 (white-collar workers), and most females retired at the age of 50 (workers) or 55 (white-collar workers). Thus, by the age of 64, the overwhelming majority of the employed workers have formally retired, even though a portion of the retired persons proceeded to take jobs for pay (bu-cha).

[7] The high response rate is typical for surveys in China. At present, being interviewed remains a novel and flattering experience. The interview survey bore no official sponsorship.

Occupational Prestige

and agricultural sectors, located primarily in agricultural districts in cities and rural counties.

The mean ages for the nonfarm employed population (19 and older) in the nation were 37.46 for males and 33.61 for females (1982). The older ages of the sampled respondents (46.5 for males and 42.2 for females) reflect again the concentration of professionals, managers, and administrators, compared with the factory workers in the sampled area.

The mean education level for the employed population (15 and older) in the country was slightly less than eight years. The higher education level of the sampled respondents (9.6 years) in part reflects the concentration of a more educated population in the Beijing metropolitan area, ranked first in China in terms of the percentage of university-trained population (49 per 1,000 in Beijing, compared with six per 1,000 in the country). It also reflects a difference owing to the higher age limit (20 and older) imposed for the sampled respondents.

The occupational distribution among the sampled respondents reflects the heavy concentration of professionals, managers, and administrators in the central city districts of Beijing. Almost half of the sampled respondents were professionals or managers and administrators ("cadres"). For the Beijing metropolitan area, the corresponding figure was only slightly less than a quarter (23.4%). On the other hand, only slightly more than a third (37.1%) of the sample respondents were manufacturing, transportation, or kindred workers. The comparable figure for the Beijing metropolitan area was 55.6%. The mean annual salary (excluding bonuses and other fringe benefits) was ¥ 781.90 for the sampled respondents, and ¥ 716.50 for all urban Chinese. The difference between Beijing residents and urban Chinese also appears in annual incomes. Thus, the differences reflect the contrast between Beijing and the rest of urban China, rather than that between the sample and the Beijing population.

In summary, the sampled respondents probably are representative of the employed population in the central districts of the largest urban centers of China. It overrepresents professionals, managers, and administrators and underrepresents manufacturing, transportation, and kindred workers in the urban areas.

SAMPLING OF OCCUPATIONS

Fifty occupations were selected for rating. Selection of the occupations began with an examination of the Occupational Classification System of the Census of China (1982), which contains eight summary categories (see these categories, except the farm category, in table 1), 64 major groups, and 301 separate categories of occupations. The initial principle of selecting one occupation from each of the major groups had to be adjusted to

American Journal of Sociology

accommodate two criteria: (1) familiarity of the general public with the occupation in Beijing and (2) a significant number of incumbents in the occupation. Furthermore, in the Occupational Classification System, the first of such compilations in modern China, some major categories (e.g., under "professionals") contain many diverse occupations, whereas other categories contain too detailed a listing of occupations (e.g., "manufacturing, transportation, and kindred workers" differentiates workers in terms of types of industries—mining, metal, chemical, rubber and plastics, textile, leather, clothing, food, tobacco, etc.). In consultation with experts of the Bureau of Statistics, more than one occupation was selected from some major groups (e.g., university, middle school, and elementary school teachers from the major group "teachers" in the professionals), and other major groups were eliminated (e.g., eight major categories of farm occupations, unclassified jobs, and occupations with few incumbents in Beijing). On the final list of selected occupations (see table 2), of the eight summary categories, six are represented (excluding the "farm" and "other-n.e.c." [not elsewhere classified] categories). Of the 64 major categories, 36 are represented in the sampled occupations.

Some of the selected occupations require discussion, since they may have different social meanings in China than elsewhere. For example, social scientists in China denote both social scientists and humanists. However, the total number of social scientists is quite small, and the general public is much more familiar with the general term "social scientists" than with specialists such as economists or linguists. Similarly, natural scientists include both mathematicians and computer scientists, besides physicists, chemists, and so on. Writers include novelists, poets,

TABLE 2

RESPONDENTS' OCCUPATIONAL PRESTIGE SCORES

Occupation	Summaries Code*	Major Groups Code	Prestige Score	SD
Physicians	0	7	86.2	19.1
Electrical and electronics engineers	0	3	84.9	22.0
Teachers, university	1	1	83.8	22.4
Natural scientists	0	2	83.8	23.1
Social scientists	0	1	82.7	25.1
Writers	1	2	81.7	24.1
Reporters	1	4	81.1	22.0
Civil engineers	0	3	79.4	22.3
Teachers, secondary school	1	1	72.9	23.5
High-ranking officials	2	1	69.1	31.1
Librarians	1	4	67.4	21.6

(*Continued overleaf*)

TABLE 2 *(Continued)*

Occupation	Summaries Code*	Major Groups Code	Prestige Score	SD
Middle-ranking officials	2	2	67.1	30.9
Electricians	8	6	66.7	18.8
Accountants	0	9	66.4	19.1
Secretaries, administrative	3	1	66.4	25.3
Drivers	9	5	63.2	22.4
Low-ranking officials	2	3	63.0	29.7
Athletes	1	3	62.8	24.4
Mechanics	8	5	61.4	20.9
Jewelers, gold- and silversmiths	9	1	60.1	23.2
Teachers, elementary school	1	1	59.8	25.6
Actors	1	2	57.7	27.2
Checkers, examiners, inspectors—manufacturing	9	6	57.4	19.5
Machinists	8	4	56.9	22.5
Typists	3	1	56.2	23.0
Nurses	0	7	55.3	23.5
Clerical workers	3	9	53.5	23.5
Installers of electrical equipment	8	6	51.3	23.6
Pressmen	8	2	50.0	20.9
Textile operatives	7	5	49.9	21.7
Purchasers	4	2	48.2	22.5
Mail carriers	3	3	46.3	20.2
Sewers and stitchers—manufacturing	7	7	46.0	22.7
Operatives and kindred workers—food and kindred products	7	8	44.6	21.0
Ticket, station, and express agents	5	1	43.8	18.9
Police officers	3	2	43.8	24.5
Cooks	5	3	43.5	18.9
Plumbers	8	8	43.4	17.8
Painters	9	0	42.2	19.2
Sales clerks	4	1	42.1	22.1
Operatives and kindred workers—chemical products	7	3	40.5	22.2
Construction workers	9	1	39.4	25.0
Waiters and attendants	5	1	39.0	24.5
Furnacemen, smeltermen, and pourers	7	2	35.1	19.8
Barbers	5	1	32.4	21.1
Miners	7	1	31.6	22.3
Loaders	9	4	26.0	21.3
Cleaners and garbage collectors	5	2	25.9	23.1
Pedicab pullers and drivers	9	5	22.2	17.9
Housemaids	5	1	18.9	18.3

Note.—*N* = 1,632.

* Both 0 and 1 codes are used for professionals; 7, 8, and 9 all cover manufacturing and transportation workers.

American Journal of Sociology

essayists, and dramatists. The high-ranking officials in our sample include the heads of regional offices (each province consists of several regions) and the heads of subcabinet offices in the central government and the Communist party. The middle-ranking officials include officials at levels lower than the regional and subcabinet offices. The low-ranking officials include heads of the lowest offices (e.g., accounting offices). Drivers include drivers of cars, trucks, and public transportation. Mechanics refer to general machine repairmen, whereas machinists refer specifically to workers involved in the production of machines. Typists include typists using both Chinese and Western typewriters. Housemaids refer mostly to women who live in with a family and have many household responsibilities, including taking care of children, cooking, washing, cleaning, and grocery shopping. Pedicab pullers are primarily pullers of carts and pedicabs carrying goods rather than people. Pedicab drivers are drivers of tricycle carts carrying either people or goods.

RATINGS OF OCCUPATIONAL PRESTIGE

To estimate initial rankings of the 50 occupations, a pretest was conducted with 50 raters (professionals from the Municipal Bureau of Statistics of Beijing, the Chinese Academy of Social Services, university faculty, factory workers, and others). Each rater was asked to rate the 50 selected occupations in terms of their prestige, ranking the occupations from the best to the worst with values from one to 50. The mean rating for each occupation was used as the initial ranking for each of the 50 occupations. The ratings provided a list of the 50 occupations in descending rank order (from the highest to the lowest mean rating).

It would have been difficult in the main study to ask respondents to rate the prestige of all 50 occupations in a single list. Therefore, the 50 occupations were divided into five sets, each of which contained 10 occupations. Each set of 10 occupations should have approximately the same ranking distribution as those in other groups. Beginning from the top of the list of the initial rankings, each set of five contiguous occupations was grouped as having approximately the same prestige ranking. This resulted in 10 groups of occupations with approximately equivalent prestige. From each group, one occupation was randomly selected and put into a set of 10 occupations. Thus, five sets of 10 occupations each were formed. For each set, the 10 occupations were randomly ordered (for the five sets of 10 occupations, see App. A).

In the survey, each respondent was presented with the five sets of 10 occupations each and asked to rank the 10 occupations in each set according to their prestige, with values from one to 10, one being the value for highest prestige, and 10 for the lowest. The wording was as follows:

Occupational Prestige

> Since there are different jobs, people have different views about the
> jobs. We would like to ask you to compare the following 50 occupations and
> tell us which ones are relatively better than others.
>
> In order to make easy comparisons, we have arranged the 50 occupa-
> tions into five sets, each of them having 10 occupations. Please arrange the
> 10 occupations in each set from the best to the worst according to your own
> judgment. (The best receives a "1," the next best receives a "2," . . . and the
> last receives a "10.") Each rank should apply to only one occupation.[8]

Each response was then multiplied by 10, and the order of ranking
reversed so that the value of 100 represented the highest possible prestige
and 10 the lowest. The lower boundary was set at 10 rather than zero on
the assumption that, when such a scale is applied in the future to the rural
population, occupations of even lower prestige may be identified.

The final mean scores of the prestige ratings for the 50 occupations are
listed in table 2. As can be seen, professional occupations (e.g., physicians, scientists, engineers, professors, writers, and reporters) are the top-
rated occupations, followed by school teachers, officials, office professionals (accountants and administrative secretaries), sports people (athletes),
and artists (actors). Also in this group are drivers, electricians, mechanics, and jewelers. These are highly skilled occupations that have access to
resources highly valued in China. Slightly less prestigious are a mixed
group of skilled and semiskilled professionals (i.e., nurses, typists, clerical
workers, mail carriers, and police officers), workers and operatives (i.e.,
inspectors, machinists, installers, pressmen, cooks, plumbers, painters),
and sales workers (purchasers, ticket sellers, and sales clerks). The least
prestigious occupations include heavy-labor workers (construction, foundry, chemical, mining, loading, sanitation, pedicab pulling) and service
workers (waiters and attendants, barbers, and housemaids).

DEMOGRAPHIC DIFFERENTIATION OF PRESTIGE RATINGS

The next step is to examine the sensitivity of the ratings. This will be
addressed in two ways. One approach is to examine variations in ratings
according to respondents' characteristics. In China, several demographic
characteristics may be salient for differences in perceptions of occupational prestige: gender, age cohort, and occupation. Analysis of the rat-

---

[8] The Chinese wording, in phonetic spelling, is as follows: *"Youou zhiyechabie de
cunzai, renmen dui gezhong zhiye de kanfa shi butong de. Women xiang quing nin dui
xiamian 50 zhong zhiye jinxing bijiao, kankan nazhong zhiye xiangdui haoyixue,
nazhong xiangdui huai yixie. Weile bijiao qulai fangbian, women ba 50 zhong zhiye
fencheng 5 zu, meizu geyou 10 zhong zhiye. Qing nin ziji anzhao cong hao dao hui de
shuenxu ba meizuzhong de 10 zhong zhiye pailie yixia (zuihao de tian 1, qici tian 2, . . .
zuihuai tian 10, yige shuzi zhineng yong yici)."*

American Journal of Sociology

ings will be conducted for each set of respondents categorized according to these characteristics. A second approach is to compare the ratings with existing ratings on prestige and socioeconomic scales constructed primarily in the United States, such as the Siegel scale, the Treiman scale, the Duncan SEI, the Nam and Powers OSS scale, and the Bose scale. One could also compare the Chinese ratings with occupational ratings obtained in both Western and non-Western societies.

These comparisons are made to examine the extent of similarity of perceptions of occupational prestige ranks across demographic and cultural/social boundaries, as well as to uncover significant discrepancies. These discrepancies, if found, must make conceptual sense in terms of the stratification and mobility processes in the particular subpopulation or society as linked to the strands of its social, cultural, and demographic elements. In this sense, a good scale is one that makes conceptual sense both in its consistency with other known scales and respondent characteristics and in its sensitivity to specific and different meanings attached to certain occupations in different groups and societies. Thus, the following examination should be considered as a series of sensitivity tests of the newly constructed scale.

Gender

We first compare the mean prestige ratings of the 50 occupations by male and female respondents. Since 1949, China has espoused a national policy of sexual equality. However, distribution of male and female occupants in various strata remains uneven. It is important to assess the extent to which such differential structural opportunities affect occupational prestige ratings.

The significance between each pair of prestige scores for each occupation was examined. Occupations that show significant rating differences between men and women are presented in table 3. None of the other occupations showed any significance in gender difference on prestige ratings.

The zero-order correlation ($N = 50$) for the mean scores for men and women was extremely high, .985. While the pattern of rankings was similar for male and female respondents, there were significant rating differences for specific occupations. Females tended to give the following occupations higher prestige scores than did males: typist, nurse, elementary school teacher, and librarian. On the other hand, males tended to rate such occupations as natural scientist, athlete, driver, and mechanic more highly in prestige than did females. These differences reflect the structure of occupational opportunity in China. The tendency is for each gender to rate more highly an occupation it has a better chance of work-

Occupational Prestige

TABLE 3

OCCUPATIONS WITH SIGNIFICANT RATING DIFFERENCES BY MALE AND
FEMALE RESPONDENTS

	MEAN PRESTIGE SCORE		
OCCUPATION	Male (N = 1,030)	Female (N = 602)	DIFFERENCE*
Natural scientists	85.27	81.25	4.02
Civil engineers	79.96	78.04	1.92
Athletes	64.55	59.53	5.02
Drivers	64.36	59.88	4.48
Mechanics	63.02	58.89	4.13
Machinists	57.74	55.47	2.27
Installers of electrical equipment	52.11	49.53	2.58
Pressmen	50.69	48.40	2.29
Police officers	44.81	42.10	2.71
Cooks	44.56	42.32	2.24
Plumbers	44.14	42.37	1.77
Painters	43.03	41.25	1.78
Construction workers	40.84	37.45	3.39
Furnacemen, smeltermen, and pourers	35.92	33.68	2.24
Miners	32.49	30.11	2.38
Loaders	27.43	24.24	3.19
Pedicab pullers and drivers	23.07	21.43	1.64
Physicians	85.16	87.90	−2.74
Teachers, secondary school	71.56	75.00	−3.44
Librarians	65.36	70.78	−5.42
Secretaries, administrative	64.97	68.21	−3.24
Accountants	64.86	69.03	−4.17
Jewelers, gold- and silversmiths	58.69	62.27	−3.58
Teachers, elementary school	57.73	63.71	−5.98
Typists	53.04	60.78	−7.74
Nurses	53.00	59.36	−6.36
Sewers and stitchers—manufacturing	45.05	47.38	−2.33
Ticket, station, and express agents	42.66	45.36	−2.70

* All differences are significant at the .05 level.

ing in. When we took the employment opportunity ratio in China into account (the percentages of the males and females participating in the labor force were 64.3% and 35.7%, respectively—a factor of 1.8) so that the entire structure of employment opportunity was normalized to 100 for both males and females, we found that, for every 100 employed males in the same occupation, there were 103 female elementary teachers, 65 female secondary school teachers, and 63 female university teachers (Statistical Bureau of China 1984*b*). For every 100 male waiters and attendants,

American Journal of Sociology

there were 210 female waiters and attendants. For every 100 male drivers, there were only 19 female drivers.

However, structural opportunity may not be the only explanation for these differences, since other occupations (e.g., electrical and electronics engineers and officials) with few opportunities for females (for every 100 males, there were fewer than 38 female engineers and technicians and 21 female officials) received similar prestige ratings from both males and females.[9] Another factor may be the traditional normative view of occupational aspirations for males and females. Chinese males seem to aspire more to be natural scientists, athletes, mechanics, and drivers, whereas Chinese females, at present, are more likely to aspire to be nurses, elementary school teachers, and librarians.

Thus, there is evidence that the general rankings of occupational prestige are similar for males and females. However, absolute prestige scores show gender variations for occupations that can be interpreted in terms of differential gender occupational opportunities and aspirations.

Age

For historical reasons, we wish to evaluate the differences in the occupational prestige ratings for different age cohorts. The intention here is to assess the extent to which different age cohorts in 1983 still carried the occupational values formulated during their different historical experiences in the occupational structure. The age groups were established according to the age when a person was most likely to enter for the first time the occupational structure in urban China. This age was determined to be 18. It is also the age at which a person in China acquires the legal status of adulthood (voting, criminal responsibility, and military service).

As discussed in a previous section, five periods are generally considered significant in the history of contemporary China: (1) The pre-1949 period saw 40 years of war and struggle. (2) The 1950–57 period saw a new era inaugurated in 1949 with the establishment of the People's Republic of China, the beginning of urban and rural economic development, and the rapid development of Beijing itself. This was considered a period of steady growth and industrialization. (3) The 1958–65 period included the Antirightist movement, the Great Leap Forward, and the communalization movement, with subsequent economic and food crises and a three-year period of recovery. (4) In the 1966–76 period, the Cultural Revolution, the entire occupational structure underwent disruption and change, and the values attached to many occupations were reversed. For ex-

[9] The zero-order correlation between the percentage of females in each of the 50 occupations and the prestige rating of the occupation was .004, not significant.

Occupational Prestige

ample, the intellectual and nonmanual occupations were the focus of attacks, and incumbents, the targets of abuse (the intelligentsia were labeled "smelly no. 9," along with the other "smelly" groups, such as landowners, rich peasants, antirevolutionaries, robbers, and gangsters). On the other hand, another group of occupations gained status because of their access to resources. These included cadres and officials at various levels, drivers, purchasers, and the police. Another group of occupations retained their desirability because of light work load, office location, nonmanual status, and general availability in the urban areas (e.g., librarians, typists, and secretaries). (5) In the post-1976 period, regular entrance examinations to universities were restored (by the end of 1977). The high status of the intellectuals was again recognized. The urban youths who had been sent to rural and border regions began to return to the cities. The more traditional Chinese attitudes toward nonmanual occupations returned. Recent years have seen an acceleration of this "normalization" process.

However, not all five periods correspond to significant changes in occupational structure and process. For example, the 1957–65 period was characterized more by economic and rural changes than by changes in the evaluation of various occupations. The Antirightist movement and the shift of populations from urban to rural areas were more focused on the political ideology of certain intellectuals than on the general status accorded skilled and professional occupations. The post-1976 era also poses some problems. Those who entered the occupational structure for the first time after 1976 actually grew up during the Cultural Revolution. Sociopolitical participation of the youth (mostly teenagers) during this era accelerated the social maturation process for this generation. Many of their values and beliefs were molded in the Cultural Revolution. Thus, we suspect that, as far as occupational prestige is concerned, this cohort's perceptions might not be significantly different from those of the previous cohort.

These considerations led us to examine the data for respondents from these five age cohorts. In all the major analyses reported in the remainder of this paper, we found a lack of significant difference between the 1949–57 and the 1958–65 groups and between the 1966–76 and the post-1976 cohorts. Thus, we decided to divide the male and female respondents into three age cohorts: (1) 21–35, who turned 18 during the period 1966–80; (2) 36–51, who turned 18 during the period 1949–65; and (3) 52–64, who turned 18 before 1949.

Mean occupational prestige for each of the 50 occupations was computed for each gender by age group. We found only slight differences in the means between the oldest (52–64) and the middle-aged (36–51) cohorts; therefore, we collapsed the two groups. Therefore, the compari-

811

American Journal of Sociology

sons, presented in table 4, are between those who entered the labor force before 1966 (the beginning of the Cultural Revolution) and those who entered the labor force in 1966 and since.

For the males, prestige ratings between the two groups showed significant differences (at .05 or less) for several occupations. The occupations that have higher prestige among the younger respondents, compared with the older, can be classified into several groups: (1) those who have legitimate power (e.g., the officials), (2) those who have access to scarce resources (e.g., drivers and electricians, manufacturing checkers, purchasers, and cooks), and (3) those who have greater freedom of physical mobility and more public recognition (writers, reporters, and athletes).

On the other hand, the occupations that have less prestige among the younger male respondents include (1) professional occupations with relatively low earning power and high physical demands (physicians, nurses, and middle and elementary school teachers) and (2) heavy manual labor occupations (foundry, textile, chemical, and construction workers; miners; garbage collectors; pedicab pullers; and drivers).

For the females, similar patterns were found. The occupations with more prestige (significant at .05 or less) among the younger respondents include (1) those who have legitimate power (the three levels of officials and the police), (2) those who have access to scarce resources (drivers, electricians, purchasers, manufacturing and industrial inspectors), (3) those who have greater freedom or lighter work loads (clerical workers, typists, librarians, and secretaries). Several of these occupations were also preferred occupations for males, as mentioned before. The occupations with less prestige among the younger females include (1) professional occupations with relatively low earning power and high physical demands (i.e., physicians and elementary and middle school teachers) and (2) heavy manual labor occupations (foundry, textile, chemical, and construction workers; miners; garbage collectors; and loaders).

By examining sex and age cohorts, we have identified two general trends regarding the changes in prestige of various occupations. First, there has been a general tendency to give higher prestige to those occupations that have gained favorable positions in the social structure, either because of their legitimate power or access to resources or because of the positions' greater freedom and lighter work loads. Second, within this structure, gender differences in the prestige ratings of certain occupations emerge because of the dominance of one gender in those occupations. For example, the younger males gave higher prestige to writers, cooks, electricians, and athletes, but the females, to librarians and secretaries. Similarly, elementary school teachers were given lower ratings by the younger males, whereas their ratings did not vary significantly among the females.

What is striking and yet understandable is the overwhelming prefer-

TABLE 4

OCCUPATIONS WITH SIGNIFICANT RATING DIFFERENCES BY SEX AND AGE OF RESPONDENTS

	Mean Prestige Score					
	Male			Female		
	Age			Age		
Occupation	21–35 (N = 316)	36–64 (N = 714)	Difference*	21–35 (N = 247)	36–64 (N = 355)	Difference*
Writers	83.50	80.32	3.18	83.09	81.27	1.82#
Reporters	83.03	80.08	2.95	83.37	79.85	3.52
High-ranking officials	73.41	67.47	5.94	71.38	67.17	4.21
Middle-ranking officials	71.74	65.83	5.91	69.55	65.92	3.63
Drivers	69.97	62.04	7.93	62.48	58.33	4.15
Electricians	68.74	66.25	2.49	67.64	65.04	2.60
Secretaries, administrative	66.69	64.22	2.47	70.29	66.84	3.45
Low-ranking officials	65.99	62.25	3.74	64.88	60.23	4.65
Checkers—manufacturing	58.52	56.39	2.13	60.45	55.80	4.65
Clerical workers	55.55	52.49	3.06	57.44	50.58	6.86
Typists	55.27	52.10	3.17	64.39	58.51	5.88
Purchasers	52.27	46.40	5.87	50.94	45.06	5.88
Cooks	46.28	43.83	2.45	41.14	43.01	-1.87#
Police officers	45.21	44.62	-.59#	44.11	40.94	3.17
Physicians	83.47	85.76	-2.29	85.98	89.22	-3.24
Teachers, secondary school	66.18	73.42	-7.28	71.87	77.01	-5.14
Teachers, elementary school	53.66	59.33	-5.67	63.01	64.15	-1.14#
Nurses	51.23	53.66	-2.43	59.59	59.29	.30#
Textile operatives	45.36	51.27	-5.91	45.94	52.51	-6.57
Operatives—chemical products	37.45	42.52	-5.07	38.46	41.75	-3.29
Construction workers	35.93	42.80	-6.87	32.44	40.46	-8.02
Furnacemen, smeltermen, and pourers	32.65	37.21	-4.56	30.61	35.65	-5.04
Miners	28.52	34.07	-5.55	26.83	32.18	-5.35
Loaders	26.28	27.89	-1.61#	20.98	26.13	-5.15
Cleaners and garbage collectors	22.97	27.35	-4.38	23.21	28.18	-4.97
Pedicab pullers and drivers	21.51	23.69	-2.18	19.88	22.30	-2.42

* All differences are significant at the .05 level, except those marked with #.

American Journal of Sociology

ence among the younger respondents for jobs typically found in cities and urban areas (i.e., drivers, officials, purchasers, office workers) to jobs that can be found in both urban and rural areas or predominantly in rural areas (i.e., construction workers, teachers, and factory workers). The forced migration during the Cultural Revolution and the rigid residential registration system have clearly hardened the prestige of urban occupations, at least among urban residents. In summary, the occupational prestige ratings seem to show consistency and variation across gender and age cohorts according to interpretable historical and structural factors.

Occupational Groups

A further sensitivity test of the occupational prestige ratings was conducted for different occupational groupings. The Chinese census defines (see table 1) three major categories of occupations as nonmanual occupations (the professionals and the administrative and managerial occupations), one major category as "semi-nonmanual" (mixed nonmanual and manual) occupations (e.g., clerical workers), and four other major categories as manual occupations. We thought that the professionals might be differentiated from the administrative and managerial occupations, as they might represent different structural responsibilities and educational requirements. Therefore, three groupings were identified: (1) the professionals (the first major census category), (2) the administrators, managers, and clerical workers (the second and third major census categories), and (3) all other occupations (all other major census categories except the sixth category, farm workers, which was not represented in the data). However, subsequent analysis showed only slight differences in prestige ratings between professionals and administrative, managerial, and clerical workers. Therefore, we combined these two groupings and compared them with the manual worker grouping. Table 5 presents those occupations whose ratings by male and female respondents show significant differences between nonmanual (professionals, administrative and managerial workers, and clerical workers) and manual workers.

The general trend seems to be that higher ratings were given to occupations of the same occupational type as the respondent's. For example, for males, the nonmanual workers tended to give higher ratings to physicians, writers, reporters, civil and electrical engineers, teachers (university and middle and elementary school), social scientists, and librarians than manual labor male respondents did. On the other hand, the manual male respondents had a tendency to give higher ratings to sales clerks, drivers, barbers, electricians, and waiters. There are exceptions. For example, the male nonmanual workers also gave higher ratings than their manual counterparts to textile and construction workers and to miners.

814

TABLE 5

OCCUPATIONS WITH SIGNIFICANT RATING DIFFERENCES BY SEX AND OCCUPATIONAL GROUPINGS OF RESPONDENTS

	MEAN PRESTIGE SCORE					
	Male			Female		
OCCUPATION	Nonmanual (N = 546)	Manual (N = 484)	Difference*	Nonmanual (N = 338)	Manual (N = 264)	Difference*
Physicians	87.42	82.42	5.00	90.54	84.71	5.83
Electrical and electronics engineers	87.87	82.70	5.17	86.14	81.93	4.21
Teachers, college and university	86.90	79.37	7.53	88.57	80.37	8.20
Natural scientists	86.85	83.54	3.31	84.17	77.85	6.32
Social scientists	84.71	80.10	4.61	84.23	80.69	3.54
Writers	82.92	79.76	3.16	81.74	82.19	-.45#
Reporters	82.58	79.13	3.45	82.71	79.23	3.48
Civil engineers	82.25	77.30	4.95	79.40	76.50	2.90
Teachers, secondary school	76.47	65.79	10.68	80.20	68.36	11.84
Librarians	67.60	62.99	4.61	73.46	67.52	5.94
Teachers, elementary school	60.02	54.92	5.10	68.23	57.08	11.15
Textile operatives	51.60	47.11	4.49	53.00	46.57	6.43
Construction workers	43.30	38.03	5.27	39.29	35.07	4.22
Miners	34.70	29.96	4.74	31.11	28.58	2.53#
High-ranking officials	67.47	71.34	-3.87#	68.00	69.85	-1.85#
Electricians	65.87	68.25	-2.38	65.12	67.01	-1.89#
Drivers	61.48	68.17	-6.69	55.51	65.51	-10.00
Athletes	62.70	66.59	-3.89	57.26	62.48	-5.22
Typists	50.85	55.41	-4.56	59.57	62.34	-2.77#
Clerical workers	51.62	55.26	-3.64	52.91	53.94	-1.03#
Purchasers	43.99	52.72	-8.73	43.37	51.46	-8.09
Ticket agents	41.46	53.82	-12.36#	43.69	47.15	-3.46
Sales clerks	39.44	44.55	-5.11	39.14	46.90	-7.76
Waiters and attendants	36.36	41.42	-5.06	36.54	45.11	-8.57
Barbers	30.51	33.62	-3.11	33.11	33.58	-.47#

* All differences are significant at the .05 level, except those marked with #.

American Journal of Sociology

Perhaps, the manual workers gave these occupations lower ratings than the nonmanual workers did because of their greater familiarity with the heavy physical demands required in these occupations. The male manual respondents gave higher ratings to high-ranking officials, athletes, typists, clerical workers, and purchasers than did nonmanual males. These ratings seem to point to those occupations in the nonmanual group that are attainable or aspired to from the manual workers' point of view. These occupations do not generally require high education levels.

For the female respondents, similar differences show up. The nonmanual workers favored teachers, physicians, engineers, natural and social scientists, whereas the manual respondents gave higher ratings to drivers, purchasers, waiters, and sales clerks. Thus, the ratings seem sensitive to the occupational positions of the respondents. There is a slight tendency for people to give higher ratings to occupations of one's own type of work (nonmanual or manual) and for manual workers to give higher ratings to lower nonmanual occupations.

In summary, examination of the occupational scale by respondents' age cohort, gender, and occupational grouping indicates that the scores reflect realistic and interpretable responses from the sampled respondents in one particular Chinese urban area.

COMPARISON WITH RATINGS IN OTHER SCALES

We now compare the Chinese occupational prestige scale with several ratings of both prestige and socioeconomic status available for the United States and other societies. The purpose is not to validate the Chinese scale, since discrepancies cannot be interpreted as measures of cross-cultural invalidity. Rather, it is again intended as a sensitivity test to ascertain whether differences, if any, would reflect different structural (including economic and political) elements in the two societies. If the Chinese prestige scale indeed is sensitive to that society, then we would expect that significant prestige differences should occur for those occupations that reflect power positions and access to resources unique to each society.

For our purpose, we selected five Western occupational scales: (1) the Treiman Standard International Occupational Prestige Scale (Treiman 1977), (2) the Siegel-NORC prestige scale (Siegel 1971), (3) the Duncan Socioeconomic Status index (Duncan 1961), (4) the Bose index (Bose and Rossi 1983; Bose 1985), and (5) the Nam-Powers scale (Nam and Powers 1983). The Treiman scale (SIOPS) is derived from multinational data and is the most widely accepted international prestige scale. The Siegel-NORC scale is probably the most popular prestige scale in use in the United States. Likewise, the Duncan SEI is probably the most used

Occupational Prestige

North American socioeconomic index of occupations. These scales and indices were initially constructed from responses of primarily male respondents or both male and female respondents. Two recent scales, the Bose index and the Nam-Powers scale, were constructed with the intention of tapping prestige ratings of occupations by females. In our study, as well as in most other studies, there is a strong correspondence in the pattern of relative prestige rankings of occupations between male and female respondents. However, such correspondence does not eliminate differences in absolute ratings for certain occupations, nor can it anticipate possible divergence in the future. We decided, therefore, also to include these two female-specific scales as part of the comparison.

Not all the sampled occupations in the Chinese scale have their exact counterparts on these scales. We tried to match occupations according to the actual work involved. The three categories of officials were most problematic. Thus, the matchings at times are approximate at best. The comparative analysis mainly provides heuristic clues for identifying major societal differences in perceiving occupations.

We first compared the Chinese scale with the Treiman, Siegel, and Duncan indices. This comparison was conducted for the male respondents in the sample, 20–64 years of age, to make it compatible with the samples for which these scales were constructed. For comparative purposes, we standardized the Chinese ratings in terms of the Treiman SIOPS.[10] Zero-order correlation coefficients between the Chinese scale scores for the 50 occupations and the Treiman, Siegel, and Duncan scale ratings are .90, .89, and .88, respectively. Thus, there is a strong correspondence in the general pattern of rankings between Chinese and other societies.

Analyses were then performed to identify those Chinese occupations that showed significantly (t-test at .01 level of significance) different ratings compared with those scores obtained for other societies. Table 6 shows the occupations that were significantly scored higher or lower in China compared with the international scores computed with the Treiman SIOPS.

As can be seen, the Chinese males tended to give higher prestige than did males in other societies to electrical engineers, writers, reporters, electricians, drivers, mechanics, checkers, textile operatives, and waiters. Thus, the Chinese seem to assign higher ratings to jobs (1) that require

[10] The procedure used was to identify 50 occupations in the SIOPS comparable with the sampled Chinese occupations and then to calculate the mean and standard deviation of their score values. Using the formula proposed by Treiman (1977, p. 166), we converted the standardized score for each corresponding Chinese occupation. This standardization was conducted for the male and female groups separately.

American Journal of Sociology

TABLE 6

OCCUPATIONS OF SIGNIFICANT RATING DIFFERENCE (≤ .01) BY MALES BETWEEN THE
CHINESE SCALE AND TREIMAN'S INTERNATIONAL SCALE

Occupation	Standardized Chinese Scale (1)	Treiman's SIOPS (2)	(1) − (2)
Higher rating by Chinese males:			
Electrical and electronics engineers	72.6	65	7.6
Writers	69.1	62	7.1
Reporters	68.6	56	12.6
Electricians	55.5	44	11.5
Drivers	53.7	31	22.7
Mechanics	51.5	43	8.5
Checkers, examiners, and inspectors—			
manufacturing	46.4	39	7.4
Textile operatives	39.4	29	10.4
Waiters and attendants	28.9	21	7.9
Lower rating by Chinese males:			
Teachers, university	70.6	78	− 7.4
High-ranking officials	57.6	74	− 16.4
Middle-ranking officials	55.5	63	− 7.5
Accountants	53.2	62	− 8.8
Teachers, elementary school	46.7	57	− 10.3
Purchasers	38.2	46	− 7.8
Operatives and kindred workers—			
chemical products	31.0	41	− 10.0
Furnacemen, smeltermen, and pourers	26.6	38	− 11.4
Barbers	22.9	32	− 9.1
Miners	23.6	34	− 10.4

special skills (engineers, electricians, and mechanics) or a combination of skills and also possession of desirable resources (drivers); (2) that command desirable resources (writers and reporters) for physical mobility and freedom and perceived light manual labor, for routine household and life needs (waiters), and for authority (checkers); or (3) textile operatives, who are not as discriminated against in China as in other societies in terms of salaries and fringe benefits relative to other types of blue-collar workers.

On the other hand, Chinese males tended to give lower prestige to university teachers, high- and middle-ranking officials, accountants, elementary teachers, purchasers, chemical workers, furnacemen, barbers, and miners. They seem to fall into three categories: (1) those whose salaries do not differentiate them from other occupations as sharply as in most other societies, such as university and elementary teachers, accountants, and purchasers; (2) those whose prestige apparently suffered because of

Occupational Prestige

recent political and historical events, such as the high- and middle-ranking officials; and (3) those whose jobs involve heavy and sometimes dangerous physical labor, such as chemical workers, furnacemen, barbers, and miners.

Similar results were obtained when we compared the Chinese ratings with the Siegel and Duncan scales, shown in table 7. For the Chinese female respondents aged 20–64, we compared their ratings with the Bose and Nam-Powers scales. The zero-order correlation coefficients between the standardized (à la Treiman's SIOPS) Chinese rankings and the Bose and Nam-Powers scales of the 50 occupations are .77 and .81, respectively. These correlations are not as high as those for the male ratings, reflecting perhaps in part the looser fit between the Treiman scale and the two scales developed specifically for females. We are not in a position to make further evaluations regarding this issue in the present paper and leave it for investigations in the future. Occupations that show significant differences ($P < .01$) between the SIOPS standardized scores and the two Western scales are shown in table 8.

Chinese females gave relatively higher prestige than Westerners did to the following occupations: electricians, jewelers, typists, drivers, nurses, checkers, clerical workers, textile operatives, sewers, and cooks. They gave lower ratings to elementary school teachers, actors, ticket agents, mail carriers, plumbers, police officers, construction workers, furnacemen, barbers, miners, and pedicab pullers and drivers. Again, these ratings reflect preference for jobs with special skills and resources and dislike of jobs involving heavy manual labor and relatively low fringe benefits, and those affected by recent historical events (e.g., police).

COMPARISON WITH RATINGS FROM OTHER
COUNTRIES/SOCIETIES

Further comparisons between the Chinese occupational prestige rankings and ratings obtained in other countries, especially in developing and noncapitalist countries, would be informative. We have selected four countries/societies for such comparison: Japan, Taiwan, the Soviet Union, and Poland. Japan is a developed country in Asia, with cultural and social norms substantially similar to both traditional and, in many ways, contemporary China. Taiwan is a Chinese society with a different recent political and economic history from mainland China's, yet with historical and cultural norms substantially similar to those in mainland China. The Soviet Union and Poland are two representatives of the socialist system. Thus, these four countries/societies offer useful comparisons of political, economic, cultural, and ecological variations that may affect norms and values concerning ratings assigned to occupations. The

TABLE 7

Occupations of Significant Rating Difference (≤ .01) between Chinese and U.S. Males

Occupation	Standardized Chinese Scale (1)	Standardized Siegel NORC Scale (2)	(1) − (2)	Standardized Duncan SEI Scale (3)	(1) − (3)
Higher rating by Chinese males:					
Electricians	55.5	48.9	6.6	46.3	9.2
Drivers	53.7	33.2	20.5	29.8	23.9
Jewelers, gold- and silversmiths	47.8	38.1	9.7	39.6	8.2
Checkers, examiners, and inspectors—manufacturing	46.4	37.1	9.3	28.0	18.4
Textile operatives	39.5	33.0	6.5	23.7	15.8
Sewers and stitchers—manufacturing	35.2	26.4	8.8	28.0	7.2
Cooks	34.5	27.4	7.1	26.8	7.7
Lower rating by Chinese males:					
Actors	47.9	55.7	−7.8	54.6	−6.7
Teachers, elementary school	46.7	60.6	−13.9	61.5	−14.8
Purchasers	38.2	48.9	−10.7	48.1	−9.9
Mail carriers	36.7	43.2	−6.5	49.9	−13.2
Police officers	34.8	48.9	−14.1	42.0	−7.2
Barbers	22.9	39.1	−16.2	29.5	−6.6
Housemaids	10.7	19.5	−8.8	23.1	−12.4

TABLE 8

OCCUPATIONS OF SIGNIFICANT RATING DIFFERENCE (≤ .01) BETWEEN CHINESE AND U.S. FEMALES

Occupation	Standardized Chinese Scale (1)	Standardized Nam and Powers Scale (2)	(1) − (2)	Standardized Bose Scale (3)	(1) − (3)
Higher rating by Chinese females:					
Electricians	54.3	47.0	7.3	47.1	7.2
Jewelers, gold- and silversmiths	50.9	28.7	22.2	33.2	17.7
Typists	49.5	41.8	7.7	34.2	15.3
Drivers	48.8	40.2	8.6	36.0	12.8
Nurses	48.2	37.6	10.6	37.0	11.2
Checkers and examiners—manufacturing	46.7	30.3	16.4	35.1	11.6
Clerical workers	43.1	36.4	6.7	36.0	7.1
Textile operatives	40.0	22.5	17.5	26.7	13.3
Sewers and stitchers—manufacturing	37.6	20.4	17.2	22.9	22.9
Cooks	32.6	17.8	14.8	25.7	6.9
Lower rating by Chinese females:					
Teachers, elementary school	52.0	63.7	−11.7	63.2	−11.2
Actors	45.1	61.6	−16.5	71.7	−26.6
Ticket, station, and express agents	38.7	59.0	−20.3	50.1	−11.4
Mail carriers	35.7	51.7	−16.0	50.1	−14.4
Plumbers	32.8	47.0	−14.2	46.4	−13.6
Police officers	32.7	57.5	−24.8	51.0	−18.3
Construction workers	28.2	36.6	−8.4	37.9	−9.7
Furnacemen, smeltermen, and pourers	25.1	39.2	−14.1	32.3	−7.2
Barbers	24.4	31.4	−7.0	34.2	−9.8
Miners	21.8	34.0	−12.2	44.5	−22.7
Pedicab pullers and drivers	13.7	20.4	−6.7	33.2	−19.5

American Journal of Sociology

ratings of occupations for these countries/societies come from the compilation by Treiman (1977). A number of other countries were also considered (e.g., India, Yugoslavia, Ghana, and Iraq). However, there were not sufficient numbers of rated occupations from these countries comparable with those rated in our study to warrant analysis.

Since comparisons could only be made when same or similar occupations were rated in the other countries/societies, the number of occupations used was 28 for Poland, 30 for Taiwan, 32 for Japan, and 34 for the Soviet Union. We standardized the rating scores for each occupation in terms of the occupations available for comparison from each country.

Because the number of occupations available for such comparisons is extremely small, the results should be interpreted with caution. Nevertheless, it is clear that the Chinese ratings are much closer to those from Taiwan ($r = .89$) and Japan (.90) than to those from Poland (.74) and the Soviet Union (.69). Our initial interpretation is that this might reflect significant similarities of cultural and historical norms in the Asian countries with respect to occupational prestige in these countries, despite their differing current political and economic systems.

Further examination of the data revealed the specific occupations receiving significantly different ratings between the Chinese raters and raters from the other countries/societies. The results of this comparison appear in table 9. The Russian ratings, compared with those from China, tend to downgrade electricians, secretaries, accountants, clerical workers, and typists and to upgrade furnacemen and miners. The Polish ratings also tend to favor furnacemen and miners while downgrading typists, clerical workers, reporters, and drivers. These ratings clearly reflect the higher social regard for heavy-industry workers in the Soviet Union and Poland. It should be noted that heavy industry was a major focus in China during the 1950s. However, after the various movements (e.g., the Great Leap Forward and communalization) of the late 1950s, great effort had to be made to recover from the economic distress, and attention shifted to the daily needs of the population. Thus, heavy industry and its associated occupations have not achieved the level of rewards and incentives evident in the Soviet Union and the Eastern European countries. Treiman (1977, chap. 6) has also noted that Poland and the Soviet Union had unusually high ratings for jobs in heavy industry. The relatively high ratings of heavy-industry workers and low ratings for female-dominated office jobs (secretaries, clerical workers, and typists) largely account for the overall lower correspondence of ratings between China and the Soviet Union and Poland.

On the other hand, ratings in Japan and Taiwan are more in favor of scientists, teachers, nurses, police, painters, and chemical workers and less favorable toward drivers, reporters, electricians, engineers, writers,

822

Occupational Prestige

TABLE 9

OCCUPATIONS OF SIGNIFICANT RATING DIFFERENCE (≤ .05) BETWEEN CHINA AND
FOUR COUNTRIES/SOCIETIES

		DIFFERENCE BETWEEN CHINESE SCALE AND OTHER SCALES			
OCCUPATION	CHINA	USSR	Poland	Japan	Taiwan
Higher rating by Chinese:					
Electrical and electronics engineers ...	72.6	6.9	...	8.9	...
Writers	69.1	(−3.8)	10.0	9.1	...
Reporters	68.6	...	12.7	12.2	9.4
Electricians	55.5	15.4	(2.6)	12.7	...
Librarians	54.0	9.2	...	...	...
Secretaries	53.9	25.9	7.3	(3.3)	(6.5)
Drivers	53.7	6.5	12.0	18.1	15.1
Accountants	53.2	29.2	(5.9)	...	(1.8)
Mechanics	51.5	6.7	...	7.7	23.9
Machinists	46.8	(.4)	(−1.1)	9.0	(5.4)
Clerical workers	42.8	14.8	14.4	(−3.4)	(−4.6)
Typists	42.7	14.7	15.8	(−1.1)	(−4.7)
Lower rating by Chinese:					
Natural scientists	72.5	(−5.2)	...	−8.6	(3.9)
Teachers, university	70.6	(1.7)	(−4.6)	−7.0	−8.9
Teachers, elementary school	46.7	−7.0	−15.8	−8.8	...
Nurses	42.3	(−.2)	−8.3	−7.5	...
Police officers	34.8	...	(1.8)	−10.8	−9.8
Painters	33.0	(2.6)	...	...	−8.4
Operatives and kindred workers— chemical products	31.0	−13.8	...	...	−10.4
Furnacemen, smeltermen, and pourers	26.6	−28.7	−28.2	...	...
Miners	23.6	−32.5	−29.3	(1.9)	(6.2)
Barbers	22.9	...	−11.6	−8.6	(−5.5)

NOTE.—The differences, in parentheses, are insignificant at the .05 level.

mechanics, and machinists. These seem to reflect differences in the relative availability of such workers and the resources they possess in the respective societies.

As a whole, therefore, the ratings given to occupations by Chinese males and females are very similar in general pattern to ratings in other societies. Where they differ reflects preference for jobs with special skills and resources considered desirable in China today and downgrading of jobs because of their leveled socioeconomic treatment in the Chinese occupational structure and pay scales or because of recent historical and political events.

823

American Journal of Sociology

The general conclusions we draw from these comparisons are (1) that there is indeed a general invariant pattern of occupational prestige ratings that seems to transcend cultural and political boundaries and (2) that within the general invariant pattern of ratings there are significant rating differences assigned to jobs in each society reflecting both (*a*) the perceived desirable skills and resources and (*b*) evaluated gaps between nonmanual and manual work required or leveling/extending socioeconomic benefits associated with certain jobs in the society because of the society's unique recent historical events and current changes.

ESTIMATION EQUATIONS FOR PRESTIGE OF ALL OCCUPATIONS

In Appendix B, we propose a series of equations to estimate the prestige of every occupation in China, based on a selected set of predictors. Such a scale is important for further studies of occupational stratification and mobility in China. The strategy we followed was similar to the Duncan SEI scale construction. However, because of the lack of detailed education and income statistics for various occupational groupings, we had to make estimates from sample data.

SUMMARY AND DISCUSSION

This study presents perhaps the first community-based attempt to measure occupational prestige in mainland China. The results strongly support the universal pattern of occupational rankings among sampled occupations in other societies reported by Treiman. There is evidence of stable and universal evaluations of contemporary occupations across cultural, political, and ecological boundaries. This universal pattern seems largely undisturbed, even after a society has experienced recent revolutionary movements specifically aimed at revamping stratification and mobility patterns, which has been illustrated by the recent history of China.

Within the general universal pattern of rankings, however, our data also suggest that the specific rankings of certain occupations may be affected by structural and cultural aspects of a given society. In China, the rankings of certain occupations seem to be affected by skills and resources valued at the particular historical moment in the development of the society as well as by recent political events.

Thus, in the analysis of the occupational prestige rankings, researchers can anticipate a general correspondence of a society's overall pattern with those of other societies, especially ones with similar geopolitical characteristics. At the same time, attention must be given to specific ranking differences owing to the society's recent history. Without such sensitivity, it would be too easy to detect recent and current trends and, thereby, to fail to anticipate changes.

In the case of China, we are mindful of the rapid social and economic changes taking place in urban and rural areas. Because of the large-scale implementation of the self-responsibility system and market-oriented organizations and processes, the value and prestige of certain occupations are sure to change. As certain resources become more accessible, occupations commanding such resources may likely receive lower prestige (e.g., drivers). There is also a clear trend toward assigning better benefits to certain professional positions in the modernization movement (e.g., university teaching). We also speculate that, in the next decade or so, if the current policies persist, income will become a more reliable predictor of occupational prestige, especially in urban China. This will in turn make estimations of occupational prestige more precise.

Another expected change is the shift in rural-urban population distribution in China. Until recently, rural residents were restricted in moving to towns and cities. Its effect can be seen in the strong preference of the younger respondents for jobs associated with urban areas. Since the end of 1984, however, new policies have allowed rural residents to live in towns, county government sites, and certain cities. In conjunction with the industrial and commercial development currently taking place in towns and cities, it is quite conceivable that we may witness one of the largest rural–small town transfers in any modern society. This does not suggest that the urban-rural distribution would in the foreseeable future reach the proportional shift of the past four decades in North America. Nevertheless, this anticipated shift will increase the generalizability of occupational prestige measures examined in the urban areas of China.

Another trend also worth noting here is that the bureaucratic structure and positions may continue to change in the future. There have been ongoing discussions on the separation of the party structure and the administrative structure in enterprises as well as in bureaucracies and institutions. This trend was perhaps significantly set back, as the campaign against "bourgeois liberalization" begun in early 1987 has expanded to reassert the authority of the party in all spheres (reflected in the insistence on the four guiding principles: socialism, dictatorship of the proletariat, the thoughts of Marx and Mao, and the leadership of the Communist party). It is too early to tell how long it will take and how the separation of the party and the administration will take place. Nonetheless, such changes will remain topics for debate and struggle.

In any event, occupational mobility in terms of employment on a contractual basis and permission for job changes is now more than a thought. These practices are becoming quite common in most middle- and small-

American Journal of Sociology

size enterprises. Continuation and even acceleration of these changes may be anticipated as long as the political reversal does not grow stronger. Their effects on occupational prestige and mobility will be far-reaching.

Finally, we have some concern regarding a potential trend toward more gender segregation in the occupational structure. As China moves toward a market orientation in its economy and ideology, it might also experience acceleration of the gender differentiation generally associated with such a labor market. We have found, for example, in our data, a trend toward a more skewed distribution of party members in favor of males over females in the younger age cohort. Percentages of party members for males and females for the cohort entering the labor force before 1949 were 47 and 50, respectively. The party memberships generally declined for younger cohorts as expected. But the decline was significantly steeper for female workers. For the cohort entering the labor force during 1966–76, the respective percentages were 28.6 and 16.6. For the youngest cohort, those entering the labor force after 1976, party membership dropped to 17.9% for males and 3.3% for females (Xie and Lin 1986). What explains this differential trend and what its implication will be for occupational stratification and mobility for males and females are unclear but deserve policy and research attention.

If these current trends continue, we predict that China will move toward an occupational prestige–ranking pattern and mobility pattern even more similar to those in many societies following a general market-driven economic policy, and especially those in so-called capitalist societies.

To set the stage for future comparisons, we are analyzing the status-attainment process with data obtained in the same survey and estimating the relative contributions of various personal and social resources, as well as of structural factors (labor sector, party membership, gender, etc.), to status attainment as measured by the Lin-Xie prestige scale outlined in the present paper.

APPENDIX A

Occupation Sets Used in Questionnaire

The five sets of 10 occupations were presented in the following sequence in the questionnaire (ranking in the total set is in parentheses):

Set 1: (1) *baomu*—housemaids (50)
(2) *zhugon*—furnacemen, smeltermen, and pourers (44)
(3) *yisheng*—doctors (1)
(4) *yianyuan*—actors (22)
(5) *shouhuoyuan*—sales clerks (40)
(6) *tushu guanliyuan*—librarians (11)

Occupational Prestige

(7) *jizhe*—reporters (7)
(8) *guangong*—plumbers (38)
(9) *jiqi xuligong*—mechanics (19)
(10) *chanpin jianyangong*—checkers, examiners, and inspectors (manufacturing) (23)

Set 2: (1) *zhongxue jiaoshi*—teachers, secondary school (9)
(2) *fangzhi gongren*—textile operatives (30)
(3) *jianzhu gongren*—construction workers (42)
(4) *jingcha*—police officers (36)
(5) *chuji ganbu*—middle-ranking officials (12)
(6) *daziyuan*—typists (25)
(7) *chushi*—cooks (37)
(8) *qiche siji*—drivers (16)
(9) *shehui kexuejia*—social scientists (5)
(10) *lifayuan*—barbers (45)

Set 3: (1) *dianqi gongchengshi*—electrical and electronics engineers (2)
(2) *mishu*—secretaries (15)
(3) *youqi gongren*—painters (39)
(4) *sijuji ganbu*—high-ranking officials (10)
(5) *kuaiji*—accountants (14)
(6) *diangong*—electricians (13)
(7) *shoupiaoyuan*—ticket, station, and express agents (35)
(8) *renliche gongren*—pedicab pullers and drivers (48)
(9) *kuanggong*—miners (46)
(10) *oiangong*—machinists (24)

Set 4: (1) *fuwuyuan*—waiters and attendants (43)
(2) *zuojia*—writers (6)
(3) *yundongyuan*—athletes (18)
(4) *zhuangxie gongren*—loaders (47)
(5) *ziran kexuejia*—natural scientists (4)
(6) *youdiyuan*—mail carriers (32)
(7) *yinshua gongren*—pressmen (29)
(8) *fengren gongren*—sewers and stitchers, manufacturing (33)
(9) *hushi*—nurses (26)
(10) *xiaoxue jiaoshi*—teachers, elementary school (21)

Set 5: (1) *yewu banshiyuan*—clerical workers (27)
(2) *huaxue gongren*—operatives and kindred workers, chemical products (41)
(3) *daxue jiaoshi*—teachers, college and university (3)
(4) *caigouyuan*—purchasers (31)

827

American Journal of Sociology

  (5) *qingjie gongren*—cleaners and garbage collectors (48)
  (6) *shipin gongren*—operatives and kindred workers, food
      and kindred products (34)
  (7) *shougongyipin gongren*—jewelers, gold- and silver-
      smiths (20)
  (8) *jianzhu gongchengshi*—civil engineers (8)
  (9) *keji ganbu*—low-ranking officials (17)
  (10) *dianqishebei anzhuanggong*—installers of electrical equip-
      ment (28)

APPENDIX B

The Lin-Xie Indices of Occupational Prestige for China

The task is to construct one or several equations using certain easily
obtainable variables as predictors so that prestige scores for occupations
other than the 50 sampled occupations can be estimated. Two criteria
guide our selection of predictive variables in the construction of the indices. First, the variables must be easily accessible in census documents.
For example, age, gender, education, and occupation (e.g., manual vs.
nonmanual) are such variables. Second, the variables must be easily
collectible in social surveys and not too sensitive to meet respondent or
other data-source resistance for cultural or other reasons. The usually
available data include the already-mentioned variables as well as basic
monthly salary (but not bonuses or fringe benefits, including pay for extra
hours of work, food inflation adjustments, transportation, baths and
haircuts).

   There are two sampling frames in which such estimation equations can
be constructed: the respondent sample and the occupation sample. We
decided to use our sample of 50 selected occupations. This method is
similar to the one used by Duncan (1961), Nam and Powers (1983), and
Bose (1985). Subsequent work on the respondent sample showed almost
identical results.

   Selection of predictors.—For predictors, we chose the following variables: education, income (monthly salary), manual/nonmanual work,
age, and gender ratios. The census publications have not reported the
average education for each detailed category of occupation. Therefore,
we adopted the average (mean) education for each major group of occupations in which the sampled occupation fell. For example, the mean
education for the category of clerical occupations was used as the education level for typists. There are several exceptions to this rule when other
sources provided the information for the specific detailed sampled occupations. For example, the average education levels of the university,

Occupational Prestige

secondary school, and elementary school teachers were available else-where, as were the average education levels of physicians and nurses.

However, one problem in using basic monthly salary as an estimator for Chinese occupational prestige is that the information is much harder to obtain from Chinese secondary sources. The Chinese census of 1982 did not contain any item on income, for example. Therefore, there might be some practical problems in creating an index of occupational prestige using income as a predictor. In this case, we had to use the mean income (monthly salaries) of the sampled occupations from the respondent data. That is, the mean income of all respondents in the same major group of occupations was used as the estimated average income for each sampled occupation.

The decision to use the manual/nonmanual distinction as a predictor was based on the earlier finding that the universal preference for non-manual jobs remains dominant in determining the prestige of an occupa-tion in China. The traditional honor accorded nonmanual occupations also seems to have persisted. Therefore, it is reasonable to expect that it contributes to the ratings of occupations today in China. Also, there is a significantly greater gradation of resources and rewards between entry and high positions among nonmanual occupations than within manual occupations. A nonmanual jobholder may have income similar to a manual jobholder's at a given moment, but the chances of further eco-nomic and intragenerational mobility are much greater for the former than for the latter. For these reasons, we felt that the manual/nonmanual distinction could contribute to the prestige ratings of occupations. We used the crude classifications provided by the census (see table 1) to group the professionals (the 0's and 1's), the administrators (2's), and the cleri-cals (3's) as the nonmanual occupations. These occupations are termed the "mental workers" (0, 1, and 2) and the "mental-and-physical workers" (3) by the Chinese census. The remaining categories (sales, service, farm-ing, and manufacturing and transportation workers) were classified as manual occupations.

The average age given in the census data for each major occupational group to which the sampled occupation belonged was used as the esti-mated age of workers in that sampled occupation. From the census data, the percentage of female workers for each major group to which the detailed sampled occupation belonged was used as the estimated sex ratio of workers in the sampled occupation. The sex ratio variable is used to examine the potential effect of gender segmentation on occupational pres-tige. The age variable was included because earlier analysis showed that age cohorts were related to differential ratings of certain occupations. Further analysis incorporating these predictors did not improve the R^2,

829

American Journal of Sociology

nor were the coefficients meaningful (F values were .02 for age and .09 for sex ratio).

Construction of estimation equations.—The first equation constructed uses two predictors: education and income. The education variable is measured with the levels of education in the national census: (1) no school, (2) elementary school, (3) junior high (middle) school, (4) high school, (5) vocational college, and (6) college and higher. Income is measured by the actual Chinese yuan earned as basic monthly salary at the time of the 1983 survey. The resulting equation for this education-income index (EII) is

$$\text{EII} = -5.188 + 13.874 \text{ (education)} + .262 \text{ (income)}.$$

This socioeconomic index has an R^2 of .72, with partial standardized regression coefficients of .67 and .26 for education and income, respectively. The zero-order correlation coefficient between prestige and education is .82 and between prestige and income, .65. Duncan, in his socioeconomic index of occupational status for men in the United States (1961), found an R^2 of .83, with zero-order correlations between status and education at .85 and between status and income at .84.

Relatively speaking, therefore, prestige ratings in China were more affected by education levels than by income levels. This reflects, in part, the relatively restricted range of income differences in China, as observed by Parish (1984), and, in part, the significant differentiation of education levels, as discussed earlier. Also, Treiman (1977, p. 115), using the International Scale metric measures, found higher standardized coefficients for education (about .52) than for income (about .36) in a study of five countries, including the United States and Taiwan. Our finding is consistent with his after the scale measures are standardized.

The next index involved the addition of the manual (0)/nonmanual (1) distinction as a predictive variable, along with education and income. The resulting estimation equation for the manual/nonmanual–education-income index (MEI) is as follows:

$$\text{MEI} = 1.604 + 7.795 \text{ (nonmanual)} + 11.041 \text{ (education)} + .239 \text{ (income)}.$$

The R^2 for the MEI index is .74, and the standardized coefficients are .21 for manual/nonmanual, .53 for education, and .23 for income. The R^2 was not appreciably higher than that for the EII equation. However, the contribution of education was substantially reduced because of the manual/nonmanual specification. Therefore, it can be inferred that the manual/nonmanual classification may serve as an intermediary variable between education and occupational prestige. The education level dictates the likelihood of entering a particular segment of the labor force (the zero-order correlation between education and manual/nonmanual classi-

Occupational Prestige

fication is .70), and this segmental position determines occupational prestige.

These analyses suggest that the simplest, yet reasonable, estimation of occupational prestige can be obtained by using the education, income, and manual/nonmanual variables as predictors (eq. [MEI]). Furthermore, if the manual/nonmanual specification is not used, the resulting prediction remains reasonably high (eq. [EII]).

With the use of easily accessible or collectible variables—education, income, and manual/nonmanual—as predictors, estimation of prestige for all occupations becomes possible. This estimation is sufficiently precise for our purpose (explained variance being in the range of .75).[11]

REFERENCES

Beijing Review. 1984. "Decision of the Central Committee of the Communist Party of China on Reform of the Economic Structure (Adopted by the 12th Central Committee of the Communist Party of China at Its Third Plenary Session on October 20, 1984)." *Beijing Review* 27, no. 44 (October 29): 2–15.

Blau, P., and O. D. Duncan. 1967. *The American Occupational Structure*. New York: Free Press.

Bose, C. 1985. *Jobs and Gender: A Study of Occupational Prestige*. New York: Praeger.

Bose, C., and P. Rossi. 1983. "Gender and Jobs: Prestige Standings of Occupations as Affected by Gender." *American Sociological Review* 48:316–30.

Chang, K. C. 1986. "Continuity and Rupture: Draft of a Theory on the Rise of Civilizations." *China Culture Quarterly* 1 (1): 1–8.

Cheng, Lucie, and Alvin So. 1983. "The Reestablishment of Sociology in the PRC: Toward the Sinification of Marxist Sociology." Pp. 471–98 in *Annual Review of Sociology*, vol. 9. Edited by R. H. Turner and J. F. Short, Jr. Palo Alto, Calif.: Annual Reviews.

Duncan, O. D. 1961. "A Socioeconomic Index for All Occupations." Pp. 109–38 in *Occupations and Social Status*, edited by A. J. Reiss. New York: Free Press.

Goldthorpe, J. H., and K. Hope. 1972. "Occupational Grading and Occupational Prestige." Pp. 19–79 in *The Analysis of Social Mobility: Methods and Approaches*, edited by K. Hope. London: Oxford University Press.

Hauser, R., and D. Featherman. 1977. *The Process of Stratification: Trends and Analysis*. New York: Academic.

[11] The decision to place the manufacturing and transportation workers in a category between clerical workers and sales workers was based on the observation that the mean salaries of these categories followed such a sequence. However, the mean education level of the manufacturing and transportation workers was actually between those of the sales workers and the service workers. Therefore, we recalculated all the estimation equations by another occupational grouping variable in which the manufacturing and production workers were placed between sales workers and service workers. Results showed little variation in estimations from those presented in the paper. However, alternative rankings of these occupations should be kept in mind for the future, as the education and income levels of these workers may undergo ranking changes.

American Journal of Sociology

Lan, C., and Z. Chang. 1982. "The Aspirations of Graduating Students in Senior High School." *Society* (Shanghai), May, pp. 22–25.
Lin, N. 1986. "Flourishing Exchanges between Chinese and American Sociologists." *ASA Footnotes*, August, pp. 10–11.
Nam, C., and M. Powers. 1983. *The Socioeconomic Approach to Status Measurement*. Houston: Cap and Gown.
North, C., and P. Hatt. 1947. "Jobs and Occupations: A Popular Evaluation." *Opinion News* 9:3–13.
Parish, W. 1984. "Destratification in China." Pp. 84–120 in *Class and Social Stratification in Post-Revolution China*, edited by J. Watson. New York: Cambridge University Press.
Robinson, R., and J. Kelley. 1979. "Class as Conceived by Marx and Dohrebdorf: Effects on Income and Political Inequality in the United States and Great Britain." *American Sociological Review* 44:38–58.
Rossi, A. S., ed. 1985. *Sociology and Anthropology in the People's Republic of China: Report of a Delegation Visit, February–March 1984*. Washington, D.C.: National Academy.
Siegel, P. 1971. "Prestige in the American Occupational Structure." Ph.D. diss., University of Chicago.
Statistical Bureau of China. 1984a. *10 Percent Sampling Tabulation on the 1982 Census of the People's Republic of China*. Beijing: Statistical Press in China.
———. 1984b. *Annual of Chinese Statistics (1983)*. Beijing: Statistical Press in China.
———. 1984c. *Annual of Beijing's Statistics (1983)*. Beijing: Statistical Press in China.
Treiman, D. 1977. *Occupational Prestige in Comparative Perspective*. New York: Academic.
Weber, M. (1922) 1957. *The Theory of Social and Economic Organization*. Edited by T. Parsons. New York: Free Press.
Wright, E. 1979. *Class Structure and Income Determination*. New York: Academic.
Xie, W., and N. Lin. 1986. "The Process of Status Attainment in Urban China." Paper presented at the annual meeting of the American Sociological Association, August–September, New York.
Xuan, Z., J. Chang, and W. Xie. 1984. "An Inquiry into Occupational Evaluation." *Society* (Shanghai), August, pp. 20–23.

PART IV

REFLECTIONS

Lessons learned from lifelong studying and conducting research

Nan Lin

After I successfully defended my dissertation, my committee members congratulated me. One of them said, "Nan, you should feel good. This is probably the high point of your knowledge!" I was shocked because I was impatient to finish the dissertation so that I could move on to a number of projects. I felt that there was so much more to be learned, and I was eager to learn it. His remarks taught me a great lesson: while respecting and learning from senior scholars and authorities, never accept their wisdom in their entirety. For the next five decades I followed this lesson and continued to benefit from it. In this reminiscent chapter, I recount some of the highlights of my lifelong learning and share this pleasure with the readers.

Learning from masters

Early on in my career, I had the opportunity to meet some of the masters of scholarship and learned some important academic and professional practices from them.

Ev Roger was the first master I met as a graduate student. Ev was a pleasure to know, and to work for and with. He always treated his colleagues and students well, was willing to share and accept ideas, truly collaborative in work, and always gave them credit in publications. I was flattered to be a coauthor and enjoyed seeing my name appear in a publication for the first time. The lessons I learned from Ev were how to build research teams and to collaborate and share credit with graduate students. I have followed these practices in my career, and I have derived pleasure from doing so.

As I started my professional career as a young faculty, I was fortunate to be in a department with Jim Coleman. I had admired Jim from a distance as a great scholar. After some hesitation, I decided to share some of my draft writings with him. Jim was a very busy man and I rarely had a chance to talk to him in person, so I made appointments (usually very short) to see him and seek his feedback on my work. When we met, he would pull out my writing, give it a quick reading and make some short but always useful points. While in his office on one occasion, I noticed that several of his cabinet drawers were labeled "rejected manuscripts." This was a surprise because I assumed that all writings of a scholar of Jim's stature must be good and NOBODY would turn down his manuscripts. The fact that some of his manuscripts were turned down and that he openly labeled them as such in his office was an eye-opener for a young scholar. The lesson I learned was that it was no big deal to be rejected, and to just keep working on manuscripts. Revising and resubmitting manuscripts has become a pleasure rather than a pain – most of the time.

As a young sociologist, I worked on some data sets and realized that Merton's homophily principle was a very powerful proposition. I drafted a paper, and decided it would be great to get some feedback from Merton himself. I did not know him and wasn't sure whether it would be appropriate to mail him the manuscript (no Internet at the time). I decided to do it, thinking that the worst-case scenario would be that he would never reply. I was therefore surprised that he not only responded a couple of weeks later, but he also sent back a carefully and thoroughly edited manuscript. I was flattered and surprised. His editing and comments were very helpful in my revision of the manuscript. I am sure he had done this numerous times for young sociologists who did not know him in person. The lesson I learned was that a senior scholar could provide enormous encouragement to young scholars by commenting on their work, even if he/she did not know them.

Grabbing opportunities
Research opportunities come from a variety of venues, some of them rather unexpected. I cite a few experiences that came my way early in my career. One opportunity came from a student in my class at Hopkins on innovation diffusion. During the course he told me that his father, a physician, was organizing an immunization campaign in rural communities in Central America, and he wondered if we could do a diffusion study. I readily agreed, and applied for a research grant from the National Science Foundation. At that time no junior scholars could apply for a grant from NSF, so I sought the help of a senior faculty in the department. He signed on as the senior scholar for the grant application sponsoring my research. I received the grant and proceeded to conduct fieldwork in Costa Rica and Honduras along with the student and several others. Eventually we extended the work to Haiti. We gained research experience in conducting house-to-house surveys and mapping sociometric patterns, from which we identified the "opinion leaders" in the diffusion of the immunization campaign. The study gave me an opportunity to design and conduct fieldwork and benefited the students. Some of them eventually became top scholars in their own right, among them Gerald Zaltman, Ron Burt, and Ralph Hingson.

In another class I taught at Albany, a student told me that his office (NY Office of Health) was investigating a possible social spread of an infection. With some funding from that office, we created a small-world study to demonstrate how information could be transmitted through social connections. Complementing Milgram's original "six-degree" connection study, we constructed a field experiment in which four targets (a white male, a white female, a black male, and a black female) at about the same socioeconomic level were randomly assigned to starters. The results confirmed the inequality hypothesis (more packets reached white targets) and the social-resource hypothesis (i.e., packets were forwarded to weaker ties but higher-status intermediaries were more likely to succeed). I gained some insights into how contacts and resources were linked (e.g., weak ties led to higher social positions and resources that were associated with eventual success) and was able to convince myself and others that such connections were "real" (i.e., real time and actual behaviors).

Social gatherings also led to unexpected research opportunities and collaborations. At one informal occasion I met a sociologist working at the Albany Medical College (Al Dean) and we started chatting about our mutual interest – how social connections could enhance health and mental health. We decided to put together a paper reviewing the research literature and proposing the social-support hypothesis. As it turned out, two other groups of social scientists were also independently looking into the social support notion at about the same time. We submitted the paper and it was soon accepted. We followed up with a research application to the National Institute of Mental Health. This was the beginning of a sustained project conducted with a panel of community residents over more than a decade. The funded projects drew in many students who became coauthors and authors in their own right (e.g., Walter Ensel, Mark Tausig and Gina Lai).

In 1979, as China and the United States re-established diplomatic relations, my wife, Alice, and I decided to visit some relatives in China. As we were embarking on the trip, I noticed in the news media that sociology was being reinstituted there (it had been banned in 1951). I sent a letter to the sociological group in China stating that as a sociologist I would like to meet them when we arrived in Beijing and how they could contact me. The contact was made, and I gave a talk to the sociological group. I suspect my taped talk received approval because my request to meet Professor Fei Xiao-tong, the leading sociologist in China, was arranged. When Fei and others subsequently organized a national class to train a new class of sociologists, Peter Blau, my colleague at Albany at the time, joined me in teaching that class at Nankai (more details in Bian's chapter in this book, Chapter 8). The connections with China expanded in multiple ways (e.g., the first Ph.D. training program for Chinese sociologists at Albany; numerous research projects between American and Chinese scholars; and my own research programs in China). Many students in that class became prominent scholars and institutional leaders (e.g., Yanjie Bian, Xueguang Zhou, Li-ping Sun, Song Lin-fei, Cai He, Wang Si-bin, Li You-mei). I subsequently served as a conduit between Chinese and western scholars and academic programs (e.g., ASA delegations to China, Ford Foundation grants programs).

Lessons on the development of research opportunities: (1) there are always "unintended consequences" from non-research circumstances. Some came to me unexpectedly and others due to my taking the initiative, (2) following up on some initial connections and efforts can pay off in big ways, for myself and others, and (3) researching in other societies enlightened my knowledge – finding the boundaries and limitations of studying in a single society/culture and learning to expand conceptual and operational schemes across multiple societies and cultures.

Multitasking, hands-on work, and participating in teamwork

Different people have different working styles. Some prefer to focus on a limited number of notions and issues and explore them deeply throughout their careers. I prefer multitasking – I am always curious about different ideas, whether I am exploring them or not. I tended to get involved in several projects or programs, probably no more than a handful, sometimes sequentially and other times simultaneously.

I am a practitioner of research. While I shared data gathering and data analyses with others, I took pleasure in the actual tasks of designing, gathering, and analyzing data. I gained a better appreciation of the patterns emerging from data analysis and gave immediate attention and consideration to what needed to be done next. Sometimes independently and sometimes with other participants, I would then launch the next series of data collection and/or analyses and anxiously watch the emerging patterns. This interaction between data analysis and thought process is central to my pleasure in research. When using secondary data I was always involved in data analyses and writing up reports. I never considered such tasks as secondary in importance or delegated this "dirty" work to others. I am pleased to report that all my former students have acquired this practice – they always participate in data design, data gathering, data analyzing, and writing up reports.

While mainly working closely with students, I also enjoyed working with others on book projects. Sharing broad issues with others and bringing in multiple contributors have been a delight. For example, coediting books with Peter Marsden, Ron Burt, Karen Cook, Bonnie Erickson, Yang-chih Fu, Jay Chih-jou Chen, and Ray-May Hsung not only affirmed the importance and benefits of scholarly collaboration, but also presented others in my network to the professional community. I was happy to be part of social capital in such networks.

On the shoulders of giants – but selectively
I never believed in inventing ideas. We take on ideas developed by others and build on them. Throughout my career I have benefited from the ideas developed by many others. Most notably, I have benefited from ideas at different stages of development from George Homans, Robert Merton, Peter Blau, Karl Marx, Pierre Bourdieu, James Coleman, Adam Smith, Karl Polanyi, and many others. I appreciated learning from them, but I never became a "true believer." George Homans taught me the reciprocal associations of interactions and activity (social) and sentiment (sociopsychological) in explaining human behaviors and human groups, but I was not inclined to believe that psychological factors were the ultimate causal factors, as Homans subsequently proposed. When I added the homophily factor from Merton's work to this scheme, social factors became just as important as the ultimate causal factors. Merton's homophily was so powerful and important, yet his writing on this issue was buried in an obscure book and sometimes mistaken as or confused with Larzarsfeld's work. To me Merton's homophily and heterophily principles are probably the most important sociological principles (as explicated by Rogers, McPherson, and so on) and yet were barely amplified in his later works. Blau and Duncan provided me with the framework of stratification and mobility on which I built the significance of social connections. Thus I was able to contribute the integration of social mobility and social networks/capital. Marx enlightened me with his notion of capital and the unequal relations between capitalists and labor in accounting for the production, reproduction, and accumulation of capital. However, his expectation that such exploitative relations would lead to revolutions, especially in developed economies, was unrealized. I argued instead (see Chapter 1 in Lin 2001a) that labor acquires other forms of capital (human capital, social capital, and cultural capital) and is able to demand better wages and compensation to accumulate surplus value for their own benefit. Bourdieu offered a precise definition of social capital and described how it produced benefit and gain for individual actors, but he then proceeded to argue that social capital mainly benefited the nobility class. So was social capital a component of individual action or a structural element for him? Coleman also shed light on social capital for individual actions. He then proceeded to describe it as a collective property and proclaimed that it could not be measured. I amended and clarified the notion and measurement of social capital so that it became clear to me that it is a concept based on microdynamics and is eminently measurable.

In the eighteenth century Adam Smith offered great insights on how moral sentiment provided the collective foundation of society and on which individual actions, for self-interest, made a difference. His self-interest thesis has dominated scholarly and political arenas for more than three hundred years, yet he never integrated these two fundamental elements of human society together. Why did he not do it? Polanyi provided a "correction" to Smith's "fictitious" scenario of free market and self-regulation by suggesting two counter-movements: state regulations and social relations (i.e., embeddedness). Unfortunately at the time of the publication of *The Great Transformation* (1944), the socialist state of the Soviet Union, for which he was hoping to provide a counter movement, was turning into a dictatorial state and destroying social relations and communities (Stiglitz 2001).

In my mind, each of these giants laid the foundation for understanding human behavior and human society. I built my work on their concepts and theories, even though I found each lacking or incomplete in some aspects. Nobody is perfect, and scholarly giants are no exception. When we recognize the imperfections we actually gain a greater appreciation of what they have accomplished and how we can benefit from their works. So what have I learned from these giants? A lot. First, I learned that understanding and appreciating history is important. Whether the history spans days, months, or years, it offers a firmer, though always tentative, grasp of potential cause–effect relations among concepts. Second, empirical work is important. Empirical work never ascertains cause–effect relationships for certain, but it does provide some assurance that a certain cause–effect relationship may hold. Third, integration is important. It offers opportunities for readers like me to bring different ideas from different giants together and contemplate "added" or "merged" ideas. Standing on the shoulders of the giants offers us a top-down view of a multitude of ideas and the exciting possibility of converging and/or emerging ideas.

Integrating theory, measurements, and research

Early in my career I taught and wrote about research methods. I always stressed that as researchers we should strive to integrate theory, measurements, and research in our work and not treat them as separate tasks for different scholars. This emphasis is difficult and not always attainable to our satisfaction. As I proceeded in my career, absorbing other scholars' works and ideas, observing in fieldwork, understanding patterns in data, and gleaning ideas from multiple projects, I learned the pleasure (and difficulties) of integrating ideas, specific measures, and empirical work guided by theory and employing the measures.

One example: in the early 1970s I read the recently published Blau–Duncan volume *The American Occupational Structure* (Blau and Duncan 1967) and Mark Granovetter's weak-tie piece (Granovetter 1973). I was intrigued by the Blau–Duncan path model of socioeconomic attainment that largely confirmed the education effect (achieved factor) rather than father's SES (ascribed factor), and wondered whether and how social connections and resources might "intervene" this process. Integrating stratification and mobility and network theories, I was curious whether social connections contributed to social mobility. This integrative thinking turned into a lifelong interest and effort (see Ronald Burt's contribution in this book, Chapter 2). Another example: involved in the development of the notion of social support, I wondered if and how much social relations sustained mental health and reduced the risk of symptoms and illnesses. Social resources/capital should thus affect expressive behaviors (e.g., attaining better well-being and alleviating life stresses) as well as instrumental behaviors (e.g., getting better jobs). However, these effects might trigger different mechanisms of social resources/capital (see Lijun Song's contribution in this book, Chapter 5).

By conducting work in different cultures and societies, I gained understanding of how various structural or institutional factors differentially affected individual and collective behaviors in different societies, and how to tease out the "cultural" or institutional factors in accounting for these differences. Thus structure and institutions act as contingent factors in understanding individual and group behaviors (see Yanjie Bian's contribution in this book, Chapter 8).

Integration work is fun, but it is hard work conceptually. It is even harder to collect data since such integration inevitably requires data that is not provided in previous data sets and requires data from multiple societies (see Lin et al. 2014a). To me, integration not only means bringing together different ideas from different perspectives and forging coherent and "innovative" schemes and theories, it also means integration of theory, measurement, and research. Too often each of these three segments of scholarship is seen as an independent aspect of scholarship. Scholars specialize as theorists, measurement experts, or empirical researchers. Theorists develop and integrate concepts and schemes; measurement experts take on such concepts and schemes, propose instruments, and test their validity or reliability; researchers apply theories and schemes, and employ measurement instruments to specific research contexts. To me, integration means bringing all three segments together.

While I had all three aspects in mind as I proceeded with my scholarship and career, it has taken me about three decades to be able to claim that I may have done it (or at least tried): social capital as a theory with specific measurements (contact resources in mobility studies and position generator as a general measure) and applied to different research settings (stratification, mental health, and so on). It was not consistently smooth sailing. Often my work seemed to have plateaued and shown little forward movement, though publications with collaborators kept coming. When I was moving from Albany to Duke, Harrison White, a casual (weak?) but important tie, teased, "Nan, now that you are moving to Duke to enjoy better resources, you are not abandoning your work, are you?" and urged me to consolidate my work into a book. This was the timely warning and stimulation I needed, but it still took me almost ten years to produce the integrative book he urged me to do (Lin 2001a). I am very grateful to him for pushing me to take on this task.

Live and learn – research as a hobby
There is a Chinese saying, "Living to an old age, and learning to the old age" (活到老, 学到老). How true and valuable it is. Now that I am retired, I have often been asked if I still work or care to work. Well, I do. Living to an old age offers more opportunities to learn and learning while aging enhances older life with happiness. In fact, without the obligation to show up in classes and meetings or writing the many required manuscript reviews and personnel evaluations, research has become a delightful hobby that still offers the opportunity to choose readings and engage in interactions with many colleagues and former students. I choose the pace of my work, but integrate work into my daily routine on both weekdays and weekends. My lifelong lesson has been and continues to be "Live and learn."

References

Acheson, James M. (1988), *The Lobster Gangs of Maine*, Lebanon, NH: University Press of New England.
Acock, Alan C. and Jeanne S. Hurlbert (1993), 'Social networks, marital status, and well-being', *Social Networks*, **15** (3), 309–34.
Adler, Paul S. and Seok-Woo Kwon (2002), 'Social capital: prospects for a new concept', *Academy of Management Review*, **27** (1), 17–40.
Andrews, Gavin, Christopher Tennant, Daphne M. Hewson and George E. Vaillant (1978), 'Life event stress, social support, coping style, and risk of psychological impairment', *Journal of Nervous and Mental Disease*, **166** (5), 307–16.
Aneshensel, Carol S. (1992), 'Social stress: theory and research', *Annual Review of Sociology*, **18**, 15–38.
Aneshensel, Carol S. and Ralph R. Frerichs (1982), 'Stress, support, and depression: a longitudinal causal model', *Journal of Community Psychology*, **10** (4), 363–76.
Aral, Sinan, Lev Muchnik and Arun Sundararajan (2009), 'Distinguishing influence-based contagion from homophily-driven diffusion in dynamic networks', *Proceedings of the National Academy of Science*, **106** (51), 21544–9.
Aral, Sinan and Marshall Van Alstyne (2011), 'The diversity-bandwidth trade-off', *American Journal of Sociology*, **117** (1), 90–171.
Asch, Solomon E. (1951), 'Effects of group pressure upon the modification and distortion of judgments', in Harold Guetzkow (ed.), *Groups, Leadership and Men*, Pittsburgh, PA: Carnegie Press, pp. 177–90.
Barker, James R. (1993), 'Tightening the iron cage: concertive control in self-managing teams', *Administrative Science Quarterly*, **38** (3), 408–37.
Barrera, Manuel, Jr. (1981), 'Social support in the adjustment of pregnant adolescents: assessment issues', in Benjamin H. Gottlieb (ed.), *Social Networks and Social Support*, Beverly Hills: Sage Publications, pp. 69–96.
Barrera, Manuel, Jr. (1986), 'Distinctions between social support concepts, measures, and models', *American Journal of Community Psychology*, **14** (4), 413–45.
Barrera, Manuel, Jr. (2000), 'Social support research in community psychology', in Julian Rappaport and Edward Seidman (eds.), *Handbook of Community Psychology*, New York: Kluwer Academic/Plenum, pp. 215–45.
Barrera, Manuel, Laurie Chassin and Fred Rogosch (1993), 'Effects of social support and conflict on adolescent children of alcoholic and nonalcoholic fathers', *Journal of Personality and Social Psychology*, **64** (4), 602–12.
Becker, Gary (1975), *Human Capital*, New York: Columbia University Press.
Beggs, John J., Valerie A. Haines and Jeanne S. Hurlbert (1996), 'Situational contingencies surrounding the receipt of informal support', *Social Forces*, **75** (1), 201–22.
Berkman, Lisa F. (1984), 'Assessing the physical health effects of social networks and social support', *Annual Review of Public Health*, **5**, 413–32.
Berkman, Lisa F. and Thomas Glass (2000), 'Social integration, social networks, social support and health', in Lisa F. Berkman and Ichiro Kawachi (eds.), *Social Epidemiology*, New York: Oxford University Press, pp. 137–73.
Berkman, Lisa F., Thomas Glass, Ian Brissette and Teresa E. Seeman (2000), 'From social integration to health: Durkheim in the new millennium', *Social Science & Medicine*, **51**, 843–57.
Bernstein, Lisa (1992), 'Opting out of the legal system: extralegal contractual relations in the diamond industry', *Journal of Legal Studies*, **21** (1), 115–57.
Bian, Yanjie (1994), *Work and Inequality in Urban China*, Albany, NY: State University of New York Press.
Bian, Yanjie (1996), 'Chinese occupational prestige: a comparative analysis', *International Sociology*, **11** (2), 161–86.
Bian, Yanjie (1997), 'Bringing strong ties back in: indirect ties, network bridges, and job searches in China', *American Sociological Review*, **62** (3), 366–85.
Bian, Yanjie (1999), 'Getting a job through a web of *Guanxi* in urban China', in Barry Wellman (ed.), *Networks in the Global Village*, Boulder, CO: Westview, pp. 255–77.
Bian, Yanjie (2000), 'Making sense of China's transformations', *Contemporary Sociology*, **29** (4), 613–24.
Bian, Yanjie (2001), '*Guanxi* capital and social eating: theoretical models and empirical analyses', in Nan Lin, Karen Cook and Ronald Burt (eds.), *Social Capital: Theory and Research*, New York: Aldine de Gruyter, pp. 275–95.
Bian, Yanjie (2002), 'Chinese social stratification and social mobility', *Annual Review of Sociology*, **28**, 91–116.
Bian, Yanjie (2003), 'Sociological research on reform-era China', *Issues & Studies*, **38–39** (4–1), 139–74.
Bian, Yanjie (2008) 'The formation of social vapital among Chinese urbanites: theoretical explanation and empirical evidence', in Nan Lin and Bonnie Erickson (eds.), *Social Capital: An International Research Program*, Oxford and New York: Oxford University Press, pp. 81–104.

Bian, Yanjie (2009), 'Sociology', in Karen Christensen (ed.), *The Berkshire Encyclopedia of China*, Great Barrington, MA: Berkshire Publishing, pp. 2031–5.

Bian, Yanjie (2018), 'The prevalence and increasing significance of *guanxi*', *China Quarterly*, **235**, 597–621.

Bian, Yanjie (2019), *Guanxi, How China Works*, Cambridge, UK and Medford, MA: Polity Press.

Bian, Yanjie and Song Ang (1997), '*Guanxi* networks and job mobility in China and Singapore', *Social Forces*, **75** (3), 981–1005.

Bian, Yanjie, Ronald Breiger, Deborah Davis and Joseph Galaskiewicz (2005), 'Occupation, class, and social networks in urban China', *Social Forces*, **83** (4), 1443–68.

Bian, Yanjie and Xianbi Huang (2009), 'Network resources and job mobility in China's transitional economy', *Research in the Sociology of Work*, **9**, 255–82.

Bian, Yanjie and Xianbi Huang (2015a), 'The *guanxi* influence on occupational attainment in urban China', *Chinese Journal of Sociology*, **1**, 307–32.

Bian, Yanjie and Xianbi Huang (2015b), 'Beyond the strength of social ties: job search networks and entry-level wage in urban China', *American Behavioral Scientist*, **59** (8), 961–76.

Bian, Yanjie, Xianbi Huang and Lei Zhang (2015a), 'Information and favoritism: the network effect on wage income in China', *Social Networks*, **40**, 129–38.

Bian, Yanjie and Ken'ichi Ikeda (2014), 'East Asian social networks', in Rada Alhajj and Jon Rokne (eds.), *The Encyclopedia of Social Network Analysis and Mining*, New York: Springer, pp. 417–33.

Bian, Yanjie and Lulu Li (2012), 'The Chinese general social survey (2003–8): sample designs and data evaluation', *Chinese Sociological Review*, **45** (1), 70–97.

Bian, Yanjie and John R. Logan (1996), 'Market transition and the persistence of power: the changing stratification system in urban China', *American Sociological Revie*, **61** (5), 739–58.

Bian, Yanjie, Xiaoling Shu and John R. Logan (2001), 'Communist party membership and regime dynamics in China', *Social Forces*, **79** (3), 805–41.

Bian, Yanjie, Yu Sun and Yinghui Li (2018a), 'On the accumulative effects of social capital', *Academics* **240** (5), 5–17. In Chinese.

Bian, Yanjie and Yang (2018), 'Forty years of sociological development in the reform era', *Journal of Xi'an Jiaotong University* (Social Sciences), **38** (6), 9–18. In Chinese.

Bian, Yanjie and Lei Zhang (2008), 'Sociology in China', *Contexts*, **7** (3), 20–31.

Bian, Yanjie and Lei Zhang (2014), 'Corporate social capital in *guanxi* culture', *Research in the Sociology of Organizations*, **40**, 417–39.

Bian, Yanjie, Lei Zhang, Yinghui Li, Yipeng Hu and Na Li (2018b), 'Income inequality and class stratification', in Weiping Wu and Mark Frazier (eds.), *Sage Handbook of Contemporary China*, New York: Sage Publications, pp. 1022–41.

Bian, Yanjie, Lei Zhang, Wenbin Wang and Cheng (2015b), 'Institution-spanning social capital and its income returns in China', in Yaojun Li (ed.), *Handbook of Research Methods and Applications in Social Capital*, London, UK: Routledge, pp. 344–57.

Bian, Yanjie and Wenhong Zhang (2001), 'Economic regime, social networks, and occupational mobility', *Social Sciences in China*, (2), 77–89. In Chinese.

Bian, Yanjie, Wenhong Zhang and Cheng (2012), 'A social network model of job-search processes: testing the *guanxi* effect hypothesis', *Society*, **32** (3), 24–7. In Chinese.

Bian, Yanjie and Zhanxin Zhang (2002), 'Marketization and income distribution in urban China: 1988 and 1995', *Research on Social Stratification and Mobility*, **19**, 375–415.

Blau, Peter M. and Otis Dudley Duncan (1967), *The American Occupational Structure*, New York: John Wiley and Sons.

Blau, Peter M. and Danching Ruan (1990), 'Inequality of opportunity in urban China and America', *Research in Stratification and Mobility*, **9**, 3–32.

Blau, Peter M., Danching Ruan and Monika Ardelt (1991), 'Interpersonal choice and networks in China', *Social Forces*, **69** (4), 1037–62.

Blazer, Dan G. (1982), 'Social support and mortality in an elderly community population', *American Journal of Epidemiology*, **115** (5), 684–94.

Boisot, Max and John Child (1996), 'From fiefs to clans and network capitalism: explaining China's emerging economic order', *Administrative Science Quarterly*, **41** (4), 600–628.

Bolger, Niall and David Amarel (2007), 'Effects of social support visibility on adjustment to stress: experimental evidence', *Journal of Personality and Social Psychology*, **92** (3), 458–75.

Bonacich, Philip (1972), 'Factoring and weighting approaches to status scores and clique identification', *Journal of Mathematical Sociology*, **2** (1), 113–20.

Bonacich, Philip (1987), 'Power and centrality: a family of measures', *American Journal of Sociology*, **92** (5), 1170–82.

Bourdieu, Pierre (1986 [1983]), 'The forms of capital', in John G. Richardson (ed.), *Handbook of Theory and Research for the Sociology of Education*, Westport, CT: Greenwood Press, pp. 241–58.

Borgatti, Stephen P. (2002), *NetDraw*, Boston, MA: Analytic Technologies.

Bourdieu, Pierre and Loic J.D. Wacquant (1992), *An Invitation to Reflexive Sociology*, Chicago, IL and London, UK: University of Chicago Press.

Brashears, Matthew E. and Eric Quintane (2018), 'The weakness of tie strength', *Social Networks*, **55**, 104–15.

Brissette, Ian, Sheldon Cohen and Teresa E. Seeman (2000), 'Measuring social integration and social networks', in Sheldon Cohen, Lynn G. Underwood and Benjamin H. Gottlieb (eds.), *Social Support Measurement and Intervention: A Guide for Health and Social Scientists*, New York: Oxford University Press, pp. 53–85.

Burger, Martijn J. and Vincent Buskens (2009), 'Social context and network formation: an experimental study', *Social Networks*, **31** (1), 63–75.

Burt, Ronald S. (1980), 'Autonomy in a social topology', *American Journal of Sociology*, **85** (4), 892–925.

Burt, Ronald S. (1982), *Toward a Structural Theory of Action: Network Models of Social Structure, Perception, and Action*, New York: Academic Press.

Burt, Ronald S. (1984), 'Network items and the General Social Survey', *Social Networks*, **6**, 293–339.

Burt, Ronald S. (1987), 'A note on strangers, friends and happiness', *Social Networks*, **9** (4), 311–31.

Burt, Ronald S. (1992), *Structural Holes: The Social Structure of Competition*, Cambridge, MA and London: Harvard University Press.

Burt, Ronald S. (1997), 'The contingent value of social capital.' *Administrative Science Quarterly*, **42** (2), 339–65.

Burt, Ronald S. (1999), 'The social capital of opinion leaders', *Annals of the American Academy of Political and Social Science*, **566**, 37–54.

Burt, Ronald S. (2000), 'The network structure of social capital', *Research in Organizational Behavior*, **22**, 345–423.

Burt, Ronald S. (2004), 'Structural holes and good ideas', *American Journal of Sociology*, **110** (2), 349–99.

Burt, Ronald S. (2005), *Brokerage and Closure: An Introduction to Social Capital*, New York and Oxford, UK: Oxford University Press.

Burt, Ronald S. (2007), 'Secondhand brokerage: evidence on the importance of local structure for managers, bankers, and analysts', *Academy of Management Journal*, **50** (1), 119–48.

Burt, Ronald S. (2010), *Neighbor Networks: Competitive Advantage Local and Personal*, New York and Oxford, UK: Oxford University Press.

Burt, Ronald S. (2012), 'Network-related personality and the agency question: multirole evidence from a virtual world', *American Journal of Sociology*, **118** (3), 543–91.

Burt, Ronald S. (2017), 'Social network and temporal discounting', *Network Science*, **5** (4), 411–40.

Burt, Ronald S. (2019), 'Network disadvantaged entrepreneurs: density, hierarchy, and success in China and the West', *Entrepreneurship Theory and Practice*, **43** (1), 19–50.

Burt, Ronald S. and Bat Batjargal (2019), 'Comparative network research in China', *Management and Organization Review*, **15** (1), 3–29.

Burt, Ronald S., Yanjie Bian and Sonja Opper (2018), 'More less guanxi: trust is 60% network context, 10% individual difference', *Social Networks*, **52**, 12–25.

Burt, Ronald S. and Katarzyna Burzynska (2017), 'Chinese entrepreneurs, social networks, and guanxi', *Management and Organization Review*, **13** (2), 221–60.

Burt, Ronald S., Kenneth P. Christman and Harold C. Kilburn (1980), 'Testing a structural theory of corporate cooptation: interorganizational directorate ties as a strategy for avoiding market constraints on profits', *American Sociological Review*, **45** (5), 821–41.

Burt, Ronald S., Martin Kilduff and Stefano Tasselli (2013), 'Social network analysis: foundations and frontiers on network advantage', *Annual Review of Psychology*, **64**, 537–47.

Burt, Ronald S. and Jennifer Merluzzi (2014), 'Embedded brokerage: hubs versus locals', in Daniel J. Brass, Giuseppe Labianca, Ajay Mehra, Dan S. Halgin and Stephen P. Borgatti (eds.), *Contemporary Perspectives on Organizational Social Networks*, Bingley, UK: Emerald, pp. 161–77.

Burt, Ronald S. and Sonja Opper (2017), 'Early network events in the later success of Chinese entrepreneurs', *Management and Organization Review*, **13** (3), 497–537.

Buskens Vincent and Arnout van de Rijt (2008), 'Dynamics of networks if everyone strives for structural holes', *American Journal of Sociology*, **114** (2), 371–407.

Cao, Yang (2001), 'Careers inside organizations: a comparative study of promotion determination in reforming China', *Social Forces*, **80** (2), 683–711.

Campbell, Karen E., Peter V. Marsden and Jeanne S.Hurlbert (1986), 'Social resources and socioeconomic status', *Social Networks*, **8**, 97–117.

Caplan, Gerald (1974), *Support Systems and Community Mental Health*, New York: Behavioral Publications.

Caplan, Gerald (1976), 'The family as support system', in Gerald Caplan and Marie Killilea (eds.), *Support Systems and Mutual Help: Multidisciplinary Explorations,* New York: Grune & Stratton, pp. 19–36.

Caplan, Robert D. (1979), 'Social support, person–environment fit, and coping', in Louis A. Ferman and Jeanne P.

Gordus (eds.), *Mental Health and the Economy*, Michigan: W.E. Upjohn Institute for Employment Research, pp. 89–138.

Carnabuci, Gianluca and Eric Quintane (2018), 'Does bridging structural holes increase innovative performance? Evidence from a field experiment', Paper presented at 8th Intra-Organizational Networks Conference, University of Kentucky Links Center, April 7.

Cassel, John (1974), 'An epidemiological perspective of psychosocial factors in disease etiology', *American Journal of Public Health*, **64** (11), 1040–43.

Cassel, John (1976), 'The contribution of the social environment to host resistance', *American Journal of Epidemiology*, **104** (2), 107–23.

Centola, Damon and Michael Macy (2007), 'Complex contagions and the weakness of long ties', *American Journal of Sociology*, **113** (3), 702–34.

Chang, Xiangqun (2010), *Guanxi or Lishang Wanglai? Reciprocity, Social Support Networks, & Social Creativity in a Chinese Village*, Taipei: Airiti Press.

Chen, Chih-Jou Jay (2014), 'Job search chains and embedded resources: a comparative analysis among Taiwan, China and the US', in Nan Lin, Yang-chih Fu and Chih-Jou Jay Chen (eds.), *Social Capital and Its Institutional Contingency: A Study of the United States, China and Taiwan*, London and New York: Routledge, pp. 283–330.

Chen, Wenhong (2014), 'The internet implications for social capital: stock, changes and tie strength', in Nan Lin, Yang-chih Fu and Chih-jou Jay Chen (eds.), *Social Capital and its Institutional Contingency: A Study of the United States, China and Taiwan*, New York and London: Routledge, pp. 150–65.

Chen, Wenhong (2015), 'Mediatizing the network model of cultural capital: network diversity, media use, and cultural knowledge along and across ethnic boundaries', *Social Networks*, **40**, 185–96.

Chen, Wenhong, Justin Tan and Fangjing Tu (2015), 'Minding the gender gap: social network and internet correlates of business performance among Chinese immigrant entrepreneurs', *American Behavioral Scientist*, **59** (8), 977–91.

Chen, Wenhong, Fangjing Tu and Pei Zheng (2017), 'A transnational networked public sphere of air pollution: analysis of a Twitter network of PM2.5 from the risk society perspective', *Information, Communication & Society*, **20** (7), 1005–23.

Cheng, Lucie and Alvin So (1983), 'The reestablishing of sociology in the PRC: toward the signification of Marxian sociology', *Annual Review of Sociology*, **9**, 471–98.

Cobb, Sidney (1974), 'Physiologic changes in men whose jobs were abolished', *Journal of Psychosomatic Research*, **18**, 245–58.

Cobb, Sidney (1976), 'Social support as a moderator of life stress', *Psychosomatic Medicine*, **38** (5), 300–314.

Cohen, Sheldon, Benjamin H. Gottlieb and Lynn G. Underwood (2000a), 'Social relationships and health', in Sheldon Cohen, Lynn G. Underwood and Benjamin H. Gottlieb (eds.), *Social Support Measurement and Intervention: A Guide for Health and Social Scientists*, New York: Oxford University Press, pp. 3–25.

Cohen, Sheldon and Garth McKay (1984), 'Social support, stress and the buffering hypothesis: a theoretical analysis', in Andrew Baum, Shelley E. Taylor and Jerome E. Singer (eds.), *Handbook of Psychology and Health*, Hillsdale, NJ: Lawrence Erlbaum, pp. 253–67.

Cohen, Sheldon, Lynn G. Underwood and Benjamin H. Gottlieb (eds.) (2000b), *Social Support Measurement and Intervention: A Guide for Health and Social Scientists*, New York: Oxford University Press.

Cohen, Sheldon and Thomas Ashby Wills (1985), 'Stress, social support, and the buffering hypothesis', *Psychological Bulletin*, **98** (2), 310–57.

Cole, Jonathan R. and Stephen Cole (1971), 'Measuring the quality of sociological research: problems in the use of the Science Citation Index', *American Sociologist*, **6** (1), 23–9.

Cole, Stephen and Jonathan R. Cole (1967), 'Scientific output and recognition: a study in the operation of the reward system', *American Sociological Review*, **32** (3), 377–90.

Coleman, James S. (1961), *The Adolescent Society*, New York: Free Press.

Coleman, James S. (1973), *Mathematics of Collective Action*, Chicago, IL: Aldine.

Coleman, James S. (1988), 'Social capital in the creation of human capital', *American Journal of Sociology*, **94** (S), S95–S120.

Coleman, James S. (1990), *Foundations of Social Theory*, Cambridge, MA and London: Harvard University Press.

Coleman, James S. (1991), 'Reflections on schools and adolescents', in Jon Clark (ed.), *James S. Coleman*, London: Falmer Press, pp. 17–22.

Coleman, James S., Elihu Katz and Herbert Menzel (1957), 'The diffusion of an innovation among physicians', *Sociometry*, **20** (4), 253–70.

Comte, Auguste (1875 [1852]), *System of Positive Polity*, London: Longmans & Co.

Cook, Karen S., Richard M. Emerson, Mary R. Gilmore and Toshio Yamagishi (1983), 'The distribution of power in exchange networks: theory and experimental results', *American Journal of Sociology*, **89** (2), 275–305.

Cook, Karen S. and Joseph M. Whitmeyer (1992), 'Two approaches to social structure: exchange theory and network analysis', *Annual Review of Sociology*, **18** (1), 109–27.

Cornwell, Benjamin (2003), 'The dynamic properties of social support: decay, growth, and staticity and their effects on adolescent depression', *Social Forces*, **81** (3), 955–82.

Cothran, Tanya (2011), 'Google Scholar acceptance and use among graduate students: a quantitative study', *Library and Information Science Research*, **33** (4), 293–301.

Cotten, Shelia R., Melinda Goldner, Timothy M. Hale and Patricia Drentea (2011), 'The importance of type, amount, and timing of internet use for understanding psychological distress', *Social Science Quarterly*, **92** (1), 119–39.

Cross, Jennifer L. Moren and Nan Lin (2008), 'Access to social capital and status attainment in the United States: racial/ethnic and gender differences', in Nan Lin and Bonnie H. Erickson (eds.), *Social Capital: An International Research Program*, New York and Oxford, UK: Oxford University Press, pp. 364–93.

Cutrona, Carolyn E. (1990), 'Stress and social support: in search of optimal matching', *Journal of Social and Clinical Psychology*, **9** (1), 3–14.

Davis, Deborah (1995), 'Inequalities and stratification in the nineties', *China Review*, **19**, 1–25.

Davis, Deborah (1999), 'Self-employment in Shanghai: a research note', *China Quarterly*, **157**, 22–43.

Dean, Alfred and Walter M. Ensel (1982), 'Modelling social support, life events, competence, and depression in the context of age and sex', *Journal of Community Psychology*, **10** (4), 392–407.

Dean, Alfred and Nan Lin (1977), 'The stress-buffering role of social support', *Journal of Nervous and Mental Disease*, **165** (2), 403–13.

Dean, Alfred, Nan Lin and Walter M. Ensel (1981), 'The epidemiological significance of social support systems in depression', *Research in Community & Mental Health*, **2**, 77–109.

Deelstra, Janna T., Maria C.W. Peeters, Wilmar B. Schaufeli, Wolfgang Stroebe, Fred R.H. Zijlstra and Lorenz P. van Doornen (2003), 'Receiving instrumental support at work: when help is not welcome', *Journal of Applied Psychology*, **88** (2), 324–31.

Deng, Xiaoping (1994), *Deng Xiaoping's Selected Works*, Beijing: People's Press. In Chinese.

Delgado López-Cózar, Emilio, Nicolás Robinson-García and Daniel Terres-Salinas (2014), 'The Google Scholar experiment: how to index false papers and manipulate bibliometric indicators', *Journal of the Association for Information Science and Technology*, **65** (3), 446–54.

deVaan, Mathijs, Balazs Vedres and David Stark (2015), 'Game changer: the topology of creativity', *American Journal of Sociology*, **120** (4), 1144–94.

Dohrenwend, Barbara Snell and Bruce P. Dohrenwend (1981), 'Life stress and illness: formulation of the issues', in Barbara Snell Dohrenwend and Bruce P. Dohrenwend (eds.), *Stressful Life Events and Their Contexts*, New York: Prodist, pp. 1–27.

Doreian, Patrick (2006), 'Actor network utilities and network evolution', *Social Networks*, **28** (2), 137–64.

Drentea, Patricia and Jennifer L. Moren-Cross (2005), 'Social capital and social support on the web: the case of an internet mother site', *Sociology of Health and Illness*, **27** (7), 920–43.

Duncan, Otis Dudley (1961), 'A socioeconomic index for all occupations', in Albert J. Reiss (ed.), *Occupations and Social Status*, New York: Free Press, pp. 109–38.

Easley, David and Jon Kleinberg (2010), *Networks, Crowds, and Markets: Reasoning about a Highly Connected World*, Cambridge, UK and New York: Cambridge University Press.

Eckenrode, John and Elaine Wethington (1990), 'The process and outcome of mobilizing social support', in Steve Duck and Roxane C. Silver (eds.), *Personal Relationships and Social Support*, London: Sage Publications, pp. 83–103.

Ensel, Walter M. and Nan Lin (1991), 'The life stress paradigm and psychological distress', *Journal of Health and Social Behavior*, **32** (4), 321–41.

Ensel, Walter M. and Nan Lin (1996), 'Distal stressors and the life stress process', *Journal of Community Psychology*, **24** (1), 66–82.

Ensel, Walter M. and Nan Lin (2000), 'Age, the stress process, and physical distress: the role of distal stressors', *Journal of Aging and Health*, **12** (2), 139–68.

Ensel, Walter M. and Nan Lin (2004), 'Physical fitness and the stress process', *Journal of Community Psychology*, **32** (1), 81–101.

Entwisle, Barbara and Gail Henderson (eds.) (2000), *Redrawing Boundaries: Gender, Households, and Work in China*, Berkeley, CA: University of California Press.

Everett, Martin and Stephen P. Borgatti (2005), 'Ego network betweenness', *Social Networks*, **27** (1), 31–8.

Fei, Xiaotong (1992 [1947]), *From the Soil, the Foundations of Chinese Society*, Berkeley, CA: University of California Press, Translated by Gary G. Hamilton and Wang Zheng.

Fei, Xiaotong (1994), 'On Chinese sociology', *Sociological Studies*, (1), 2–8. In Chinese.

Fei, Xiaotong (1999), *Fei Xiaotong's Works*, Beijing: Qunyan Press. In Chinese.

Feng, Junqi (2010), *Cadre in Central County*, Doctoral dissertation, Department of Sociology, Peking University, Beijing. In Chinese.

Festinger, Leon, Stanley Schachter and Kurt W. Back (1950), *Social Pressures in Informal Group: A Study of Human Factors in Housing*, Stanford, CA: Stanford University Press.

Fischer, Claude S. (1982), *To Dwell Among Friends: Personal Networks in Town and City*, Chicago, IL and London,

UK: University of Chicago Press.

Fleming, Lee and Matt Marx (2006), 'Managing creativity in small worlds', *California Management Review*, **48** (4), 6–27.

Fleming, Lee, Santiago Mingo and David Chen (2007), 'Collaborative brokerage, generative creativity, and creative success', *Administrative Science Quarterly*, **52** (4), 443–75.

Foster, Jacob G., Andrey Rzhetsky and James A. Evans (2015), 'Tradition and innovation in scientists' research strategies', *American Sociological Review*, **80** (5), 875–908.

Fraser, David (2000), 'Inventing oasis: luxury housing advertisements and reconfiguring domestic space in Shanghai', in Deborah Davis (ed.), *The Consumer Revolution in Urban China*, Berkeley, CA: University of California Press, pp. 25–53.

Freeman, Linton C. (1977), 'A set of measures of centrality based on betweenness', *Sociometry*, **40** (1), 35–40.

Freeman, Linton C. (1978), 'Centrality in social networks: conceptual clarification', *Social Networks*, **1** (3), 215–39.

Freeman, Linton C. (1992), 'Filling in the blanks: a theory of cognitive categories and the structure of social affiliation', *Social Psychology Quarterly*, **55** (2), 118–27.

Freeman, Linton C. (2011), 'The development of social network analysis – with an emphasis on recent events', in John Scott and Peter J. Carrington (eds.), *The Sage Handbook of Social Network Analysis*, London and Thousand Oaks, CA: Sage Publications, pp. 26–39.

Freeman, Linton C., Stephen P. Borgatti and Douglas R. White (1991), 'Centrality in valued graphs: a measure of betweenness on network flow', *Social Networks*, **13** (2), 141–54.

Fried, Morton H. (1953), *Fabric of Chinese Society: A Study of the Social Life in a Chinese County Seat*, New York: Octagon Books.

Fu, Qiang, Shenjing He, Yushu Zhu, Si-ming Li, Yanling He, Huoning Zhou and Nan Lin (2015), 'Toward a relational account of neighborhood governance: territory-based networks and residential outcomes in urban China', *American Behavioral Scientist*, **59** (8), 992–1006.

Fu, Qiang and Nan Lin (2013), 'Local state marketism: an institutional analysis of China's urban housing and land market', *Chinese Sociological Review*, **46** (1), 3–24.

Fu, Qiang and Nan Lin (2014), 'The weaknesses of civic territorial organizations: civic engagement and homeowners associations in urban China', *International Journal of Urban and Regional Research*, **38** (6), 2309–27.

Fu, Yang-chih (2005), 'Measuring personal networks with daily contacts: a single-item survey question and the contact diary', *Social Networks*, **27** (3), 169–86.

Fu, Yang-chih (2009), 'Immediate returns on time investment in network overlapping: evidence from contact diaries', in Ray-May Hsung, Nan Lin and Ronald L. Breiger (eds.), *Contexts of Social Capital: Social Networks in Markets, Communities, and Families*, London, UK: Routledge, pp. 327–47.

Fu, Yang-chih and Nan Lin (2015), 'Using the position generator in cross-national surveys: challenges and potentials (1975–2016)', Paper presented at 6th Conference of the European Survey Research Association, Reykjavik, Iceland, July 16.

Fukuyama, Francis (1995), *Trust: Human Nature and the Reconstitution of Social Order*, New York: Free Press.

Gans, Herbert J. (1962), *The Urban Villagers: Group and Class in the Life of Italian-Americans*, New York: Free Press.

Giddens, Anthony (2001), 'Elites and power', in David B. Grusky (ed.), *Social Stratification: Class, Race, and Gender in Sociological Perspective*, Boulder, CO: Westview Press, pp. 212–15.

Goldberg, Amir, Sameer Srivastava, V. Govind Manian, William Monroe and Christopher Potts (2016), 'Fitting in or standing out? The tradeoffs of structural and cultural embeddedness', *American Sociological Review*, **81** (6), 1190–222.

Gore, Susan (1978), 'The effect of social support in moderating the health consequences of unemployment', *Journal of Health and Social Behavior*, **19** (2), 157–65.

Gore, Susan (1981), 'Stress-buffering functions of social supports: an appraisal and clarification of research models', in Barbara Snell Dohrenwend and Bruce P. Dohrenwend (eds.), *Stressful Life Events and Their Contexts*, New York: Prodist, pp. 202–22.

Gottlieb, Benjamin H. (1978), 'The development and application of a classification scheme of informal helping behaviours', *Canadian Journal of Behavioural Science*, **10** (2), 105–15.

Gould, Roger V. and Roberto M. Fernandez (1989), 'Structures of mediation: a formal approach to brokerage in transaction networks', *Sociological Methodology*, **19**, 89–126.

Gouldner, Alvin W. (1957), 'Cosmopolitans and locals: toward an analysis of latent social roles', *Administrative Science Quarterly*, **2** (3), 281–306.

Goyal Sanjeev and Fernando Vega-Redondo (2007), 'Structural holes in social networks', *Journal of Economic Theory*, **137** (1), 460–92.

Granovetter, Mark (1973), 'The strength of weak ties', *American Journal of Sociology*, **78** (6), 1360–80.

Granovetter, Mark (1974), *Getting a Job: A Study of Contacts and Careers*, Chicago, IL and London, UK: University of Chicago Press.

Granovetter, Mark (1983), 'The strength of weak ties: a network theory revisited', *Sociological Theory*, **1**, 201–33.
Granovetter, Mark (1985), 'Economic action, social structure, and embeddedness', *American Journal of Sociology*, **91** (3), 481–510.
Granovetter, Mark (1992), 'Problems of explanation in economic sociology', in Nitin Nohria and Robert G. Eccles (eds.), *Networks and Organizations: Structure, Form and Action*, Boston, MA: Harvard Business School Press, pp. 29–56.
Greif, Avner (1989), 'Reputation and coalitions in medieval trade: evidence on the Maghribi traders', *Journal of Economic History*, **49** (4), 857–82.
Haines, Valerie A. and Jeanne S. Hurlbert (1992), 'Network range and health', *Journal of Health and Social Behavior*, **33** (3), 254–66.
Haines, Valerie A., John J. Beggs and Jeanne S. Hurlbert (2011), 'Neighborhood disadvantage, network social capital, and depressive symptoms', *Journal of Health and Social Behavior*, **52** (1), 58–73.
Haines, Valerie A., Jeanne S. Hurlbert and John J. Beggs (1996), 'Exploring the determinants of support provision: provider characteristics, personal networks, community contexts, and support following life events', *Journal of Health and Social Behavior*, **37** (3), 252–64.
Hampton, Keith N. and Barry Wellman (2018), 'Lost and saved ... again: the moral panic about the loss of community takes hold of social media', *Contemporary Sociology*, **47** (6), 643–51.
Hannum, Emily and Yu Xie (1994), 'Trends in educational gender inequality in China: 1949–1985', *Research in Social Stratification & Mobility*, **13**, 73–98.
He, Xuefeng (2007), 'The mode of differential associations and regional differences in governance of village community', *Journal of Jianghai*, (4), 114–17. In Chinese.
Henderson, Scott (1977), 'The social network, support and neurosis: the function of attachment in adult life', *The British Journal of Psychiatry*, **131**, 185–91.
Henderson, Scott, Donald Glenn Byrne and Paul Duncan-Jones (1981), *Neurosis and the Social Environment*, New York: Academic Press.
Hicks, John R. (1939), *Value and Capital*, New York and Oxford, UK: Oxford University Press.
Honig, Emily and Gail Hershatter (1988), *Personal Voices*, Stanford, CA: Stanford University Press.
House, James S. (1981), *Work Stress and Social Support*, Reading, MA: Addison-Wesley.
House, James S., Debra Umberson and Karl R. Landis (1988), 'Structures and processes of social support', *Annual Review of Sociology*, **14**, 293–318.
Hsung, Ray-May and Ronald L. Breiger (2013), 'Similarities and differences in relation-specific social resources among three societies: Taiwan, China and the United States', in Nan Lin, Yang-chih Fu and Chih-jou Jay Chen (eds.), *Social Capital and Its Institutional Contingency: A Study of the United States, Taiwan and China*, London: Routledge, pp. 103–18.
Hummon, Norman P. (2000), 'Utility and dynamic social networks', *Social Networks*, **22** (3), 221–49.
Hurlbert, Jeanne S., Valerie A. Haines and John J. Beggs (2000), 'Core networks and tie activation: what kinds of routine networks allocate resources in nonroutine situations?', *American Sociological Review*, **65** (4), 598–618.
Hwang, Kwang-kuo (1987), 'Face and favor: the Chinese power game', *American Journal of Sociology*, **92** (4), 944–74.
Jackson, Matthew O. (2008), *Social and Economic Networks*, Oxford and Princeton, NJ: Princeton University Press.
Jackson, Matthew O. and Asher Wolinsky (1996), 'A strategic model of social and economic networks', *Journal of Economic Theory*, **71** (1), 44–74.
Jackson, Pamela Braboy (1992), 'Specifying the buffering hypothesis: support, strain, and depression', *Social Psychology Quarterly*, **55** (4), 363–78.
Jacobs, Bruce (1979), 'A preliminary model of particularistic ties in Chinese political alliances: Kan-ch'ing and Kuan-hsi in a rural Taiwanese township', *China Quarterly*, **78**, 237–73.
Jang, Sujin (2018), 'Cultural brokerage and creative performance in multicultural teams', *Organization Science*, **29** (6), 993–1009.
Janicik, Gregory A. and Richard P. Larrick (2005), 'Social network schemas and the learning of incomplete networks', *Journal of Personality and Social Psychology*, **88** (2), 348–64.
Kahn, Robert L. and Toni C. Antonucci (1980), 'Convoys over the life course: attachment roles and social support', in Paul B. Baltes and Orville G. Brim (eds.), *Life-Span Development and Behavior*, Vol. 3, New York: Academic Press, pp. 253–86.
Kana'Iaupuni, Shawn Malia, Katharine M. Donato, Theresa Thompson-Colon and Melissa Stainback (2005), 'Counting on kin: social networks, social support, and child health status', *Social Forces*, **83** (3), 1137–64.
Kaniasty, Krzysztof and Fran H. Norris (1993), 'A test of the social support deterioration model in the context of natural disaster', *Journal of Personality and Social Psychology*, **64** (3), 395–408.
Kaplan, Berton H., John C. Cassel and Susan Gore (1977), 'Social support and health', *Medical Care*, **15** (5), 47–58.
Katz, Elihu and Paul F. Lazarsfeld (1955), *Personal Influence: The Part Played by People in the Flow of Mass Communications*, New York: Free Press.

Kawachi, Ichiro and Lisa Berkman (2000), 'Social cohesion, social capital and health', in Lisa F. Berkman and Ichiro Kawachi (eds.), *Social Epidemiology*, New York: Oxford University Press, pp. 174–90.

Kawachi, Ichiro, Daniel Kim, Adam Coutts and S.V. Subramanian (2004), 'Commentary: reconciling the three accounts of social capital', *International Journal of Epidemiology*, **33** (4), 682–90.

Kearns, Michael, Siddharth Suri and Nick Montfort (2006), 'An experimental study of the coloring problem on human subject networks', *Science*, **313** (5788), 824–7.

Keister, Lisa (2000), *Chinese Business Groups: The Structure and Impact of Interfirm Relations during Economic Development*, New York: Oxford University Press.

Keister, Lisa A. and E. Paige Borelli (2012), 'Market transition: an assessment of the state of the field', *Sociological Perspectives*, **55** (2), 267–94.

Kessler, Ronald C. and Jane D. McLeod (1985), 'Social support and mental health in community samples', in Sheldon Cohen and S. Leonard Syme (eds.), *Social Support and Health*, San Diego, CA: Academic Press, pp. 219–40.

Kessler, Ronald C., Richard H. Price and Camille B. Wortman (1985), 'Social factors in psychopathology: stress, social support, and coping processes', *Annual Review of Psychology*, **36** (1), 531–72.

Kilduff, Martin and David Krackhardt (1994), 'Bringing the individual back in: a structural analysis of the internal market for reputation in organizations', *Academy of Management Journal*, **37** (1), 87–108.

Killworth, Peter D. and H. Russell Bernard (1978), 'The reverse small world experiment', *Social Networks*, **1**, 159–92.

King, Ambrose (1985), 'The individual and group in Confucianism: a relational perspective', in Donald J. Munro (ed.), *Individualism and Holism: Studies in Confucian and Taoist Values*, Ann Arbor, MI: Center for Chinese Studies, University of Michigan, pp. 57–70.

King, Ambrose (1994), 'Kuan-Hsi and network building: a sociological interpretation', in Wei-Ming Tu (ed.), *The Living Tree: The Changing Meaning of Being Chinese Today*, Stanford, CA: Stanford University Press, pp. 109–26.

Kipnis, Andrew (1997), *Producing Guanxi: Sentiment, Self, and Subculture in a North China Village*, Durham, NC: Duke University Press.

Kleinbaum, Adam M. (2012), 'Organizational misfits and the origins of brokerage in intrafirm networks', *Administrative Science Quarterly*, **57** (3), 407–52.

Kleinbaum, Adam M. and Toby E. Stuart (2014), 'Inside the black box of the corporate staff: social networks and the implementation of corporate strategy', *Strategic Management Journal*, **35** (1), 24–47.

Kleinberg, Jon (1999), 'Authoritative sources in a hyperlinked environment', *Journal of the Association for Computing Machinery*, **46** (5), 604–32.

Kleinberg, Jon (2000a), 'The small-world phenomenon: an algorithmic perspective', Proceedings of the thirty-second annual ACM symposium on theory of computing, pp. 163–70.

Kleinberg, Jon (2000b), 'Navigation in a small world', *Nature*, **406** (6798), 845.

Kleinberg Jon, Siddharth Suri, Éva Tardos and Tom Wexler (2008), 'Strategic network formation with structural holes', Proceedings of 9th ACM Conference on Electronic Commerce.

Kogut, Bruce (ed.) (2012), *The Small Worlds of Corporate Governance*, Cambridge, MA and London: MIT Press.

Kogut, Bruce and Gordon Walker (2001), 'The small world of Germany and the durability of national networks', *American Sociological Review*, **66** (3), 317–35.

Korte, Charles and Stanley Milgram (1970), 'Acquaintance networks between racial groups: application of the small world method', *Journal of Personality and Social Psychology*, **15** (2), 101–8.

Krackhardt, David (2009), 'A plunge into networks', *Science*, **326** (5949), 47–9.

Kraus, Richard C. (1981), *Class and Class Conflict in Contemporary China*, New York: Columbia University Press.

Kwon, Seok-Woo and Paul S. Adler (2014), 'Social capital: maturation of a field of research', *Academy of Management Review*, **39** (4), 412–22.

Lai, Gina (1995), 'Work and family roles and psychological well-being in urban China', *Journal of Health and Social Behavior*, **36** (1), 11–37.

Lai, Gina, Odalia Wong and Xiaotian Feng (2015), 'Family, school, and access to social capital among high school students in urban Nanjing', *American Behavioral Scientist*, **59** (8), 946–60.

Lan, Chengdong and Zhongru Zhang (1982), 'The aspirations of graduating students in senior high school', *Society*, (2), 22–5. In Chinese.

Laumann, Edward O. (1966), *Prestige and Association in an Urban Community: An Analysis of an Urban Stratification System*, New York: Bobbs-Merrill.

Laumann, Edward O. (1973), *Bonds of Pluralism: The Form and Substance of Urban Social Networks*, New York: Wiley Interscience.

Leavitt, Harold J. (1951), 'Some effects of certain patterns of communications on group performance', *Journal of Abnormal and Social Psychology*, **46** (1), 38–50.

Lee, Min-Ah and Ichiro Kawachi (2017), 'The company you keep: is socialising with higher-status people bad for mental health?', *Sociology of Health & Illness*, **39** (7), 1206–26.

Lee, Nancy Howell (1969), *The Search for an Abortionist*, Chicago, IL and London, UK: University of Chicago Press.

Li, Bobai and Andrew G. Walder (2001), 'Career advancement as party patronage: sponsored mobility into the Chinese administrative elite, 1949–1996', *American Journal of Sociology*, **106** (5), 1371–408.

Li, Chunling (2005), 'Prestige stratification in contemporary China: occupational prestige and socioeconomic status index', *Sociological Studies*, (2), 74–102. In Chinese.

Li, Debin (2000), *My Twenty Years with Chinese Sociology: Review of the First Workshop of Chinese Sociology*, Shenyang: Shenyang Publishing House. In Chinese.

Li, Peilin (2016), 'The historical responsibility of Chinese sociology', *Sociological Studies*, (5), 1–9. In Chinese.

Li, Shi, Hiroshi Sato and Terry Sicular (eds.) (2013), *Rising Inequality in China: Challenges to a Harmonious Society*, New York: Cambridge University Press.

Li, Stan Xiao, Xiaotao Yao, Christina Sue-Chan and Youmin Xi (2011), 'Where do social ties come from: institutional framework and governmental tie distribution among Chinese managers', *Management and Organization Review*, **7** (1), 97–124.

Li, Youmei (2018), 'Forty years of growth and development of Chinese sociology', *Chinese Social Sciences News*, June 28.

Liang, Shuming (1949), *The Essential Meanings of Chinese Culture*, Hong Kong: Zheng Zhong Press. In Chinese.

Liang, Yucheng (2018), 'A reassessment of the thesis "going out of the misunderstanding of the indigenization of Chinese sociology"', *Expanding Horizons*, (4), 49–54. In Chinese.

Liang, Yucheng, Wen Zhou, Lingxin Hao and Heqing Liu (2015), 'Methods of population outmigration: theory and practice of rural migrant population surveys', *Central University of Science and Technology Journal of Social Science*, (4), 113–23. In Chinese.

Lin, Nan (1982), 'Social resources and instrumental action', in Peter V. Marsden and Nan Lin (eds.), *Social Structure and Network Analysis*, London and Beverly Hills, CA: Sage Publications, pp. 131–45.

Lin, Nan (1983), 'Social resources and social actions: a progress report', *Connections*, **6** (2), 10–16.

Lin, Nan (1986a), 'Conceptualizing social support', in Nan Lin, Alfred Dean and Walter M. Ensel (eds.), *Social Support, Life Events, and Depression*, New York: Academic Press, pp. 17–29.

Lin, Nan (1986b), 'Modeling the effects of social support', in Nan Lin, Alfred Dean and Walter M. Ensel (eds.), *Social Support, Life Events, and Depression*, New York: Academic Press, pp. 173–209.

Lin, Nan (1986c), 'Epilogue: in retrospect and prospect', in Nan Lin, Alfred Dean and Walter M. Ensel (eds.), *Social Support, Life Events, and Depression*, New York: Academic Press, pp. 333–42.

Lin, Nan (1989), 'Measuring depressive symptomatology in China', *Journal of Nervous and Mental Disease*, **177** (3), 121–31.

Lin, Nan (1990), 'Social resources and social mobility: a structural theory of status attainment', in Ronald Breiger (ed.), *Social Mobility and Social Structure*, Cambridge, UK and New York: Cambridge University Press, pp. 247–71.

Lin, Nan (1992), 'Social resources theory', in Edgar F. Borgatta (ed.), *Encyclopedia of Sociology*, Vol. 4, New York: MacMillan Publishing, pp. 1936–42.

Lin, Nan (1994), 'Action, social resources and the emergence of social structure', in Barry Markovsky, Jodi O'Brian and Karen Heimer (eds.), *Advances in Group Processes*, Vol. 11. Greenwich, CT: JAI Press, pp. 67–85.

Lin, Nan (1995), 'Local market socialism: local corporation in action in rural China', *Theory and Society*, **24** (3), 301–54.

Lin, Nan (1999a), 'Social networks and status attainment', *Annual Review of Sociology*, **25**, 467–87.

Lin, Nan (1999b), 'Building a network theory of social capital', *Connections*, **22** (1), 28–51.

Lin, Nan (2000), 'Inequality in social capital', *Contemporary Sociology*, **29** (6),785–95.

Lin, Nan (2001a), *Social Capital: A Theory of Social Structure and Action*, Cambridge, UK and New York: Cambridge University Press.

Lin, Nan (2001b), 'Building a network theory of social capital', in Nan Lin, Karen S. Cook and Ronald S. Burt (eds.), *Social Capital: Theory and Research*, New York: Aldine de Gruyter, pp. 3–29. Included as Chapter 4 in this book.

Lin, Nan (2001c), '*Guanxi*: a conceptual analysis', in Alvin Y. So, Nan Lin and Dudley Poston (eds.), *The Chinese Triangle of Mainland, Taiwan, and Hong Kong*, Westport, CT: Greenwich, pp. 153–66.

Lin, Nan (2004), 'Job search in urban China: gender, network chains, and embedded resources', in Henk Flap and Beate Volker (eds.), *Creation and Return to Social Capital*, New York: Praeger, pp. 145–71.

Lin, Nan (2008), 'A network theory of social capital', in Dario Castiglione, Jan van Deth and Guglielmo Wolleb (eds.), *Handbook on Social Capital*, Oxford: Oxford University Press, pp. 50–69.

Lin, Nan (2011), 'Capitalism in China: a centrally managed capitalism (CMC) and its future', *Management and Organization Review*, **7** (1), 63–96.

Lin, Nan (2017), '*Guanxi*: social relationships based on sentiment (*renqing*)', Keynote speech delivered to the annual meeting of Chinese association for social network and social capital research, Beijing, June 1–3.

Lin, Nan and Dan Ao (2008), 'The invisible hand of social capital: an exploratory study', in Nan Lin and Bonnie H. Erickson (eds.), *Social Capital: An International Research Program*, New York and Oxford, UK: Oxford University Press, pp. 107–32.

Lin, Nan, Dan Ao and Lijun Song (2009), 'Production and returns of social capital: evidence from urban China', in Ray-May Hsung, Nan Lin and Ronald Breiger (eds.), *Contexts of Social Capital: Social Networks in Communities, Markets and Organizations*, New York: Routledge, pp. 107–32.

Lin, Nan and Chin-jou Jay Chen (1999), 'Local elites as officials and owners: shareholding and property rights transformation in Daqiuzhuang industry', in Andrew Walder and Jean Oi (eds.), *Property Rights and Economic Reform in China*, Stanford, CA: Stanford University Press, pp. 145–70.

Lin, Nan, Chih-jou Jay Chen and Yang-chih Fu (2010), 'Types and effects of social relationship in a three-way comparison: Taiwan, the United States, and Chinese mainland', *Taiwanese Journal of Sociology*, **45**, 117–62. In Chinese.

Lin, Nan, Karen Cook and Ronald S. Burt (eds.) (2001), *Social Capital: Theory and Research*, New York: Aldine de Gruyter.

Lin, Nan, Paul W. Dayton and Peter Greenwald (1977), 'The urban communication network and social stratification: a small world experiment', in Brent D. Ruben (ed.), *Communication Yearbook*, Vol. 1, New Brunswick, NJ: Transaction Books, pp. 107–19.

Lin, Nan, Paul W. Dayton and Peter Greenwald (1978), 'Analyzing the instrumental use of relations in the context of social structure', *Sociological Methods and Research*, **7** (2),149–66.

Lin, Nan and Alfred Dean (1984), 'Social support and depression: a panel study', *Social Psychiatry*, **19** (2), 83–91.

Lin, Nan, Alfred Dean and Walter M. Ensel (1981c), 'Social support scales: a methodological note', *Schizophrenia Bulletin*, **7** (1), 73–89.

Lin, Nan, Alfred Dean and Walter M. Ensel (eds.) (1986), *Social Support, Life Events, and Depression*, New York: Academic Press.

Lin, Nan and Mary Dumin (1986), 'Access to occupations through social ties', *Social Networks*, **8** (4), 365–85.

Lin, Nan and Walter M. Ensel (1984), 'Depression-mobility and its social etiology: the role of life events and social support', *Journal of Health and Social Behavior*, **25** (2), 176–88.

Lin, Nan and Walter M. Ensel (1989), 'Life stress and health: stressors and resources', *American Sociological Review*, **54** (3), 382–99.

Lin, Nan, Walter M. Ensel and John C. Vaughn (1981a), 'Social resources and strength of ties: structural factors in occupational status attainment', *American Sociological Review*, **46** (4), 393–405. Included as Chapter 3 in this book.

Lin, Nan and Bonnie H. Erickson (eds.) (2008a), *Social Capital: An International Research Program*, New York and Oxford, UK: Oxford University Press.

Lin, Nan and Bonnie H. Erickson (2008b), 'Theory, measurement, and the research enterprise on social capital', in Nan Lin and Bonnie H. Erickson (eds.), *Social Capital: An International Research Program*, New York and Oxford, UK: Oxford University Press, pp. 1–24.

Lin, Nan, Yang-chih Fu and Chih-jou Jay Chen (eds.) (2014a), *Social Capital and Its Institutional Contingency: A Study of the United States, China and Taiwan*, New York: Routledge.

Lin, Nan, Yang-chih Fu and Ray-May Hsung (2001), 'The position generator: measurement techniques for investigations of social capital', in Nan Lin, Karen S. Cook and Ronald S. Burt (eds.), *Social Capital: Theory and Research*, New York: Aldine de Gruyter, pp. 57–81.

Lin, Nan and Gina Lai (1995), 'Urban stress in China', *Social Science & Medicine*, **41** (8), 1131–45.

Lin, Nan, Hang Young Lee and Dan Ao (2014b), 'Contact status and finding a job: validation and extension', in Nan Lin, Yang-Chih Fu and Chih-Jou Chen (eds.), *Social Capital and Its Institutional Contingency: A Study of the United States, Taiwan and China*, London: Routledge, pp. 21–41.

Lin, Nan, Victor Nee, William Parish and Elena Yu (1992), 'The development of sociology in China: a delegation report', Washington, DC: Committee on Scholarly Communication with China.

Lin, Nan and M. Kristen Peek (1999), 'Social networks and mental health', in Allan V. Horwitz and Teresa L. Scheid (eds.), *A Handbook for the Study of Mental Health: Social Contexts, Theories, and Systems*, Cambridge: Cambridge University Press, pp. 241–58.

Lin, Nan, Ronald S. Simeone, Walter M. Ensel and Wen Kuo (1979), 'Social support, stressful life events, and illness: a model and an empirical test', *Journal of Health and Social Behavior*, **20** (1), 108–19. Included as Chapter 6 in this book.

Lin, Nan, John C. Vaughn and Walter M. Ensel (1981b), 'Social resources and occupational status attainment', *Social Forces*, **59** (4), 1163–81.

Lin, Nan and Jeanne Westcott (1991), 'Marital engagement/disengagement, social networks, and mental health', in John Eckenrode (ed.), *The Social Context of Coping*, New York: Plenum Press, pp. 213–37.

Lin, Nan, Mary W. Woelfel and Stephen C. Light (1985), 'The buffering effect of social support subsequent to an important life event', *Journal of Health and Social Behavior*, **26** (3), 247–63.

Link, Bruce G. and Jo C. Phelan (1995), 'Social conditions as fundamental causes of disease', *Journal of Health and Social Behavior*, **35** (Extra Issue), 80–94.

Liu, Weifeng, Yunsong Chen and Yanjie Bian (2017), 'Occupational interactions and income level: a social capital study using the first-order difference method', *Sociological Studies*, **31** (2), 34–56. In Chinese.

Logan, John R. (2018), 'People and plans in urbanising China: challenging the top-down orthodoxy', *Urban Studies*, **55** (7), 1375–82.

Logan, John R. and Yanjie Bian (1993), 'Access to community resources in a Chinese city', *Social Forces*, **72** (2), 555–76.

Lu, Yao, Danching Ruan and Gina Lai (2013), 'Social capital and economic integration of migrants in urban China', *Social Networks*, **35** (3), 357–69.

Marsden, Peter V. (1987), 'Core discussion networks of Americans', *American Sociological Review*, **51** (1), 122–31.

Marsden, Peter V. (2011), 'Survey methods for network data', in John Scott and Peter Carrington (eds.), *Sage Handbook of Social Network Analysis*, London and Thousand Oaks, CA: Sage Publications, pp. 370–88.

Marsden, Peter V. and Karen E. Campbell (1984), 'Measuring tie strength', *Social Forces*, **63** (2), 482–501.

Marsden, Peter V. and Nan Lin (eds.) (1982), *Social Structure and Network Analysis*, London and Beverly Hills, CA: Sage Publications.

Marx, Karl (1835), 'Reflections of a young man on the choice of a profession', first published in German in 1925, which was translated from the Latin by Sally Ryan. http://marxists.anu.edu.au/archive/marx/works/1837-pre/marx/1835-ref.htm (accessed 10th October, 2018).

Masuda, Yuta J., Yuqing Liu, Sheila M.W. Reddy, Kenneth A. Frank, Kyle Burford, Jonathan R.B. Fisher and Jensen Montambault (2018), 'Innovation diffusion within large environmental NGOs through informal network agents', *Nature Sustainability*, **1** (4), 190–97.

Matthews, Rebeca and Victor Nee. (2000), 'Gender inequality and economic growth in rural China', *Social Science Research*, **29** (4), 606–32.

McDonald, Steve, Feinian Chen and Christine A. Mair (2015), 'Cross-national patterns of social capital accumulation: network resources and aging in China, Taiwan, and the United States', *American Behavioral Scientist*, **59** (8), 914–30.

McDonald, Steve, Nan Lin and Dan Ao (2009), 'Networks of opportunity: gender, race, and job leads', *Social Problems*, **56** (3), 385–402.

McPherson, Miller, Lynn Smith-Lovin and James M. Cook (2001), 'Birds of a feather: homophily in social networks', *Annual Review of Sociology*, **27**, 415–44.

Mehra, Ajay, Martin Kilduff and Daniel J. Brass (2001), 'The social networks of high and low self-monitors: implications for workplace performance', *Administrative Science Quarterly*, **46** (1), 121–46.

Merton, Robert K. (1949), 'Patterns of influence: local and cosmopolitan influentials', in Robert K. Merton (ed.), *Social Theory and Social Structure*, 3rd edn. (1968), New York: Free Press, pp. 441–74.

Michelson, Ethan (2007), 'Lawyers, political embeddedness, and institutional continuity in China's transition from socialism', *American Journal of Sociology*, **113** (2), 352–414.

Mills, C. Wright (1959), *Sociological Imagination*, Oxford, UK: Oxford University Press.

Milgram, Stanley (1967), 'The small world problem', *Psychology Today*, **1** (May), 61–7.

Mitchell, J. Clyde (ed.) (1969), *Social Networks in Urban Situations: Analyses of Personal Relationships in Central African Town*, Manchester: Manchester University Press.

Mitchell, J Clyde (1974), 'Social networks', *Annual Review of Anthropology*, **3** (1), 279–99.

Mizruchi, Mark S., Peter Mariolis, Michael Schwartz and Beth Mintz (1986), 'Techniques for disaggregating centrality scores in social networks', *Sociological Methodology*, **15**, 26–48.

Moen, Phyllis, Donna Dempster-McClain and Robin M. Williams, Jr. (1989), 'Social integration and longevity: an event history analysis of women's roles and resilience', *American Sociological Review*, **54** (4), 635–47.

Moody, James and Pamela Paxton (2009), 'Building bridges: linking social capital and social networks to improve theory and research', *American Behavioral Scientist*, **52** (11), 1491–506.

Moore, Spencer, Ulf Bockenholt, Mark Daniel, Katherine Frohlich, Yan Kestens and Lucie Richard (2011), 'Social capital and core network ties: a validation study of individual-level social capital measures and their association with extra- and intra-neighborhood ties, and self-rated health', *Health and Place*, **17** (2), 536–44.

Moore, Spencer, Mark Daniel, Lise Gauvin and Laurette Dubé (2009a), 'Not all social capital is good capital', *Health and Place*, **15** (4), 1071–7.

Moore, Spencer, Mark Daniel, Catherine Paquet, Laurette Dubé and Lise Gauvin (2009b), 'Association of individual network social capital with abdominal adiposity, overweight and obesity', *Journal of Public Health*, **31** (1), 175–83.

Moore, Spencer, Ana Teixeira and Steven Stewart (2014), 'Effect of network social capital on the chances of smoking relapse: a two-year follow-up study of urban-dwelling adults', *American Journal of Public Health*, **104** (12), e72–6.

Moreno, Jacob L. (1934), *Who Will Survive?*, Washington, DC: Nervous and Mental Disease Publishing.

Nahopiet, Janine and Sumantra Ghoshal (1998), 'Social capital, intellectual capital, and the organizational advantage', *Academy of Management Review*, **23** (2), 242–56.

Nahum-Shani, Inbal, Peter A. Bamberger and Samuel B. Bacharach (2011), 'Social support and employee well-being:

the conditioning effect of perceived patterns of supportive exchange', *Journal of Health and Social Behavior*, **52** (1), 123–39.

Naughton, Barry (2006), *The Chinese Economy: Transition and Growth*, Cambridge, MA: MIT Press.

Nee, Victor (1989), 'Theory of market transition: from redistribution to market in state socialism', *American Sociological Review*, **54** (5), 663–81.

Nee, Victor (1991), 'Social inequalities in reforming state socialism: between redistribution and markets in China', *American Sociological Review*, **56** (3), 267–82.

Nee, Victor (1996), 'The emergence of market society: changing mechanisms of stratification in China', *American Journal of Sociology*, **101** (4), 908–49.

Nee, Victor and Rebecca Mathews (1996), 'Market transformation and societal transformation in reforming state socialism', *Annual Review of Sociology*, **22**, 401–35.

Nee, Victor and Yang Cao (1999), 'Path dependent societal transformation: stratification in hybrid economies', *Theory and Society*, **28** (6), 799–834.

Newman, M.E.J. (2006), 'Modularity and community structure in networks', *Proceedings of the National Academy of Sciences*, **103** (23), 8577–82.

Noh, Samuel and William R. Avison (1996), 'Asian immigrants and the stress process: a study of Koreans in Canada', *Journal of Health and Social Behavior*, **37** (2), 192–206.

Parish, William L. (1981), 'Egalitarianism in Chinese society', *Problems of Communism*, **30** (1), 37–53.

Parish, William L. (1984), 'Destratification in China', in James L. Watson (ed.), *Class and Social Stratification in Post-Revolution China*, New York: Cambridge University Press, pp. 84–120.

Parish, William and Ethan Michelson (1996), 'Politics and markets: dual transformations', *American Journal of Sociology*, **101** (4), 1024–59.

Parish, William L., Tianfu Wang, Edward O. Laumann, Suiming Pan and Ye Luo (2004), 'Intimate partner violence in China: national prevalence, risk factors, and associated health problems', *International Family Planning Perspectives*, **30**, 174–81.

Pearlin, Leonard I. (1989), 'The sociological study of stress', *Journal of Health and Social Behavior*, **30** (3), 241–56.

Pearlin, Leonard I. (1992), 'Structure and meaning in medical sociology', *Journal of Health and Social Behavior*, **33** (1), 1–9.

Pearlin, Leonard I. and Mary E. McCall (1990), 'Occupational stress and marital support: a description of microprocesses', in John Eckenrode and Susan Gore (eds.), *Stress between Work and Family*, New York: Plenum Press, pp. 39–60.

Pearlin, Leonard I., Elizabeth G. Menaghan, Morton A. Lieberman and Joseph T. Mullan (1981), 'The stress process', *Journal of Health and Social Behavior*, **22** (4), 337–56.

Pearlin, Leonard I., Joseph T. Mullan, Shirley J. Semple and Marilyn M. Skaff (1990), 'Caregiving and the stress process: an overview of concepts and their measures', *The Gerontologist*, **30** (5), 583–94.

Peng, Yusheng (2004), 'Kingship networks and entrepreneurship in China's transitional economy', *American Journal of Sociology*, **109** (5), 1045–74.

Perry-Smith, Jill E. (2006), 'Social yet creative: the role of social relationships in facilitating individual creativity', *Academy of Management Journal*, **49** (1), 85–101.

Peek, M. Kristen and Nan Lin (1999), 'Age differences in the effects of network composition on psychological distress', *Social Science & Medicine*, **49** (5), 621–36.

Pescosolido, Bernice A. (2006), 'Of pride and prejudice: the role of sociology and social networks in integrating the health sciences', *Journal of Health and Social Behavior*, **47** (3), 189–208.

Pevalin, David (2003), 'More to social capital than Putnam', *British Journal of Psychiatry*, **182** (2), 172–3.

Podolny, Joel M. (1993), 'A status-based model of market competition', *American Journal of Sociology*, **98** (4), 829–72.

Podolny, Joel M. (2001), 'Networks as the pipes and prisms of the market', *American Journal of Sociology*, **107** (1), 33–60.

Podolny, Joel M. (2005), *Status Signals: A Sociological Study of Market Competition*, Oxford and Princeton, NJ: Princeton University Press.

Polanyi, Karl (1944), *The Great Transformation: The Political and Economic Origins of Our Time*, Boston, MA: Beacon Press.

Pool, Ithiel de Sola and Manfred Kochen (1978), 'Contacts and influence', *Social Networks*, **1** (1), 5–51.

Portes, Alejandro (1998), 'Social capital: its origins and applications in modern sociology', *Annual Review of Sociology*, **24**, 1–24.

Putnam, Robert D. (1993a), *Making Democracy Work: Civic Traditions in Modern Italy*, Oxford and Princeton, NJ: Princeton University Press.

Putnam, Robert D. (1993b), 'The prosperous community: social capital and public life', *American Prospect*, **13** (Spring), 35–42.

Putnam, Robert D. (2001), *Bowling Alone: The Collapse and Revival of American Community*, New York: Simon & Schuster.

Putnam, Robert D., Robert Leonardi, Raffaella Y. Nanetti and Franco Pavoncello (1983), 'Explaining institutional success: the case of Italian regional government', *American Political Science Review*, **77** (1), 55–74.

Quintane, Eric and Gianluca Carnabuci (2016), 'How do brokers broker? Tertius gaudens, tertius iungens, and the temporality of structural holes', *Organization Science*, **27** (6), 1343–60.

Rabkin, Judith G. and Elmer L. Struening (1976), 'Life events, stress, and illness', *Science*, **194**, 1013–20.

Rapoport, Anatol and William J. Horvath (1961), 'A study of a large sociogram', *Behavioral Science*, **6** (4), 279–91.

Reagans, Ray and Bill McEvily (2003), 'Network structure and knowledge transfer: the effects of cohesion and range', *Administrative Science Quarterly*, **48** (2), 240–67.

Reagans Ray E. and Ezra W. Zuckerman (2008), 'Why knowledge does not equal power: the network redundancy trade-off', *Industrial and Corporate Change*, **17** (5), 903–44.

Ren, Qiang and Donald J. Treiman (2015), 'Living arrangements of the elderly in China and consequences for their emotional well-being', *Chinese Sociological Review*, **47** (3), 255–86.

Rider, Christopher I. (2009), 'Constraints on the control benefits of brokerage: a study of placement agents in U.S. venture capital fundraising', *Administrative Science Quarterly*, **54** (4), 575–601.

Ross, Catherine E. and John Mirowsky (1989), 'Explaining the social patterns of depression: control and problem solving – or support and talking?', *Journal of Health and Social Behavior*, **30** (2), 206–19.

Rossi, Alice S. (ed.) (1985), *Sociology and Anthropology in the People's Republic of China: Report of a Delegation Visit, February–March 1984*, Washington, DC: National Academy Press.

Ruan, Danching (1998), 'The content of the GSS discussion networks: an exploration of GSS discussion name generator in a Chinese context', *Social Networks*, **20**, 247–64.

Ruan, Danching (2001), 'A comparative study of personal networks in two Chinese societies', in Alvin So, Nan Lin and Dudley L. Poston (eds.), *The Chinese Triangle of Mainland, Taiwan, and Hong Kong: Comparative Institutional Analysis*, Westport, CT: Greenwich, pp. 189–205.

Russell, Daniel W. and Carolyn E. Cutrona (1991), 'Social support, stress, and depressive symptoms among the elderly: test of a process model', *Psychology and Aging*, **6** (2), 190–201.

Ryall Michael D. and Olav Sorenson (2007), 'Brokers and competitive advantage', *Management Science*, **53** (4), 566–83.

Salganik, Matthew J., Peter Sheridan Dodds and Duncan J. Watts (2006), 'Experimental study of inequality and unpredictability in an artificial culture market', *Science*, **311** (5762), 854–6.

Sampson, Robert J., Stephen W. Raudenbush and Felton Earls (1997), 'Neighborhoods and violent crime: a multilevel study of collective efficacy', *Science*, **277**, 918–24.

Sarason, Irwin G., Henry M. Levine, Robert B. Basham and Barbara R. Sarason (1983), 'Assessing social support: the social support questionnaire', *Journal of Personality and Social Psychology*, **44** (1), 127–39.

Sasovova Zuzana, Ajay Mehra, Stephen P. Borgatti and Michaéla C. Schippers (2010), 'Network churn: the effects of self-monitoring personality on brokerage dynamics', *Administrative Science Quarterly*, **55** (4), 639–70.

Sauder, Michael, Freda Lynn and Joel M. Podolny (2012), 'Status: insights from organizational sociology', *Annual Review of Sociology*, **38**, 267–83.

Shen, Jing and Yanjie Bian (2018), 'The causal effect of social capital on income: a new analytic strategy', *Social Networks*, **54**, 82–90.

Shinn, Marybeth, Stanley Lehmann and Nora W. Wong (1984), 'Social interaction and social support', *Journal of Social Issues*, **40** (4), 55–76.

Shirado, Hirokazu and Nicholas A. Christakis (2017), 'Locally noisy autonomous agents improve global human coordination in network experiments', *Nature*, **545** (7654), 370–74.

Shu, Xiaoling, Yifan Zhu and Zhanxin Zhang (2013), 'Patriarchy, resources, and specialization marital decision-making power in urban China', *Journal of Family Issues*, **34**, 885–917.

Shumaker, Sally A. and Arlene Brownell (1984), 'Toward a theory of social support: closing conceptual gaps', *Journal of Social Issues*, **40** (4), 11–36.

Smith, Edward B., Tanya Menon and Leigh Thompson (2012), 'Status differences in the cognitive activation of social networks', *Organization Science*, **23** (1), 67–82.

Snow, David L., Suzanne C. Swan, Chitra Raghavan, Christian M. Connell and Ilene Klein (2003), 'The relationship of work stressors, coping and social support to psychological symptoms among female secretarial employees', *Work & Stress*, **17** (3), 241–63.

So, Alvin Y., Nan Lin and Dudley Poston (eds.) (2001), *The Chinese Triangle of Mainland, Taiwan, and Hong Kong: Comparative Institutional Analysis*, Westport, CT: Greenwood.

Soda, Giuseppe, Pier V. Mannucci and Ronald S. Burt (2018), 'Networks, creativity, and time: staying creative through time and space', Paper presented at the Insead Network Evolution Conference, 28 October.

Son, Joonmo (2013), *Social Capital and Institutional Constraints: A Comparative Analysis of China, Taiwan, and the U.S.*, New York: Routledge.

Son, Joonmo (forthcoming), *Social Capital (Key Concepts Series)*, Cambridge, UK: Polity Press.
Son, Joonmo, Nan Lin and Linda K. George (2008), 'Cross-national comparison of social support structures between Taiwan and the United States', *Journal of Health and Social Behavior*, **49** (March), 104–18.
Song, Lijun (2011), 'Social capital and psychological distress', *Journal of Health and Social Behavior*, **52** (4), 478–92.
Song, Lijun (2013a), 'Social capital and health', in William C. Cockerham (ed.), *Medical Sociology on the Move: New Directions in Theory*, Dordrecht, the Netherlands: Springer, pp. 223–57.
Song, Lijun (2013b), 'Institutional embeddedness of network embeddedness in the workplace: social integration at work and employee's health across three societies', *Research in the Sociology of Work*, **24**, 323–56.
Song, Lijun (2014a), 'Is unsolicited support protective or destructive in collectivistic culture? Receipt of unsolicited job leads in urban China', *Society and Mental Health*, **4** (3), 235–54.
Song, Lijun (2014b), 'Bright and dark sides of who you know in the evaluation of well-being: social capital and life satisfaction across three societies', in Nan Lin, Yang-Chih Fu and Chih-Jou Chen (eds.), *Social Capital and Its Institutional Contingency: A Study of the United States, Taiwan and China*, London: Routledge, pp. 259–78.
Song, Lijun (2015a), 'Does knowing people in the positional hierarchy protect or hurt? Social capital, comparative reference group, and depression in two societies', *Social Science & Medicine*, **136–137** (9), 117–27.
Song, Lijun (2015b), 'Does knowing people in authority protect or hurt? Authoritative contacts and depression in urban China', *American Behavioral Scientist*, **59** (9), 1173–88.
Song, Lijun and Tian-Yun Chang (2012), 'Do resources of network members help in help seeking? Social capital and health information search', *Social Networks*, **34** (4), 658–69.
Song, Lijun and Wenhong Chen (2014), 'Does receiving unsolicited support help or hurt? receipt of unsolicited job leads and depression', *Journal of Health and Social Behavior*, **55** (2), 144–60.
Song, Lijun and Nan Lin (2009), 'Social capital and health inequality: evidence from Taiwan', *Journal of Health and Social Behavior*, **50** (2), 149–63.
Song, Lijun and Philip J. Pettis (2018), 'Does whom you know in the status hierarchy prevent or trigger health limitation? Institutional embeddedness of social capital and social cost theories in three societies', *Social Science & Medicine*, https://doi.org/10.1016/j.socscimed.2018.09.035.
Song, Lijun, Cleothia G. Frazier and Philip J. Pettis (2018), 'Do network members' resources generate health inequality? Social capital theory and beyond', in Sherman Folland and Eric Nauenberg (eds.), *Elgar Companion to Social Capital and Health*, Cheltenham, UK and Northampton, MA, USA: Edward Elgar Publishing, pp. 233–53.
Song, Lijun, Philip Pettis and Bhumika Piya (2017), 'Does your body know who you know? Multiple roles of network members' socioeconomic status for body weight ratings', *Sociological Perspectives*, **60** (6), 997–1018.
Song, Lijun, Joonmo Son and Nan Lin (2010), 'Social capital and health', in William C. Cockerham (ed.), *The New Companion to Medical Sociology*, Oxford, UK: Wiley-Blackwell, pp. 184–210.
Song, Lijun, Joonmo Son and Nan Lin (2011), 'Social support', in John Scott and Peter J. Carrington (eds.), *The Sage Handbook of Social Network Analysis*, London: Sage Publications, pp. 116–28.
Stiglitz, Joseph E. (2001), 'Foreword', in Karl Polanyi, *The Great Transformation: The Political and Economic Origins of Our Time*, Boston: Beacon Press, pp. vii–xvii.
Sun, Liping (1996), '*Guanxi*, social relations, and social structure', *Sociological Studies*, (5), 22–32. In Chinese.
Sun, Liping (2000), 'In search of the development of sociology in the scholarly community', *Social Sciences in China*, (1), 24–7. In Chinese.
Sun, Yu and Yanjie Bian (2017), 'Favoritism as causal mechanisms in occupational status attainment', *Journal of Social Science Front*, (5), 189–99. In Chinese.
Sutherland, E.H. (1939), *Principles of Criminology* (3rd edn), Chicago, IL: University of Chicago Press.
Thoits, Peggy A. (1982), 'Conceptual, methodological, and theoretical problems in studying social support as a buffer against life stress', *Journal of Health and Social Behavior*, **23** (2), 145–59.
Thoits, Peggy A. (1984), 'Explaining distributions of psychological vulnerability: lack of social support in the face of life stress', *Social Forces*, **63** (2), 453–81.
Thoits, Peggy A. (1995), 'Stress, coping, and social support processes: where are we? What next?', *Journal of Health and Social Behavior*, **35** (Extra Issue), 53–79.
Thoits, Peggy A. (2011), 'Mechanisms linking social ties and support to physical and mental health', *Journal of Health and Social Behavior*, **52** (2), 145–61.
Tian, Felicia and Nan Lin (2016), 'Weak ties, strong ties, and job mobility in urban China: 1978–2008', *Social Networks*, **44**, 117–29.
Tortoriello, Marco and David Krackhardt (2010), 'Activating cross-boundary knowledge: the role of Simmelian ties in the generation of innovations', *Academy of Management Journal*, **53** (1), 167–81.
Tortoriello, Marco, Ray Reagans and Bill McEvily (2012), 'Bridging the knowledge gap: the influence of strong ties, network cohesion, and network range on the transfer between organization units', *Organization Science*, **23** (4), 1024–39.
Travers, Jeffrey and Stanley Milgram (1969), 'An experimental study of the small world problem', *Sociometry*, **32**

(4), 425–43.

Treiman, Donald J. (1970), 'Industrialization and social stratification', *Sociological Inquiry*, **40** (2), 207–34.

Treiman, Donald J. (1977), *Occupational Prestige in Comparative Perspective*, New York: Academic Press.

Treiman, Donald J. and Andrew G. Walder (1996), 'Life histories and social change in contemporary China', Distributed by the UCLA Social Science Data Archive. http://www.sscnet.ucla.edu/issr/da/, retrieved August 26, 2018.

Treiman, Donald J. and K.B. Yip (1989), 'Educational and occupational attainment in 21 countries', in Melvin L. Kohn (ed.), *Cross National Research in Sociology*, Newbury Park, CA: Sage Publications, pp. 373–94.

Tsai, Shuling and Haiyuan Chiu (1991), 'Occupational hierarchies in Taiwan: construction of scales', *Research in Social Stratification and Mobility*, **10**, 229–53.

Turner, J. Blake and R. Jay Turner (2013), 'Social relations, social integration, and social support', in Carol S. Aneshensel, Jo C. Phelan and Alex Bierman (eds.), *Handbook of the Sociology of Mental Health* (2nd edn), New York: Springer, pp. 341–56.

Turner, R. Jay (1981), 'Social support as a contingency in psychological well-being', *Journal of Health and Social Behavior*, **22** (4), 357–67.

Turner, R. Jay (1983), 'Direct, indirect, and moderating effects of social support on psychological distress and associated conditions', in Berton H. Kaplan (ed.), *Psychosocial Stress: Trends in Theory and Research*, New York: Academic Press, pp. 105–55.

Turner, R. Jay and Robyn Lewis Brown (2010), 'Social support and mental health', in Teresa L. Scheid and Tony N. Brown (eds.), *A Handbook for the Study of Mental Health: Social Contexts, Theories, and Systems* (2nd edn), Cambridge: Cambridge University Press, pp. 200–212.

Turner, R. Jay and Samuel Noh (1988), 'Physical disability and depression: a longitudinal analysis', *Journal of Health and Social Behavior*, **29** (1), 23–37.

Uchino, Bert N. (2009), 'Understanding the links between social support and physical health: a life span perspective with emphasis on the separability of perceived and received support', *Perspectives on Psychological Science*, **4** (3), 236–55.

Umberson, Debra and Jennifer Karas Montez (2010), 'Social relationships and health: a flashpoint for health policy', *Journal of Health and Social Behavior*, **51** (S), S54–S66.

Uzzi, Brian (1996), 'The sources and consequences of embeddedness for the economic performance of organizations: the network effect', *American Sociological Review*, **61** (4), 674–98.

Uzzi, Brian (1997), 'Social structure and competition in interfirm networks: the paradox of embeddedness', *Administrative Science Quarterly*, **42** (1), 35–67.

Uzzi, Brian (1999), 'Embeddedness in the making of financial capital: how social relations and networks benefit firms seeking financing', *American Sociological Review*, **64** (4), 481–505.

Van der Gaag, Martin and Tom A.B. Snijders (2005), 'The resource generator: social capital quantification with concrete items', *Social Networks*, **27** (1), 1–29.

Van der Gaag, Martin, Tom A.B. Snijders and Henk Flap (2008), 'Position generator measures and their relationship to other social capital measures', in Nan Lin and Bonnie H. Erickson (eds.), *Social Capital: An International Research Program*, New York and Oxford, UK: Oxford University Press, pp. 27–48.

Verhaeghe, Pieter-Paul and Gindo Tampubolon (2012), 'Individual social capital, neighbourhood deprivation, and self-rated health in England', *Social Science & Medicine*, **75** (2), 349–57.

Verhaeghe, Pieter-Paul, Elise Pattyn, Piet Bracke, Mieke Verhaeghe and Bart Van De Putte (2012), 'The association between network social capital and self-rated health: pouring old wine in new bottles?', *Health and Place*, **18** (2), 358–65.

Von Hippel, Eric (1994), 'Sticky information and the locus of problem solving: implications for innovation', *Management Science*, **40** (4), 429–39.

Walder, Andrew G. (1986), *Communist NeoTraditionalism: Work and Authority in Chinese Industry*, Berkeley, CA: University of California Press.

Walder, Andrew G. (1989), 'Social change in post-revolution China', *Annual Review of Sociology*, **15** (1), 405–24.

Walder, Andrew G. (1992), 'Property rights and stratification in socialist redistributive economies', *American Sociological Review*, **57** (4), 524–39.

Walder Andrew G. (1995), 'Career mobility and the communist political order', *American Sociological Review*, **60** (3), 309–28.

Walder, Andrew G. (2002), 'Markets, economic growth, and inequality in rural China in the 1990s', *American Sociological Review*, **67**, 231–53.

Walder Andrew G., Bobai Li and Donald J. Treiman (2000), 'Politics and life chances in a state socialist regime: dual career paths into the urban Chinese elite, 1949–1996', *American Sociological Review*, **65** (2), 191–209.

Wang, Barbara X. and Chris Rowley (2016), 'Business networks and the emergence of *guanxi* capitalism in China: the role of the "invisible hand"', in Jane Nolan, Chris Rowley and Malcolm Warner (eds.), *Business Networks in East Asian Capitalisms*, London: Chandos, pp. 93–118.

Wang, Feng (2008), *Boundaries and Categories: Rising Inequality in Post-Socialist Urban China*, Stanford, CA: Stanford University Press.

Watts, Duncan J. and Steven H. Strogatz (1998), 'Collective dynamics of "small-world" networks', *Nature*, **393** (6684), 440–42.

Webber, Martin P. and Peter Huxley (2004), 'Mental health and social capitals (letter)', *British Journal of Psychiatry*, **184** (2), 185–6.

Wellman, Barry (1979), 'The community question: the intimate networks of East Yorkers', *American Journal of Sociology*, **84** (5), 1201–31.

Wellman, Barry (1981), 'Applying social network analysis to the study of social support', in Benjamin H. Gottlieb (ed.), *Social Networks and Social Support*, Beverly Hills: Sage Publications, pp. 171–200.

Wellman, Barry (2001), 'Computer networks as social networks', *Science*, **293** (5537), 2031–4.

Wellman, Barry and Scot Wortley (1990), 'Different strokes from different folks: community ties and social support', *American Journal of Sociology*, **96** (3), 558–88.

Wellman, Barry, Janet Salaff, Dimitrina Dimitrova, Laura Garton, Milena Gulia and Caroline Haythornthwaite (1996), 'Computer networks as social networks: collaborative work, telework, and virtual community', *Annual Review of Sociology*, **22** (1), 213–38.

Wheaton, Blair (1985), 'Models for the stress-buffering functions of coping resources', *Journal of Health and Social Behavior*, **26** (4), 352–64.

White, Harrison C. (1970), 'Search parameters for the small world problem', *Social Forces*, **49** (2), 259–64.

Whyte, Martin King (1984), 'Sexual inequality under socialism: the Chinese case in perspective', in James L. Watson (ed.), *Class and Social Stratification in Post-Revolution China*, New York: Cambridge University Press, pp. 198–238.

Whyte, Martin King (2000), 'The perils of assessing trends in gender inequality in China', *Redrawing Boundaries: Gender, Households, and Work in China*, **25**, 157–67.

Whyte, Martin King and William L. Parish (1984), *Urban Life in Contemporary China*, Chicago, IL and London, UK: University of Chicago Press.

Whyte, Martin King, Ezra F. Vogel and William L. Parish (1977), 'Social structure of world regions: mainland China', *Annual Review of Sociology*, **3** (1), 179–207.

Williams, Ann W., John E. Ware and Cathy A. Donald (1981), 'A model of mental health, life events, and social supports applicable to general populations', *Journal of Health and Social Behavior*, **22** (4), 324–36.

World Bank (2018), https://tradingeconomics.com/country-list/disposable-personal-income, retrieved on September 19, 2018.

Wortman, Camille B. and Darrin R. Lehman (1985), 'Reactions to victims of life crises: support attempts that fail', in Irwin G. Sarason and Barbara R. Sarason (eds.), *Social Support: Theory, Research, and Applications*, Dordrecht, the Netherlands: Martinus Nijhoff, pp. 463–89.

Wu, Wei (2015), 'Income gap in China and an international comparison', *Survey Research World*, (9), 11–21. In Chinese.

Wu, Xiaogang (2002), 'Work units and income inequality: the effect of market transition in urban China', *Social Forces*, **80** (3), 1069–99.

Wu, Xiaogang (2013), 'Redrawing the boundary: work units and social stratification in urban China', *Chinese Sociological Review*, **45** (4), 6–28.

Wu, Xiaogang (2019), 'Inequality and social stratification in post-socialist China', *Annual Review of Sociology*, forthcoming.

Wu, Xiaogang and Donald J. Treiman (2004), 'The household registration system and social stratification in China, 1955–1996', *Demography*, **41** (2), 363–84.

Wu, Xiaogang and Donald J. Treiman (2007), 'Inequality and equality under Chinese socialism: the *kukou* system and intergenerational occupational mobility', *American Journal of Sociology*, **113** (2), 415–45.

Wu, Xiaogang and Xi Song (2014), 'Ethnic stratification and China's economic transition: evidence from the Xinjiang Uyghur autonomous region', *Social Science Research*, **44**, 158–72.

Wu, Xiaogang and Yu Xie (2003), 'Does the market pay off? Earnings returns to education in urban China', *American Sociological Review*, **68** (3), 425–42.

Wu, Xiaogang and Bingdao Zheng (2018), 'Household registration, urban status attainment, and social stratification in contemporary urban China', *Research in Social Stratification and Mobility*, **53**, 40–49.

Wu, Zheng, Samuel Noh, Violet Kaspar and Christoph M. Schimmele (2003), 'Race, ethnicity, and depression in Canadian society', *Journal of Health and Social Behavior*, **44** (3), 426–41.

Xi, Juan, Sean-Shong Hwang and Patricia Drentea (2013), 'Experiencing a forced relocation at different life stages: the effects of China's three gorges project-induced relocation on depression', *Society and Mental Health*, **3** (1), 59–76.

Xiao, Yang and Yanjie Bian (2018), 'The influence of *hukou* and college education in China's labour market', *Urban Studies*, **55** (7), 1504–24.

Xiao, Ying (2014), 'The mode of differential associations and the transition of Chinese society toward modernity', *Exploration and Contention*, (6), 48–54. In Chinese.

Xie, Yu (2018), 'Going out of the misunderstanding of the indigenization of Chinese sociology', *Sociological Studies*, (2), 1–13. In Chinese.

Xie, Yu and Emily Hannum (1996), 'Regional variation in earnings inequality in reform-era China', *American Journal of Sociology*, **101** (4), 950–92.

Xie, Yu and Jingwei Hu (2014), 'An introduction to the China family panel studies (CFPS)', *Chinese Sociological Review*, **47** (1), 3–29.

Xie, Yu and Xiangang Wu (2008), '*Danwei* profitability and earnings inequality in urban China', *China Quarterly*, **195**, 558–81.

Yan, Yunxiang (1996), *The Flow of Gifts Reciprocity and Social Networks in a Chinese Village*, Stanford, CA: Stanford University Press.

Yang, Ching Kung (1959), *The Chinese Family in the Communist Revolution*, Cambridge, MA: Harvard University Press.

Yang, Hsieh-Hua, Shu-Chen Kuo, Hung-Jen Yang and Jui-Chen (2013), 'Social capital and health literacy in Taiwan', *Health*, **5** (5), 898–902.

Yang, Mayfair Meihui (1994), *Gifts, Favors, and Banquets: The Art of Social Relationships in China*, Ithaca, NY: Cornell University Press.

Yin, Zhijun, Lijun Song and Bradley A. Malin (2017), 'Reciprocity and its association with treatment adherence in an online breast cancer forum', Paper presented at the 30th IEEE (Institute of Electrical and Electronics Engineers) International Symposium on Computer-Based Medical Systems (IEEE CBMS), Thessaloniki, Greece, June 22.

Zaheer Akbar and Giuseppe Soda (2009), 'Network evolution: the origins of structural holes', *Administrative Science Quarterly*, **54** (1), 1–31.

Zang, Xiaowei (2001), 'University education, party seniority, and elite recruitment in China', *Social Science Research*, **30** (1), 62–75.

Zhai, Xuewei (2018), 'Is the indigenization of sociology a false question?', *Exploration and Free Views*, **1** (9), 49–57. In Chinese.

Zhang, Lei (2016), Sociology 'Nankai Class' (1981–1982), Master Thesis, Peking University. In Chinese.

Zhang, Yanlong and Nan. Lin (2016), 'Hiring for networks: social capital and staffing practices in transitional China', *Journal of Human Resource Management*, **55** (4), 615–35.

Zhao, Yandong (2008), 'Social networks and mental health among urban and rural residents', *Society*, **28** (5), 1–20.

Zhe, Xiaoye and Yingying Chen (1995), 'Occupation, identity, and prestige in rural China', *Chinese Social Science Quarterly*, **6**, 83–95. In Chinese.

Zhou, Feizhou (2017), 'Ethical behavior and *guanxi* society: the Chinese path to sociology', *Sociological Studies*, (1), 41–62. In Chinese.

Zhou, Xueguang (2000), 'Economic transformation and income inequality in urban China: evidence from a panel data', *American Journal of Sociology*, **105** (4), 1135–74.

Zhou Xueguang (2001), 'Political dynamics and bureaucratic career patterns in the People's Republic of China 1949–1994', *Comparative Political Studies*, **34** (9), 1036–62.

Zhou, Xueguang (2014), 'Increasing returns to education, changing labor force structure, and the rise of earnings inequality in urban China, 1996–2010', *Social Forces*, **93** (2), 429–55.

Zhou, Xueguang and Xiaomei Pei (1997), 'Chinese sociology in a transitional society', *Contemporary Sociology*, **26** (5), 569–72.

Zhou, Xueguang, Qiang Li, Wei Zhao and He Cai (2003), 'Embeddedness and contractual relationships in China's transition economy', *American Sociological Review*, **68** (1), 75–102.

Zhou, Xueguang, Nancy Brandon Tuma and Phyllis Moen (1996), 'Stratification dynamics under state socialism: the case of urban China', *Social Forces*, **74** (3), 759–96.

Zhou, Xueguang, Nancy Brandon Tuma and Phyllis Moen (1997), 'Institutional change and job-shift patterns in urban China', *American Sociological Review*, **62** (3), 339–65.

Index